D0779218

1948

Uri Avnery, the day after the crucial battle of Ibdis, July 1948

1948

A SOLDIER'S TALE
THE BLOODY ROAD TO JERUSALEM

Uri Avnery

Translated by Christopher Costello

ONEWORLD
OXFORD

A Oneworld Paperback Original

First published in English by Oneworld Publications, 2008
Part One first published in Hebrew as In the Fields of the Philistines, 1949
Part Two first published in Hebrew as The Other Side of the Coin, 1950
This edition, which was slightly revised by the author,
was first published in Germany as In den Feldern der
Philister by Diederichs Verlag

Copyright © Uri Avnery, 1949, 1950, 2008
Translation copyright © Christopher Costello, 2008

The right of Uri Avnery to be identified as the Author of this work
has been asserted by him in accordance with the Copyright,
Designs and Patents Act 1988

All rights reserved
Copyright under Berne Convention
A CIP record for this title is available
from the British Library

ISBN 978–1–85168–629–2

Typeset by Jayvee, Trivandrum, India
Cover design by designedbydavid.co.uk
Printed and bound in Great Britain by Bell & Bain

Oneworld Publications
185 Banbury Road
Oxford OX2 7AR
England
www.oneworld-publications.com

Learn more about Oneworld. Join our mailing list to
find out about our latest titles and special offers at:

www.oneworld-publications.com

Contents

CONTENTS

Illustrations

Maps

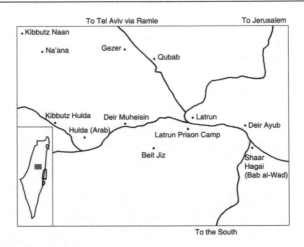

Map I: The Road to Jerusalem

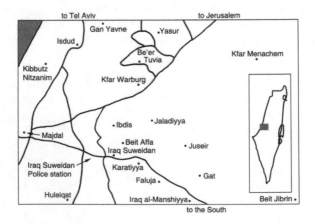

Map II: The Southern Front

Preface

"For the victims of the next round"

The preparation of this combined edition of my two books *In the Fields of the Philistines* and *The Other Side of the Coin* was a strange experience for me. For the first time in almost sixty years, I read them again.

The eighty-one-year-old Uri Avnery came face to face with the twenty-five-year-old Uri Avnery. Two different people – and yet the same man. The twenty-five-year-old is a part of the eighty-one-year-old. One cannot be separated from the memories of the other. And yet he is very remote, almost someone else, hard to recognize through the fog of years.

The eighty-one-year-old has gained experience. He has overcome many difficulties; over the years he has acquired a deeper understanding of political and historical processes. He tries to understand the twenty-five-year-old, his fears and hopes, his good and bad deeds, the spirit of those days. That wasn't always easy, just as it won't always be easy for today's reader.

If I had written this book today, it would have turned out differently. Very differently. The books portray the events as seen at the time by a participant. But I decided to leave the book as that of the twenty-five-year-old, to allow the reader to experience the events of 1948 the way he experienced them then, not as we see them now, over half a century later.

For every historical event there is a subjective and an objective truth. The first is the truth for those directly involved, the second describes the facts that crystallize out in later years. The gap between these two truths is particularly wide for the war of 1948.

In the Fields of the Philistines describes the feelings of the Hebrew fighters in this war, what they knew, what they thought, what they felt. This book almost escapes definition, arising, as it did, in very unusual conditions. It is no ordinary book. But it is also not a diary. It is something else.

At the start of the war I enrolled in the army. An acquaintance of mine, the deputy editor of a newspaper, asked if I could send occasional reports of my experiences. I answered simply "I'll try." I didn't really know what I was saying. Writing for a newspaper? In those days I had never thought of that. But in the following months writing became an obsession for me. I wrote and wrote and wrote. It helped to reduce the tension, to overcome the fear, to digest the experiences.

I wrote before the action, during the action, and after the action. When an exhausting battle was over, my comrades would lie down and snore. I picked up my pencil and paper and wrote. I wrote on the ground, in the trenches, and on the hood of a jeep. I wrote in the canteen surrounded by hundreds of noisy comrades and I wrote in bed at night.

I wasn't writing a diary. A diary is a dialogue with yourself, a record of your most intimate thoughts. But my articles were meant to be published. I knew they would appear the next day in black and white in the newspaper. All these reports appeared in the paper *Yom Yom* (*Day by Day*), the evening edition of the great Israeli daily paper *Haaretz* (*The Land*).

But how did the reports find their way to the editorial board in the distant city? That is one of the most surprising things about the whole business. I often ran to the road to stop a supply truck, and asked the driver to do me a favor and deliver something to the editors. At other times when a comrade received permission for a short furlough, I would ask him to sacrifice an hour of his precious time to get an envelope and a stamp and put the report in the post. It was a miracle: not one of the dozens of reports got lost. They all reached the editorial office.

My comrades in the company got used to my passion. They knew that Uri writes, just as Jossi plays the mouth organ, or Moshe hits on all the girls. When they got annoyed about something, they would call over to me "Uri, write this down." And when their worried parents asked them "Where are you?" and they couldn't be bothered with long explanations, they would tell them "Read Uri Avnery's reports. Then you'll know."

Every word in this book was written in clear violation of an unambiguous order: soldiers are forbidden to give interviews or to write for newspapers without express permission. My superior turned a blind eye. When a high-up officer from the base began to cause trouble, I was called to our battalion headquarters where a senior officer told me he would deliver my reports personally and secretly to the newspaper. One day, after I was yet again emphatically ordered to stop writing, I received a summons to our battalion commander. Full of trepidation I announced my presence. I was handed a small brown envelope. In it was a handwritten letter from the legendary brigade commander Shimon Avidan. He congratulated me on a report I had written about the special role of the infantry soldier. That's the kind of army we were then.

One thing should be clear. *In the Fields of the Philistines* – the first part of the present book – consists of individual reports, written by a soldier at the time the events occurred. Without my being aware of this, each report reflects the mood of the troops at that particular moment. In retrospect it seems to me that this is the distinguishing feature of this book. It describes the fluctuating morale of the fighting unit – from the initial enthusiasm as the war began, through the inhuman tension of the fighting, through to the deep disappointment at the end.

There is another special feature of this book, determined by the way it came about. The book contains the truth and nothing but the truth. But it does not contain the whole truth. There are things I did not want to describe, things one could not inflict on the parents of a soldier while the war was still going on. In addition, before publication the newspaper had to get my reports past the military censors. They cut out the parts that seemed to them to violate military secrecy or that could undermine morale. These parts have been lost, resulting in unfortunate gaps in the book.

Toward the end of the war, when I was recuperating from my wounds but still in uniform, a friend suggested publishing the reports as a book. After initial hesitation I agreed. I decided to publish the chapters as they were. I just added some lines wherever this seemed necessary to make the events easier to follow. As in the original version, any longer linking passages appear here in italics.

I still had one problem. During the war I occasionally wrote political articles which summarized my thinking at the time. One such article criticized the hatred of the Arabs, which some people harbored. I wrote that we were an "Army of Love" – love for our comrades and love for the land – and not an army of hate. In another article under the Latin heading "Pax Semitica," I proposed a Hebrew–Arab federation from Morocco to Iraq. The people at *Yom Yom* found these articles too serious for an evening paper, and passed them on to the editors of *Haaretz*. That is where they appeared. I decided to leave these articles out of the book, where they would have been foreign bodies.

I sent the manuscript to the large Israeli publishing houses, and all of them sent it back. "Yesterday's news," said one. "We've had enough of the war," wrote another. I was also told that they would print the words of well-known writers and not the reports of a simple soldier. In the end I found a small, plucky publisher which, after long consideration, decided to publish the book under the title *In the Fields of the Philistines 1948*.

To the mystification of all the experts, and much to my own surprise as well, it became an absolute bestseller overnight. It was an unprecedented phenomenon in the Hebrew literature of the time. In the course of a single year the hardback version went through ten printings. There wasn't a single wedding or bar mitzvah party that did not have several copies among the presents.

The reviews in the press were just as astonishing. One wrote that I had expressed the "Spirit of the Generation." Another suggested carving the words of the book in stone, as a reminder for later generations. Overnight I was in great demand. I was flooded with invitations to private functions as well as officers' meetings, and all branches of the Israeli bureaucracy fawned on me. I could take my pick in the media world. The chief editor of *Haaretz* offered me the chance to write the leading article of the paper, which I accepted.

It was really peculiar. Before the war I was one of the people everyone loved to hate. Eighteen months before the war I published a little magazine that I had named *Bamaavak* (*In the Struggle*). In it I wrote that we would form a new Hebrew nation in Palestine, a nation distinct from everything earlier among the Jewish people, and that we should realize our national interests and form an alliance with the Arab national movement. The attacks of *Bamaavak* on the sacred cows of official Zionism[1] caused a lot of bad blood. More than a hundred irate reactions appeared in a wide variety of papers. One of the best-known writers, in a vicious play on words, called our little journal *Bamat-Avak* (stage of dust).

That's what made my sudden popularity all the more surprising. I could have enjoyed it and lived happily ever after, if not for the following event …

* * *

A few weeks after *In the Fields of the Philistines* was published, I happened to overhear two boys sitting behind me on a bus. They were bemoaning their fate – they had been too young to fight in the war. To my horror they were quoting the "great experiences" from my book, which they had apparently missed out on.

That conversation disturbed me deeply. Until then I thought that I had described the awful side of the war. But if two young people could use it to feed their enthusiasm for war, then I had failed. I decided to write a second book that would describe the other side of the coin. For this I used the notes that I had made in the hospital after I was wounded. Since the war was over by then, I could write the whole truth. I saw that as my duty. Who else should write the truth, if not those who were there as it happened?

Under tremendous pressure I hammered away on my little Hermes typewriter, and in three or four weeks the second book was ready. The essential idea was to expose *The Other Side of the Coin*. I wanted to show the dark side of the war, as a complement to my first book. Only the two together could present the whole truth as I experienced it.

After the great success of the first book I expected no problems with the second. A big mistake. The publisher of *In the Fields of the Philistines* refused – as did all other publishers that I approached – to have anything to do with it. In the end I managed to find a small, unimportant publisher prepared to take it on.

The reaction to the publication of *The Other Side of the Coin* was also remarkable – though diametrically opposed to the first book. The new volume caused a scandal. From this developed shock, anger, and hate. Overnight I changed from hero of the day to public enemy number one.

"Lies! Deceit!" cried the patriots, who had stayed at home during the war. "Our soldiers don't swear like that! Our soldiers don't murder and rob! They didn't drive away any Arabs! It is well known that the Arabs decided to flee on their own initiative. They were just following the calls of their own leadership! Our weapons are pure! Our army is the most moral in the world!"

Everything possible was done to make the book disappear from the market. The critics ignored it. However, the first printing did indeed sell out immediately, but when the publisher wanted to reprint the book, it was blocked. At that time everything was severely rationed in the new, impoverished country. The authorities would not allocate the publisher the necessary paper.

But the three thousand copies of the first printing made up for it. They were passed from hand to hand. Only a few of the generation who were young at that time have not read the book. It took six years before I managed to get more printed. And it was over forty years before anyone else dared to portray the war of 1948 as it really was.

I always thought that both works should really appear in one book. Now this wish is realized. In order to make this possible, the books had to be shortened a little. We made sure that neither the spirit nor the content of either book was distorted by this.

The two volumes, which appear here as two parts of one book, are complementary to each other, but they are also very different. I wrote *In the Fields of the Philistines* in the course of a year, section by section. The individual articles are colored by different moods. *The Other Side of the Coin* was written in one go, and represents only one mood. The people who appear in *In the Fields of the Philistines* bear their real names, and the events are described factually. The actors in *The Other Side* appear under fictional names, even though they correspond to real people. The plot appears as a work of imagination, although everything really happened as described. I consciously cast the book as "literature," so that I would be free in my description of things without having to take account of real existing people. And since it was "literature," the manuscript was not presented to the military censor.

According to many friends the writing of this second book involved the commission of a literary sin. It ended with an up-to-date, political chapter, in which I clearly expressed my opposition to the policies of David Ben-Gurion, the absolute ruler of the young state. Ben-Gurion effectively laid down the rails on which the state of Israel has run to this day. From the direction the train was pointing I could see a collision approaching, and tried to indicate an alternative: Israel as a secular republic, democratic and liberal, an ally of the Arab national movement and a partner in the construction of a regional federation.

The experts told me that you can't just stick a political–ideological section into a literary text. I dug my heels in and put this section as an epilogue at the end of the book, so that the thoughts there might grow roots in the heads of the readers. The epilogue was headed "For the casualties of the next round."

This chapter is omitted from the present edition, since what I wrote then, in the year 1949, reflected the reality of that time. I have replaced it with an up-to-date introduction, which shows the interconnectedness of the events, and provides a historical perspective.

I am a naturally optimistic person. When I was at school in Hanover at the age of eight, the teacher talked about the monument to Hermann the Cherusker, who stands there "facing the Arch Enemy." "Children, who is the Arch Enemy?" she asked, and all the children cried in unison "France! France!" Today France and Germany both belong to the European Union, and Germans and French cross the border between their countries freely and without formalities, a border along which millions from earlier generations died.

I added the following section to the second edition of *The Other Side of the Coin:* "In the hospital I swore an oath. It may have been histrionic, or even childish. I swore to dedicate the rest of my life – which was saved by four recruits from Morocco, who rescued me under heavy fire after I was wounded – to the struggle for peace. I have often reminded myself of this oath, particularly in moments of disappointment, frustration or weakness."

I hope that I have not broken this oath, and that I will not break it, as long as I still live on this planet.

Uri Avnery
Tel Aviv

Introduction

A very special war

On 29 November 1947, thousands of people jumped out of their beds and rushed out onto the streets when the reports were broadcast on the radio. The UN General Assembly had decided to divide the land of Palestine between a Jewish and an Arab state. Still wearing their pajamas, people rejoiced, shouted, sang, and danced. I stayed in bed, feeling sad and depressed.

Sad, because I knew that a cruel war was coming, which would bring death to many of those now dancing. Depressed because I could see that this land that I loved so much, where I had grown up since the age of ten, would never be the same again.

The 635,000 Jewish inhabitants of Palestine rejoiced, because they could set up their own state in at least a part of the land. The Arab population lamented the loss of a large part of the land where their ancestors had lived for generations.

The next day the war began. It was not a normal war, where two countries fight over an area of land. The Germans and the French fought for generations over Alsace and Lorraine. But it would not have occurred to a Frenchman to eliminate Germany from the map. And no German had ever said that there was no such thing as a French nation.

And in our case? The Jews denied the existence of a Palestinian people and so obviously did not accept their right to any of this land. And the Palestinians said the Jews were no nation and had no rights in Palestine. Both sides were fully convinced that the whole area between the Jordan River and the Mediterranean Sea was their homeland and belonged to them alone. How did this situation come about?

The historian Isaac Deutscher explained it using the following parable: a man lives on the top floor of a building in which fire breaks out. To save his life, he jumps out of a window and lands on the head of a passer-by, who is severely injured. Bitter hostility develops between the two, and only gets worse day by day. That is approximately what really happened.

At the end of the nineteenth century many Jews felt that the ground was starting to burn under their feet. National movements were developing in Europe. Every national grouping, whether large or small, wanted to live in its own national state. There was a development of national culture, which was moving to fill the space left by the decline of the great dynastic conglomerates like the Austro-Hungarian and Ottoman Empires.

Almost all of these national movements were anti-Semitic. France, the homeland of Jewish emancipation, had the Dreyfus Affair. Demonstrators shouted "Death to the Jews." In the new German Reich, every level of the population was infected with anti-Semitism, an expression that was coined at the time the Reich was founded. The royal court preacher propagated this teaching. The Polish movement for national independence was just as openly anti-Semitic as the majority of the smaller peoples of Europe.

The Jews were an "anomaly" in nationalistic Europe. They were scattered over many lands and among many peoples, and had no homeland of their own. They were a remnant from an earlier age, two thousand years before. At that time the Mediterranean region was divided into ethnic-religious communities. Each community was autonomous, with its own legal system – whether in the Byzantine or the later Ottoman Empire. A Jew from Alexandria in Egypt could marry a Jew in Antioch (in today's Syria), but not the Christian woman who lived next door.

In the Europe of the late nineteenth century nobody considered the possibility of the Shoa, the Holocaust: the planned, industrial-scale destruction of the Jewish people. But the pogroms in Russia were a clear warning.

When the Jews realized that there was no place for them in the developing national movements, they decided to do the same as all the others: to form themselves into one nation on the European pattern, with a unified territory, and a common history and language. They wanted to take their fate in their own hands and found their own national state. This was the birth of the Zionist movement, which aimed to set up a Jewish state in Palestine.

The 208 delegates at the First Congress of Zionists in Basel in 1897 knew next to nothing about Palestine. With one or two exceptions, none of them had ever been there. What concerned them was the desperate situation of the Jews in Europe. This is the only way to explain how they got the idea that the land was uninhabited. Their slogan was "a land without a people for a people without a land."

But the land was not "empty." About half a million people lived there, 90% of them Muslim and Christian Arabs. They were a part of the large Arab population of the Ottoman Empire. This people too had its own national aspirations. Arab intellectuals wrote nationalistic manifestos, Arab officers set up underground cells in the Turkish-Ottoman army. The Arabs in Palestine were also swept along in this nationalist development.

This is how it happened that two national movements arose at the same time – the Zionist and the Arab – unknown to each other. When the Jews started to settle in Palestine, conflict was inevitable. The Jewish settlers were surprised to find an Arab population there, which fought with increasing violence against their presence. And the Arab population became increasingly concerned about the rapid growth of the Jewish population, which was developing into a state within a state in their land.

The two populations lived side by side. There were indeed completely mixed villages and towns, but the Jewish and Arab populations had almost no contact with each other. Both groups developed their own world of values and expressions, myths and slogans, that had nothing in common with the mental world of the other side. Through their separate and very different upbringing, a generation grew up with diametrically opposed attitudes and aspirations. The lack of contact on a commercial level ensured that the two groups lived separate lives. They spoke different languages, followed different religions, and each had their own history.

The Holocaust in Europe produced an almost irresistible pressure in support of the Jewish demands. The Arab opposition gained strength with the foundation of the Arab League in 1945. The conflict sharpened with the United Nations' declaration in 1947 on partition. The Zionist side accepted the partition, at least officially, because it gave them 55% of the land although they represented only a third of the population. The Arab side rejected partition completely. They saw it as a decision on the part of foreigners to take away a large part of their land and give it to intruders. The British government, which had been administering the Mandate for Palestine following the fall of the Ottoman Empire after the First World War, committed itself to withdraw from the land by the middle of May 1948. That's how the war began.

It was an "ethnic" war: a war between two peoples, where both tried to occupy as much of the land as possible with as few of the "enemy" population as possible. Many years before the term "ethnic cleansing" became current, it was put into practice in this war – and not just by one side.

Few Arabs remained in the areas conquered by the Jews. But no Jews remained in the Arab occupied areas, either. The expulsion of the Arabs is more prominent, because the Jews occupied a lot more of the area where Arabs lived, than the Arabs did Jewish areas (although they took the Old City of Jerusalem and Gush Etzion, a block of small settlements south of Jerusalem).

That is the background for the events described in this book. We, the soldiers, were totally convinced that we were fighting for our existence, for our lives, and the lives of the Jewish population. And the Arab Palestinians naturally felt the same. We had internalized the Hebrew mantra which was current at the time – *Ein Brerah* – "we have no choice."

Until the regular Arab armies joined the war – when the British withdrew in May 1948 – no prisoners were taken. We knew: if we surrender, we die. We saw photos at the beginning of the war showing the severed heads of our comrades being paraded on stakes through the Old City of Jerusalem. The Palestinians themselves suffered the awful massacre in Deir Yassin, a suburb of Jerusalem, where the Irgun[1] and the Lehi[2] murdered dozens of men, women and children.

We knew that 635,000 Jews were facing hundreds of millions of Arabs: "The few against the many." The armed Arab villages controlled almost all the routes of transport. The later invasion of the "seven Arab armies," with plentiful modern weapons, came on top of that.

Today we know that it wasn't quite like that. The Jewish population was cohesive, well organized, and had available informal military units that had been trained and armed in secrecy. On the other side the Arab population was divided, had no central command, and was armed only with old and simple weapons. The Arab world was almost no help to the Palestinians, and when they did intervene they spent more of their energy fighting against each other than against the common enemy.

All this became clear only later. This book shows what the soldiers then thought, as they made history, and not what later became clear and entered the history books.

If someone had told us at the end of 1948 that the Israeli–Palestinian war would still be raging sixty years later – nobody would have believed it. But that is the reality: this war still occupies the headlines, every day people are dying, and the gulf between the two sides is not reducing. The conflict has had its ups and downs. For forty years the Palestinians have been suffering under our brutal occupation. Terrible things happen on both sides. And each side is convinced that it is the victim of the other side.

The descriptions of the situation by the two sides bear no resemblance to each other. This applies to every single event of the last hundred years. For example, we Israelis talk about the "War of Liberation" or "of Independence," while the Palestinians call it simply *Nakba*, the catastrophe. Many Israelis still believe that the Palestinians want to throw us into the sea. And many Palestinians are convinced that the Israelis want to drive them into the desert. As long as people think like this, there will be no peace.

Perhaps this book will help the reader to understand what happened and why it happened – and what must be done to put an end to it all.

PART ONE

In the Fields of the Philistines

Before the Battle

29 November 1947, a few minutes after midnight

No one is sleeping. Everyone is sitting by the radio. And over the ether comes the message: the General Assembly of the United Nations has decided in favor of the founding of a Jewish and an Arab state.

Joy explodes like a wild storm. Young people stream onto the streets, collect together, go wild. Such a demonstration of mass enthusiasm has never been seen before in this land. Groups are formed, people packed together, songs are sung, and wildly dancing circles form at the crossroads. Men and women who have never met before hug and kiss each other.

Joy washes away all boundaries; limits and differences disappear. In a sea of flags, drunk with enthusiasm, the youth celebrate the great news.

* * *

In the last few months the land of Palestine had fallen ever deeper into the abyss. Order collapsed and chaos ruled everywhere.

On 29 September 1947, exactly two months before the historic decision, Jamal Husseini[1] declared, in a clear and unambiguous speech, that the Arabs would take up arms to convert the land into an Arab state. On the same day the police station in Haifa was blown up by the Irgun, with the death of ten British soldiers. The governments of Syria and Lebanon began moving their armies to the border. On 12 November the British murdered four young members of the Lehi. The next day the Lehi killed eight Englishmen in various parts of the country. Three days later the ship *Aliyah* ran the British maritime blockade and brought refugees to the beach of Nahariya.[2] On 19 November two new Jewish settlements were founded in the

9

Negev. On 21 November ten people were injured when Arabs attacked a bus on the way from Cholon to Tel Aviv.

Three different groups were fighting against each other. A British government – without any moral authority – tried to keep out the refugees, who were streaming into the land from Europe, week after week. Their refusal to allow in the fugitives on board the *Exodus*[3] sent shock waves around the world. A small group of young people, agents of the Haganah,[4] were trying to set up an underground network in Europe and the Arab states. Their attempts to find ways through this blockade gained tremendously in support from the *Exodus* affair. At the same time other small groups were fighting the British administration through acts of sabotage. A continuous cycle of terror and counter-terror eroded the basis for a normal life.

And on the other side of the border Haj Amin al-Husseini[5] was meeting with the leaders of the Arab states. They made the decision to use armed force to destroy the "Zionist danger" once and for all.

* * *

In this atmosphere of threatening crisis, the UN decision was like the first thunder announcing a refreshing storm after days of hot, sticky weather. Everyone felt instinctively: the die is cast. The uncertainty, the paralyzing indecision is at an end.

The most brilliant director would not have been capable of producing a scene of such spontaneously erupting joy. These young people were not happy about the partition, which would divide Palestine into little pieces. They were not celebrating the approaching battles. Their joy was an expression of freedom: the walls of the ghetto have fallen, the road out is clear, new horizons for activity and life are open.

But there were some who remained quiet on that night. They went around with gloomy faces, and took no part in the celebrations. They looked upon the dancing, jubilant youth and wondered: how many of these will still be living next year?

Because they knew the decisive battle was yet to come: a bloody war in the struggle between Israelis and Arabs, which had been approaching for thirty years, ever since the Balfour Declaration.[6]

30 November 1947

The enthusiasm continues. Young men and women, who didn't sleep all last night, dance, rejoice, and sing on.

Suddenly there is a moment of quiet. Shots echo through the land. A bus on the road from Netanya to Jerusalem is attacked, leaving four dead bodies on the ground. The war has begun.

Everywhere the Arab youth rush to join the fighting organizations. And from Syria, from Egypt, from Iraq, and from Transjordan,[7] volunteers come streaming into the country – along with large quantities of weapons.

The first attack is aimed at the lifeline of the Hebrew population – the lines of transport. The roads to Jerusalem and in the Negev are closed after repeated attacks by Arab groups. A bomb is placed under the water pipeline in the Negev, and after each repair it is blown up again. On 2 December an Arab mob rampages through the commercial center of Jerusalem, killing five Hebrews and chasing the Hebrew population out of remote parts of the city. At the same time the first attacks are mounted on the outskirts of Tel Aviv from the direction of Jaffa. The roads are blocked. The larger towns and also smaller villages are encircled.

The third party is also active. The British, who had decided to withdraw from the country, intended thereby to leave the Arabs to finish off the Yishuv.[8] They have no scruples about making it easier for them. With British support the Arab Legion[9] enters the country. On 14 December fourteen members of the Haganah are killed outside the barracks of the Legion in Beit Nabala, as they are escorting a convoy of lorries to Ben-Shemen. On 22 February British terrorists blow up the center of Hebrew Jerusalem in Ben-Yehuda Street. On 28 February the British disarm eight Haganah people, who are securing the road from Tel Aviv to Cholon by the Hayotzek factory, and hand over the helpless victims to the Arab murderers. The Yishuv is fighting for its life and still may not carry its weapons openly.

* * *

The Yishuv is also unprepared for this war. The Zionist institutions, which have been campaigning for years for the partition of the country, didn't believe that the Arabs would carry out their threat and go to war. They expected that the world, represented by the UN, would come to their aid and impose the division of the country by force of arms.

The rumors about huge quantities of hidden weapons, buried somewhere deep underground, pop like soap bubbles on the walls of reality. And the fairy tale of the 80,000 well-trained and armed Jewish soldiers, who would appear from the underground at the command of the national institutions, also dissipates like the morning mist.

The hope of early weapons supplies was also quickly dashed. The British blockade impeded the import of weapons, and the UN prohibited its members from arming the fighting parties. So the Yishuv was faced with two bitter alternatives: either to win the battle with whatever resources it had, or to give up without a struggle. There were only a few, light, weapons. And there were only a few organized troops, in small units. Survival was hanging from a very thin thread.

* * *

On 30 November 1947, when the first shots of the war sounded, the national institutions proclaimed the mobilization of everyone between seventeen and twenty-five years of age. With great enthusiasm the best of the youth streamed to the recruitment offices.

While small groups of the Palmach[10] and the HISH[11] accompanied the supply convoys and defended the outer parts of the city with other volunteers, a new army was being formed all over the country. An army without a name, without insignia, ranks, or a uniform – the army of the young Hebrews. In the barracks of Tel Aviv and Sarona, which the British police had vacated on 15 December 1947, hundreds and thousands were hastily trained and instructed in the use of weapons.

The first fighting units began with reprisals, storming Arab villages and blowing up houses. With only a few rifles, which were passed from hand to hand, without sufficient armored vehicles to defend the transport arteries, these young people won great victories and suffered painful defeats. On 23 February 1948, thirty-five of them fell on the road to Gush Etzion. They were on their way to an action that only a well-trained and appropriately equipped company could have carried out successfully. On 4 March, fifteen fell near Atarot. On 28 March, forty-two fell defending a supply column near Yehiam.

New fighting units were formed from freshly recruited volunteers. From the companies, battalions were formed, from the battalions – brigades. It was an army without means of transport, without aircraft, and without a supporting infrastructure in the rear. There were neither cannons nor tanks. But they were supported by the enthusiasm of the population, in a way that has not often happened in the history of humankind, perhaps only with the troops of the French and later the Russian revolution.

* * *

When I read on 30 November that the first Hebrew bus had been attacked by Arab fighters, I knew what my duty was: to report for service.

In the days leading up to my recruitment I wrote a little pamphlet about the problems of the war. Unlike the troubles of 1936 to 1939 we were now faced with a real, lengthy war with many casualties, which would decide the question of our survival.

I used what money I had left to buy a khaki uniform, a sock hat, and the clothing a soldier needs, and reported at the gate of the training camp. I became a simple soldier of the infantry.

13 February 1948
Training camp

Initiation

They arrive singly, one after the other. Some with a firm step, with the forced smile that is supposed to show self-confidence. They give the guard at the gate their call-up papers as if they are showing a bus ticket. They look at the camp, trying to absorb everything with one glance, dump their luggage on the ground, light a cigarette, and wait for what may happen. But there are others who approach the gate hesitantly, cast a last, longing look at the "civilian" street behind them, and wait like small, nervous children, as though they felt guilty about something.

These two types differ even in their clothing. One kind is dressed like a staff officer, with a uniform bought "outside" – *battle dress* (as it is also called in Hebrew), and khaki trousers. Their berets are creased, as if they had already seen a couple of years' service. The others are the civilians – colorful trousers, checkered jackets, some even wearing ties.

Now they are standing next to each other, examining each other – foreign to each other. In a few hours they will be living together, standing in line at the mess, pushing for a place to shave in the morning, borrowing shoe polish from each other, and firing off ancient curses in fourteen different languages. But now they are still foreign to each other. The distance between them is enormous – locally born, traditional Yemenites, Yekkes,[12] fat and thin, a roundish youth with glasses who was yesterday the director of finance in a factory, and little Ezra, who sold ice cream on the beach, standing there like a crooked question mark.

Here and there the barriers are overcome. The more active make contact. The lanky blond asks the little Yemeni for a cigarette, a first conversation develops with a few sentences – and a friendship begins that will be known to everyone in the whole training camp in a few weeks. In another corner they are comparing what they paid for their battle dress. The conversations drift from topic to topic, "acquaintanceships" arise – a "family."

The whistle blows. The commanding officers have arrived. They observe the "human material" which they must turn into a battalion as quickly as possible. They are very young, no older than their recruits, who from now on will stand to attention before them and obey their orders.

"Atten-shun!" Talking stops. The red-haired officer arranges the men patiently in rows of three. In a few days they will form up like this to order.

They stand in ranks. Soldiers.

What was being formed here was not just an army. It was also a youth movement, a revolutionary movement. Within a few days a new lifestyle developed, a new way of talking, of dressing, of behaving. This new style was not copied from somewhere or somebody. It arose within us, from the character of a generation.

It is possible that this youth movement would have arisen even without the war. It was the coming-of-age of a whole generation: the first generation that grew up in this land, conscious of its freedom. Even before the war there were preliminary signs. Members of the Palmach felt like new people with new goals. Intellectual circles like Bamaavak were searching for new spiritual roots – a whole range of curious groups, involved in the most disparate aspects of life.

This great movement needed a symbol, a badge, to represent the character of this army. We had no uniforms. We wore the clothes we had brought with us. But thousands suddenly began to wear the same headgear, without being told to by anyone: the sock hat.

The sock hat

18 February 1948
Training camp

The khaki bucket hat – *kova tembel* in Hebrew, meaning "idiot hat" because it makes you look particularly stupid – was the symbol of the pioneering days of Zionism. Who doesn't remember the propaganda pictures of the Zionist organizations? This war has created its own headgear – the *kova gerev* or "sock hat," that curious woolen stocking which never stays the same shape. The sock hat is the symbol of the individualist army. Its main characteristic is that it can be worn in a thousand different styles. You won't find two soldiers who wear this headgear in the same way. One wears it like a garrison cap, another makes the corners into pointy horns and looks like a Spanish bull fighter, a third flattens out the corners and looks like an Arab Fellah or a Russian Muzhik. Briefly: there is an enormous range of possibilities, limited only by the soldier's individuality and creativity.

The ordinary soldier likes this article of clothing more than any other part of his military outfit. Nobody leaves the barracks without his sock hat. Even the dandies who won't wear it to breakfast, in order to preserve the hairstyle that they spent five precious minutes of their free time arranging – they wear it too, but folded under their left shoulder strap.

The sock hat has further properties: it is extremely practical. It can be used for almost anything. When you are on sentry duty on a cold night, and feel as if you are at the North Pole, you can pull your hat over your frozen ears. If your neck is feeling chilly, it turns itself into a scarf. Or if you have secretly taken the evening off and want to get back over the fence, and the sentry is suddenly standing six feet in front of you, you pull the cap over your glimmering face. You can't see the sentry any more, and you hope that he can't see you either. On leave, on the city streets, the sock hat signals at a distance: here goes a soldier – a magnet for female eyes …

* * *

The start of the war presented everyone with a decision. And the youth divided into two groups – those who joined up and those who did not join up.

For thousands the decision was simple. They never even considered doing otherwise. They signed on immediately to the fighting units. They were not always the cleverest. Most of them were simple lads. But they formed the backbone of the generation, they had character.

But there were also those who weakened at this moment. They stayed at home and waited for the right "opportunity." The true Hebrew youth despised them deeply. We felt the deep chasm between them and us. And the longer the war lasted and the fiercer the battles raged, the deeper this division became.

28 February 1948
Training camp

Leave

He had worked everything out exactly. Just a few paces from the barracks to the barbed wire, crawl under that to the little slope, and down that on all fours. A simple plan – all you need is strong nerves.

He left the mess. "Where are you off to?" asked a friend. "A short walk – I'll be right back." On the way he threw a glance into the officer's mess. The NCOs still used to eat together at that time. The sentry is standing in the corner chatting. It is the right moment.

Everything goes to plan. It really is child's play. The hole in the barbed wire is large enough. Now he crawls on his belly to the slope, just the way he learned. His instructor would be proud of him. He smiles to himself.

The sentry post is unmanned. From here on the way is open. On the streets of the city a Sabbath-evening atmosphere. Not many people around. They look at him as though he were a strange animal. Crumpled overalls and the sock hat announce: here is a soldier … he feels like a stranger in the city, as though he has been away for years. And it is just four days since he reported to the camp. But his civilian life feels to him like something from the distant past, part of history. Hard to believe that just four days ago he was walking around like the others here, exchanging remarks with those very same girls who now appear to him like the denizens of a foreign world …

Home? His parents would be pleased. But he doesn't have enough time. If he arrived back after ten, without knowing the night password, then he would be exposed. He only has two hours. Not a minute to waste. So – straight to Rachel's.

Rachel … how often had he thought about her during these four days?

He imagined this evening in bright colors. He would ring the doorbell, she would open the door – and smile. Of course she would smile. Triumphantly he would recount his adventure. How he broke out for her sake, although twenty-four hours in the arrest cells await him if he gets caught.

That is the house. His breathing is labored – he ran half the way so as not to waste any time. Luckily he is used to running. He pauses on the stairs a moment to regain his breath. Then he rings the bell. She opens the door, looks at him with astonishment, yes, she smiles too. But it is a different smile. Not the one he expected.

"Come in" she says, and leads him into the room. Someone is sitting there. He is in civilian clothes. They introduce themselves awkwardly. Somehow they manage to talk about this and that, while she gets changed.

They walk to a little cafe. He tells them about life in the training camp, talks without stopping, so as to have no time to think. She asks if he has gone AWOL. But suddenly he finds he has lost all desire to talk about his heroic deeds.

He feels alien. They don't understand what he is trying to tell them about – the joys and troubles of a soldier's life in the training camp. What made him come here? Did he really think she would be waiting for him with open arms?

Quarter past nine. He stands up and takes his leave. He even smiles through his pain.

The way back is just the way out in reverse. Around the guard, crawling up the slope. There's a sentry standing by the gap in the wire. Five motionless minutes with his face pressed against the ground. At last he's gone. Slip under the wire, one leap to the barracks – made it!

The lights are still on in the barracks. It is warm inside. His comrades are arranging the beds. Chatting and swearing like always. As he comes in they look at him enviously. He was in their dream land: "Outside."

His friend approaches. "What was it like? See your girlfriend?"

He turns his back on his friend, arranges his bed. "Alright" he mumbles, "everything OK." He puts out the light and lies down. "I'm back" he thinks to himself "at home."

4 March 1948
On leave

We are soldiers now

A soldier is not a citizen who is familiar with the use of weapons, who moves in a particular way, and obeys particular orders. A soldier is a special kind of human creature in a world of his own.

The son, brother, or boyfriend is called up. Two weeks later he comes back home on his first leave. He doesn't appear to have changed in any way. He is tanned, the skin on his nose is peeling, and on his hands are little cuts and sores from his field exercises. But those who approach him more closely notice that something has changed. Something deep and fundamental. He feels different, talks differently, behaves differently. And they will never really understand what this change means.

For them it was just two short weeks. But for him it was an eternity. And everything from his past now seems to him to belong to a distant and alien world. What has happened to him in these two weeks? He has changed. He has lost one world and gained another. A painful process.

The first three or four days are the worst. The raw recruit entered the camp in joyful, relaxed expectation, looking forward to new experiences, which he pictures in bright colors. And the reality is gray. Dark gray. His thoughts were on automatic weapons, hand

grenades, the joy of the assault. But now he is occupied with polish-
ing boots, washing dishes in cold water, trying to shave in such
crowded conditions that he cannot move his arms, collecting
rubbish from the paths, cleaning the floor, and folding blankets
according to a very complicated scheme.

And he is not doing that of his own free will. It's all about obeying
orders. You are driven, shouted at, urged on. Each unit has its share of
the slothful and the undisciplined who increase the pressure applied
to the unit. The most striking thing about this first phase is being
completely cut off from the world outside. This is not just a physical
separation, but mental too. You lose interest in all the things that used
to be important and precious: cultural, political, and social. That all
belongs to "Outside." And "Outside" is strange and distant. In the
first few days you still try and get hold of a paper in the reading room.
But after a week you only read the headlines, and after two weeks have
gone by you don't read anything at all.

Your relationship to "Outside" is reduced to one dimension: the
family, the girlfriend, or some other person who symbolizes the
outside world. The one you think about when you dream of a short
leave. Go home and visit the girlfriend – that is as much as you can
yearn for. For that much, you are prepared to take risks – you vanish
for one evening and spend a day in the arrest cells.

The second experience is the company in which you find yourself.
"Outside" you know a relatively small number of people, who you
more or less get on with. But here young people are mixed together at
random, with no account taken of personality, job, origins, or education. At the beginning that is painful. You find it difficult to make
contact with those you are thrown together with, twenty-four hours
a day. You have no space to yourself. And whether you like it or not,
you have to make the best of it. After a while you begin to notice that
some of your comrades are nice and some less so. You discover sides
of yourself that you knew nothing about. Unexpected contacts are
made. Shared experiences, memories, and unpleasant events bring
you closer together.

Eventually, after a few days that feel like half an eternity, you find
your place. You learn quickly how to get out of unpleasant tasks, how
to get a feel for what's going on. You get used to things that not long
ago seemed to be pure bloody-mindedness and torture. All of a

sudden you begin to take pleasure in things that you would have despised "Outside" – the quantities of sweets that you chew during night exercises, or idleness: you lie on your back along with the others and stare into the sky, without saying a word.

You see new comrades coming into the camp, smile about the "green recruits," feel like a veteran and give them the benefit of your advice.

And when you go into town after two weeks, it looks strange. You talk with friends and acquaintances and notice that there is something separating you.

You have become a soldier.

On the streets we were followed by respectful looks. The state was still in the future. It was difficult to come to terms with carrying arms openly. And we – with proudly raised heads we strode along. Pride in the army and our weapons. But we had no song of joy on our lips. The great, moving song for this uplifting moment remained unwritten. For the first time I became aware that this great movement, this earthquake that gripped the youth, had not touched the intellectuals, the poets, or the writers. Those too who were known as the "young writers" stayed at home, as though nothing had happened. They did not join us on our road of suffering and endurance.

14 March 1948
Camp "Jonah"

Squad leader

The leader of a squad is the backbone of the army, as they say. The squad leader is the most pitiful command position. He has the pleasant duty at quarter to six in the morning of ripping the covers off the soldiers' beds and rounding them up for morning gymnastics. He has to keep order in the hungry cutlery-clattering line at the mess. At ten in the evening he must supervise lights out, just at the moment when the men in the tents remember the hottest stories of the last week.

In brief, the squad leader is the direct superior. He is the recipient of the juiciest curses from the ordinary soldiers. But he has none of the status of an officer at all.

We got to know various squad leaders. There were some we would have done anything for. And there were others who we used every opportunity to try and take for a ride.

Grisha was one of the first kind. He was a nice fellow. There was no prank that he didn't take part in. He was disciplined as often as our greatest rascals. He drank our stolen cognac with us and helped us with all the thousand things that make up life in the army.

Shimon, however, we didn't like at all. The man with the gigantic black mustache kept his distance. He avoided familiarity with the ordinary soldiers. During breaks in the field exercises he sat twenty meters away with his back to us. And no one ever saw him smile. Just one time I thought I detected a slight twitching at the end of his mustache, when he saw our comrade "Nail" in his long white nightshirt.

Squad leaders have a particularly difficult time if they are younger than their subordinates. A twenty-five-year-old soldier, who was some kind of a manager "outside," has great difficulty standing to attention in front of a nineteen-year-old school-leaver.

The most popular squad leader is the one who knows his job, who pays close attention to the really important things, without going an inch too far, who looks after the interests of his people, and is their friend occasionally – even in minor misdemeanors. For this kind of squad leader – and we experienced many such – one can truly say that they are the backbone of the army.

22 March 1948
Camp "Jonah"

On the eve of battle

A day of drama. We are lying on the lawns in front of the tents and enjoying the lunch break. The intellectual among us are holding a newspaper and pretending to read, while they are really staring into the empty sky. Others are complaining about their superiors and discussing how they can get out of the afternoon's exercise. In a tent two men are sitting and discussing at the top of their voices what they would do with an unofficial leave.

Then suddenly – roll call! We assemble on the parade ground. The usual orders – "Company – ... stand at – ease!" We go through the motions mechanically and wonder "what's all this about?"

Aryeh, the company commander, stands before us. As usual his head is slightly tilted forward. He is also dressed as always: that special brown battle dress. But somehow he looks different. More serious, almost solemn.

He reads out a command from the battalion commander. The company should provide fifty men as the reserve for an operation. The names are not yet decided. They will be announced in the evening. Those who take part will hold high the honor of the company etc, etc.

The roll call is over. We climb into the vehicles to return to our field exercise. Normally we lark about, shout, and laugh. This time we are quiet. Very quiet. No singing. A few of us hum a melancholy soldier's tune that reflects our mood.

Each of us is wondering: is my name on the list? Or must I take my leave from my friends? I wouldn't be able to say goodbye to my parents or girlfriend. All leave has been canceled. We will have to be ready – as soon as the command arrives – to depart within twenty minutes.

In the late afternoon we return to camp. We have hardly had time to change our clothes when there is another roll call. We line up in silence. We are waiting for the list.

The boss gives us a searching look. In his hand is a white sheet of paper. We know: the list. "I will read the names of reserve number one. The men will line up in three rows before me ..."

One name after another. After each name your heart skips a beat. A good friend: Gustav, the clown of the company. We will miss his performances in the evening. My chess opponent.

We stand there perfectly still. Each one is expecting his own name. One after another they go and form the new unit.

The list is finished. Over half the company. Those who remain are standing in sparse rows, with the gaps standing for those who were called. We look at each other – like orphans. Nobody is pleased that he was not chosen. We are all thinking of our missing comrades.

The gaps are closed and the ranks reformed. Off to the culture room to hear a lecture. But nobody is listening. From time to time we glance out of the window. See the comrades packing, see them gathering by the vehicles.

The commander can feel that we are unsettled. He gives us a few minutes to say our goodbyes. We do our best to smile, to make jokes, we offer oranges. We all know how the others are feeling. A silent handshake. Those who are leaving don't envy us. They know that we'll be following them in a few days.

The vehicles are moving. A last wave. An outsider wouldn't notice that anything has changed. But on this day it has happened to us. Those who used to be recruits are now soldiers.

Baptism of Fire

At five o'clock in the morning our commanders stormed into the dormitories to wake us. No morning gymnastics. We are in a high state of alert. Our comrades who were on night duty report that the superiors were summoned to battalion HQ around midnight. So it really is serious.

What it is about is still a secret. But most of us can guess the aim. We know that Jerusalem is cut off and that no supply convoys are getting through. This is an existential matter for the whole population. In this situation the army has no choice but to start a large-scale offensive for the first time.

In the evening we are transferred to a temporary field camp near the port of Tel Aviv. Four companies in total (at that time a tremendous force). For the first time we have enough equipment: Australian uniforms, sock hats, shoes.

Our comrades tell the most amazing stories about heavy automatic weapons that they claim to have seen somewhere: a Browning machine gun, an Italian anti-tank weapon, even a machine gun called Schwarzlose is among them! But nobody has seen simple rifles.

On the high seas a drama was being enacted at the same time. The first of the Army's munitions ships was trying to run the British blockade. In the hold of that ship are the rifles and the automatic weapons that can determine the result of that operation, the fate of the whole of Eretz Israel.[1] The British warships detected it, but it slips by in the dark. On 2 April it docks in the harbor of Tel Aviv. The hour has struck for Operation Nachshon.

In the afternoon there is a roll call for the company. We are reorganized in preparation for combat. Aryeh Spack, the company commander, holds a sheet of paper in his hand and reads out the names.

"Platoon number one. Leader: Yaakov Burstein." Yaakov, small and skinny, moved to the front of the row. "Deputy: Chaim Bulmann." Bulli, tall, broad-shouldered, always smiling, stood behind Burstein. "Squad number one. Shlomo Greimann, Uri Avnery, Moshe Shatzky ..." We look at each other. We know: from now on we will live together, rely on each other, and have faith in the commanders.

Suddenly a stir in the camp – our weapons have arrived. We run, in order not to miss this historic moment. The crates are opened and there they are, the rifles. Thickly coated in grease. With plenty of ammunition. Everyone gets his own personal rifle. As evening falls we sit and clean them without having the right equipment. And the whole time, until long after midnight, we try to come to terms with events: a personal rifle for each Israeli soldier.

Sleep is out of the question. Janek Levkovitz, a refugee from Europe who knows rifles inside out, shows us how to use these guns that we never saw in training. Nobody sleeps.

Saturday 3 April, 1948

Dawn departure

At five o'clock the next morning we have breakfast. We stand in a long line, receive our food, devour it in no time, and return to our tents. Everything is packed, the weapons have been cleaned. Four companies are standing by.

The buses arrive. We get in. Our orders are: no singing! Don't make any noise. Keep your weapons out of sight. Nobody in Tel Aviv should notice that a large body of troops is leaving the town. We drive through the empty streets of the sleeping city.

A man is standing at a corner alone. An old German Jew with a hat. He sees the bus full of young people in uniform. Suddenly he lifts his hand and raises his hat. The civilian salutes the soldiers, with a simple, spontaneous, and touching gesture. I look at my comrades. I am the only one who noticed.

We leave the city. In the distance we recognize the Arab bunkers of Jaffa and Tel a-Rish. We gather our weapons from the floor at the same moment as a rousing song bursts from our lips: "Believe me, the day will come/It will be good, that I promise you/I will hold you in my arms/And tell you – everything ..."

I think about the battle that lies before us. Will we win? And what about the next one? I am convinced that it will be a long war, and that the regular armies of the neighboring countries will cross the border.

We spend the whole day sitting in a lonely field near Ramat Aharon.[2] We are supplied with hand grenades, a very unpopular weapon. Senior officers come to inspect us. The old hands know their names. The one in the green camouflage outfit, that's Chaim Laskov,[3] and that one there with blond hair, that's Shimon "Givati".[4]

In the afternoon we each fire five shots to test our rifles. For the first time we smell the acrid aroma of cordite. For the first time our shoulders feel the kick of a rifle.

Toward evening we drive to Kibbutz Naan. Later in the evening, after dark, we should be in Hulda.

The operation is called "Nachshon."

4 April 1948
Forward base Hulda[5]

The first casualties

As soon as it is dark we set out – a long row of staff people, infantry, machine gun crews, auxiliary troops, and others. It doesn't sound like much to us – a night march of four miles. Of course we know that there are Arab villages in the area. But nobody sees any significance in that.

Now and then the line stops. It seems the scouts in front are checking something. Occasionally whispered orders are passed back along the line.

"Six feet separation from man to man!"

"Close up the gaps!"

"No noise!"

"Everyone there?"

Somewhere a light is flashing. That's where the camp is, someone tells us, the one we are heading for. But the light seems to get further away the more we walk toward it.

We cross a wadi.[6] The water is a few inches deep. I jump, slip, and scrabble to remain upright. Joske, the squad leader, is in front of me, and reaches out his hand, and I help Shlomo who is behind me.

The line stops. By the road stands a small Arab house. Presumably this is the Arab village of Na'ana which we were told about. We lie on the ground for about ten minutes. We are so tired we do not move. We are all afraid of the moment when we have to get up again. But somehow we manage it. The long line passes the house just a few paces away, without being noticed – the result of intensive training.

Again the line stops. This time the company runner appears and whispers something to Joske. He gets up and beckons to me. Our squad goes ahead, next to the long line, right up to the front. Aryeh, the company commander, is waiting for us.

"To the left – fan out!" whispers Joske to me, and I pass the command. We fan out to the left, six feet apart, forming a sharp angle with the head of the long row. Joske is in the middle of the squad, I am at the right-hand end.

"Who is that?" I recognize Aryeh's voice

"Uri." He approaches me.

"Make sure you don't lose sight of him!"

He points to a man wearing pale khaki trousers. They stand out brightly in the dark. He is carrying an automatic weapon – so he must be a commander. Probably the commander of the section at the head of the column. Our squad is defending their left flank, another squad has the same task on the right.

We walk, or rather stumble, forwards. Our rifles no longer hang from our shoulders. Within the first few steps the row is jumbled up. It is not possible to maintain a regularly spaced formation in a freshly plowed field when you are dog tired. Shlomo, who should be to the left of me, is suddenly behind me. I do my best to keep the man with the bright trousers in view. I don't know how long it goes on like this. Five minutes perhaps. Maybe half an hour. My feeling for time is long gone. I am walking mindlessly, like an automaton.

I have no idea how I fell. My body just hit the ground instinctively. On the way down I see a burst of fire. Ten yards away at the most. Bullets whistle past my ears.

Rat-tat-tat-tat rat-tat-tat-tat-tat

I lie motionless on the ground. Something is missing. My spade, where is it? Slowly and carefully I feel the area around me. There it is. I put it next to me.

I examine myself. My brain is working – I congratulate myself on my cool-headedness and try to push some earth aside so I can get my head lower. No good. The earth is as hard as stone. Slowly I lay the tarps in front of me and press my head into them. Well, it's some kind of protection …

The bullets keep whistling by. Suddenly it is quiet. Has the enemy withdrawn? Shots can be heard from near the Arab village. I can hear the Arab calls clearly – "Ahmed! Ta'al lahon!"[7]

I can see Shlomo lying diagonally behind me. Next to him is Moshe. Both are hugging the earth like me and cursing quietly. I can't see anyone else. Everyone is on the ground, keeping still.

Suddenly someone raises themselves from the ground and crawls back. From his silhouette I can recognize him: Yaakov Rachmilevitch, the company medical orderly.

Only then did I become aware that someone behind me is groaning and whimpering. I can't see who it is.

"Who has got a penknife?"

I dig out my knife and throw it to Shlomo, who crawls to the wounded man. I suppose he needs it to cut through his clothing.

The groaning continues for a while, then suddenly stops. Movement near me. The message is passed on. I hear three awful words: "… he is finished …"

Anyone else been hit?

We remain on the ground. Absolute quiet all around us. The first shock is over and I can think again. That was our baptism of fire. The platoon was OK, I say to myself. Yes really, the platoon was completely OK. I repeat this sentence over and over. It makes me calm.

"Platoon Number One withdraw!"

I grab the spade, the rifle, the tarps, and crawl backwards to where the platoon is surrounding the corpse on the stretcher. Our orders are to bring him back to Naan.

I will never forget the next two hours, even if my memory is a little hazy. In the company's history they are recorded as the "Death March."

The dead weigh a lot more than the living. We are carrying the stretcher in addition to our rifles and equipment. We walk, stumble, slip, and can't think at all. We have only one desire: to throw away the damned stretcher together with our rifles and equipment, to lie down on the wet ground and sleep, sleep, sleep.

We are alone. A platoon of infantry soldiers and a corpse. With every step death is waiting. Every bush could be hiding an enemy, or we could walk into an ambush of our own people, who could mow us down. We don't really care. We are so tired and tense that we don't mind if we live or die. Even death doesn't seem so terrible to us any more.

I still don't know who it was that died. While I am carrying the front part of the stretcher, the tarp slips from his head. I know that face. Hey, that's Yitzhak Heller, the section leader I met this morning. The tarp slips a bit further, and I see his almost white trousers – and now it all comes back to me. That's the man who I was not supposed to let out of my sight.

In the course of the action I happened to get in front of him instead of to his left. If I had kept the formation I would have been in the line of fire. That is the arbitrariness of war, that spares the life of one, and randomly kills another.

At long last we somehow get to Naan. When we see the kibbutz our last energy is drained. We lie on the ground and wait for a patrol to come by. But our suffering is not yet over. We have to wait at the gate for the convoy of heavy weapons that is also headed for Hulda. We, the infantry, have to protect its flanks. Rifles in hand, we stare into the darkness. When the trucks stop we jump out.

We arrive at Hulda at three o'clock in the morning. It is drizzling, but we don't notice. We don't notice anything at all. If artillery opened fire on us – it wouldn't make us move any faster. We don't even know where exactly we are – whether we are in the camp or outside it. We know only one thing – we can sleep. We take a blanket and lie down on the damp ground between the puddles, with our boots on. And go to sleep.

They didn't give us much time to rest. In the afternoon we are out on patrol. We circle around Hulda and reach the camp of Wadi Sarar, where Iraqi volunteers are supposed to be stationed. As we walk next to the tracks we see a train approaching. We take our positions with the automatic weapons and the grenade launchers at the ready. The train is full of English soldiers who are leaving the country for Egypt. To see our weapons pointing at them fills them with astonishment.

The trucks that are supposed to supply Jerusalem finally arrive on 4 April. Now everything is ready. We are just waiting for our marching orders.

7 April 1948
Position "Boas five" opposite Wadi Sarar

Deir Muheisin

At four o'clock in the afternoon we are called from our tents. The company sits casually in a semicircle. Keen anticipation. We know that now we'll hear the details of the operation that we have been expecting for days. Aryeh, the company commander, looks briefly at us and comes straight to the point. That's how he is – he tells it like it is, direct, unadorned.

The battalion will attack tonight. The aim: to clear the route to Jerusalem. The other companies will carry out diversionary and mining operations, along the whole section from Ramle[8] to Latrun.[9] Our company and one other have the task of capturing a position that overlooks the village of Deir Muheisin, and mining the access roads. As soon as we have completed this action, the convoy to Jerusalem can set off. If it comes under attack, we have to divert the fighters in the village. At dawn we will assault and take the village.

Deir Muheisin controls the road from Hulda to Latrun. Its capture will ensure the safety of the Jerusalem convoys from Arab attacks.

Now it is clear why the preparations for this operation have been so elaborate. The operation is on a huge, historical scale. For the first time we will be operating as a regular army, capturing a village in order to hold it. Our company has a key role in this operation.

Aryeh concludes his talk in a calm voice which fills us with confidence. "If we do our work well and each one of us fulfills his tasks, we can be successful without losses …"

* * *

We return to our little tents. I clean my rifle, check every single part, pull the oily rag through the barrel, and oil the trigger. I know that tonight my life will depend on this little part.

My preparations are complete. I have checked the hand grenades ten times. The ammunition is distributed around my pockets, within easy reach. The individual first-aid dressing is in its place. To the right of me in the tent my friend Shlomo is lying down. Neither of us says anything. I can hardly believe that just three days ago I was a recruit in the training camp. We have gone through so much since then. Being woken up in the middle of the night and told to be ready to set out in two hours. The contradictory rumors about the aim and the location of the operation. The attempts to get a message to the parents. The strange feeling when we saw the heavy weapons and realized that this time it was going to be a really big operation. The night march from Naan to Hulda – a world full of experiences.

I have a strange feeling in my belly. Is this *fear*? I ask Shlomo. He has the same feeling. This will be our first battle. Are we going to get through it alright? Yes, we are sure of that. And still there is a weight on our minds.

The time has come. We put on our equipment – a rifle, one hundred and fifty rounds of ammunition, three hand grenades, a box of rounds for the machine gun, a grenade for the grenade launcher, two dressings, the iron ration, the mines for the preliminary operation, a folding spade. We are loaded down like mules.

Then we jump up and down, to make sure that nothing rattles. Someone brings some charcoal from the camp fire so we can blacken our faces, necks, and hands, to reduce their visibility in the dark. Someone suggests that Shlomo should blacken his bald pate, or else he'll endanger the whole company. Someone else asks Yehuda, our man from Damascus, why he bothered at all. He is as black as pitch in any case.

Here and there orders are given, questions whispered and answered. "Where is the platoon orderly?" "Hey, you, radio operator, which section do you belong to?" "Platoon leaders over here!" "Damn it, where are the mines?" "For God's sake, the dressings belong in the other pocket!" "Where is the scout from the Palmach?" The command is given to set off.

* * *

We leave the village behind. The night is dark. No one talks. We walk in a long column, like a giant snake.

Our platoon is at the head. In front of me our platoon leader, Joske the redhead. I keep my eyes on him. The thing I am most afraid of is to lose touch in the dark. I have heard the most terrifying stories about people who lost contact and wandered around the whole night, till the next morning they found themselves in the middle of an Arab area.

I make a note of anything conspicuous – the shape of the hill on the horizon to the left, white stones beside the path, the direction of the Pole Star. If something happens, I will be able to find the way back to base.

We have been walking for at least an hour. Now we are deep in enemy territory. At any moment, guns could open fire on us from an ambush. It seems to me that we are making a fantastic amount of noise. Boots are tramping on the rocks, the grass is rustling, someone coughs, a rifle rattles against a water bottle, someone slips. I try to calm myself: all this noise mixes in with the sounds of the night. The enemy won't hear us.

Two hours have gone by already. Gradually the feeling that nothing matters has taken over: you don't care if someone shoots at you and kills you. The main thing is not to have to lug this weight around any more. In this situation the purpose of orders becomes clear – without orders you won't reach your target. The order drives you on, discipline gives you strength. Without them you are lost.

* * *

Our platoon leaves the long column and goes off with the scouts to mine the road between Deir Muheisin and Seidun, to cut off the route for enemy reserves. We are on our own now – twenty soldiers in the middle of Arab territory. And suddenly I notice that the feeling in my belly is gone. Strange that one is afraid only before things start. Now I am feeling fresh and relaxed. Devil knows why.

There is the path – a narrow, light strip between the meadows. Joske arranges us in a defensive circle. I am lying directly facing the Pole Star. I can't see my comrades to the right and left of me. An irrational fear overcomes me: what if they leave me here alone? Maybe they won't notice that anyone is missing? I listen. Can hear absolutely nothing. Have they already withdrawn? Then I hear the sound of digging. The scout is doing his job. I laugh to myself. You can rely on Joske.

A faint whistle. The sign to withdraw. The mines have been buried. We reform our ranks and march about one and a half kilometers back to the company. They are still lying in the same place, waiting for us.

"Who goes there?"

"Nachshon!"

Aryeh met us. Yaakov told him that everything was OK. We form up again and set off.

In front of me I can see a steep hill. That is our position. Joseph, the scout, stops the long column. The first two platoons go ahead, to occupy the top of the hill.

We space ourselves out, six feet from man to man, and walk stooped. We can hear dogs barking in the distance. That must be Deir Muheisin. I estimate the distance as about half a kilometer. If the Arabs are clever, they will set an ambush for us here. Maybe someone is lying in wait behind that white rock and aiming his Sten[10] at me.

"Faster!" – Shlomo passes on the command. I am almost running. With one hand I am keeping hold of my equipment to stop it making a noise. I am the furthest to the right. I am supposed to keep a look-out to the side. Can't see anything. The way we are moving, though, we should be recognizable from any distance.

We are there. A stone wall in front of me, about three feet high. Again I have to secure the right-hand side. I lie on the ground, facing right, and freezing miserably. I get out my watch and try to see the hands. It is just before twelve. No idea how long I have been lying here. My whole body is crying out for sleep. My eyes keep closing. But I manage to catch myself each time I am just about to go to sleep. That happens again and again. For God's sake, are they never going to relieve me? We can't sleep. We carry the responsibility for the lives of the whole company.

Far away I hear a vehicle. Light appears from behind the hill. Another one behind it, and a third. The *convoy*! It is on the way. Aryeh has apparently reported that we have taken our position.

* * *

At last I am relieved. I sit behind the stone wall. We have orders not to sleep. I rest for an hour and look ahead. I hear a call in Arabic far away. Change of the guard in the village? Now and then a dog barks.

A strange feeling – you are lying a short distance from the enemy and he knows nothing. He has no idea that in two or three hours we will be attacking.

Behind me the radio operator is talking. His monotonous voice blends in with the noises of the night. He has been trained to speak with that kind of voice. Like a machine. "Hallo, Baruch two, Baruch two, can you hear me? Can you hear me? We are ready. Waiting for orders. Waiting for orders. Over."

Steps behind us. "Who goes there?"

"Nachshon."

Nachman, the blond platoon leader, is back with the two groups who mined the road to Beit Jiz. His people are also dead tired. They sink to the ground. But everything is prepared for the assault.

Very slowly a thin light streak appears in the east. The sleepers are roused. Aryeh stands next to the radio operator. We know that soon the concert will begin. Now I see the village for the first time. I am amazed how near it is. Small brown houses stand directly in front of us on a low hill on the other side of the wadi. The people in the village haven't noticed us yet.

Yechiel, the deputy company commander, runs to the mortar platoon. They have already set up their weapons. Ephraim Makovsky, the one with the twisted mustache, barks orders in all directions. Asriel Spitz, the leader of the second platoon, checks the aiming devices.

"Two rounds on the target – fire!" shouts Yechiel at the top of his voice. The night is over. The assault has begun.

The shells whiz through the air. A moment of absolute quiet. Then they explode – at least a hundred meters in front of the village – which comes to life. We can hear the shouts. A few rifles begin to shoot. I don't hear the whistle of any bullets. The Arabs' fire is unaimed. They don't where the attack is coming from.

Two more shells. Another two. Two more. The explosions are getting closer and closer to the village. There – Asriel's shells have hit. Ephraim has not yet reached the target. In the village little figures are running to and fro. A crowd assembles around the big tree in the center. So far we have received no order to fire.

Movement behind us. The second company, which should attack in the first wave, is taking position behind our stone wall. The unaimed fire of the Arabs and our shells raise our morale. Our mood is getting better and better.

People start to joke. Red-haired Joske invites Aryeh to a good Arabic Finjan[11] in an hour. Someone suggests making a list for those who want a rendezvous with the daughter of the Mukhtar.[12]

"Target four hundred meters, five rounds – fire!"

I load my rifle and shoot. In the village some figures are running around. The medical orderly begs me to give him my rifle. He wants to have a go at shooting too. I feel light and happy.

"Cease fire!"

The second company is ready for the assault. Some of the faces are very pale. The leaders make jokes. There – they jump over the stone wall. Run. They reach the wadi. We shoot over the roofs. They are making progress. The first have reached the village. The Arabs are still shooting from the village.

We stop shooting. Our people have occupied the edge of the village. They are running from house to house, just the way they learned. I can't see whether they are taking prisoners. Now it is our turn, to take the center of the village. Our mood reaches its peak.

"Section number one – forwards!"

I jump over the wall. The second platoon jump and throw themselves on the ground.

"Platoon one – jump!"

I jump, run ten paces and drop to the ground. Bullets whistle over my head. They are not coming from the village. They are coming from the steep hill to the left. The Arabs have occupied the grave of Nebi Musa.[13] From there they have a good overview of our assault. There is also firing on the right. A few houses stand there. I can't see any movement. We jump up again, run a few steps, and throw ourselves on the ground. Between me and Bulli, the deputy company commander, a bullet hits the ground. My God, the Arab snipers know their job. To the left someone shouts something. Is he wounded? I don't have time to look. I run and throw myself on the ground again. My equipment gets in the way. Doesn't matter. I have to reach the wadi. There we'll be able to catch our breath. I run ahead, wait for my comrades to catch up, run forwards again, reach the wadi, and lie on the ground again.

I look around. The whole company is charging behind us. Squad after squad. The last are the mortar crews. Reuven, the company giant, is carrying the heavy mortar on his back as though it were a tin of sardines. Behind him fat Shalom is running. He is carrying the shells which weigh even more.

Our "heavy weapon," the machine gun, keeps up continuous fire on Nebi Musa. But the snipers are still shooting. We continue the assault. The slope is steep. I am breathing heavily. I have no strength left to run, but I keep up. We reach the left side of the village. There our comrades from the earlier group are lying. They point at a collection of houses in the center. "There the Arabs are holed up." I wait until our squad is complete. Yaakov has arrived too and assigns us a group of houses. We run over there. The doors are locked. We hammer on them with the butts of our rifles. One door gives way. Joske fires a burst from his Sten into the house. I can't see a single Arab. They cleared off when they saw us coming.

We are at the last house. I am running with the squad, my rifle in my hand. I feel that I have to shoot. A movement in front of me. A little Arab dog running away. I raise my rifle and shoot. The dog howls.

The howling wakes me up. What have I done? Have I become an animal? Shlomo, running behind me, raises his rifle and shoots. The howling stops.

That incident makes me feel sick. I want to get away. My comrades are lying on the ground drinking water. In front of me is the corner house. A ladder is leaning against it. I climb onto the roof and lie between the two domes. From here I have a better view toward the south and the west. The landscape seems peaceful. I can't see any movement. But the Arab snipers continue to shoot without interruption.

* * *

We remain in the position we have captured. Joske establishes himself in one of the rooms. Three of us form the lookout and change round every hour.

I lie on the roof. Suddenly I hear a shout and see a concerned expression on Shatzky's face. When I look at him, he laughs. Apparently I had fallen asleep, and when I didn't react to his first call he was afraid that I had been hit.

The landscape is quiet. In front of me is a field of red poppies. A remarkable contrast to the whistling bullets. I have no idea where the snipers are situated. From the noise of the shots I can estimate roughly, but I can't see anything.

My turn to be replaced. The ladder is in view of the snipers. As I climb down two bullets whistle past me. We have all become indifferent. You can't be bothered to keep your head down or to hide when you can't see the enemy.

I find a pickax and begin to break open the locked doors of the houses. We heard that a large quantity of weapons was found in one part of the village. I enter the first room. An awful stink. A torn and fouled mattress, a broken jug, a rusty sickle, goat and donkey droppings. In an old tin I find photos of a man and a woman. They are attached to naturalization certificates. Her name is Fatima, very pretty, twenty-four years old. According to the certificate she has a three-year-old son. I remove the picture and put it in my pocket.

The dirt and the poverty revolt me. They probably worked fourteen hours a day and led a dog's life. I feel sorry for them.

No time for philosophizing. I break open other rooms. The booty is disappointing: a few eggs, a tin of oil, a broken petrol stove, a pot, and a pan. At last I discover a cockerel. I go out to announce my finds. In the meantime the firing of the snipers at our area has increased. The bullets are coming from the south. An isolated house stands there on a hill. There is no doubt that this is the snipers' hideout. Now and then they are treated to a few salvos from us. The shots keep coming.

* * *

I tell Shlomo that he should take the cockerel. "Are you crazy?" he exclaims. I put the cockerel in a bag and run to the room where the platoon is. With a triumphant cry I tip the cockerel out of the bag. The cockerel jumps up and escapes through the open door. My comrades laugh. I am annoyed.

Meanwhile some eggs have been boiled. And the ever-present sardines are not absent. We eat quickly. From the house of the company commanders wafts the aroma of chicken soup. They offer me a bowlful and a chicken leg. There is also coffee. I sit down for a moment and hear the news. The snipers have killed one man so far and wounded several.

Benjamin, the runner, comes to us. He has a funny story to tell: the battalion commander turns up at the company in an armored car and asks what the people are doing. Aryeh had assured him that no plundering had taken place, that not even the hens had been touched. And just at that moment a soldier enters the room holding up two chickens – his platoon's present for the company commander.

* * *

In the afternoon our mood darkens. The Arabs are firing at us from all directions. They have occupied all the positions that dominate the village. Our machine guns answer occasionally. We are saving ammunition. The shots from the invisible enemy get on our nerves. More wounded are reported. A medical orderly is hit in the eye. We want to shoot but can't find a target.

Bad news: Aryeh, the company commander, has been wounded. An armored car is going to take him to the base. We are horrified.

At three o'clock we are called together. We are in a state of high alert and take our positions. Shlomo and I lie behind a pile of stones facing west. Uninterrupted fire is coming from that direction. I press my head against the ground. Directly in front of me is a heap of manure. I ignore it. Occasionally I raise my head and look around. I can't see anything apart from a beautiful, peaceful landscape.

* * *

"Uri!"

Joske calls me. I get up and run to him. He is sitting with Bulli behind a house. He points at the roof where I was lying this morning, and orders me to climb up again.

For a moment I am afraid. The way up and the roof itself are visible from all sides. I overcome my fear and climb up. Once there I position myself between the two domes. That way I have some kind of cover.

"Uri – tell us what kind of armored vehicles are on the road!"

I raise my head. An armored vehicle is approaching. I know the type well – one of ours. But it is behaving strangely, turning, and taking the road in the direction of Latrun. Suddenly a burst of machine gun fire hits the house. What the devil, an Arab tank. Perhaps one of those they captured on the road to Gush Etzion. Devil take them!

Suddenly I hear a familiar sound and a moment later a gigantic explosion. A mortar shell. At least three inch. It exploded in the middle of the village. So the Arabs have reinforcements.

The feeling of being surrounded depresses us. We are dog tired. We have gone at least thirty hours without sleep.

We hear that we are to withdraw under cover of darkness. We imagine that we will be brought back with armored vehicles. And this idea encourages us. At sunset we assemble at the command post, talking and even joking. Freddy and Reuven, our fat mortar crew, keep a lookout. Their rifles are at the ready, just waiting for a sign of movement from the enemy. I feel like shooting. I go over to them and take a shot at the house on the hill. Freddy curses me in Russian – I fired too close to his ear.

Our machine gun fires occasional long bursts so that the Arabs won't notice that we are preparing to withdraw.

At last Bulli comes with the order to withdraw to company HQ. I remain a while to cover the rear. We fire off a few shots "to leave a good impression" and pull out.

Suddenly the order: "No retreat!" We are to hold the village overnight and will be relieved by another company tomorrow.

My comrades are speechless. Yet another night in this place. We are depressed. Yechiel allocates rooms and positions to the platoons. In the end we have given up part of the village in order to increase our hold here.

* * *

Completely dark. Joske has organized the lookout for the night. Two comrades each have two hours' duty. The machine gun is in position. The positions are spaced out at ten-yard intervals.

We eat a slice of bread with sardines and lie down to sleep. The whole platoon in one narrow, stinking room. We are almost lying on top of each other. Someone wakes me. I feel I have just gone to sleep, but I have actually slept three hours. Shlomo and I go out. I can't keep my eyes open. They keep closing. It is a great effort to keep opening them again.

* * *

They wake us up again. It is three o'clock in the morning. The relief company has arrived. But if we believed that we were going to be brought back to base in armored vehicles, a bitter disappointment awaits us. We are returning on foot. Six kilometers' distance, with full equipment and weapons – defending ourselves along the way.

At long last we are off: squad number one of the first platoon secures the flanks. Benjamin and I form the first group. We head off over the hill and observe the area, while the platoon marches along below. Joseph, the scout, orders and drives us on. Not a spark of energy left in my body. I am surprised myself that I don't simply collapse in a heap. I keep slipping on the stony ground. My equipment keeps getting in the way.

Behind us the orchestra starts up again. It seems that Deir Muheisin is being drowned in fire. But our thoughts are already ahead of us, at the base.

As we get nearer, our morale rises. In spite of our fatigue, we start to sing. "Believe me, the day will come/it will be good, that I promise you/I will take you in my arms/and tell you about – everything ..."

* * *

I am too tired to sleep. After a cold shower I feel much better. A radio operator from the battalion tells me, confidentially, that the British have given us an ultimatum. They would use artillery to drive us out of the village if we didn't leave it by the evening, without blowing it up. If we fulfill their demands, they would ensure the safety of our convoys in the area. From the village come reports of heavy attacks, with several dead and many wounded.

* * *

Toward evening we learn exactly what was agreed with the British. We will leave the village under the condition that they will take over control and guarantee the security of the road. We feel we have achieved a great victory – we have ensured the safety of the road to Jerusalem through this area, we have shown that we can capture and hold a village, and we have dealt the Arabs in this region a decisive blow. Arab Hulda, which dominates the whole area, has been occupied by us, after the whole Arab population fled – and remains in our hand.

Around midnight I go to the mess. Sitting there is the whole company that was in Deir Muheisin this morning. The atmosphere is lousy and depressive. The troops were under continuous attack. The Arabs had heavy weapons and were under the command of German or Polish officers. They got to within twenty yards of the village and even occupied a few houses. In the end, however, they were beaten back. We suffered heavy losses.

We held Deir Muheisin until the aim of the operation was attained.

Operation Nachshon achieved its goal. But the army did not have enough men to hold the positions on the road to Jerusalem. Near Latrun and Bab al-Wad,[14] the road was undefended. That was effectively an invitation to the enemy.

We sat in Arab Hulda, a gigantic natural fortress overlooking the road to Latrun, fought the fleas, poured whole containers of DDT over ourselves, and made occasional visits to the "Boaz" position between Hulda and Wadi Sarar. There we hung around in the stifling heat, almost motionless, hidden between the rocks, dug in in the fields. We spent our time telling each other the secrets of our lives. Our real task was to disrupt any Arab traffic between Latrun and Wadi Sarar, and to defend the road to Jerusalem in a southerly direction.

In the evening the "Cameri Theater"[15] came to us. After the performance I and some other comrades volunteered to accompany the actors to Rehovot. They needed this escort, since the village of Akir was still in the hands of the Arabs. Before the actors left us, I asked them to write their names on the stock of my rifle. And so for several weeks the bleached wood shimmered with the names of Batyah, Chanah, and Rosa ...

Around two in the morning we arrived back in a good mood. After three hours' sleep we were awoken. The convoy was waiting for us.

19 April 1948
On leave in Tel Aviv

Convoy to Jerusalem

A cry of joy escapes from the barracks. If there is one thing that infantry soldiers dream about (apart from a trip home), then it is going to the front. But our joy had an even deeper source. For weeks we had been fighting for a breakthrough to Jerusalem. But the reward for our efforts, the "result," we did not see. We read in the paper about the reception of the convoys in Jerusalem and we envied our comrades who drove through the town in a victory parade. Finally we too would enjoy the fruits of victory. Somewhere in the capital a pretty Jerusalem girl was waiting for each one of us – bursting with admiration.

They wake us at two in the morning. We spring from our mattresses and within a few minutes we are dressed and armed. In one corner of the camp we get cocoa, bread, and hardboiled eggs. Such is our joy that we crack open the eggshells on each other's heads.

Fate, in the form of Bulli, our deputy platoon leader, allocates to my squad a truck full of Tnuva cheese.[16] Some of us see this as disadvantageous: fresh cheese is not a particularly effective protection against bullets. But most are in agreement with Nachman, our blond squad leader, who explains the appetizing aspect of the situation. After our stomachs have just about turned into aquariums from the quantity of sardines we eat all the time, a good helping of cheese would make a nice change.

We quickly move the boxes to the sides of the cargo area and construct a nice hiding place in the middle which we like to hope is protected from bullets.

* * *

The fabled silver streak on the horizon announces "Zero Hour." The head of the convoy starts to move. As we climb the hill, a fantastic view opens up – innumerable vehicles, one after another: buses, trucks, armored cars, private cars. In every second or third vehicle we see the faces of Nachshon people and next to them their rifles and grenade launchers.

We reach the limits of the captured area, the front that we formed over the last weeks. Every hill and every shrub brings back memories.

Deir Muheisin! All heads are raised, despite our orders. A sea of memories: the house where we ate the chickens, the house with the two domes where I lay, the house where we spent a whole day under sniper fire.

We feel fine. The exchange of memories wakens our appetite. Nachman opens a pack of cheese. We touch the yellow mass as though it were something sacred. Our stomachs, used only to sardines and bully beef,[17] rejoice.

Latrun. We examine the great prison with curiosity. Memories of a bygone epoch.[18] A group of Arab police stare at the enormous convoy and its armed escort with wide eyes.

Shaar Hagai.[19] Immediately we tense up. To both sides the land rises steeply. If we are attacked from the heights, all we can do is to jump into the ditch and wait. To climb up the slope under fire from above would be simply suicidal. But nothing happens.

Abu-Ghosh. For the first time we see an Arab village where the inhabitants are working peacefully. Some children run in to the road to look at us as we drive by. The adults try and behave as though they don't see us.

A discussion begins on the truck. How should we behave to the Arabs? Moshe and Nachman are in favor of a hard line. I tend to support tolerance.

On the hill to the right a figure is standing and waving. On his head he is wearing a sock hat. We reply with a cheer. We have reached the eastern part of Nachshon, the position that our comrades captured while we were securing the road from the west.

* * *

From here on it is a friendship tour. From all the positions along the road our bearded comrades shout something to us.

Someone points to a steep mountain to the right of us, with a flag waving. I take the field glasses. It is a blue-white flag. That is the famous Castel.[20]

We are a bit annoyed about this Castel. It became famous and overshadowed our victories although we saw them as the peak of military success. The people from Castel have climbed down to us on the road. Someone raises a tin of sardines in our honor: the symbol of the army at the front. Together we have fought to clear this road. They have suffered the same as us, made the same sacrifices, fought like us with grenade launchers, rifles, against fleas and sardines. A silent friendship unites us. We don't need many words. A rough curse and a smile are enough.

In the distance we can see the suburbs of Jerusalem. We prepare ourselves for the high point of our journey – the ceremonial entry into the city. We are riding on the boxes of cheese. Nachman combs his blond quiff. Moshe gives his sock hat the right dashing line. Yehudah puts on his American goggles and looks like a company commander at the very least.

* * *

None of us will ever forget this moment: hundreds of vehicles and their escorts drive into the waiting city to the cheers of the inhabitants who collect in groups on the streets, on balconies, on the roofs.

It must have been like this when de Gaulle entered liberated Paris, or the Red Army Kiev and Odessa.

They see their own soldiers who fought to open the roads into their besieged city, the soldiers who suffered, attacked, and fought to provide them with food and equipment. And we – we see "our" citizens, the people for whom we fought.

This entrance into Jerusalem has made up for everything we went through in recent weeks. And even if none of the daughters of Jerusalem have come to kiss us, even if instead of pretty girls a shaven-headed military policeman climbs into the truck, still it was a wonderful experience.

* * *

We were in the city for about two hours. We helped to unload the cheese, we drank milk until our stomachs could take no more, and attracted cheers and applause to the point of exhaustion.

The vehicles arrived at the collection point, ready for the return trip. A crowd of people gathered there. One asked for his greetings to be passed to someone, a woman wants us to take a letter for Tel Aviv. Our photo is taken and our photo is taken and our photo is taken. Standing, sitting, on the trucks, with rifles, without rifles, with girls, without girls, in groups and singly ...

* * *

The way back. We are tired and talk about politics. The talk comes back to our treatment of the Arabs, and we talk about the Etzel action in Deir Yassin.[21] The discussion becomes heated and gets on everybody's nerves. In the end nobody knows what we are arguing about.

On the way we meet a British convoy driving in the opposite direction. A strange experience: Israelis with rifles and automatic weapons exchange dark looks with British soldiers, who have rifles and automatic weapons with them. With a certain admiration they stare at our weapons. The length of the convoy seems to impress them.

On the next day it is reported: "A big convoy of 235 vehicles has reached Jerusalem safely."

A few days later we drove to Tel Aviv. Our first leave since we started active operations. The city received us with open arms. Our title, the "Nachshonim," was on everybody's lips. Those were the glory days of the people's army. We came to feel that the fighting was not for nothing and that the citizens on the road appreciated our spirit of self-sacrifice.

* * *

When we returned from leave, the news came in that the fourth convoy had been attacked near Bab al-Wad. Joseph of the Palmach, our scout before Deir Muheisin, had saved the convoy by an amazingly daring feat. He climbed up, with a few others, to the top of the slope and drove away the attackers. He himself fell and the convoy reached Jerusalem. But the road remained blocked.

Qawuqji's[22] soldiers held the stretch of road near Bab al-Wad and built up a gigantic concrete barrier. The aim of our operation was to clear that barrier. A Palmach unit from the "Harel" brigade was coming from Jerusalem to capture the villages of Deir Ayub and Beit Mahsir on the north and south of the road. When this operation was complete we were to advance down the road to the barrier, giving the scouts cover so that they could destroy the barrier, and then accompany the next convoy to Jerusalem. The operation bore the name "Maccabi."

17 May 1948
Forward base in Hulda

The first battle for Latrun

Like every large-scale operation, this one is preceded by superfluous activity. For a civilian it may sound ridiculous. But in the life of a soldier, the operations that don't get carried out play as great a role as those that you read about in the newspaper. So for example we were alerted one night, and set off to shock the enemy with enormous firepower in a particular village – only to learn, a few hundred meters from our target, that the operation had been called off. Hardly had we made it back to our base camp when we were put into trucks and taken off to a forward camp to take part in the capture of another village. And after a quarter of an hour we learned that our comrades had already taken the village.

After these "successful" operations we got a few hours' rest. Then another alert, and we were told that this time the real operation was about to begin. Is it any surprise that we were disappointed to hear that we were just a reserve for another unit that had already set out?

We are no particular heroes and are no more enthusiastic than any other normal person about the dangers that face us. But after a series of such "joke actions" the real order to set out is like a liberation.

We lay on the road and cursed ourselves and the whole world, while our comrades got into the armored vehicles in order to check the road to Bab al-Wad. After half an hour we heard the rumble of distant artillery. But that didn't stop us eating jam and reading cheap novels.

The situation changed from one second to another as suddenly a pickup truck appeared at 100 km/h and stopped just long enough to call out to us that we must ready ourselves for immediate action. And he was gone, followed by an armored car that looked like a sieve. Armor-piercing rounds had penetrated it from all sides. In it sat Aryeh, our company commander, bleeding from five wounds. He only said two words: "Immediate action!"

We knew: it's our turn.

* * *

On the road our armored cars line up. Now and then ambulances drive past, bringing back the dead and wounded of the first patrol. We quickly complete our last preparations. All private possessions and supplies are left behind. All we take with us are our weapons and military equipment. In the last moment Asriel, the squad leader for this operation, appoints me his deputy. That doesn't make me happy. Experience has taught me it is better in combat to be free and independent, without responsibility for the lives of others.

Someone tells me what happened. The armored convoy drove past Latrun. Before the Hartuv crossroads they met Arab tanks that were equipped with two-pound guns. Before the heavy vehicles could turn around, they were penetrated one by one by cannon shells. Most of the men were hit. Only one vehicle, the last in the row, was not hit.

We drive off. The vehicles are spaced out about forty meters apart. Our morale is high. We tell jokes and play tricks. The first time we went into battle, in Operation Nachshon, we were excited and nervous. Now we feel none of that. Combat is no longer a strange and frightening world, it is now a more or less known factor. We have learned that not every bullet hits. In brief – we have become "experienced frontline soldiers." Or at least that is how it seems to us.

We drive past Deir Muheisin, the scene of our baptism of fire. The houses are deserted. Our curious eyes seek out "our" positions. I even manage to take a picture of "my" house as we drive quickly past.

* * *

Between Deir Muheisin and Latrun we come under fire. In the armored vehicle it is hard to judge the direction the shots are coming from. Some say that they are coming from Latrun. To me however it seems – wrongly, as it turns out – that the shots are coming from Beit Jiz, to our right. The people in the first vehicles jump out and storm up the hill in front of us. They run as if in a field exercise. It is a pleasure to watch them. Somewhere nearby, a machine gun barks. As our comrades reach the summit, the firing stops. The enemy escapes.

This little battle has delayed us. Meanwhile it has got dark. It is clear to us that we will not make it to Bab al-Wad. We consider what we should do – return to base or set up a position here?

* * *

Esra, the company runner, brings us the command: forward. The armored car moves cautiously. Around us it is pitch dark. We drive without lights. After another five hundred meters we stop. The command: get out! We jump – as agreed, Asriel takes the right-hand side and I, with my group, the left. We lie at the edge of the road in a defensive position.

A few bullets whistle over our heads. I press my head against the ground and dig a little hollow with my hands. Aryeh and Peretz, the members of my group who haven't been exposed to live fire before, lie there motionless. I reassure them – the bullets are flying too high to threaten us. And in the dark the enemy can't see us anyway.

* * *

Bulli calls me. We cross the road. One after the other we jump across. In front of me is a little white hut behind a peculiar form of barbed wire fence. What is that? Then it dawns on me: we are by the internment camp of Latrun. A strange feeling – not so long ago some of us were threatened with an extended period of rest in there. Now we are breaking our way in, in the middle of the night. The words of a song come to me, that I have read somewhere: "Even Latrun is part of the land of Israel …"

We manage to get in through a hole in the fence. I understand the intention: we will spend the night here. A good idea. As long as we are here, the enemy cannot send reinforcements to his troops who are fighting with our comrades up on the road. Here we can block the enemy's supply routes from Ramle and Lod.

We feel our way forwards. Most of the buildings are destroyed. Only here and there is a white house still standing. Behind one of these houses our platoon stops. We gather blocks of stone from other ruins and build a little position. It is not very convincing. We have no digging equipment, and the protection of the stones is rather questionable.

* * *

Behind us an armored bus is being converted into a staff room. We draw sheets over the viewing ports to prevent any light escaping. Meanwhile some squads have been stationed for perimeter defense. I look at the clock. It is past midnight. We have only a few hours left for sleeping. But there is no chance of that. We have no blankets. Since midday we have not changed our clothing, so we are now wearing short-sleeved khaki shirts. It is unbelievably cold. But the total fatigue of battle has not overcome us, that tiredness that would allow us to sleep in any place, in any position, and without any covering.

* * *

It is light. From our position we have a wonderfully panoramic view. I can see the wooded hills of Bab al-Wad, the deserted Beit Jiz, Arab Hulda, and Deir Muheisin in the south. In all directions the enemy has very good positions for snipers. But the area seems deserted. I can't make out any movement at all.

Little Yakov, who is lying by himself in his position a few paces away, finds it boring. He comes over to ask for a cigarette against the hunger and forgets to go back. Little Yakov is a refugee who came here just two months ago from a German concentration camp. He has some stories to tell.

He is interrupted in the middle by the morning concert which we were already expecting. The enemy fires at us with rifles and automatic weapons. During the night we have "annoyed" him. He shot at us, but we did not reply. That makes any enemy nervous. As long as we don't return fire, he doesn't know where we are hiding and how many of us there are.

This time we give an answer. Our heavy machine gun fires a short salvo now and again. This explains some of our success. The enemy fires like a madman with everything he has got, without having a definite target. We reply with a few bullets, but only when we can see clearly what we are shooting at. Not for nothing did they tell us the story of comrades who ran out of ammunition while they were surrounded by the enemy, and who used their last hand grenade to evade capture.

Suddenly we hear a new instrument in the orchestra. A kind of explosion we haven't heard before. I raise my head and see a cloud of smoke. Shlomo and Yakov also get up and look around. For the first time we are being bombarded by artillery.

The heavy guns fire without interruption, for almost two hours. They are methodically covering the whole area. The instinct for self-preservation tells me to stay on the ground. But curiosity demands the opposite and wins. My ears get used to the shells. As soon as I hear the whistling, I throw myself on the ground. And after the explosion I raise my head again. That way I can follow the impacts exactly.

The fire is now concentrated on the road to Hulda and on the field in the south. The intention is clear: they want to cut off our retreat. The explosions take place directly in my field of view, but don't approach our position closer than thirty meters. Apparently the enemy doesn't know that we have taken this position.

Now we begin to shoot with everything we have. Heavy machine guns, automatic weapons, and mortars. We aim for the centers of concentration of the enemy, but can do nothing about the artillery. All our vehicles have been destroyed.

I crawl to Nachman Shmueli, who is now in command of fourteen people. We have a machine gun which fires regular salvos at an enemy artillery piece. He too has no contact with HQ. I ask him what he is going to do. He gives me a typical soldier's answer: he will not withdraw without orders, but will provide cover for the other units. He has already sent out a runner to find the HQ. If he finds them maybe he will return with new orders.

I return to my position. For some reason I am not worried about the situation. I am not even excited. There is nothing for me to do apart from observing the impacts of the shells and occasionally to duck.

One unit withdraws from the field that lies in front of me. They are rather disorderly until the deputy section leader sorts them out. Quite soon I begin to admire this Ovadia Treblov from Be'er Tuvia. He is very calm, rearranging the platoon. Someone asks him if it is OK to leave some things behind. This earns him just a cutting look, then the answer: "You can throw away all your clothes. But you dare leave behind a single cartridge!!"

Ovadia suggests that we should withdraw together with him. But Nachman decides to stay. After a while the platoon withdraws. This is where the qualities of the commander become clear: he doesn't withdraw along the road, but around the hill in front of us. That is a safer route. But still, one of his people is wounded by shrapnel in the open field. After treatment he is carried by his comrades.

Other wounded are brought to the rear, and lie next to the road. The enemy notices the movement and concentrates his fire. There is no alternative. That is the shortest route, and the lives of the wounded depend on the speed in getting them to a place where they can be treated.

Now and then a group appears carrying one of the wounded. The shells land near them. I can see that some of the bearers are also wounded. Later we hear about a tragic incident: Abraham Bendarski, our medical orderly, a well-known football player, was carrying a dying soldier on his back. He hears an incoming shell, lays the wounded man on the ground and throws himself down next to him. The explosion flings Abraham several meters, but he is not hurt. When he goes back to the wounded man, he is not there.

The fire on the road is murderous. Asriel Spitz, my platoon leader, who had ended up in another place, wanted to salvage three vehicles. The enemy observed what was happening and concentrated its fire on that area. Asriel jumped out of the vehicle. A moment later it received a direct hit.

One after another our units withdraw. In the end we are the only ones left. Two machine guns and five infantry with rifles. Nachman is in command of the heavy weapons. A company commander I don't know is in command of the second machine gun, which belongs to another unit. I lie next to it and try my hand as a sniper.

From this position I can now see the enemy quite clearly. A tank is standing next to the monastery of Latrun. Hundreds of Arabs are coming toward us through the wheat fields. They are still about eight hundred meters away. They are well trained. Move in accordance with the art of war. Meanwhile reinforcements for the Arabs are streaming in from Ramle. They are approaching from the left. It is clear that we will be lost within half an hour. We keep up continuous fire on the enemy in front of us so that our comrades can get the wounded to safety. The Arabs are advancing in a broad line, and our automatic weapons are hitting many of them.

The enemy is getting closer and closer. One of our machine guns withdraws. Moshe's is the only one left. But just as the Arabs present a wonderful target silhouetted against the horizon, the gun jams. Moshe almost goes crazy. Nachman flies into a rage. But the machine gun goes on strike again. Moshe picks it up and heads toward the rear. On the way he will take it apart and try to get it working again. I want to try out an old ruse.

We have to hold the enemy off at least a quarter of an hour. We have only four soldiers with rifles. I explain the trick to them. We must shoot one after the other in quick succession, so that it sounds like a salvo from an automatic weapon. It works. Rat-tat-tat-tat. Rat-tat-tat-tat. Like a machine gun. The enemy lies on the ground and waits. We have won the necessary minutes.

Meanwhile Yaakov, our chief, has turned up. At first he wants to stay. But when he sees the enemy to the left and right of us, he realizes that the time has come to withdraw. We go toward the south-east, to go around the hill and meet the road about a kilometer further down.

On the way we meet two comrades standing next to a wounded man. He has a shrapnel wound in the chest and is covered in blood. His dressing and his clothes are red and dripping, but he is fully conscious. We take turns in carrying him on our backs. After two hundred meters we are exhausted. We shout out to some comrades who are walking in front of us. They come back and help us. Under covering fire some other comrades get the wounded man to the road. We are all bloody. Bulli looks like a butcher with his hands and arms all red.

When we reach the road we can hear our heavy machine gun shooting again. Suddenly an armored car races across the road in the direction of our base. We don't know if it is one of ours or not. If it belongs to the Arab Legion then we are cut off in this direction too. Then we would have to find our way back through the hills. We are the last ones facing the enemy – slightly more than a dozen soldiers and officers from a variety of units. If we don't manage an orderly withdrawal …

We hear calls from the other side of the road. We cross over in an easterly direction. The heavy machine gun joins us. We take position on the road and have a rest. The wounded man is still clearheaded. I give him some water from my canteen. At last we see one of our vehicles in the distance. We call to them. They come nearer, so that we can put the wounded man in. He is saved.

Now begins our return march: about eight kilometers through the mountains back to our base. We are exhausted, not having eaten or drunk in the last twenty-four hours and slept only two or three hours in the last thirty. The sun is merciless. The ammunition is heavy. But it is a matter of life and death. We are the last of the rearguard before the enemy. We make an orderly withdrawal.

* * *

In the distance we can see a convoy of armored vehicles forming up, but can't tell whether they are Arab or British. We take up a position, even though we know that our weapons are useless against their guns. We advance while giving each other cover. Some of us take the position, while the others withdraw further – alternately. At last the armored convoy comes nearer. It belongs to the British. We don't know what their intentions are. But they drive past without opening fire. Probably they are as afraid of us as we are of them. Later we hear that one of our mortars hit a British tank in the morning, mistaking it for an Arab one. When the mistake became apparent, one of our officers took care of the wounded. Since then the British have not been very active in this area.

The last two hundred meters are the worst. We got to know that stretch during our withdrawal from Deir Muheisin about a month ago. The path is as steep as a wall. The village looks as though you could reach out your hand and touch it, but getting there is torture. I feel that I have reached my absolute limit. I clench my teeth and reach the goal.

Opinions are divided about this action. No one knows for sure whether it was a victory or a defeat. For almost twenty-four hours we interrupted the enemy's lines of supply at a decisive point and prevented the movement of reinforcements for the battle in Bab al-Wad. There our comrades from Jerusalem are still fighting. On the other hand we had to retreat before the enemy's greater firepower.

We returned from Latrun with troubled thoughts. In the first confrontation with heavy weapons we had to give way. The road to Jerusalem remained closed. And that meant Operation Maccabi had failed.

But after a few days we learned some secret information. Between Beit Jiz and Beit Mahsir, in the area captured during Operation Maccabi, while we held off the enemy in Latrun, a new road had been built. A "Burma Road"[23] to Jerusalem. The heavy losses at Latrun were not in vain.

On 15 May, English hegemony over the land is supposed to end. Somewhere, far, far away, in the civilian world, a heated discussion was going on – should we form our own government or not? A faint echo of this debate reached us. It was said that Ben-Gurion was in favor and Shertok[24] against.

On the afternoon of 14 May one of our comrades stormed into our tent encampment and told us what he had just heard on the radio: the Israeli state had been declared. We crowded into the large dining room of the Hulda Kibbutz – which soldiers were forbidden to enter – and heard Ben-Gurion's speech in English. We had missed the transmission in Hebrew.

Even though we were far away from politics and from the speeches of politicians, the news still moved us. The battles were not for nothing, then. We looked at each other and all had the same thought: we were the ones who founded this state! With our blood and our sweat. When Ben-Gurion spoke about the contribution of the defense forces to this historic moment, we accepted his words as the gratitude of the Yishuv.

After the transmission we lay on the lawn behind the dining room. We were informed that this evening we would again be going into action. Issar Barsky, a nineteen-year-old company commander, organized his people for the operation. We also heard that company number one, under the command of Aryeh Kotzer, had captured the village of Abu Shusha near Gezer. We could guess the aim of the new operation.

Qubab

We didn't hear the end of Ben-Gurion's speech on the *Kol Israel* station.[25] We were ordered out to prepare for an operation. We took our equipment, rifles, and automatic weapons and climbed into the vehicles. We set off toward Gezer along field paths.

Ben-Gurion's words still ring in my head. Weren't they too dry for this event? After all, today we became a regular army of an independent state. From now on we can buy the heavy weapons we need and use them. After our experience of artillery yesterday in Latrun we have come to appreciate heavy guns and armored cars.

The light of a petrol lamp illuminates Matti Arazi, who now commands the company, and his platoon commanders. They are having a discussion, examining maps and aerial photos. I listen. And from the fragments that I hear, I make my own picture of the operation: the task is to assault and capture the village of Qubab, which dominates the road between Ramle and Latrun. It is one of the larger villages in the area and according to the information of the Shaj[26] houses a large number of fighters and weapons.

Three units will take part in the attack on the village. Simultaneously with the assault, a few armored cars will drive into the middle of the village to draw enemy fire. Before the operation mortar fire will "soften up" the village. A rumor spreads quickly: our unit will be assigned to the armored cars. We stand around in little groups and discuss things.

We used to think, before we had any experience, that sitting in an armored vehicle was better than carrying all that heavy equipment on your back as an infantryman. Since then we have learned. When you are on foot, you can move as you like and change position, stay under cover, and confuse the enemy. But when you are sitting in a vehicle you are stuck there, in full view of the enemy and offering a first-class target for his heavy weapons

While we are still exchanging opinions, Akiva comes to tell us that my platoon will not be taking part in the operation because of a shortage of armored vehicles. Instead we are to take a position next to the road and to hold it.

Without success I try and persuade the platoon leader and the corporal to take me with them. There is no room for us. Why did I do it? I don't know. Is it curiosity, the hope for material to write about? Or is it the misery of lying in an isolated position while your comrades are storming a fortified village?

My comrades climb in. It turns out that there is room for two more riflemen. I grab the opportunity, and they take me too. We set off along winding dirt roads without lights. Yaakov, the platoon leader, and Ezra, the company runner, are sitting in the first vehicle. We are in the second vehicle.

Then we hit a tarred road. The road from Tel Aviv to Jerusalem. Strange feeling: going for a drive in the middle of the Arab area, on a road we've been fighting over for weeks.

The vehicles drive terribly slowly. You can hardly hear the motors. We get tenser and tenser. In front of us a signal rocket climbs into the air. We think the village is about a hundred meters ahead. A few bullets whistle past above us. The Arabs have certainly noticed that we are up to something, but they don't know exactly what.

The vehicles stop. Ezra, the runner, jumps out and runs to the last vehicle. Something is happening there. Some people get out and carry something heavy into the field by the road. I understand: they are setting up the mortar. Moments of expectation. But it doesn't work.

A command comes from the third vehicle, where Matti Arazi and the commanders are sitting – drive forward. We realize that the moment has arrived. We will have to storm the village without waiting for the mortar fire. The vehicles start moving. The rifles, the Sten guns, and the machine guns are ready for action. I load my rifle and slip off the safety catch.

An unattended roadblock. We drive around it. I look at the time. It is exactly twelve. "This is the very moment of the founding of the State of Israel" I say to Bulli, who is sitting in front of me next to the driver. "OK," he answers, without turning round. "Maybe we'll find some wine in Qubab."

The driver closes the steel shutter in front of him. Now only a small slit is left. That feels better: when the shutter is open we are directly in the line of fire.

We drive into the center of the village. We all lower our heads a little. Through the slit I can see the houses and trees next to us. "The village appears to have been deserted" says Israel Gossek, the platoon medical orderly. It is only now that we become fully aware that we have met no resistance. There is no doubt – the village has been abandoned. Suddenly some armed figures appear from nowhere. I raise my rifle.

"Maccabi!" – our password.

We have run into Aryeh Kotzer's company, which was supposed to attack the village from the other side. The village is in our hands.

In front of us is a house with the lights on. Bulli, Nachman, and I jump out to investigate. We provide Nachman with cover and he storms in. There is nobody in the house, but a petroleum lamp is burning: a sign that the inhabitants and the fighters have only just fled. We quickly look through the cupboards and discover some boxes of Italian ammunition.

We go back to our vehicle. A new task is already waiting for us there. We are to return to the entrance to the village and secure the road in the direction of Ramle. We swear. What a prospect: yet again we have to hang around a sandy position while our comrades are gathering souvenirs.

We repair the road block, set up the machine gun, and build a lookout, just as the sun is rising. We can only look through the few houses in the immediate area. We break open the doors one after the other. Here the houses are much prettier and cleaner than the ones we know from Arab Hulda or Deir Muheisin. Almost everywhere we discover military equipment and ammunition.

Another problem is food. We know from experience that one can eat well in Arab villages. The chickens of Deir Muheisin are already legendary, and quite often, when we are sitting down to sardines and bully beef, someone will say "Come on, let's raid an Arab village."

We quickly organize four hens and about twenty pigeons. While I stand in the lookout post, keeping an eye on nearby Ramle, and stopping vehicles, my comrades prepare the meals.

For breakfast I eat a roast pigeon. We are not used to them yet. The outside of the bird is charred and the meat is almost raw in the middle.

Someone relieves me at the lookout. I go for a sleep. My comrades have found a bicycle and take turns riding around the village. They report that the other platoon is just lying in their position and cursing the commanders. Midday arrives without any sign of the enemy, apart from an armored car coming from the direction of Qawuqji's camp. It quickly leaves the area under our heavy fire.

The chickens are cooking on the Primus.[27] We each get a quarter. It is true: on the foundation day of the state we ate really well.

The main road now looks like Allenby Street in Tel Aviv. Buses bring reinforcements and drive here and there. Non-commissioned officers, quartermasters, the medical service, and other institutions establish themselves.

But naturally we are not left to enjoy life for long. We are relieved from our duties at the roadblock and sent to another position where we should remain with the rest of the company. They get us to dig trenches for protection from artillery. The day before yesterday, in Latrun, we learned to appreciate that. But that doesn't mean that we enjoy the work involved. The jokers see that as a sign that we will soon be leaving this position. It has happened to us so often already that we were ordered to dig trenches, and no sooner was the work complete than the order came to move elsewhere. Lo and behold – the jokers were right. The order arrives for us to collect our equipment and leave the village.

Man against Steel

*O*n the day after the founding of the state of Israel the regular troops of the Arab states marched into the Land of Israel. We were faced with a new enemy – equipped with aircraft, artillery, tanks. What I had been afraid of was now reality – the population of Israel now found itself at war with the whole of the Middle East.

Our newly created army did not have the weapons to win the battle with the enemy's destructive machine. We had no artillery and no aircraft fit for combat. We had no tanks, apart from the few that were "confiscated" from the British. With almost empty hands, with rifles, machine guns, and hand grenades, the Israeli soldier had to hold off well-trained armies equipped with heavy weapons.

From the first day the whole Givati Brigade directed its attention toward the south. There the strongest and most modern Arab army, the Egyptian, was just beginning to set up its "springboard" in the area between Gaza and Majdal. This enemy was facing a choice: either to march ahead toward Tel Aviv, or to link up with the Arab Legion around Hebron and cut off the Negev. The task of the Givati Brigade was to prevent both these possibilities.

Between Majdal and Hebron, near the Negba kibbutz, stands a fortress on high ground, that dominates the whole area. It can be seen from almost any point in the south of the country. This gigantic fortress, the police station of Iraq Suweidan,[1] was recently handed over to the Arabs by the British as they pulled out. Our first task was to capture this fortress before the Egyptian army could establish itself there.

The first attacks on Iraq Suweidan

The order to stand by comes in the afternoon. As usual we make use of the time before an operation to collect the things that we are most deprived of in combat: sleep and food. We also clean our weapons.

* * *

Matti Arazi takes over command of the company after Aryeh Spack's wounding in Latrun. He explains the operation: a night attack on the police station of Iraq Suweidan, which controls the important roads to Gat and Gal'on. Our role in the operation will be to capture the crossroads between Majdal and Julis and prevent the Egyptian army sending reinforcements from Majdal.

We drive south toward Negba. Here we take it easy until it gets dark. Mirah is the little soldier with the plaits; she serves us tea and sandwiches.

My name is called. The company radio operator is standing next to the armored vehicle. They want me to take on a new function: to become the radio operator of the unit. It's a shock at first. I have always pitied the radio operator. Staggering around with a thirty-five-pound box on your back, the antenna waving around and announcing your presence for miles. But they reassure me – they're talking about a Type-21 radio which weighs less than five pounds.

I am not sure whether to feel pleased or sorry for myself. On the one hand it is very awkward. You have to keep an eye on the antenna when you are walking under branches or crawling under wire. It is dangerous in combat, presenting a target for the enemy while your comrades are safely hidden. On the other hand it is an interesting job. As a radio operator you can follow the progress of the battle in detail, you hear all the orders and the discussions among the commanders.

The operator explains the equipment to me and gives me general instructions. My code name for the operation is Lea One. I learn the standard terms. "Avor"[2] ("Over"), or "Radio Check."

We set off in a long column. I have to follow Amnon, the new deputy company commander, a scrawny, blond youth, together with Israel Gossek, the medic, and Ezra Cohen, the runner. I belong to the staff.

Walking with the radio is uncomfortable. It keeps distracting my attention. The antenna tends to fall out, and when you bend down to pick it up, you stumble over stones that you hadn't noticed. When you cross barbed wire you turn into an acrobat. You have to crouch and turn this way and that if you want to avoid damaging the device. And that continuous voice in your ear: "Hello Lea One – message for you – are you making progress? Have you crossed the fence? ..."

And between the individual messages you keep hearing atmospheric noises, occasionally a weak English voice disturbs reception, and from time to time the beeping of Morse Code. After half an hour you have a headache.

Together with Israel the medic, I take a position about twenty meters behind the unit. We arrange ourselves in a defensive circle around the hill. To the left of me is the police station. I estimate that it is about a kilometer away.

I can't dig myself a trench. In one hand I keep hold of the mouth-piece of the radio, which I must not let go. The connection may not be broken even for one moment. I try to dig a little hollow with my heels, and with my free hand I move some lumps of earth as a protection for my head – a symbolic protection.

Amnon comes back. He digs himself a waist-deep hole.

"Hello Lea One, hello Lea One. We are ready, we are ready. The weapons are set up, the weapons are set up. Avor."

We wait. People take it in turns to sleep. In each trench one sleeps while the other is awake. But as radio operator I am not allowed to sleep. And that continuous crackling in my ear is a guarantee of my obedience.

"Booooooom!"

I look at the time. It is exactly one thirty in the morning. The attack has begun. The people in the police station wake up. They fire off one flare after another, and in their light our mortar crews can see their targets clearly. The machine guns and rifles bark. There is no way to distinguish our fire from the enemy's.

I know the plan. The sappers must now be crawling toward the fence. Two hundred meters crawling on your belly, under continuous fire. Not a pleasant job. Particularly when you're carrying enough explosive on your back to blow up a whole battalion.

From our position we can follow the progress of the bitter fighting which is now in its full frenzy. Now and then a shell explodes directly on the police station, which lights up the whole building. When the building is taken, then our task here is complete.

The fighting lasts over an hour. It seems that there is some hitch somewhere. There is continuous fire coming from the police station. The building is lit up as bright as day. An island of light in a sea of darkness.

The Arabs have ignited a prepared fire barrier. How will the sappers and the assault get through the burning area?

All is quiet where we are. Just the occasional few shots whistling over our heads more or less by chance.

Suddenly I notice that Amnon is tense, and hear the rattle of a motor. There – two lights of a vehicle from the direction of Majdal! The Egyptian reinforcements are coming. Without waiting for instructions I speak into the handset "Hello Lea One, hello Lea One, important message, important message, over!"

No answer. I check the antenna and the connections. Everything OK.

"Hello Lea One, hello Lea One, can you hear me? Can you hear me? Answer without delay. Over."

No answer.

The vehicle is getting closer. Amnon looks at me. I am going crazy. Now Lea Three is calling. I can hear him clearly: "Hello Lea Three, hello Lea Three, message for you. Over."

Nobody answers him either.

What's the matter? Trouble with the radio or has the operator been hit?

"Lea One here, Lea One here, enemy vehicle on the road. Repeat: enemy vehicle on the road. I see the lights. I see the lights. Can you hear me? Can you hear me? Over!"

I cannot contact the center.

"Hello Lea Two. Message for Lea One. Over!"

"Hello Lea One. OK, OK, OK. Over."

Apparently the second platoon had made contact with the company commander using a runner. "Here is Lea Two, calling Lea One, the command is only open fire when the target is quite clear. The sign for opening fire is a long burst of automatic fire. Understood? Over!"

Meanwhile the enemy vehicle has come to a stop about a hunded meters away and extinguished its lights. They may not have seen us, but they know that we are in the area. If they were to drive on fifty meters they would reach the mines laid by our sappers and our PIAT[3] would destroy them.

Suddenly our machine gun barks. Has the man gone mad?

The enemy replies immediately. The bullets come directly at us. We duck down in our trenches. Someone crawls over and whispers to Amnon: "One of the men got nervous. He heard a noise and thought the enemy was coming." Devil take it. That's the way operations fail.

The enemy keeps up his fire. My radio is driving me mad. I've lost contact with Lea Three. Then I have an idea – maybe the battery is flat? I stand up to change it. Amnon shouts at me to get down. But I ignore him. After all the lives of many men depend on the functioning of this damned box. As soon as the new battery is connected I notice the difference. It is nearly three o'clock. It will be light around four. If we don't manage to capture the police building, we will have to withdraw. In the daylight we will be easy prey for the enemy in these positions. There's no way we would get out alive.

"Hello Lea Two, message for Lea One, Matti is here, Matti is here, message for you, Lea One, over!"

At last. The company commander has taken over the functioning radio.

The retreat begins. First the sappers remove the mines. The squads withdraw in order – first the most forward squad with the sappers, the machine gun, and the PIAT.

We return on foot, with me talking continuously on the radio. The withdrawal goes according to plan. The police station is very near. At the moment there is no shooting from there, but the fire barrier is still burning. It seems that the building was not taken despite all our efforts. In this light it would really have been madness to approach the enemy.

* * *

Two days later the fortress again came under attack. This time our platoon was in the front line of assault. The plan is to assault the building from two directions after a heavy mortar barrage. While the two platoons crawl toward the fence, a column of armored vehicles will drive from the road toward the police station to draw enemy fire.

Nachman's squad will form the first assault wave, under the command of Menachem, our platoon leader. David's squad will form the second wave, together with Amnon's staff, the radio operator, the runner, and the medic. The people in the police station are alert. The lights that identified the building for us the day before yesterday cannot be seen.

After the three units have taken their start positions, the first wave starts crawling forwards. People swear. All three units come under rifle and automatic weapon fire. The armored vehicles attract the heaviest fire.

The first wave of our platoon crawls forwards. After a hundred meters people are exhausted. They throw caution to the winds and start to jump. Jump – lie down. Jump – lie down. The PIAT crew are the first to jump. The scouts with the explosive for bringing down the fence hesitate a little. The fire is heavy. In the open field there is no cover. But for some reason the enemy is aiming at the second wave rather than the first.

The first wave has reached the fence, which is only about thirty meters from the building. But they make no more progress. Where are the scouts? Eliyahu Keil has set up his PIAT and fires. The explosions are enormous. Every shot hits the building squarely. We can hear the cries of the wounded inside.

Our armored vehicles are blocked. The drivers of the first two vehicles have been hit. The column cannot advance.

The first assault wave has no radio operator. The second wave is far behind – almost three hundred meters. Between the two waves there is almost no contact. Shalom and Ezra are in the space between and try to transmit commands by shouting.

The people at the fence are angry. They are very near the building. The fence just needs to be breached so the second wave can come, and then the success of the attack is certain. From the building the cries of the Arabs can be heard "La ilaha illa Allah wa Muhammad rasul Allah."[4] They are preparing for death.

Menachem Brotzki, the leader of the first wave, orders a withdrawal of thirty meters, so that the sappers can blow the fence. The men crawl backwards. When you crawl backwards, you can't keep your head as low as when you go forwards. The enemy fire is unrelenting. Menachem shouts his commands, but they can hardly be heard above the noise of the firing. All weapons, both ours and those of the enemy, are giving everything they can.

Suddenly Menachem falls silent. Nachman calls to him but gets no answer. He crawls over and finds him sitting with lowered head. He touches him and his hand is covered in blood. For a moment Nachman loses his composure.

Menachem groans. Micki and Reuven take him on their backs and walk back through the hail of bullets. They know that every minute is critical with a head wound. But they also know that the wounded man should be kept as still as possible. They lie him on the ground, and Micki runs back to get the medic from the second assault wave.

Israel runs over. He bandages Menachem's head. He is still alive, but seems to have lost consciousness. He is put on a stretcher and moved away as quickly as possible.

Only ten men remain from the first assault wave. Nachman takes over command. The men have steadied themselves. They want to attack, now, immediately! The desire for revenge is burning in them. They are sure that the building can be taken. But the order does not come. Amnon, in command of the second assault wave, is in radio contact with the commander of the operation. He does not advance. He has received the order to retreat.

* * *

Everyone is thinking of Menachem. Everyone knows that he is dead.

Menachem was in the platoon for only a few days. But in this short time he won the hearts of the men. Just ten days ago – after an exhausting night of battle – we had to transport heavy stone blocks from one side of the camp to the other. He took off his shirt and joined in.

And another picture of him remained with us. A very disturbing picture. The day before yesterday, after the first attack on the cursed police, Menachem permitted us an "unofficial" leave. Instead of driving back to the base, we simply spent two hours in Tel Aviv. For almost a month we hadn't seen the town or our parents. Menachem himself got out in Allenby Street to catch a bus. Suddenly there was a cry of "Menachem" and a small, roundish, older woman fell on him, hugging and kissing him in the middle of the street. The collection of people around were moved – a mother and her son from the front. And tomorrow or the next day she will hear "Fallen in the battle to open the road to the Negev, the company commander Menachem Brotzki …"

In the darkest hours, as the invading enemy tried to advance into the heart of the State of Israel from all directions, the defense army[5] had only one thing to oppose the enemy's superior weapons – the human being.

And the human being stood firm. He knew that he was standing with his back to the wall. He knew that there was no area to withdraw into. He knew that his home, bombarded day and night by the Egyptians, was in danger. They were no "heroes." They were simple youths who took the fighting spirit of the real people's army to the limit of its possibilities. In this society of fighters they could do nothing less.

25 May 1948
Battalion HQ

A man and his weapon

Elisha was the curse of the company. If complaining and moaning is an art, then the whole army couldn't offer an artist to compare with him. If the order came to turn out for an exercise, then he would curse the commanders who had no concern for human life. If he was allowed to take it easy the whole day, then he cursed those who send men into battle without enough training.

A professional moaner like that can make your life into hell. Even without that, it is hard enough. The food is not the best. And nobody really enjoys being under fire. If all that is hard enough to bear, even if one jokes about it, it becomes completely intolerable if comrades complain and pull a sour face.

Elisha arrived here recently from Poland, and thinks that even here he is being pursued and oppressed by everybody. He always thinks he has had a raw deal – whether it is the distribution of cigarettes or the rota for guard duty.

No, Elisha was not born to be a soldier. On the return from Latrun, after three hours under artillery bombardment, Elisha was next to me in the rearguard. Our comrades were carrying a wounded man, whose chest had been opened up by a piece of shrapnel. He was covered in blood. Elisha took one glance at the wounded man and threw his rifle away. He refused to take one step more. It took a whole canteen of water, which we poured over his head, in his mouth, nose, and ears, to bring him to his senses and get him to walk on.

And so, when David, the deputy company commander, told us that we were getting a PIAT and that Elisha would be the "Number One PIAT operator," we took it as a good joke. Elisha of all people ...

The PIAT is a weapon with a very short range. To fire it effectively, you have to get very close to the enemy – whether tank, building, or defensive emplacement. For that you need bravery and ingenuity. And apart from that the PIAT weights thirty-five pounds. More than a two-inch mortar. Could anyone imagine Elisha with such a weight on one of our forced marches? Elisha, who whines and complains if he has to carry a five hundred round reserve for the machine gun?

But an order is an order, there's nothing to be done. And with all the joking none of us noticed that Elisha was not complaining, didn't see himself hard done by, and didn't even ask why it had to be him ...

After a while we couldn't overlook it any more – something had happened to Elisha. He complained less and less. Sometimes a whole meal would pass without the slightest murmur from him. One could almost believe that he was content with our commanders. And when we, for the third night in succession, were due to go for a pointless march of twenty kilometers, and even the strongest fellows were showing signs of insubordination – Elisha shouldered his PIAT without a word and got ready.

A strange relationship developed between Elisha and his PIAT. He treated his weapon like a young and pretty woman. After a tiring night march, when the rest of us were already in our beds snoring, he would kneel on the ground, take the weapon apart, clean it, and oil it, and put it tenderly back together again.

And woe to anyone who dared to insult the honor of this weapon. According to Elisha, the PIAT was the best of all weapons, superior to any artillery piece and even to aircraft. And with a few more PIATs the war would been won long ago.

In that night when we assaulted that damned fortress, Elisha and his PIAT were in the first wave. Or more correctly: Elisha ran in front of the others. The bullets whistling around him did not concern him. He probably didn't even notice them. He had only one thought in his head: to get as close to the building as possible, so his PIAT could perform its task. And the PIAT did work. When it raised its voice, the rifles and the automatic weapons seemed to fall silent. Like in the jungle, where all the animals fall silent when the lion roars. It was less than fifty meters range. Elisha fired at will. Every shot a hit. We couldn't see the holes in the wall. But the ground shook.

After that Elisha didn't grumble any more. He was balanced, content with the world, with the army, and most of all with his PIAT.

For a whole week we felt dejected. Every day we heard the news of the Egyptian advance toward Tel Aviv. We on the front knew what the people in Tel Aviv did not know – that this invading army, with its tanks and aircraft, was faced by a defensive army of no more than one thousand lightly armed soldiers.

* * *

Between patrols we unloaded the first combat aircraft that our army had received. We loaded ammunition and equipment onto transport aircraft for the Old Town of Jerusalem where a desperate battle was taking place.

Before our eyes appeared that terrible monster: the tank. We knew that we would have to fight against it tomorrow or the next day. We were all terrified of it. We were told that everyone who knocked out a tank would get two weeks' leave. And everyone developed their own method. Shalom Cohen wanted to jump on top of the armored vehicle and throw a hand grenade inside. Janek Levkovitz was of the opinion that the Molotov cocktail was the best method. We discussed this question for hours. Underlying this was the bitter truth: we did not have suitable weapons to engage the tanks that were descending on Tel Aviv, apart from Molotov cocktails and a few PIATs.

* * *

On the evening of 29 May came the red-haired Jerachmiel Fingermann, and called us to a meeting. Following the death of Menachem Brotzki he had taken command of the platoon. For the first time we heard a comprehensive summary of the situation. We sat there, appalled.

The enemy was dug in at Isdud, about thirty kilometers from Tel Aviv. Their vanguard had reached Yavne, about twenty kilometers from Tel Aviv, and it was possible that they had advanced even further. The Givati Brigade had received the order to stop them at all costs.

An explosives expert entered the room and placed a bottle on the table. He introduced us to this weapon which we were supposed to destroy the enemy with – the Molotov cocktail. After the lecture we were ordered to get ready for immediate action. We prepared ourselves for a week of fighting: blanket, washing things, changes of clothing.

We didn't sleep that night. We were too excited and too worried. We lay in bed and talked till after midnight. We discussed the chances of stopping the enemy's advance in time. And like all soldiers' talk we began with strategy and ended with women.

* * *

At eight o'clock in the morning of 30 May came the alarm – in the vehicles within ten minutes. No time for breakfast. Just a cup of black coffee.

In Gedera we got out. You could feel that the front was approaching. Groups of refugees stood around in the streets, evacuees from Be'er Tuvia and Kfar Warburg. Young women went from house to house and made lists of women and children. The news spread from mouth to mouth that the commander of the Givati Brigade had issued a harsh order for the population: no man was to leave the area.

We walked through the streets. This was no ceremonial march – we walked in fighting order, steel helmets on our heads, in one long column. The inhabitants and the evacuated women looked at us. They didn't cheer, but their eyes followed us. They also knew that the thin rows of khaki shirts were the last defense for their house, for Tel Aviv, for the state of Israel.

Our morale was high all the same. We were gripped by the feeling of battle approaching. Some girls were standing along the street. I waved and blew kisses to them. They smiled.

* * *

About a kilometer south of Gedera, where the road to Kibbutz Yavne joins the main road, we stopped. Our orders were to dig in and expect an attack with tanks, artillery, and aircraft. We knew that there was no way back. Now and then an Egyptian reconnaissance plane appeared, and we hid ourselves in the trenches. Our morale was back down at zero.

In the course of the day we were relieved from the trenches at Gedera. We spent a few hours in our base camp. There we were informed of the offensive that would begin this evening, the biggest attack that we had ever taken part in. This was our signal to go to bed and pull the covers over our heads. At least we could have a reasonable sleep before this tremendous attack.

1 June 1948
Battalion camp

Operation called off

We got out of the buses at Gan-Yavne. In a large field all participating forces were assembled for tonight's attack on the enemy rear: companies one and two, the support company of our battalion as well as an additional company under the command of Josh.

At the last moment the appearance of Dov Feit and Ephraim Makovsky was like a miracle. These two squad leaders had fought with us in Deir Muheisin and were now training recruits in another unit. Their people were not yet ready for combat, and so they had literally fled. Deserters of a special kind – leaving their unit to take part in action. They could expect to be punished on their return. Is there another army in the world with such soldiers?

* * *

In the field the special atmosphere before battle. Comrades squat on the ground. Some are cleaning their weapons. Contact between those from different units, getting to know each other.

At the last moment I am again appointed radio operator. I test the new radio apparatus and try to make contact with other operators, when silence falls.

Abba Kovner speaks. He came to us directly from the partisans in Russia and is the information officer of the brigade. It is the first time that someone from Brigade HQ has spoken directly to us. This underlines the importance of the upcoming operation more than anything else. The special mood is also reflected in the faces of the soldiers squatting on the ground.

Abba Kovner explains the operation. Tonight the whole brigade will be in action, together with other units of the Negev Brigade of the Palmach and a battalion of the Irgun. The Palmach units will attack the village of Isdud from the south and the Irgun will engage the Egyptians from the east. At the same time we will approach the Egyptian armored units from their rear, from the direction of the sea. Our four companies will attack the enemy directly and destroy them in man-to-man fighting. Before the attack the enemy will be softened up by artillery and aircraft.

The aim is not to capture a single village or a particular area. The aim is to destroy the Egyptian armored units.

"Tonight we will hear for the first time the thunder of our heavy guns … the air force, the artillery, and the infantry will operate in coordination … what could have been prepared and planned has been prepared and planned … now everything depends on your courage in the assault …"

The words have their effect. Nobody ever talked to us like this before. For a long time there has been a lack of concrete military information. The Israeli soldier wants to know what he is doing, he wants to understand his role in the battle.

Today I feel fresh and cheerful. The damned radio may be a bit of a weight, but it is lighter than a machine gun or a PIAT. We walk and walk and walk. It is some consolation to know for sure that we won't have to come back this way. After capturing and destroying the Egyptian camp we will stay there and take up a position.

After two hours' march we are tired. Occasionally the scout at the head of the gigantic column calls a halt and we lie on the ground. In training we would keep an eye out to left and right in such a case. Here we look at the stars in the sky, if anything.

We walk over a field, cross a road, the railway line, and a wadi, and arrive at the dunes. We can hear the sea in the distance. I know that we will soon be in the enemy's rear.

Marching on sand is particularly tiring. It gets into your shoes and socks. Occasional shots from the Egyptians permit us to estimate the reducing distance between us and them.

At last we reach our planned starting point, due west of the enemy. We are three or five hundred meters away from them at the most. Unit by unit we leave the long column, to take our planned positions. Here and there, friends shake hands and whisper "Good luck!" – which under these conditions means: "Come back alive!"

I have to establish radio contact. I put on the headphones, pull out the antenna, and speak into the microphone:

"Hello Yitzhak, hello Yitzhak, can you hear me?"

No answer.

Is the story of Iraq Suweidan going to repeat itself, when radio contact was broken just as direct fighting with the enemy started? I swear into the microphone. May the Devil take whoever it was who invented this damned contraption!

Yitzhak appears, the radio operator of the second platoon. One of our radios is not working. Before we set off they were both OK. Now there is nothing we can do about it. We fold up the antennas and return to our units. The company will just have to do without internal radio contact.

Suddenly there is a stir around Amnon, who is in command of the company today. His radio operator is in contact with Brigade HQ. What has happened?

The news spreads like wildfire. Order from HQ: return to base ...

Damn! Now we remember that a ceasefire was supposed to begin tonight. We heard about it in the camp, but no one took it seriously. In our imagination a ceasefire means two weeks' leave in Tel Aviv with many visits to the cinema and pretty girls, and then a crash course in modern weapons and new techniques, suited for modern warfare.

But now, at this instant, the ceasefire is a scandal. We are five hundred meters from the enemy and about ten kilometers from our forward base. We want to deal with the Egyptians once and for all, and we don't even want to think of the march back.

"Maybe we have agreed a price with the Egyptian commanders," I suggest as an explanation. "Maybe," says Jerach, "after all we were supposed to reach our aim 'at any price'..."

Back at the base we learn that the Egyptians have attacked and heavily bombarded Kibbutz Negba. There was a misunderstanding about the beginning of the ceasefire. Fighting will continue until a definite date is set down by the UN.

The platoon is outraged. We were relying on the ceasefire and the two weeks' leave to follow it. "Damn them all!" said Shalom Cohen, summing up the feelings of all of us. "They will pay for this lost leave."

Toward evening the new standby order arrived. We were certain that the operation would not be canceled this time. But at the same time we knew that it would be much more difficult and dangerous this time. The enemy must certainly have noticed what was going on last night. After all, the first company had already dug in directly in front of the enemy lines, before the order to withdraw arrived.

2 June 1948
Orange plantation near Gan-Yavne

The battle for Isdud

We are lying in the big field near Gan-Yavne. Soon we will be setting off. In the dusk one of our planes is flying a reconnaissance mission over enemy positions. Anti-aircraft guns fire tracer shells and every now and then it looks as though one has hit. But the pilot continues circling as if nothing had happened. We watch, fascinated.

Our last preparatory task is aided by Shalom, who grew up in Egypt: we have to learn a couple of Arabic words, so that we can tell the enemy soldiers to surrender – "Sallim nafsak!"[6]

Since we are not going to use the radio for company internal communication this time, I am appointed the company runner. This has a good and a bad side. The good is that the runner only needs to carry his personal weapon. He doesn't have to drag along heavy weapons or extra ammunition. On the other hand it is a dangerous job. The runner is always racing around the battle area while his comrades can remain under cover. Since I am more frightened of carrying heavy weights than the dangers of battle, I am pleased with this task. In addition it will help me to follow events on the battlefield. I leave behind all unnecessary items like a pullover or a towel, and do without spare clothing. And above all: I'm not taking the steel helmet. Yesterday the thing really got on my nerves.

We set off. The password is "Beat Egypt!"

Now we have to save time. The scouts go further than usual toward the south. I miss the conspicuous points that I noticed earlier, in case we had to make a quick withdrawal. Still it takes a long time. It is over an hour before we cross the road and the railway tracks. The Arabs are very quiet today. Hardly a shot to be heard.

In front of me is Jerach, and behind me Israel the medic. Behind him Salomon and Jaakobi, the two sappers with the explosives. If a bullet hits their backpack, the whole staff will be heading for heaven …!

We reach the wadi. I have an unpleasant feeling – something is not right. We didn't go this way last time. The distance between the tracks and the wadi is too short. The banks of the riverbed are very steep here. It takes time to cross them. The seconds stretch like rubber. The gaps are growing between the individual soldiers, the units could lose eye-contact with each other. Those in front don't notice and walk on at normal speed. This is the classical mistake in a night operation. It has already cost many victims and will continue to do so in the future.

Someone behind shouts to us to halt. We can't do that without losing contact with those ahead. What to do? Jerach sends me ahead to the company commander. The radio operator is there. He should order the units at the head to halt. I run ahead and look for the antenna of the radio. Asher Dromi, who is in command of the operation today, must be with him. While I am running I notice that a hand grenade has come loose from my belt and fallen to the ground. I bend down to pick it up. The devil take ...

rat-tat-tat-tat-tat-tat-tat-tat-tat ...

I automatically drop to the ground. Someone falls on top of me. "Damn ..." I start, but stop in the middle of the sentence. The man is moving strangely. I realize he must be wounded.

"Medic!" I call quietly. That is an alarm call in combat. One medic is directly behind me. He crawls forwards. The wounded man was hit in the back. It is Yaakov Rachmilevitch, the company medic. He was hit at exactly the moment I bent down for the hand grenade. If I hadn't bent down ...

We were now under heavy enemy fire: at least one machine gun, several handguns, and any number of rifles. The bullets whistled over our heads and all around us. I press my head against the ground and dig holes with my hands and feet. Did we run into an ambush? No. We simply marched into the middle of the enemy position.

The whole company is lying on the ground. Bullets are hailing down. But I have a task, I have to be with the platoon commander. I get up and run, crouching, toward the rear. But my section is not lying on the ground. The men are sprinting back to the wadi. I manage to find Jerach running and follow him. The Arabs are still shooting with all they've got. But they are now aiming in the wrong direction. The bullets are now flying past us to the right.

We have reached the wadi. The bank is as sheer as a wall. We sit on the rim and simply slide down. No idea how the mortar and PIAT bearers manage it, but somehow they too arrive at the bottom. Yaakov too, now bandaged, is back with us.

Down below is chaos. I run around looking for the units. We form up again in a long line and set off to the north, in the wadi. We travel in a long arc to the north and the west. The Egyptians are still shooting at the place we were when we first made contact.

While we are marching through the dunes toward the south, the rumble of our artillery meets our ears. One shell after another explodes in the Egyptian camp. Our hearts leap. That is our revenge for Latrun.

To the sound of artillery we march on, until we reach our goal. We lie on the ground in a circular defensive position. At the same time the Irgun unit joins the battle. Their task is to harass the enemy from the other direction and to tie up his forces. The Irgun orchestra produces a sound we have never heard before: hundreds of rifles, handguns, heavy machine guns, and mortars make an unbelievable racket.

The Arabs respond and also fire red and green rockets into the air.

Asher Dromi has now completed his preparations. He arranges the company for the assault. Our section on the northern wing, two squads directly facing the enemy. The third squad as a reserve behind. Jerach and I in the middle of the front row. The whole company advances on a broad front.

After a hundred meters we halt. According to the plan, Kotzer's platoon should capture the left wing and Josh's the right, before we in the center begin the decisive assault.

We are lying in soft sand and freezing. From both sides come the typical sounds of close combat. Shots from rifles and heavy weapons mingle with human shouts and cries. Our comrades are storming the fortified positions of the enemy at this very moment.

We wait for the command to start the assault. The ground here is unpleasant. You can't run on this sand. Now and then a salvo of machine gun fire comes in our direction – thirty to fifty tracer rounds.

"It will be light in twenty minutes" remarks Shmulik, the squad leader.

We know what that means. In daylight we cannot remain in this area. There is no cover at all and you can't even dig yourself in properly. As long as we are in his rear area, the enemy can easily cut off our retreat.

It is getting light.

The enemy bullets are now flying directly over us. Salvo after salvo. Yaakov Burstein, the acting deputy company commander, crawls to us and gives Jerach the order to withdraw. I am a kind of traffic policeman – slow down one squad, hurry the other one up, pass commands to take cover. We climb over a hill that is within full view of the enemy. We are inundated in fire, but cross the danger area without losses. On the north wing a wild close-combat battle is raging, which distracts the enemy a little from our part of the front.

It is six thirty.

After a few hundred meters we are exhausted. Jerach tries to get us to go faster, explaining that the danger for our lives is growing from minute to minute. But we are back in that stage of exhaustion where arguments have lost their effect. We reach the wadi and hide in it. We are almost out of danger here – the bullets fly past over our heads.

To the left we can see a white two-storey house. That's where Kotzer's company is fighting. Every few minutes the house disappears from view in the smoke of a shell.

The company had initially managed to set up a half-way fortified position. Now they are withdrawing in the direction of the white house. Aryeh reports from there that they have heavy losses. All our medics, including Israel, the section medic, are sent there. Yaakov Rachmilevitch, the company medic, who was lightly wounded in the back earlier, got a whole salvo in the chest this time.

Of all frontline soldiers, the medics are the real heroes. Behind the lines they are sometimes regarded as non-combatants. But nobody exposes themselves to more danger than they do in the attempt to save human life.

We crawl wearily through the fields toward Gan-Yavne. Near the road Moshe Shatzky, our lanky machine gunner, is wounded. A bullet in the leg hit the bone. Reuven, Micki, and Freddy take it in turns to carry him on their backs, each about fifty meters. Moshe rides piggyback and cracks jokes. From behind they are calling us. In Kotzer's company some wounded men are lying on the ground, and there are not enough people there to rescue them. We leave all our equipment and ammunition reserves in the field before we go over there. We can pick the things up later.

We carry five wounded men. One has a shrapnel wound in the chest, another in the back. A third was wounded in both legs by one bullet. We only have a stretcher for one of them. The others will be carried on tarps.

Those who haven't seen these wounded men can't imagine the heroism the human being is capable of. They were wounded in the field and are in danger of remaining there. Some of them are seriously wounded and won't live to reach a hospital. They are all in great pain. But none of them complains. They try to crack jokes and to make suggestions for the best way to transport them.

Like always after a battle we have to tell someone about it. That way a complete picture can be formed. One talks in particular about the heroism of the wounded. There were not enough stretchers and blankets. People take off their shirts and trousers. We tell each other the names of the wounded and the fallen. It is clear that the "supporting" unit suffered heavy losses and that Kotzer's company was almost wiped out.

Each name is a living figure for us, a person who shared the ups and downs of life with us for months, in operations and celebrations. Someone whose most private secrets, desires, and preferences we know. And every one of them leaves behind a gap that cannot be filled.

Some feel that we have suffered a defeat. But we know that the outcome of a single confrontation doesn't mean much. The battle as a whole is all that counts. Whether this or that engagement ended in defeat or victory is not important. What is decisive is the losses of men and material on the two sides and whether, in the end, the enemy advance was stopped or not. But one thing is certain: we have stopped the Egyptian advance. The danger is no longer acute. That is the most important lesson of the battle of Isdud.

* * *

After this battle we remained in the camp for a few days to reorganize. We didn't get any leave. But we didn't wait for written permission. We could check that no action was planned for the next twenty-four hours, find a hole in the fence, and disappear for a day.

Back at camp, I was requested, with all due politeness, to accompany two battalion policemen – and the gates of the "Calabush"[7] closed behind me.

4 July 1948
In battalion jail

Intermezzo in the Calabush

In the memoirs of former prisoners one reads about that terrible moment: you enter the cell, the door slams behind you ... I had no such feelings of fear. When I entered the Calabush I was greeted with a cheer – from my comrades, who were in here for the same misdemeanor: absence without leave. Those who are used to sleeping in a soft bed, with clean bedclothes, won't regard the Calabush as a high-class residence. But anyone who has slept in flea-infested Arab villages will find the Calabush a pleasant place to stay.

My "more experienced" comrades showed me around. Up on the wall was a long screed: "Here vegetate the prisoners of Zion: the mortar man Yitzhak P., the machine gunner Moshe A., the scout David M., the conquerors of Qubab, the heroes of Latrun, the liberators of Jerusalem ... "

Time passes. We get hungry. The military policemen bring us food. We eat and drink and amuse ourselves at their expense. We call them military waiters.

We lie on our backs in contentment. After a few hours visiting Tel Aviv, you return in a good mood. Only if you spend two or three days there and find out what's really going on, if you meet old friends who are making a military career for themselves behind the lines, then you come back in a bad mood, depressed and annoyed.

We belong to different units, but we are all veterans. Each one of us has lived through at least a dozen battles. And without noticing it, we begin to discuss strategy. There is hardly a better place than the Calabush for concentrated thinking. In the unit there is no time for such discussions.

It is late. We talk quietly so as not to disturb the sleeping guards. We cover a wide range of subjects and discuss the questions that really concern us. When will the war be over? Are we really doing everything to overcome the enemy? Will we be able to adapt to civilian life again after everything that we have experienced here?

Late in the night I hear a quiet voice.

"Uri!"

"Yes"

"You OK? Need anything?"

"A cool beer wouldn't be bad"

He laughs and disappears, but not before throwing me something. A piece of chocolate. In the last battle I carried his rucksack after he had collapsed with exhaustion.

A strange experience, this Calabush. Actually you can't really be punished if you are already in a fighting unit. What can they do to you? Withdraw your leave? You don't get any anyway. Cut your pay? Very well. The two lira that you get ... In any case the Calabush is nothing to fear if you have just come back from a dirty position where you were bombarded for hours by mortars and artillery.

Discipline in a fighting unit depends only on the personality of the commanders and the will of the ordinary soldiers. There is nothing more dangerous than the feeling of an ordinary soldier that he has been unjustly treated, that things are happening behind his back, that he hasn't been given what he deserves. A fighting soldier is effectively a volunteer, even when he has been conscripted.

The battle for Isdud inflicted serious losses on the battalion. The first company was completely out of action. Its commander, Aryeh Kotzer, was already a legendary figure on the front. The fate of his people had shaken him so badly that he had to be transferred to a post at HQ for the time being. Our company was lucky and was the only experienced unit remaining in the battalion. The third company consisted mainly of young recruits.

Since we had not succeeded in destroying the armored column at Isdud, we were now given the task of confronting it and blocking its further advance. In the night of 6 July we tried to reach Kibbutz Nitzanim,[8] which was under heavy fire. In the darkness we passed Hill 69, where our people had started to dig in. But even before we had reached Nitzanim we got the news that the kibbutz had surrendered. We received the order to withdraw.

8 June 1948
Beit Daras

A little job

What made me volunteer? It sounded interesting. And since I happened to be there when they were asking for volunteers, I joined them "just like that." Predictably, my comrades said that I had done it just to have something to write about in the paper. Jerach, our platoon commander, told us that they were looking for four volunteers for a special and very important job. I said I was prepared to go.

It happened about ten o'clock in the morning. Three Egyptian tanks, a howitzer, and an armored car attacked our position in Beit Daras from the direction of Isdud. Our platoon returned their fire. The first Egyptian shells fell near our positions, but then we suddenly noticed that they had changed their aim. Two trucks of ours, probably from Be'er Tuvia, had lost their way and driven into range of the Egyptians.

I was sent to the command post which had been set up under the trees of the village. Meanwhile the number of volunteers had risen to six. David Shani, our deputy battalion commander, explained our task: the two trucks were carrying howitzers and ammunition, which we needed critically. There were also explosives, which could detonate. We must do all we could to get the vehicles out. If we couldn't move them, we should unload the artillery pieces and get them to a safe area.

We watched the proceedings through our binoculars. The Egyptian shells were exploding all around the vehicles. The enemy was only a few hundred meters away and it was a miracle that the trucks had not long since been hit. Visibility was unobstructed over the whole area.

We looked at each other – six young men from two companies who had volunteered for a job whose importance we didn't need explaining to us.

Six men: Siff, the broad-shouldered, black-haired squad leader, like someone from the front page of a weekly magazine; Ovadia, the driver, a man with "guts," who hides the fact that he is a squad leader; Benjamin, thin and pale, and David, dark skinned, with glasses – who both took part in the heroic retreat from Hartuv; Janek, the refugee who spent half his life in concentration camps, small, quick, but a slow talker; and me.

The enemy artillery kept firing. "What do you think?" I asked Janek. "Fifty–fifty" he answered in his thick Polish accent. I was more optimistic – if the trucks were not seriously damaged ...

* * *

We are off. There is no boss here. We don't have to prove ourselves. That's the way we like it – a few comrades who understand one another and know that we can rely on each other. We travel in a wide detour, for maximum safety. So we will creep up from the south. From this direction we can get to within two hundred meters of the vehicles under cover of the cactus plants. Every few meters we stand before a hedge of cacti, which we break through with the butts of our rifles. And the beautiful knife, a present I was given the day before yesterday, serves well.

The sun is burning down. This time I have brought my helmet with me, and it's a burden. Our clothes are running with sweat, but we make good progress. Every minute is important, because one of the vehicles could be hit at any moment. But even this short distance takes us more than half an hour.

At last – the end of the wall of cacti. From here the way to the vehicles is straight and in full view. For some reason the Egyptian firing has stopped for the moment. We advance in two groups.

Ovadia jumps into the first truck. His first attempt to start it fails. Janek makes some suggestions. Suddenly the engine fires up. I jump on, the truck is moving. I glance at Ovadia. We can both see the problem: should we wait until the second truck is started, or set off as fast as we can toward Be'er Tuvia and then come back? At any moment the enemy fire can restart. We know that we are being watched through two pairs of binoculars: those of our commander and his Egyptian counterpart. We decide to drive straight off.

Four stay behind. As we drive off, we can see that the other truck is not moving. We will have to bring a recovery vehicle from Be'er Tuvia. We drive fast. The tires are flat, the doors full of holes. So what?

A jeep comes toward us from the direction of Be'er Tuvia. Only one man in it, with a beret on his head. "Hey, you, where are you heading?" I ask him. Maybe he could get to Be'er Tuvia quicker and call help. It is too late that I notice that it is Czera Czertenko,[9] my battalion commander.

We receive a hero's welcome in Be'er Tuvia. They have heard what happened. The tow-truck is ready to go. We jump on and race back to the second truck. There the four are still struggling with the engine that won't start. They have already begun to unload the truck, but reload it quickly when they see us coming. On the way back I notice a steel helmet with a camouflage net, lying by the roadside. We stop briefly so I can pick it up.

We couple the two vehicles together, and they move off. We don't accompany the vehicles. Our task is complete. Now we have to disappear. Quickly. A miracle that we haven't been shot at. But our machine guns have distracted the enemy.

On the way back we take a shorter route. We have lost our caution. A result of the little victory. We have done our job.

Back at camp we have a triumphant reception. Jerach shakes Janek's and my hand. Our comrades whisper that they have it from a "reliable source" that we will be mentioned in dispatches. The main thing that we are happy about is to be back safely. During the operation we had no time to think about the dangers. Now we love life all of a sudden. We don't feel like heroes, but we do feel particularly good.

While we were sitting in Beit Daras, the battle for Hill 69 began. A fairly low position with three peculiar water towers on the top, about a kilometer away from Beit Daras, the hill had a special importance for the Egyptians. From there one controlled the road between Isdud and Majdal. One could practically cut off the Egyptian forces from their HQ. The Egyptians committed their strongest forces to this battle – tanks, aircraft, and artillery made the earth shake. In this terrible bombardment Issar Barsky, the nineteen-year-old section leader, was wounded. The ambulance couldn't reach him. His condition worsened. Thanks to the outstanding bravery of Shraga Gafni and Joseph Waadjah he was brought down from the hill and taken to a hospital, where he died.

The crisis began when Danni Dalugi, the deputy commander of the company there, fell. The company commander lost his self-control and the willpower of the soldiers collapsed. They pulled back.

At the last moment our company was hurriedly ordered onto the hill, to give the retreating company covering fire. We reached the edge of an orange grove about two hundred meters from the hill. That's where we saw the heavy tanks. Elijahu Keil and Yaakov Levkovitz, the PIAT crew, braved the heavy fire to get in a close shot at one of the tanks. But under the double bombardment from our own and the enemy artillery, we were forced to withdraw. In this time the men from the hill managed to reach Beit Daras. They brought their wounded with them.

The news of the loss of the hill was a heavy blow for the whole brigade. For the first time our fighters had come across enemy tanks, and they lost their nerve and retreated. From then on the number "69" troubled us all. It was engraved on the heart of the brigade – we didn't want to forget it. We wanted to free ourselves from this disgrace.

Finally. Finally we were informed that the ceasefire was supposed to begin at ten o'clock in the morning. None of us believed that the Egyptians would respect it.

In the middle of the night we were roused from our sleep. Five volunteers were needed for a tank ambush on the path from Hill 69 to Beit Daras. I set off with four of my comrades. In the darkness of the night we dug a trench next to the road. We put the Molotov cocktails next to us, camouflaged ourselves with twigs, and waited for sunrise.

No tanks came. But at exactly ten o'clock the Egyptians began shooting wildly. At first we were certain: they had violated the resolutions of the UN again. Then we noticed that no bullets or shells were coming in our direction. It was an oriental "Fantasia." The Egyptians had accepted the ceasefire.

Around midday we were relieved. We spent the day in Beit Daras, before returning to our base camp.

Eleven Days of Decision

The thirty days of the ceasefire were days of preparation. It was clear from the beginning that the whole thing would start up again. We knew that the decisive battles would be fought on the southern front. We also knew that our brigade would have to confront the full strength of the Egyptian army, and that we could rely only on ourselves. The brigade set to work to prepare itself. The quality of training was improved. A special brigade HQ for combat situations was set up, to command the units directly during the fighting.

In the last battles at Beit Daras and Hill 69, Palmach units had supported the brigade, using jeeps and half-track vehicles. The soldiers were impressed by the power and potential of such units, by their combination of speed, agility, and immense firepower. A "motorized assault company" was set up, and provided with all the brigade's jeeps and the odd armored vehicle "confiscated" from other battalions.

Our company was chosen. Those of us who had been transferred to Jerusalem during the war returned. For the first time since the start of hostilities our company was "complete" – fully manned in accordance with the organization chart.

* * *

On one of the early days of the ceasefire period we were summoned to the mess hall. Before us stood Aryeh, who had recovered and resumed command of the company. The news that we would henceforth be the "motorized commando company of the southern brigade" filled us with enthusiasm. A new spirit gripped us. We were ready for anything.

Urgent job

"Respond immediately … important message … maximum speed … "

We jump into our jeep, Elimelech slams it into gear, five kilometers per hour, ten, fifteen, twenty …

It is a hot, clear day. The sun is burning down, but when we are moving we don't feel it. A squad of infantrymen are marching next to the road. They are sweaty and tired with their weapons and equipment on their backs. We think of the days when we were poor sods like that.

The infantry lead a bitter life. When they arrive on the battlefield they are already dog tired. They are so tired that it doesn't really matter to them what will happen. And though they suffer more than the others and work harder than the others, they are treated like inferior beings. The Palmach despises the army, the artillery and the men of the air force laugh at it, and only writers who were never in the field sometimes show sympathy for those who "are occupying positions" or "our young men in Arab villages."

Thirty kilometers per hour.

The road is lined by orange groves. Here and there we see a young girl, and wave at her. Sometimes she will smile, or turn her back on us. Life is great.

We keep a casual hand on the machine gun mount. We all wear an ammunition belt over our shoulder. The cartridges shine like gold in the sun – a poseur's dream.

Forty kilometers per hour.

It really was a stroke of luck for us, becoming the motorized company. It might mean more danger in combat. But you quickly forget this little drawback when you consider the advantages: a comfortable drive to the action, with weapons and equipment just lying there; pleasant words of recognition from HQ; and an almost aristocratic status in the estimation of civilian friends.

And what about danger? You go on an extremely dangerous mission, attack the enemy from the rear or from the flank, and return without losses. And on the next day you undertake a boring routine patrol, run into an ambush, and lose half the unit. Our experience teaches us: mobility is more important than thickness of armor, firepower more decisive than the number of soldiers, and surprise much more effective than a fortified position.

Fifty kilometers per hour.

Fatima slowly wakes up. Fatima is our jeep. The name comes from the picture of the pretty girl that I "captured" in Deir Muheisin. Since then I have carried it with me. It wasn't easy to choose a name for the jeep. There were many suggestions. Melech wanted to call it "Flash," I suggested "Devil," "Flea," or "Beetle." Sali Kreismann liked the sound of "The Merry Widow" or "Modest Rose." In the end we decided unanimously: our jeep is called Fatima.

Seventy kilometers per hour.

The speed is shaking our bones. The muscles of the face begin to tense. Without our noticing it, a smile of enjoyment spreads over our faces. We lean forward and urge Melech on. But he doesn't need any encouragement. He is already drunk with speed.

Eighty kilometers per hour.

The jeep flies over the road. The wind tears at our faces and whistles like a thousand rifle bullets. Sometimes we get hit by small stones, which feel like bullets.

Ninety kilometers per hour.

Our eyes are watering. Melech is the only one with the necessary goggles. We blink and try ineffectively to recognize the landscape around us. In the distance a motorbike appears, coming in our direction. It is dancing strangely up and down. A sharp *voooom* and it is behind us.

Everything is dancing – even the trees along the road. They are swaying like a swing boy[1] in Tel Aviv, dancing his last rumba. We have to hold on with all our strength to the machine gun support, or we'll fall out the back onto the road.

Ninety-five kilometers per hour.

It's like being drunk. A wonderful intoxication. A conscious euphoria that wakes all the senses. The blood is buzzing in our veins. The jeep sings. The world around us sings. Fragments of verse appear in my head, only to disappear immediately. "The wheels roll to victory," "the jeep races the wind …" They appear and vanish like the clouds in the sky.

We are approaching a populated area. Melech takes his foot off the accelerator. Sixty, fifty, forty. We awake from our dreamlike state, look at each other in amazement. I rub my eyes. Slowly our face muscles relax.

The people on the road stare at us. We are covered in dust, our faces radiant, the machine guns pointing upwards, our cartridge belts gleaming.

For the jeep teams there was no ceasefire. We had a lot to do: test the enemy lines along the front, probe the enemy's preparedness for the next round in "aggressive patrols," put pressure on the Arab villages east of the Hulda–Kfar Menachem line.

19 June 1948
Routine patrol

Our orders were to patrol the ceasefire line and test the troop strength of the Arabs. When we run into Arabs, to provoke a confrontation.

We mount the weapons on the jeeps and are ready. At the last moment I am appointed radio operator, to maintain communication between the jeep commander and Aher Asherov, the platoon commander. Three jeeps set out. That might sound like a small unit, but the firepower is enormous.

The jeep leaps along the road like a frisky foal. We hang on to the machine gun mounts. I hug the radio as if it were a baby. Within a few minutes we are moving in a cloud of white dust. Hardly anyone has the goggles we need, and we can see almost nothing. The dust gets up your nose, in your mouth, and into your ears. Shalom, who is in the jeep in front, has tied a handkerchief over his nose and mouth. We all follow suit.

"Hello Hagar One – message for Hagar Two – Over …" It's Reuven Huber's first time with a radio. We don't actually need any code names because we are only using two radios. But I don't want to spoil his fun.

"Hello Hagar Two – message for Hagar One – how do you like the dust? Over …"

"Hello Hager One – Ruth – out"

We have now reached the border area and are following the dividing line. We know this area from earlier deployments. Every hill and every path wakes memories. In front of us is a ruined bridge. I get out and examine the wadi. It is deep and steep, but we have to get across. Slowly, in the crawling gear, the first jeep drives down, while the soldiers in the second provide cover. At the bottom the first jeep gets stuck at first, then thinks better of it, the engine coughs and shakes, then it drives back up on the other side. The slope is almost fifty degrees, and the men are almost lying down. Pity I don't have my camera with me. The second and then the third vehicle make it across the wadi. Once on the road again we drive fast. Albert and Dov crouch behind their weapons. This is a dangerous area and we don't want to be dependent on the carelessness of the Arabs.

In the distance we see a few Arabs with camels who have strayed into our area. They run away when they see us, but the first jeep leaves the road and races after them. They stop and raise their hands, shaking with fear. Simple Fellaheen[2].

Shalom Cohen, our Arabic speaker, searches their clothes for weapons and interrogates them. They tell him something about the region. When we let them go, they run away fast.

* * *

We are approaching the village of Ssajad, a well-known hide-out for Arab fighters. We stop behind a hill, with only our heads and our weapons visible to the enemy. They don't take the geography of the ceasefire too seriously and open fire without announcement. The bullets whistle over our heads. We are pleased. Finally we have the chance of showing what our weapons can do. Asher gives the sign and we fire away.

"Cease fire!"

We drive back and disappear. It is not worth fighting a long, drawn-out battle. We are supposed to look around the area. So we drive close to the village of Gazaza and position ourselves behind a hill again. The village is quiet. But from Sajad they are still shooting in our direction. Pity about the ammunition.

* * *

We have done our job. We race back along the road to the ruined bridge. Albert Mandler,[3] sitting in front of me, looks like a baker after a hard day's work. He is covered in white dust. Ephraim, our driver, is wearing a sock hat pulled hard down over his forehead, goggles, and a cloth over his face – with a thick layer of dust over everything. The weapons too are covered in dust. A miracle they still work.

The jeeps race along at over 100 kilometers per hour. We are within range of the enemy, who are still shooting at us. But there is almost no chance that we will be hit. Speed is the best armor. With both hands I hold onto my hat, my rifle, and the radio. The muscles of my forehead are aching from squinting, and my eyes are red and watering.

The wadi once more. We position ourselves to give covering fire if necessary. This time we get across quicker. We have learned from experience. In Ekron[4] there is a little soldiers' club. Two cute girls are sitting there as we come in, and they get quite a shock from our appearance, covered in dirt and dust from head to foot, but then they laugh. Hearing their laugh, we forget our tiredness. We drink lemonade and beer and feel like heroes. The jeeps with their dust-encrusted weapons look as though they have been through a heavy battle. What a great impression!

Back to the base. We have only two things in our heads: a cold shower and bed. We have been spoiled by the ceasefire. It is about time we accustomed ourselves again to the rigors of combat.

* * *

Ceasefire …

One of our duties forced us to spend some days in Camp Sarafand.[5] There we had the chance to live alongside the Palmach people. The battalions of the Harel Brigade were stationed there. Relations between us and the Palmach were rather curious. At the beginning of the war we got annoyed at the attention all their actions attracted, while hardly anyone showed any interest in us.

But as time went on we began to like the Palmach on account of the attitude of their soldiers and their discipline. Friendly relations developed between the Givati brigade and the Harel, Yiftach, and Sergei brigades after we had fought side by side in several operations. This mutual sympathy was also based on a similar attitude to military hierarchy and discipline.

22 June 1948
Sarafand

The tents of the Palmach

It was ten in the evening when we arrived back from our patrol. We had spent the whole day in our jeeps. A very boring task. We will have to report again for duty at two in the morning, and don't feel like wasting the few remaining hours in our barracks. We need some diversion. But our own base is far away and we don't know our way around here.

Somehow we hear that the Cameri Theater is performing "He Walked Through The Fields," a successful theatrical production of the novel by Moshe Shamir. We read about it in the paper and are keen to see it.

"They won't let anyone in," says somebody. "Even Palmach people from other units were kept out. They certainly wouldn't let the army in."

"Are we commandos or not?" asked Dov Kirschenbaum.

"Yes, but ..."

"So? We'll storm the place!"

The big sports hall is surrounded by people. No more room inside. Bearded young soldiers, the victors of many a battle, cannot force their way into the hall. Laughable ...

Inside the lights go out. The performance is beginning and we are still outside. Dov and I go to the back entrance to the hall. I try out a really old trick. I knock on the rear stage door and ask naively: "Excuse me. Is Batya Lanzet there?" But on the other side is a muscular soldier who is not naive, and who slams the door in my face. That annoys me. What is this all about? Are we commandos or not? A group from the Fourth Battalion is standing by one of the side doors. When they are let in we squeeze through with them. Finally we have made it.

All the seats in the hall are taken, and you can't see anything from the standing places. Dov gets two boxes. When we stand on them we can see the stage. But hear anything? The honorable spectators won't even consider making do with the passive role of an audience. "A play direct from the life of the Palmach" as it says on the billboards in Tel Aviv. And here it is concrete reality.

Only a small part of the audience is sitting. The majority are strolling around the sides and walking up and down the aisles. Others have found a place on the bars that are fixed to the walls. Others sit ten feet up on the window ledges. And at least twenty are sitting fifteen feet above our heads on the wooden beams that cross the room. They are climbing up and down the ropes in a good impersonation of Tarzan. It looks as though they might fall on our heads at any moment. But they are well trained ...

The audience is paying attention. But the people are too active just to listen. So Chanah and Immanuel are acting on the stage, and Joseph, Eytan, and Danni are acting in the hall. And they don't disturb each other. Perfect harmony – a play straight out of the life of the Palmach ...

Our many patrols during the time of the ceasefire were good practice. We learned how to use our new weapon: the jeep. We learned how to take advantage of its special feature – speed. We learned how to protect ourselves in moments of danger. And even if some of us were more or less severely wounded in the process, it was worth it. This experience saved our lives more than once after the fighting broke out again.

1 July 1948
Battalion base

Tuition fees

The first jeep had already passed the point when I got a message from Reuven, the operator in the last jeep: "Hello Nesher Three, hello Nesher Three, message for Nesher One – I can see Arabs in the field, Arabs in the field, over!" Our orders were to capture all Arabs we came upon.

* * *

Ovadia turned and raced back. While we are still driving we hear the shots and see three Arabs running away across the open field. The excitement of the chase grips us. We drive into the field to cut off their escape route. Jerucham, the operator of the forward machine gun, fires off a few single shots. But the Arabs keep running.

The jeep begins bumping around. The field is covered in tall bushes. You can hardly see the shape of the ground. We can just hope for the best. Our task is important.

The jeep jumps around madly. I am hugging the radio with both arms and can't hang on anywhere. I just manage to fold down the antenna. A big bump. We are tearing along a small wadi. I am thrown three feet into the air, but land back in my place, the radio still in my arms. Then another bump. Nobody has seen this wadi before. I feel a heavy blow, fly into the air, another hefty blow, and I fall backwards. In the air I collide with Dov. I land on my back about ten feet behind the jeep which is skidding to a halt. I stand up. My brain is not working. Automatically I walk a few steps. Nothing is broken. My arms and legs are working. My head is buzzing. I walk up and down in a daze. My whole body is in pain. As if through a fog I see Dov, who is also staggering around. I see something red, bright red. Blood.

He is injured. I get a dressing and bandage his neck. He looks as though his throat has been cut. He curses me. The bandage is too tight. I remove it and start again. Only then do I notice that my face is bloody. A small cut on the nose, which I ignore. My leg hurts. I pull up my trouser leg. A long cut, but not very deep. Ovadia and Jerucham are unhurt.

"Shall we go?" shouts Ovadia.

"Let's go!" answers Jerucham.

The jeep drives on, but gets stuck again after a few meters. This time it is Jerucham who is hurt. He bangs his head with full force against the machine gun. But there is no visible wound.

I notice that my shirt is torn. I take it off – a long, deep wound on my shoulder. I call Ovadia, who bandages my wound hastily. Slowly I am coming to myself. I remember that I had to do something. Where is the radio? It is lying in several pieces, some in the vehicle and others strewed around nearby. I reassemble it laboriously. "Hallo Nesher One, message for Nesher Two, over!" A tense moment. "Hello Nesher Three ..." It is working!

Suddenly Dov falls down. He is out cold. We sit him up and he comes to. Jerucham's condition is worsening. He doesn't talk any more. Just sits there with his head bowed.

Somehow we manage to get back in the jeep. I can't sit down. The relevant part of my body has taken a beating. Each bump is hell. Still, we make it back onto the road. The other jeeps drive up. They have two young Arab prisoners, and Asherov is interrogating them. Then they are sent away. One of them has a bullet wound which one of us has bandaged.

Our medic takes off our bandages and puts on new ones. Jerucham lies motionless on the road, Dov sits there as if asleep, I stagger around. We are all in shock.

Asher allows Ovadia to drive us to the medical station. Ovadia sets off at high speed. Occasionally we have to leave the road and drive around damaged bridges. On the way we pick up Shalom, who is wounded when the Arabs fire at us, and we have to zigzag to put the snipers off their aim. The bullet hit him in the nose, and his blood sprays over the whole jeep. It is a painful drive over these rough paths. Each pothole is like a hammer blow. Now and then Ovadia looks round. He wants to see if we are still alive.

When we get closer and the medics in the station see our bandages, they jump up. Aviva, Ovadia's wife, cleans the wounds and puts some ointment on them. I want to take some photos, but Jerucham and Dov are already in the ambulance. Aviva pushes me in too. We drive to the hospital. There we are received by a nice doctor and the pretty nurse Jocheved. The doctor is a volunteer from an English-speaking country. Dov and Jerucham are put straight to bed. My wounds are to be sewn up after lunch. I am hungry and the food here is first class – roast chicken, soup, potatoes, white bread. That is enough to make it worthwhile getting wounded.

* * *

I am lain on the operating table and given an anesthetic injection in the shoulder. The doctor sews. I feel nothing, but have to laugh. A strange idea, being sewn up like a torn shirt.

The excitement is over and I am dog tired. I go back to the base wearing only a vest. I want to sleep, though I don't know which side to lie on. The rumor goes round the camp that we are half dead. When I am spotted, they want to know every detail – the typical curiosity of bored soldiers, who know that their comrade likes telling stories. I make my excuses and go off to sleep. I can expect two or three days of peace and quiet.

The ceasefire officially ended at ten o'clock in the morning of 9 July. On 6 July Aryeh called us together in the mess hall. He read out our operational commands. On the night of 9 July we would be going into action.

In the early morning hours of 8 July the alarm was sounded. No breakfast. Within minutes we have collected our combat equipment and are ready. In Be'er Tuvia we hear that the Egyptians have broken the ceasefire in the night – thirty hours before it officially ends. They surprised our troops in Beit Daras with a massive attack. Shimon's company was responsible for defense there. In vicious hand-to-hand fighting the attack was beaten off. One comrade, Matitjahu Borochin, who remained at his post after his rifle jammed, had four hand grenades thrown at him. He picked them up and threw them back at the Sudanese attackers – both he and his comrade, Noam Kascher, were rescued.

But the Egyptians committed their reinforcements. The attack was just the start of a large-scale offensive. Our task was to reinforce the defense at Beit Daras. But the road there from Be'er Tuvia was blocked by Egyptian tanks. Only later did we find out that most of them were fakes – made of wood and cloth – just decoys.

The jeeps were to attack the enemy from the rear, from the direction of Sawafir. Their sudden appearance completed the work of the infantry and the Sudanese withdrew in panic. Due to a mistake in radio communications the leader of the jeeps failed to understand that he had the unique chance to drive the enemy before him and perhaps even reach Hill 69.

At the end of the operation we returned to Be'er Tuvia. We helped to transport the mass of weaponry captured at Beit Daras and waited for new orders. The large-scale offensive was due to start in the night.

9 July 1948
In the trenches near Sawafir

Night without compass

"Guess what I have brought you," said Shaul Potruk, the sarge. He showed us a packet of strings with little metal tags attached. "You know what these are? The tickets to heaven, or to hell – with compliments of Farouk."[6]

So that's what they look like: the famous dog tags.

"Don't talk nonsense!"interrupted Ovadia, "that is for the girls, so you don't have to introduce yourself."

"What girls? Where can you find girls around here? Here there is only Fatima, and she can recognize me without a tag."

Fatima, the Arab fantasy girl, who came into our minds before every operation. The first time we "met" her was before our assault on Deir Muheisin during the Nachshon operation. Somehow it is preferable to imagine the enemy as a pretty girl than as tanks and aircraft.

The whole thing reminds us a bit of the Nachshon days. In those days we came from the training camp, and now we are starting again after a month's ceasefire. We are well rested. Last night we slept through to the morning, and we are well fed. Still, it is not the same atmosphere. Then, we were "green," full of expectations, and doing our very best not to show our nervousness. Now we are supposedly "experienced," fatalists who don't get excited. Even the approaching "rendezvous" with Fatima leaves us cold.

* * *

"Pay attention, lads," says Aryeh Spack. He begins every talk with these three words. It is an amusing sight. We are sitting in the dining hall of Be'er Tuvia in the little children's chairs, with our elbows leaning on the minute desks. A real kindergarten, with the company commander as the nursery school teacher.

"Right. While our comrades attack Iraq Suweidan and Beit Affa," says the "nursery school teacher," "we will distract Hatta and Karatiyya. Ahijah with two jeeps will deal with Hatta, Albert with two jeeps will drive on and handle Karatiyya. Radio contact will be maintained with MK 21."

The kindergarten yawns. We have known this operational plan backwards for at least a week. "We start in Jassir. The area around the village is mined. You will have to drive back along the road. Our recognition signal is three whistles or three flashes of the headlights." Most of us are looking out of the window. "Pity there aren't any girls here" Israel whispers to me.

* * *

We are driving very slowly. A wadi. We cross it. Another wadi. Chadad, our driver, gets out to have a look. We drive across at an angle. Karatiyya is not far away, but we are not taking a direct route. We have lost at least a quarter of an hour.

A brief flash of light ahead of us. At last. We drive on a bit, then stop in the middle of a field. "Lea Three for Lea Two. We are ready. Over!" Silence all around us. You could think we were in the middle of an uninhabited desert.

Rat-tat-tat-tat-tat – tat-tat – rat-tat-tat-tat-tat – tat-tat

In the whole world there is only one person who can fire such musical salvos. Our friend Chalek. So the fighting in Hatta has begun. We too open fire.

From the village comes return fire. Pitiful fire. Just a few rifles, two submachine guns. That's just a few local fighters, no army. We don't even relocate our position, as we were taught to do. We stay where we are and keep on shooting. The whole thing is rather boring.

"Hold your fire!" It is eleven o'clock. In Hatta too there is no more shooting. "Ask if we should continue or return."

I put the cartridge belt to one side and pick up the radio. "Hello Lea Three for Lea One. Can you hear me? Over." No answer. I try again. "Hello Lea Three for Lea One. Can you hear me? Over." I can just hear a faint murmur. Then that stops. The battery is dead.

* * *

Asher discusses with Albert, the section commander. They decide to drive back to Jassir. To avoid getting within firing range of Hatta, we make a wide detour to the west.

"Pay attention to the stars," says Albert to me. He knows my passion.

The new route is more difficult than the old one. We cross deep wadis. It is difficult to stay on course. Cassiopeia is sometimes to our right and sometimes to the left of us. Ursa Major and the Pole Star have completely disappeared.

The sky is darkening. It is getting cloudy. I can only see two stars in Cassiopeia. They are to the right of us. In the middle distance, directly ahead of us, is a green Egyptian rocket.

"What direction are we heading?" asks Albert casually. "To the west," I answer.

"Good" says Albert. Then he is suddenly wide awake and brings the jeep to a halt. "What did you say?"

"We are driving toward the west, and have been for about twenty minutes."

Albert says nothing. For a moment he switches on the darkened flashlight and looks at the map. Then he turns the jeep around and we drive in the opposite direction. After quarter of an hour we discover a compacted sand road. Albert stops again, switches on his flash lamp, examines the map.

"Where are we?" asks Hadad. "God knows" answers Albert. "I don't." It is two o'clock in the morning.

Slowly we realize: we have lost our way. We – eight men in two jeeps – are somewhere in the south of the country, either in our own area or in one under Arab control.

"What do you suggest?" asks Asher. "How do we get out of here without a compass?" Asher Asherov got his military training in the British Army. He is good at organizing things, but doesn't have much of a sense of direction. Albert Mandler, on the other hand, the youth from Ramat Gan,[7] blond and blue-eyed, grew up in Gadna.[8] He is a genius at finding his way around the battlefield. And he is blessed with a healthy self-confidence. "There are the stars," he answers.

The truth is, there are not many stars. In front of us there are two stars to be seen, that I recognize as belonging to Cassiopeia. But Reuven Huber, who is sitting behind the machine gun in the second jeep, has settled on another star in exactly the opposite direction. And there is no discussing with him. He is as stubborn as a mule. Albert wants to rely on me. Asher supports Reuven. And the others too, who never in their lives observed a single star, join in the discussion. Everyone chooses his own star and swears that that is Cassiopeia. The discussion might have been amusing, if only our lives hadn't depended on the outcome.

We drive. Every few minutes we stop and look around. On this level plain you can't recognize anything. Again we come to a wadi. Again we cross it. But no one knows if it is a new wadi, or one we have crossed twenty times already this night. Someone starts to complain to Albert. We shut him up immediately. Of course we know the situation we are in. But we also know that grumbling and moaning will get us nowhere.

I look at my watch. It is three o'clock. We have been driving for four hours. Now Albert gives up too. To our right he spots a wheat field and suggests we wait here till the morning. We all agree. We park the jeeps between the tall stalks, remove the high machine guns, and camouflage the mountings. Albert and Asher take their rifles and disappear into the darkness – they want to reconnoiter the area.

"We must be quite near Hebron," claims Reuven. He still believes that "his" Cassiopeia is the right one. "Rubbish," answers Israel, a Holocaust survivor from Poland. "We are near Beer Sheva." I myself believe that we are near Faluja.

"What do we do tomorrow?" asks Hadad nervously.

"Either or ..." laughs Micki. "If we are near Farouk, we will be slaughtered. If not, we'll drive home."

"Shut your mouth!" says Reuven. "I'm dog tired." Israel is prepared to stay awake. Reuven and Micki fall asleep. I hear their first snores, then my eyelids close ...

* * *

"Get up!" Someone is shaking me. I wake up. On the horizon is the first faint light. My comrades are all awake already, their rifles in their hands, and the hand grenades hanging from their belts.

My first feeling is satisfaction. The sun is rising in exactly the right place – according to "my" Cassiopeia estimation. But I don't have any time to savor my victory. Everyone is staring at a large, dark block in front of us, that is getting more definite the lighter it gets. It is an Arab village. In the middle is the minaret of a mosque with a very unusual form. We only know one single village with such a remarkable minaret – Jaladiyya. The village is in our hands.

We stare at it, at first skeptical and confused, then humor wins the upper hand. We laugh until we cry. We were already thinking of an epic battle, flight, imprisonment, or worse. And now we find ourselves two hundred meters away from Jaladiyya, five hundred meters from our Jassir base. "Get in the jeep!" Albert manages to say through his laughter. It is a small step between the ridiculous and the heroic ...

* * *

In Jassir they stare at us like ghosts. Compared with our grinning faces our comrades look like convalescents from some serious illness. They gather round us, climb on the jeeps, hug us, and kiss us. Then Aryeh appears. He stammers, screws up his face, tries to say something, and can't make a sound. The radio operator tells us what happened: when we got lost eight hours ago they were sure that we had been killed. Aryeh had already informed the battalion commander. When they then saw a cloud of dust and our jeeps appeared, they couldn't believe their eyes. "OK, you are not really so important," laughed Aryeh, "but the two expensive jeeps!"

"What happened to your Cassiopeia?" I asked Reuven. I couldn't help myself. "If all our scouts were like you, we would long since be in heaven."

"Me?" asked Reuven with surprised naivety, "without me you would never have got out of that hole."

That night our armored units, together with some infantry companies, attacked the villages of Ibdis, Iraq Suweidan, and Beit Affa. All of them quickly fell. Only the Palmach unit that attacked the police fortress of Iraq Suweidan failed. And as long as this key position remained in the hands of the enemy, there was no point trying to hold the villages of Beit Affa and Iraq Suweidan. They were abandoned in the morning. Only Ibdis, where an Egyptian battalion HQ was wiped out, remained in our hands.

* * *

In the morning the Egyptians launched a massive counter-attack, based on the fortress of Iraq Suweidan. The scale of this attack showed that they had originally planned to start their great offensive there. Their aim was to break through our lines and join up with Egyptian forces which should have preceded them at the front near Beit Daras. If they had succeeded in this plan – the way to Tel Aviv would have been wide open.

Two obstacles stood in their way: the position at Ibdis and Kibbutz Negba. The whole of the enemy's force was concentrated on them.

The greatest battle in the history of this war had begun.

11 July 1948
A trench near Sawafir

The battle for Ibdis and Negba

An apricot orchard near the village of Sawafir. My comrades are lying in small, freshly dug foxholes, next to the camouflaged jeeps. Their snores can be heard from far away. They are tired. Yesterday they helped to repel the heavy attack on Beit Daras. In the night they harassed Hatta and Karatiyya with their machine guns. When they got back in the early morning, they had to work hard: They dug foxholes and camouflaged their vehicles. Artillery is thundering nearby – ours and the enemy's. Rumors are circulating among the commanders of heavy fighting around Negba. Another name is also mentioned: Ibdis. Czera Czertenko, the battalion commander, suddenly appears. Czera, as he is known to everyone, is fresh and smiling as always. God knows when he sleeps. He needs four jeeps to accompany him to Negba. It is a unique opportunity to find out what is going on in the area. Such chance duties go to those who grasp them first. I wake my team. We set off.

About a kilometer before Negba I see the people in the first jeep lowering their heads: the typical movement of experienced soldiers who feel the approach of danger. What is it? I look around and see it. Near Beit Affa five little dots are moving over a field, and rapidly getting larger. Tanks! They are heading for us. Separating us is a bend in the road, that leads to Negba.

Our commander has only a tenth of a second to make a decision. He has three possibilities, each one of which is actually an impossibility. He can race ahead, toward the tanks, in the hope of reaching the bend before them. He can leave the road and drive across country directly to the gate of Negba, but the field might be full of mines and wadis. Or he can turn round and drive back.

Czera looks like a student of the humanities, wears glasses, and smiles a lot. But inside he is a real old warhorse, brave, cool headed, and decisive. He knows that our army has no surplus of battalion commanders. And he also knows that Negba needs us.

He leaves the road and races like the wind. The tanks have noticed our turn and drive toward us. At this moment our lives are in the hands of Ovadia, our driver. We keep our heads down, as much as we can, making ourselves as small as possible.

As we are getting near to the gate the Egyptian tanks realize that they will not be able to catch us up. They come to a halt about two hundred meters away and start firing at us. The shells fly over us and to either side of us. It is very difficult to hit a fast-moving jeep.

* * *

We have only just arrived when the enemy opens up an artillery barrage. The lookouts in the police station of Iraq Suweidan have seen us.

The trenches are full of every kind of soldier – radio operators, medics, mechanics, mortar crews. They call to us to join them. We laugh at them. We are used to the whistle of shells and stay by our vehicles. We throw ourselves on the ground as soon as we hear the whistle of an approaching shell. This is a kind of sport for us.

One after another the shells are exploding around us. Directly in front of us a wooden hut is hit and collapses. We are enveloped in the typical smell of battle: a mixture of the smoke from powder, corpses, burning trees, and dead animals. A wounded soldier runs past us. His left arm is covered in blood. He is holding it with his right hand, his eyes staring. He runs mutely to the collection point. Time for us to jump into the trench.

* * *

"Jeep crew out!"

David Shani, the deputy battalion commander, and Aryeh Segal, the company commander of the resupply unit, are standing by the jeeps. A heavy machine gun and ammunition have to be taken to Ibdis immediately. The supply troops pack the vehicles so full that we can hardly move.

As soon as we are out of the gate, the dust from the shell impacts starts to swirl around us. The position at Ibdis is not very far, something like two kilometers. But the earth is shaking from the impact of the shells.

"Faster!" we shout at Ovadia. The jeeps race along, bump over ditches, and try to confuse the artillery with a crazy zigzag path. We arrive at the low, bare hill. There are some trenches there. Gray figures are sitting there – the company that captured the position of the Egyptian battalion HQ at dawn, and the men of the armored car platoon of our company.

We unload the heavy weapon and the ammunition. Nobody pays us any attention. They are all looking toward Beit Affa. There, a scene is developing like a Hollywood movie. Eighteen tanks are driving slowly, in a broad front, straight toward us. Behind them are running rows and rows of infantry. It looks like a large scale maneuver.

Somewhere our artillery begins to thunder. We see the shrapnel shells exploding in the air, but the rows of soldiers run on. We estimate their distance as about six hundred meters. All our machine guns bark at the same time. The theories of aimed bursts and conservation of ammunition are forgotten. The gunner keeps his trigger finger firmly pressed until the cartridge belt is expended. The others reload the belts. We have enough ammunition on the jeeps. The tank shells whistle around our ears. Our position here is uncomfortable. We drive behind the hill so that only our weapons are visible. Our automatic weapons start to bark again.

The tanks approach us to within a hundred meters. There they stop. The infantry behind them lie on the ground and don't move.

This is the moment for the PIATs. Two tanks are hit by the first two shots. Shlomo Kochmann, an educated young man, a squad leader, dances for joy and rubs his hands together. He has just destroyed a tank with a PIAT, he tells us enthusiastically, and goes straight back to his weapon. The tanks slowly reverse.

* * *

Three jeeps drive back to the base. We stay with our jeep, without any special task – just in case we are needed. After a while it seems senseless to us to lie by the jeep listening to the sounds of battle. We jump into the trenches, and our comrades update us on events. Joseph Siff, who had driven out with me to fetch the field guns at Beit Daras, was hit this morning by a sniper. Ephraim Makovsky ran to him to get him out, and was himself fatally hit. Moshe Ben-Moshe crawled over to help the two, and was hit by the same sniper.

* * *

Two small aircraft appear and start circling above us. I can make out two white rings on the wings of one of them, with some kind of symbol inside that I can't identify for sure. They seem to me to be stars of David.

"Idiot! Stay on the ground!" Ovadia Rechtmann shouts at me. "They are ours!" I shout back and stand up. At that moment both of the machines dive at our position and four bombs whistle down and explode nearby. I lie on the ground. Damn these symbols – they are so similar …

* * *

Ovadia Rechtmann has discovered a special trench – a sort of cave, enclosed on three sides and only open at the top of the fourth side. A few paces away from us the commander, the radio operator, and our friend Jerucham are lying in a rather questionable trench.

Ovadia is hungry. I find a tin of meat and open it with a knife.

"Curious that I never feel like eating when fighting is going on …" I think aloud. Ovadia mumbles something and keeps eating. "We need something to drink with it," he says after a moment and gets up. Ten feet away from us is a big earthenware jug full of water. I think of his wife who works in the medical center of the battalion. "I feel sorry for her. She always knows about it when you are in the middle of a battle." I am not sure whether I said the words or just intended to say them. Just then we hear the whistling of a shell. It is especially loud. I duck, and there is a loud explosion. The shell lands about five feet from our trench.

I raise my head and see Ovadia lying in the commander's trench. I start to laugh, but break off immediately. Blood is dripping from Ovadia's sleeve.

"I am hurt" he calls to me. I jump up, wrap a bandage around his arm. The wound is not so terrible. A fragment has gone right through his arm, but apparently missed the bone. I force myself to eat. In situations like that you never know when you'll next get the chance.

* * *

The damn shelling gets heavier again. The Egyptians have apparently given their forces a pep talk. The tanks are moving again. And the rows of infantry are following, jumping forwards and lying flat, jumping forwards and lying flat. The hill holds its breath – these are decisive moments.

David Shani runs back and forth between the trenches and the command post. Someone notices that his shirt is bloody.

"You are wounded!" they shout to him.

"It's nothing" he replies, clenching his teeth. A fragment has hit him in the shoulder, so they bandage him up.

"You'll have to get out of here" says the one remaining unwounded commander. David refuses. That is no empty heroic gesture. He knows that everything now depends on the commander. He thinks of Hill 69 that was lost a month ago due to the incompetence of the commander. He knows that the morale of the soldiers might collapse if he now disappears. So he stays. And with him stay Nehemiah Rotholz, the platoon leader, and Levy Kolker, our deputy company commander – both of them wounded.

* * *

Again the attack is repelled. The order to return to base comes over the radio.

In Sawafir they let us sleep the night. Despite our tiredness it is difficult to get to sleep. Twenty meters away from us an artillery battery is thundering without pause. The next morning we watch the work of the gunners and find it fascinating. They sit there quietly while their boss, Dr Wolfgang von Weisl, tells them jokes in his typical Austrian accent. With one hand he keeps the earpiece of the field telephone pressed to his ear. In mid-sentence he breaks off and calls "group fire – one shrapnel …!"

The gunners around him jump up. With astonishing speed they go about their work. Next to every gun one of them is standing, and shouts "Number one ready!" "Number two ready!" …

"Fire!" shouts the old man. A bang, some smoke, the shells are on their way. The people sit down again. They have done their job, with almost Olympian calm, without seeing the enemy, without knowing the target of their shots.

We stand and admire the "Napoleons" – that's what we call the old guns that look as though they haven't been used for a hundred years. That is so remote from war as we know it – fatigue, pain, the tension of the infantryman who sees the enemy face to face. Still, we love the gunners. We are feeling generous these days. Anyone who finds themselves between Sawafir and Negba can be sure of our love.

"Up you get, people!"

Another drive to Ibdis – ammunition to be delivered, wounded to be evacuated. This damned position cannot be reached without being observed by the enemy lookouts. But we have now got used to it, driving through a field under fire. We have learned that the danger of being hit is rather low under these conditions. You just have to rely on speed and luck.

In Ibdis all hell has broken loose. The earth shakes from the impact of shells. Yesterday we waited for the whistling of shells before throwing ourselves on the ground. Now you can't even hear the individual shells, they follow each other in such quick succession – twenty-five-pounder shells and heavy mortar bombs. Yesterday aircraft, artillery, and tanks took their turns. Today they are all in action at once. The aircraft dive at us while we are shooting at the tanks, and the impacts of shells spray us with earth when we get up to shoot at the aircraft.

Just as we arrive the horror reaches a climax. A wild being, smeared with dirt and blood, jumps out of one of the trenches. He no longer looks human, more like a wild animal fighting for its life. He exchanges a few words with Asher Asherov, who decides to dismount two machine guns from the jeeps and set them up here. This order means that the situation is hopeless. The regulations for jeeps, that one should on no account abandon the vehicles, are no longer in force. We look at each other. Reuven leaves one of the vehicles. David and I get out of the second jeep. The vehicles cannot remain here. Under this fire it would just be a matter of time. We load them up with dead and wounded and then the jeeps race away.

Nobody takes any notice of us. It is up to us to know what we should do. Our task is clear: We have to reach the forward position. The only way is the one connecting trench which leads there. But it is not deep enough for our purposes. The lads who captured the hill yesterday from the Egyptians have simply taken over their positions. Since then they have had no time to dig any deeper. Part of it is no deeper than half a meter. It is not even worth crouching there – all you can do is run and pray. The first one gets through OK. A sniper's bullet whistles between the legs of the second. I jump and get through without being hit.

The next part of the trench is deeper, and branches in several directions. In one of these continuations two figures are lying as if they were hugging each other. But their heads are missing. I feel ill.

Later I hear that this happened in the morning, but there was no way to get the corpses out. All the fighters on the hill have been past this place at least once. The shell fell directly in the trench. A direct hit. A third comrade sitting next to them was flung right out by the force of the explosion. But he was otherwise OK.

I look for a place and David and I move into it. Reuven takes a position nearby. Six people in the trench. People? They are filthy, their eyes dusty and reddened. It is a long time since they had a thought, or hunger and thirst. Four of them are wounded and patched up with bandages. The other two hold rifles in their hands. The automatic weapon is out of order.

David sets up our machine gun and fires off a salvo. The immediate reply is a shower of bullets around us. He loses his grip on the machine gun, which falls in the dirt and is now full of mud. It doesn't work any more. I duck down, pull the weapon into the bottom of the trench and have a go at cleaning it. My hands are shaking. I set it back up and pull the trigger. Nothing happens. All the time the whistling, screaming and roaring of shells, bullets, and bombs. The very air seems to be alive and trembling. The whole hill is covered in thick smoke and dust.

And in the middle of this cacophony there are people living and breathing. A sort of command structure is still functioning. Every few minutes I hear calls from position to position: "Joseph, take over command!" And even before there is time for anyone to bandage the wounded commander, there is a whistling and a shell bursts, spraying earth everywhere. Joseph calls with a shaking voice: "Shmuel – you take over …!"

* * *

I take the rifle from a wounded man, and for a fraction of a second my view clears and I shoot. Immediately bullets pepper the ground around us. I function by instinct alone. Have stopped thinking.

One of the wounded men hangs his helmet over his rifle and raises it above the edge of the trench. A whistling bullet knocks two holes in it. Rifle and helmet fall into the trench. The wounded man laughs.

I look up again and suddenly see – nothing. Twenty yards away a white wall is forming. They are firing smoke shells into the no-man's-land between us. A chilling moment. The decisive attack is imminent. Everyone who is still capable gets up and shoots into the smoke. There are not many of us left. One machine gun and perhaps thirty rifles are all the defense that Ibdis has at this moment. The rifle is overheating. We are firing shot after shot. At any moment ranks of Sudanese infantry with fixed bayonets will appear out of the smoke a few meters ahead of us. Slowly the fog thins. Nothing moves. Probably the snipers, who are hiding in the field, just moved to new positions.

* * *

Then I notice that something has happened to David. He is sitting on the floor, pale and motionless. It would be better to withdraw behind the hill and try to repair the machine gun. Maybe new orders have come in from the company. David gets up like a zombie. When we come to the dangerous part of the connecting trench he hesitates and stops walking. I give him a push and he jumps and crosses over. I follow him.

We go to the trench where I was sitting with Ovadia the day before. I dismantle and reassemble the weapon. David just sits there. I try and shoot. Nothing happens.

An aircraft above us has noticed the antenna of the nearby radio operator, and dives toward us with machine guns barking. Of all the awful noises in the world this is the very worst. We try to hide behind what little cover there is. The plane flies past, climbs again, and goes back to flying its leisurely circles.

Suddenly Reuven appears. I can hardly recognize him. Reuven is the ultimate in coolness under fire. Now he looks like a lunatic. His face is green and he is foaming at the mouth. I call to him, and he joins us.

* * *

The radio operator reports to the commander that a company is on its way to relieve him. He hardly reacts. He is no longer even capable of being pleased.

Reuven and I decide that the time has come to return to our own company. We wake David from his trance and climb into a deep wadi by the rearward hill. In the wadi about thirty wounded are lying. Most of them are "lightly" injured, with bullet or shrapnel wounds in their arms or legs. The seriously wounded have already been removed by our jeeps in a ride of death across the open field. Most of the wounded lie there silently, looking at the sky. Some are groaning, others recount how they were wounded. All are smeared with blood.

* * *

The relief force has arrived. A company from the same battalion. Around one hundred healthy lads. How many of them will still be healthy in an hour's time? They know how things are. But still they march forwards, into the deadly trenches. The vehicles arrive one by one. The men jump out and go straight to the front. After a few minutes the ones who are being replaced climb into the wadi. How many of them? Less than thirty. They arrived here twelve hours ago. Then there were more than a hundred. But in these twelve hours of 10 July Ibdis stood firm – while the surrounding world raged, the air shivered, and the earth shook.

* * *

We load some of the wounded into a pickup and climb on ourselves. Someone is lying between my legs. I look at his face. He is dead. His eyes stare emptily at me. One of the defenders of Ibdis. He was just an ordinary soldier. One little ant in the great ant-hill of the front. He is unknown at HQ. There they don't even know the name Ibdis. But still this dead man has made history on this day.

The heavy vehicle struggles across the cratered ground, rolling from side to side, but somehow manages to reach the road. We breathe in deeply as though we have just awoken from a nightmare. But no more than five hours have passed since we arrived on that hill.

Three Spitfires[9] fly in our direction. The driver accelerates and we hold onto the wounded to stop them falling out. But the aircraft take no notice of us. They fly to the hill, circle once, and drop their bombs. Above the hill of Ibdis smoke and dust clouds rise into the air.

The battle for Negba and Ibdis raged for four days. It was the Israeli infantryman, bleeding and red-eyed, who held this narrow strip of ground that the Egyptians needed at any price. He was the real hero of the most terrible battle of this war, the simple rifleman of the infantry. He stood against tanks, aircraft, artillery, and mortar shells. He stood up to them – and he did not give in.

The jeeps raced back and forth between the infantry positions. The seven jeeps of the "Motorized Company." They achieved true miracles. In these four days they drove across the open fields so many times. They brought the fighters urgently needed ammunition, saved the lives of hundreds of wounded, and drove the enemy back again and again with unexpected bursts of fire.

Along with the ammunition boxes, the PIAT rounds, and the mortar bombs, the jeeps also transported small packets of printed papers. The frontline fighters were as impatient for these as for the ammunition itself. The papers went from hand to hand and were read under fire and in the most critical moments. Read until the soldiers knew the text by heart.

During the battle for Ibdis the brigade bulletin evolved into its final form. For us it was like a motivating crack of the whip. It explained our modest contribution in the context of the whole front. It forged the companies and the battalions into one unit, into one beating heart – the Givati Brigade.

The bulletin appeared daily. At the top were two brutal words – the brigade motto, "Mavet LaPolshim!" (Death to the Invaders!). A special relationship developed between the bulletin and the brigade. It was as if the heartbeat of the whole brigade and its feelings were put into words, which echoed across the whole region of the south.

On 10 July the bulletin published a portrait of the fighters of Beit Daras. On 11 July it described the Negba fighters and our motorized company. And on 14 July the bulletin invented a new name: "Samson's Foxes."[10]

For four days and three nights Negba and Ibdis stood firm. For four days and three nights the Givati Brigade, four pitiful, undermanned battalions and a reserve battalion of foreign volunteers, withstood the concentrated power of the most modern Arab army. Resisted, and did not give way.

On the fourth day of the battle, 12 July 1948, an Egyptian unit managed to sneak out of the police fortress of Iraq Suweidan and occupy Hill 105. This position controlled the road to Negba. For the first time Kibbutz Negba was completely cut off. The decisive moment had arrived, the desperate fight, man against man, to determine the outcome of the war.

13 July 1948
A trench near Sawafir

Hill 105

In the last five days we have not washed, we haven't slept more than two or three hours at a stretch, and eating we have only done on occasion and in a terrible hurry. We are tired enough to drop. The tension of combat is the only thing that rescues us for a few hours from our total mental exhaustion.

Shortly before midnight the jeeps are readied. There was bad news during the day. Negba managed to fight off a heavy attack which lasted for ten hours. Ibdis too, the position overlooking the Kibbutz, came under continuous attack. The whole day long we heard the noise of battle, the artillery and the shells.

We lay next to the jeeps and tried to get a bit of sleep. The roaring of the heavy guns, theirs and ours, did not disturb us. We have got used to it, just as one can get used to the waves of the sea.

* * *

"Jeep teams – in the vehicles!"

We put on our helmets, try to find a half-way comfortable

position to sit in, check the machine guns one last time – and we're off. Our tiredness is gone. We are wide awake. The jeep leaps along the road, which has been severely damaged by shelling, toward Julis – our starting point in the direction of Negba.

The jeep stops. Czera, the battalion commander, is taking part in the operation this time. He talks quietly with a mysterious figure that has slipped out of the darkness. The infantry there are getting ready for their part in the operation: our company number one under the command of Asher Dromi. We slide forwards. Our tension is rising. It must be somewhere around here. I press the machine gun against my shoulder, ready for action.

* * *

A red Egyptian rocket. The vehicles stop. A short moment of quiet while the landscape is dimly illuminated by the reddish glow. And then the order, in the calm, clear voice of Aryeh Spack:

"Fire!"

All the machine guns start rattling simultaneously. The red flames from the barrels are visible a long way away. The noise is deafening, despite our ear plugs.

I empty one cartridge belt after the other. Two hundred, three hundred, four hundred rounds. The weapon is working fine. The Egyptians are shooting at us, and we can identify their positions very clearly. We can't hear the whistling of the bullets, but we know that they are flying all around us. The distance is fifty meters at the most.

"Hold your fire!"

I hardly hear the command when the jeeps drive off. We heave a sigh of relief. With one hand we hold on, with the other we refill the cartridge belts.

The commanders confer. Czera thinks that one volley is insufficient. The infantry is in difficulties. So – once again into action. The Egyptians are still shooting. They have a lot of firepower. That must be several companies over there. And this time we won't have the advantage of surprise – the most important thing in engagements with the jeeps. But we have no choice: Negba and Ibdis are fighting for their life.

* * *

We arrive back where we were before. About twenty meters ahead of us is a red rocket, directly on the road. "Forwards!" calls the battalion

commander in the vehicle ahead of ours, the second in the column.
"At them! Wipe them out!"

Without thought, without hesitation, the jeeps drive into the illuminated area. Ephraim Regenstreif, the driver of the first jeep, notices figures moving just next to the jeep, no more than two paces away. We have stumbled right into the middle of the enemy position! Both sides are surprised by this sudden encounter. Ephraim leaves the road, drives over trenches and positions, notices that the wheels are running over human bodies, puts it into reverse and returns to the road. Ahijah HaShiloni, the twenty-year-old squad leader, fires continuously with the machine gun pointed down into the trenches.

I am no longer aware of the world around me. I shoot and shoot and shoot. This feeling discharges the tension of the last five days, the days of the battles for Beit Daras, Ibdis, and Negba.

* * *

In the confusion around us I suddenly notice a big black something directly in front of our jeep, only about five yards away. An enemy tank? I turn the machine gun and shoot and shoot. "Hold your fire!" shouts Aryeh. "That is one of ours." I stop immediately. Have I hit any comrades? (Only the next morning do we learn that it was an enemy vehicle after all, a half-track that got left behind.)

Aryeh Spack gets out of the jeep and finds two of our wounded at the side of the road. We load them in and race to the collection point. I can't recognize who they are in the darkness. One is moaning pitifully. In Julis we try to bandage them up. I cut off their clothes with my knife. One of them has had a bullet through his arm. He is bleeding heavily. The blood drips on the floor of the jeep. I also get blood all over me. The other has a shrapnel wound in the belly.

* * *

We bandage them up as best we can and drive at one hundred kilometers per hour to the medical center at Sawafir. It is a dangerous drive, but the lives of the wounded depend on every minute that passes.

The medics at the station are prepared. The doctor opens the bandages. We don't wait for the result, but race back to the collection point at Julis. More wounded and the other jeeps have already arrived. Two of the vehicles are damaged.

Unbelievable happenings are recounted. The quiet Amnon

Steinschneider leapt from his jeep to shoot into a trench full of Egyptians, returned to the vehicle to bandage Freddy Glückmann, and suddenly noticed that his back was wet. It turned out that he had been hit some time earlier, in the jeep, by four shell fragments. David Kalkess, the radio operator of the first jeep, told the story for the tenth time of how Freddy Regenstreif left the road, how he drove over bodies, through the middle of the enemy position, without a single person in the jeep being hit.

The most incredible of all is the story of the third jeep. The driver, Yitzhak Neuhaus, was hit in the chest by a burst of fire, collapsed dead, and fell out of the jeep. Asher Asherov, who sat next to him, was also hit. So the two soldiers sitting behind had to do something. Reuven Huber, who had never in his life driven a jeep, took the controls. Micki Rosenblatt got out – ten feet from an enemy position – recovered Yitzhak's corpse and only then did Reuven drive backwards to the other jeeps which had already withdrawn.

* * *

Two jeeps drive to Julis, where company number one is assembled. We are afraid that they may have more wounded. The soldiers are dog tired. One of their officers, the same Dov Feit who "fled" from his unit to take part with us in the attack on Isdud, is sitting there. Two bullets have hit him in the arm after he had finished off eleven Egyptians with two hand grenades.

* * *

As dawn breaks we reach our forward base. But something is missing. It takes us a while to notice what it is: the usual background of enemy firing. It has stopped.

Our mood has its ups and downs. It's always the same after heavy fighting. First it sinks. Our best comrades have been killed or wounded, people we were swearing and joking with yesterday. Some had been with the company since it was formed. Without them the unit is no longer what it was. But slowly the bad mood dissipates and is replaced with simple, primitive joy. We are glad to be still alive and to see the sun! We know that death was very near. Only chance has arranged for one to be hit and another not.

It is Micki Rosenblatt's birthday. "You've got a lovely present," we tell him. "A lovely present." "What sort of present?" he asks in puzzlement. "Your life, my friend. Your life!" We sit together and tell how one was wounded and another saved. We know all the details already. But it is compulsive: after fighting, everyone who comes by must hear, over and over again, what we have done and what happened to us. Otherwise we can't dissipate the tension and mull over our impressions.

After a few hours the picture changes completely. The first reports filter through and the rest is forgotten. We won! A victory! A victory that no one dared to hope for. We have destroyed almost a whole Egyptian battalion. In the enemy camp panic has broken out, the soldiers have fled, leaving a lot behind them: two artillery pieces, four half-track vehicles, ten PIATs, several heavy machine guns, and huge quantities of ammunition. The fields are full of dead, and the position that is so important to the defense of Negba is in our hands.

For five days we have been fighting against an enemy that is many times better equipped than we are. And we have dealt them a decisive blow. A few men have gained the upper hand over this army. We have forced a turning point on the southern front. That is the sign for the salvation of Negba, that heroic rock in the storm.

And if something was missing from our happiness, we got even that. Four hours without action, to shower and relax. A shower – the peak of happiness! And it is urgently needed. When I appeared at breakfast, I looked like a butcher – bloody stains on my trousers, and dried blood up to my elbows. One of our comrades turned away and spewed on the floor ...

The battle for Position 105 was the decisive victory, the turning point for the whole southern front. And our unit got its new name. This is how it was reported in the "battle bulletin" of 14 July 1948:

Samson's Foxes

SOUTHERN FRONT: DEATH TO THE INVADERS!
BATTLE BULLETIN
HQ GIVATI BRIGADE
SAMSON'S FOXES

... at zero hours thirty a company of our infantry, supported by the motorized commando unit, began the attack on enemy units which had taken new positions in the Negba–Julis–Hill 113 triangle. The attack lasted the whole night. The firepower of our units smashed gaps in the enemy lines, destroyed the concentrated units, and the enemy fled in an unprecedented state of panic. The enemy left behind more than ten PIATs, two heavy machine guns, four half track vehicles, and much other material.

During the attack our units encountered heavy enemy fire – they were facing a whole Egyptian battalion. The enemy was defeated in tough man-to-man fighting, and "Samson's Foxes" (the brigade's motorized commando unit) spearheaded the advance. Suddenly they found themselves traveling over soft ground. Bodies! Nothing but bodies under their wheels.

The driver stopped: people under his wheels! He only hesitated for a moment. He remembered Negba and Beit Daras. Then he drove on ...

* * *

Onward drive!

In gratitude and respect for this action, the motorized unit will henceforth be known as "Samson's Foxes."

* * *

The region is quiet. For the first time since the outbreak of hostilities the Egyptian weapons are silent. They are reorganizing their forces. In our brigade, hardly a single company is still fit for action. But once again our courage and faith in ultimate victory triumphed. We cannot allow the Egyptians any time to recover. We must hit them immediately. And if only remnants of the brigade are available, then these remnants must do the attacking.

It has been decided to stage an attack this very night on the Egyptian forces regrouping around Beit Affa, the Arab village opposite Negba and Ibdis. The task again falls to company number one of our battalion, under the command of Asher Dromi. The jeeps are to divert the enemy with blows in Hatta and Karatiyya, and help in the capture of Beit Affa with supporting fire.

In an orange orchard near Sawafir we reorganized ourselves – we, the company that was today given the name "Samson's Foxes." Only half the people are still with us after the last operation. How on earth are we going to carry out three actions tonight?

Instead of four we now only have three men for each jeep. We have also been reinforced with comrades who have no experience in this type of warfare: Asriel Spitz and Yaakov Velichkovski from the armored section, Zvi Bruk, the company runner, Chaim Poltruk, the sarge, Moshe Vanzover, the quartermaster, and David Finkel, the armorer. The units are reduced to the point where we have no non-combatant soldiers.

Half the unit, under the command of Aryeh Spack, will carry out the diversionary attack against Hatta and Karatiyya, and the other half, which includes me, is allocated to the fight against Beit Affa. The jeeps will arrive from the north and start the attack with a heavy blow at point blank range, to keep the enemy forces busy while the infantry assault goes in from the south to take the village.

14 July 1948
A trench near Sawafir

Beit Affa

Quarter of an hour before midnight. Fifteen minutes till zero hour. The night is completely dark. The jeeps are creeping along, without lights. Colorful flares fly up above the village. Now we can see where our target lies. A crossroads.

Something dark looms up in front of us. The machine gunners tense up. No. It is just an isolated, deserted house. Ahijah, who is driving the first jeep, leaves the road. Without waiting for orders, the other jeeps fan out. It is a routine exercise – "long volley at close range."

I am sitting on my own in the back. Shaul is driving. Next to him sits Chaim, the NCO. It is the first time he's seen action in a jeep. We stop about two hundred meters before the village. Quiet all around us. The only noise that rises above the chirping of the cicadas is the murmur of the radio operator. Suddenly even that stops. What's up? As usual, the radio's not working. We have no connection to HQ.

Then the whole area begins to shake. Machine guns, automatic weapons, the village is lit up by flares. Damn, the infantry is attacking without waiting for us. The detour we had to make has delayed us.

Schwuk, who sits in Ahijah's jeep, starts firing, and everyone else joins in the orchestra. The weapon trembles in my hands and I press it with all my strength against my shoulder. That is the only way to avoid mechanical troubles. One, two cartridge belts. Ahijah's team stop shooting and the jeep drives on. We follow them about two hundred meters. Seconds later shells explode exactly where we were a moment before. The muzzle flash from our weapons is clearly visible in the dark. While we are moving I refill the cartridge belt. That is the main problem with the jeeps. You can't reload as fast as you can shoot.

"Fire!" shouts Ahijah. The weapons bark again. But this time the enemy is expecting it. After the first salvos, greenly glowing two-pound shells crash down around us. This game repeats itself a few times: we stop, shoot, move on. Stop, shoot, move on. The enemy is confused, fires here and there, without knowing where our shots are going to come from next.

"Cease firing!" Maybe our own infantry is already in the village? Without the radio we cannot know. We could be shooting at our own comrades. What now? Back to HQ for new orders. The jeeps turn and race back to the abandoned house, back onto the sand road, and off to Sawafir.

* * *

After a minute Ahijah comes back. With him a stooping man with slightly oriental features. We recognize Aryeh Kotzer.

"Let's go, friends!" he shouts and climbs with me into the jeep. The infantry has met strong resistance. Our supporting fire is needed.

After the battle in Isdud, Kotzer was appointed chief training officer of the battalion. But he can't sit around at HQ. Actually it is none of his business going along with us. But we are pleased with his "interference." This man has a strange power – when he is next to you, you don't feel any danger.

This time the tempo is something else. Kotzer won't let us stop. We keep driving in wide figures of eight, from right to left and from left to right. And we shoot on the move. The enemy is bewildered and fires bullets and shells with no definite aim. The air is full of whistling noises. We are going wild and our hearts are laughing. If the enemy fires to the right, we are on his left-hand side. And when he aims to the left, we are back on the right. It is a real sport.

"Forwards!" shouts Kotzer. We are about a hundred meters away from the village. "Left!" "Backwards!" "Faster!" We are drunk with speed. My gun jams. A cartridge is stuck in the breech. I manage to free it with my knife. Frantically I reload the cartridge belts.

Gradually the village quietens down. Has the infantry completed their task? Kotzer decides to drive back to HQ and find out what the situation is. Damn these stupid radios.

* * *

At HQ they are celebrating. Asher, the commander of the first company, has just reported the capture of most of the village. Six Bren carriers[1] and other vehicles have been taken. Since he intends to withdraw from the village before sunset, he asks for the "Foxes" to be sent to recover the booty. A truck accompanies us, driven by Tzvi Melnowitzer, our tall baby. This time we will drive into the village along the main road.

It is three o'clock. So we have plenty of time. I am content. An ideal operation. Bombardment, assault, capture – and without any unnecessary incidents. I remove the belt from the weapon, stretch my legs out on the place next to mine (Kotzer is now sitting in another jeep), and enjoy the drive. What a change – the day before yesterday it looked as though the whole front might collapse, and now we are driving along the main road to Beit Affa. There are the first houses already ...

A sharp whistling. A red rocket flies up and lands near us.

Suddenly it is light as day. And at the same moment the air around us starts to whistle, to roar, to howl. Tracer rounds and green shells whistle past our heads.

No time for considering. We can't turn round. Kotzer races directly into the village with us close behind.

A kind of square opens up in front of us, surrounded by houses. We are under fire but can't tell where the bullets are coming from. It feels as if they are coming from all directions. I can't understand what's going on. What happened? Did no one tell our friends that we were coming? Do they think we are Egyptians?

Kotzer's clear voice echoes through the village: "Samson – Delilah." They continue shooting. Have they forgotten the password? Now we all shout together in chorus: "S-a-m – s-o-n – D-e-l-i-l-a-h!" The firing gets heavier. We are totally confused. Something unexpected, incomprehensible has happened. Have our comrades gone mad?

(Later we find out that the connection between the infantry who captured the village and HQ was broken. They did not know that we were coming and had abandoned the village before we arrived.)

Suddenly I see Kotzer walking around in the hail of bullets. "On the ground," he commands us. He climbs onto one of the houses. Now a flashlight is shining from his hand. Is he mad too? All the firing is concentrated on him. But he has already hit the ground. And then I understand what he is doing. One of our jeeps has got stuck in a ditch outside. The diversionary tactic is successful. The jeep races into the village and joins up with us.

A heavy machine gun begins to rattle. Our infantry people have no such weapons. Without a doubt our friends have left the village. We are in the middle of a village which is occupied by the enemy.

My heart is beating like a drum. My brain has ceased to function. For the first time in many months I am overcome by fear. Simple, blind, primitive fear. What can we do? If we wait till sunrise, we will be wiped out. There is no doubt that the enemy will have his weapons aimed at the road along which we arrived in this accursed village. Where are they shooting from? What does the situation look like? None of us knows. What should we do? No one knows that either. We have all lost control of ourselves.

We need a quick decision.

* * *

Suddenly we hear a calm, clear voice of command – Kotzer's voice: "Group one – in the jeep – drive directly to Negba – forwards!" Can you stand up in this hail of bullets? Isn't it suicide? But the voice drives the soldiers on. One after the other they jump into the jeep and race off.

A green glowing shell is fired at them from ten yards' range, flies past over their heads, and disappears. A barrage of withering fire follows them. But they get through it and disappear.

* * *

"Group two – in your jeep – forwards!" The jeep races off and breaks through the circle of death.

"The truck – forwards!" Will the heavy vehicle overcome this barrier? We hold our breath. It gets through.

"Jeep three – forwards!"

I jump on. Shaul has already started the engine. The jeep accelerates. My heart has stopped beating. A tracer shell flies past a few meters away. Bullets are flying in front of us and behind us, but we are already out of danger and don't look back. We reach Negba, stop next to the ruined water tower, and breathe deeply. The three of us get out and look at each other. None of us feels like talking, none of us is capable of talking.

* * *

We wait for the two last jeeps. Five minutes, ten minutes, quarter of an hour. They don't come. Terrible thoughts haunt us. Has something happened?

Suddenly we hear a strange noise. It is not a tank, but also not a car – tak-tak-tak-tak-tak, what is that?

An odd-looking vehicle appears out of the darkness. No. That is no longer a jeep. Both back wheels have gone. The front wheels are turning. In the destroyed vehicle sits one man – Abraham Bendarski, the driver.

We rush over, drag him out of the jeep, want to ask him questions. He just mumbles a few words. He doesn't know what happened. Aryeh Kotzer and Moshe Vanzover were sitting behind. He just felt a tremendous crash, the brakes failed. He had already selected four-wheel drive. His ribs are crushed and he is suffering from shock.

While we are still questioning him, the last jeep appears. Janek is driving. The jeep is fully loaded with people. Janek tells us how he saw something happen to the jeep in front. So he drove round it. But he didn't see any people. On the way to the kibbutz he came across some wounded from the first company, and took them on board. We have a look at the wounded. Kotzer and Moshe are not among them. We send Janek with the wounded on to Sawafir. When he is gone a strange stillness falls. We all know what the situation is without having to talk about it. It is quarter past five. Within half an hour the sun will rise.

The awful fear I felt earlier returns. But my mouth says: " A jeep must go back. Who is coming?" "I will" says Yaakov Velichkovski, the dark-haired squad leader. A discussion starts. Should one jeep go or two? They talk about shells. I have a look at the damaged jeep. That doesn't look like a shell to me. The jeep was damaged from below. That is the work of a land mine. And without a doubt, where there is one mine, there will be others.

"We need a driver" says Yaakov. No answer. A pity that Janek drove on to Sawafir. He would have come for sure. Minutes pass. Suddenly a civilian speaks up. "You need a driver?" he asks quietly. "I'll do it." Can he drive a jeep? He smiles. He is a bus driver.

We jump in. Then another jeep appears at the gate. Joseph Segal is sitting in it. He is the commander of the auxiliary company, and currently deputy battalion commander. We quickly explain the situation to him. "You will all return immediately to Sawafir" he orders. We are horrified. Back to Sawafir. Now? And then we follow his gaze. On the horizon we see a light silvery stripe.

We lost two comrades, both of whom were something special. Moshe Vanzover, the quartermaster of the company, was with us in almost every action from the first day on, without being obliged to do so, and without anyone asking him. And Aryeh Kotzer, the man who had led countless assaults at the head of his men, a man whose name had long since become a symbol and a legend on the whole front. How can it happen that a bullet, a piece of shrapnel, or a mine puts an end to a life like this?

... and the fighting continued. A battalion captured Tel al-Safi, a

natural fort without parallel on the southern front. In a rapid action we took Idnibah and Muralis near Kibbutz Kfar Menachem. After the loss of Hill 105 the Egyptians give up their dream of advancing and conquering. They give up plans to take the two isolated kibbutzim of Gat and Gal'on, which seemed to threaten a repetition of the Negba story on a smaller scale. They concentrated all their efforts on a stubborn defense. We have now gained the initiative. From Isdud to Beit Jibrin and Zakariyya, along the great arc of the southern front, our decimated units have begun the attack on the fortified defensive positions of the Egyptians.

The newspapers that somehow found their way to us reported that the United Nations had decided on a ceasefire for 18 July, to start at seven in the evening. We didn't believe it. We had a superstitious belief that we would be disappointed if we believed in the ceasefire. And we knew this disappointment would be terrible. Still we couldn't keep out the thought: maybe there will be one after all?

18 July 1948
A trench near Sawafir

Wounded transport

We knew that a big offensive was coming – to open the route to the Negev before the ceasefire came into force. Everyone had the same feeling. We have seen death a hundred times, it can't scare us. But the date for a new ceasefire … "I just need to stay alive until tomorrow" is in all our minds.

It means a lot to us, the opening of the road to the Negev: the aim of all our activities these wild ten days. And we are resolutely determined to finish the job.

The commanders return from a discussion. Two infantry companies – our number one company and a company of recruits from the navy, which will act as a reserve – are going to attack Beit Affa from two directions. The jeeps will keep the enemy busy with quick volleys. But this time two of the jeeps are allocated the task of collecting the wounded. Mine is one of them.

* * *

We drive to the medical station to equip ourselves with as much bandage material as possible and enough stretchers. On the way we meet the company of recruits heading for the starting point. The lads are completely green. This will be their first battle. They are singing loudly and happily: "Believe me, the day will come ..." We stop to let them pass. It is a terrible moment. We know what Beit Affa means. We also know that the moon will be shining brightly tonight. We know that not many of them will be coming back unharmed.

* * *

We are in Negba, in wounded, bleeding Negba, and wait in the dark for the whistling of the first bullets from the direction of Beit Affa. That will be our sign to drive to the appointed place, to wait for the wounded, and then take them to the medical station. It is shortly before midnight. Everything is much too quiet. The Egyptians are also waiting for the decisive battle in the last night before the ceasefire.

The night is very bright and visibility good. A warning sign for the attackers. We think of our comrades who will have left the base an hour ago, with a song on their lips. The night is much too bright ...

Shots. First a few, then salvos. And suddenly the world around us wakes up – colorful rockets climb into the sky, artillery roars, machine guns chatter. Time for us to set off. Four men in an unarmored jeep. Our destination is about five hundred meters away from the village which is under attack. Were we earlier somewhat ashamed of this task? That was a mistake. This is a worthy job for "Samson's Foxes." The enemy is shelling the road. We leave it and drive across the open field toward the fire. The area is flat and doesn't offer even a hint of cover.

There it is! We lie on the ground and set up the machine gun. A scene in front of us could almost be described as beautiful: artillery fire, colorful rockets, glowing streams of tracer. But we don't feel comfortable. We lie there with no protection and have nothing to do apart from wait – for a bullet or a piece of shrapnel.

We don't talk. We listen and try to guess how the fighting is going from the noise of battle. We hear the occasional battle cry from our comrades. It is the first time that we have observed fighting without taking part in it. Not a pleasant feeling.

An hour passes. Two. Benjamin Friedmann has fallen asleep. Joseph, the driver, reveals to me his secret fear: that he would faint at the sight of a severely wounded man. I smile. I also said that once, and have heard the same thing more than once from other comrades. But still we carried the wounded on our backs, and the dying, and did everything necessary – the pressure of the awful moment made us forget our feelings. It will be the same with Joseph.

"David!"

We jump up. The bullets and shells are forgotten. A wounded comrade – we have to make sure that he gets to the medical station as quickly as possible.

"David – Goliath!"

He has a wound on the ear. Not a particularly serious case. We drive him in the jeep to the medical center. "We are almost there" Benjamin reassures him. "A few more minutes …" "No panic" answers the wounded man angrily. "I'm OK." I know this voice. I have often heard it singing songs in the old "Jonah camp" a long time ago, before the Great Flood. It is the voice of Zalman Kamin. He is one of the few veterans who are still with us in company number one.

The medical center of the battalion is located in one of the bunkers in Negba. Ben-Zion and Rafael, the battalion medics, are waiting for us. We deliver the wounded man and have to go back into the night, into the fire. That demands a lot of willpower.

Waiting again. But not for long. It is a hard fight and there are many wounded. Some of them come limping, supporting themselves with their rifle. Others are carried in by their comrades, on stretchers or on tarps.

The jeep becomes a bus – driving there and back, there and back. Interesting how the task suppresses your fear. None of us even thinks of ducking. Every delay can cost a human life. One of the wounded refuses to travel in the jeep. There are others there who are more seriously wounded, he says in a weak voice. He will manage on foot …

The wounded lie in a field until their turn comes to be driven away. Joseph and I load eight of them into the jeep and drive to Negba. There we ask for reinforcements. In the meantime Benjamin Friedmann and Yaakov Velichkovski have gone to the wadi near the village. There a large number of wounded, who need to be brought to the path, are lying. Finally some armored vehicles arrive. We fill them up with the wounded.

It is four o'clock in the morning. The firing is reducing. The operation seems to be almost over. But we are still busy. None of the wounded can be left in the field. That is our responsibility. And we are determined to carry out this task at any price.

The last trip. Two seriously wounded in the jeep. They groan with every bump. But the road is full of holes – it has been bombarded the whole night. It is a miracle that nothing has happened to the jeep.

Will the ceasefire come into force at seven o'clock or not?

We are lying in the new trenches. Unbelievable tension in the air. For eleven days the brigade has faced the enemy alone. Half of our company dead or wounded. We have taken part in two, three, four actions in twenty-four hours. Every one of us knows that if the fighting continues, it is just a question of days before one is hit oneself. We wait for the start of the ceasefire like the accused waiting for the verdict: life or death.

I have been talking about this and that with Shalom Cohen. Neither of us was really concentrating. Both of us kept looking at the time. The hands move very slowly. There – it is five to seven.

Suddenly wild shooting begins in the south-east, from the direction of Karatiyya. Nobody says a word. We just listen. If we hadn't been told about the ceasefire, we wouldn't be suffering so cruelly. We had become fatalists, indifferent. It was long ago that we stopped thinking about tomorrow. Nobody talks about what might happen in three days – that is much too far off in the future. But the talk about the ceasefire has really thrown us. Will we get out of here alive and healthy? Even if only this one time? The disappointment was crushing. Suddenly Aryeh Spack appeared. He is beaming fit to burst. The report has just come over the radio that the ceasefire has come into force.

18 July 1948
A trench near Sawafir

Ceasefire

It is seven in the evening. The shooting that started five minutes ago has stopped. The artillery on the southern front is silent.

They crawl out of their trenches, and the sun smiles on them from the west. They blink in the sunlight, which they haven't seen for eleven days. They are dirty, their eyes are reddened, their clothes are torn and they are dog tired.

Eleven days! Has it really been only eleven days? Every single day felt like five years. On each day they saw death in a thousand forms.

They crawl out of their trenches and they are only few. They carry on their backs dead comrades, dying comrades, wounded comrades. Comrades who can never be replaced. Every one has grown together with the unit, become a part of it – and leaves behind a painful gap.

They crawl out of their trenches – the soldiers of the southern front, who have overcome an enemy much stronger and better equipped. They held back the tanks almost with their naked hands, lived through endless battle, and did not flinch.

"Samson's Foxes!" – the commando fighters in their shot-up jeeps, who raced along under fire, who drove into enemy positions, who stormed fortified villages, saved the wounded, and delivered ammunition to remote positions. How many of the original members of this unit are still alive? How many are unwounded?

The defenders of Negba – the men who lived in stifling bunkers and threw back assault after assault of tanks and infantry, who were bombarded twenty-four hours a day by artillery and aircraft, soldiers and "civilians" who moved around, crouching behind the cover of destroyed houses and burning barracks.

The fighters from the Ibdis position – who went through a hell almost beyond description and survived. Who held themselves with their fingernails onto the shaking, heaving ground.

They crawl out of the trenches in Julis and Karatiyya, in Beit Daras and Hatta, the few against the many, the Davids who have beaten the Goliaths.

They crawl out of their trenches and want to live. Every one of them was prepared to die and every one of them is only alive by chance. Each one of them has miraculously escaped a certain death a hundred times.

They crawl out of their trenches. The few, to whom the State of Israel owes a debt it can never repay.

Even after the ceasefire had come into force, operations in the area of Karatiyya continued. The enemy attacked the newly captured village very heavily. The capture of the village was intended to open the way to the Negev and prevent the enemy forces in Majdal and Iraq Suweidan joining up with those in Faluja and Iraq al-Manshiyya.

As in the days of Ibdis the Egyptians attacked with artillery, with tanks, and with an infantry assault. The attack failed. In the evening we were sent out to collect the booty, to test the enemy positions, and to gather in the weapons of the dead left in the field.

But the hope of opening the route to the Negev was disappointed. After the Egyptians had failed to recapture the village, they occupied – in violation of the ceasefire conditions – the hill to its south. Karatiyya remained in our hands. But the Negev was still cut off.

We stayed a few more days in Sawafir, ready to react immediately to any breach of the ceasefire by the enemy. But our opponent, who had suffered enormous losses, sorted out his own positions and kept quiet.

For the first time we could think about home. For eleven days that was a remote, forgotten world. Suddenly we remembered: we have a home. We have a family. We have parents.

19 July 1948
Sawafir

For our parents

The guns are silent and the soldiers crawl out of their trenches. The desire is strong to send a few words to the parents – your own parents and the parents of friends, to the parents of all the thousands of soldiers at the front who have survived the storms of the battle on the southern front:

* * *

Your son returns for a short period of leave. He is tired and uncommunicative. And you feel that something is standing between you and him which you have no part in.

You would so dearly like to understand it. To have a role to play in everything that concerns him. You ask him questions: but he shrinks back. He falls silent and turns away from you, or he replies with a tortured smile.

And you, mother, you tell your son about your problems. About the bombing, the sleepless nights, the high prices, and the limited amount of food on sale – and he doesn't even listen. As if all that was too far away, as though he came from a different world.

Sometimes you ask each other. Why is your son so distant? Has he cut himself off from you? Has the war opened a chasm between sons and parents, a chasm too wide to bridge?

Yes. Your son is no longer that nice, smiling boy, who put on a uniform and joked about the experiences in the training camp. He has been in combat. He has seen dead and wounded comrades, he has met fear and learned to overcome it. And he has felt that terrible loneliness which comes when you are on your own in a trench under fire.

He tells you nothing about this, to save your feelings. He can't tell you about this enigmatic life and cruel death, because you belong to another world.

But, parents, on those days of battle your son was also very close. When he set off on an operation in the dead of night, he knew that you were lying sleepless in your beds and worrying about him. And his concern was with you – his parents.

You complain that he wrote so little. Wasn't that cruel of him? But what could he write? These empty words "I am fine … I look forward to seeing you again soon"? In his position those were empty, meaningless, pathetic words. Sometimes he made a ridiculous attempt to deceive you. Said he wasn't even at the front. That his unit was being held back in reserve. At the same time he knew that you wouldn't believe a word of it.

And when it happened that a friend died next to him – how terrible was the thought of the parents sitting at home without any idea that their son existed no more. Even more horrifying was the thought that tomorrow the same could happen to his own parents.

So, dear parents – if your son comes back on leave, don't make it too difficult for him. Don't ask him any questions. Don't expect any confessions from him. Know that there are things in his heart that cannot be said. Simply enjoy the simple, wonderful reality: Y-o-u-r – s-o-n – i-s – b-a-c-k.

A soldier in combat sees only the small part where he is. Even for us, in our jeeps, with our frequent activity along the whole front, we had almost no chance of comprehending the significance of our own experiences.

Only after many months did I get the chance to speak with the brigade commanders and get a high-level view of the fighting during the months of June and July 1948. And then, much too late, I was shocked by the dangers that threatened Tel Aviv and the whole state. It really was a miracle that the soldiers and officers were able to avert this danger. This is what happened:

* * *

"Hello – Hagar – Boaz – Shamir – one – five. Hello – Hagar – Boaz – Shamir – one – five ..." A monotonous voice over the radio. The operator at brigade HQ writes his report mechanically. "Urgent! ... the lookout reports ..." A young liaison officer delivers the report to the office of the commander. One of many.

* * *

A man is sitting in the room in front of a table covered in maps. Blond, gray-blue eyes, a nose like the beak of a hawk – a fighter. His face looks tired as he reads the report. "The lookout reports: two hundred Egyptian vehicles on the road going north ..."

The reports come one after another. Report from Nitzanim: four hundred vehicles have passed, six hundred, eight hundred, one thousand, one thousand five hundred Egyptian vehicles driving northwards. Gan-Yavne reports: three hundred vehicles spotted on the road north from Isdud, five hundred, eight hundred. Armored vehicles, tanks, Bren carriers. The commander covers his face with his hands. He doesn't need the map. He knows the distance from Isdud to Tel Aviv is thirty-two kilometers as the crow flies.

The door opens. A short, roundish man with brown hair enters – the chief of operations of the brigade

"And?" asks the commander and raises his eyebrows.

"I saw them" answers the other. "Over a thousand vehicles north of Isdud." He says it unemotionally, as though he is talking about getting a box of cigarettes from the quartermaster. He is not one to get excited quickly. In the morning he drove out to check the reports personally. Now he is back he can confirm the reports are accurate. A gigantic Egyptian armada is moving in the direction of Tel Aviv.

For a brief moment the two look at each other. They are two very different types, almost opposites. Shimon Avidan, the commander of the brigade, is a sensitive, quiet type. Introverted and a little nervous. A fighter with a lot of revolutionary experience. In Europe he led a resistance group against the Nazis, was a commando leader, member of the Palmach. His deputy, Me'irke Davidsohn, comes from a kibbutz, is cold blooded, athletic, and lively.

They don't need to say anything. They both know the facts. And their significance is clear to them. The Egyptians are marching on Tel Aviv equipped with all available heavy weapons. Between this force and Tel Aviv stands … stands what?

Nothing! Two companies. A thin line of young men equipped with rifles, light automatic weapons, and Molotov cocktails. What else? A bridge to the north of Isdud, that was blown up the night before last. And also? Four aircraft which are unsuited to the conditions of the land and haven't made their first test flight. These forces are all the two have to defend the south and save Tel Aviv.

*   *   *

The four pilots stand on the runway looking at the aircraft. They have just been assembled and the motors need to be tested.

Suddenly a stranger is standing among them, an infantry officer. They don't know him, but they have heard a lot about him. "Comrades," he says, "you must get in immediately and take off." The four look at him with astonishment. He is not their boss. And they know that one should never take off in a machine that has not been thoroughly checked.

"Only your aircraft can save Tel Aviv, can save the whole land. The enemy is marching on the city. Apart from your aircraft, we have nothing to hold him back." Simple words. Spoken without drama and pathos. But the four don't just understand the words, but also the language of the eyes: gray-blue eyes, intense, and still very human. The eyes say: You have no choice.

The four get in, wave, and take off. Three of them will return.

*   *   *

North of Isdud is a traffic jam of Egyptian vehicles. a destroyed bridge is holding them up. The commanders curse, but they can do nothing but wait until the bridge is repaired. Aircraft appear. Bombs fall. The damage is slight. Where did the Jews get aircraft from? That is something new, that hasn't happened before. The Egyptian is a cautious person. His military training took place in a British academy. The expensive armored equipment should not be endangered through irresponsibility. Better to wait, assemble more forces, set up anti-aircraft guns, make preparations calmly, forge new plans, prepare a new blow to destroy the Jews. The order goes out: stop, dig in, take up positions for all-round defense.

Make preparations calmly? No! We cannot allow them to prepare calmly. We have to harass them, to threaten them on all sides, not allow them a moment's peace. At brigade HQ, near Rehovot, this work goes on at a feverish pace. The commander and his operations chief are hunched over plans for new operations. Battalion commanders come in and out. The telephone and the radio are never quiet.

Night after night the boys go out and attack. The attacks are small. They are more like harassment – a blow here, a blow there. But the enemy gets nervous and uses up huge quantities of ammunition. All his weapons fire away as soon as the slightest rustling is heard. No, the Egyptians will be given no chance to make their preparations calmly.

* * *

4 June 1948. Units from all parts of the southern region assemble at Gan-Yavne and Bitzaron. Tonight they will launch a large-scale attack on the Egyptian army near Isdud.

The commander gets no sleep this night. He knows the risks of the step he is attempting. To allow the necessary concentration of forces he has to leave large areas with inadequate defense. He knows that the Egyptians have three to five heavy machine guns for every light automatic weapon he has. He also knows that the available communication system is insufficient for the five battalions that he is committing to the battle. There will be almost no connection between the units, and as soon as the battle begins there will be no possibility of coordination.

But he knows another thing: there is no alternative. We have to attack, precisely because we don't have enough forces. This goes against all the rules of the theory of war. And yet it is correct: when you don't have enough forces to defend yourself against an attack, then you have to go on the offensive yourself. Hit him, harass him, deceive him. Make it impossible for him to prepare his forces for an orderly attack. This rule has a high price. But it offers the only possibility of saving the south and the city of Tel Aviv.

Slowly the first reports are coming in. The operation has failed. All our attacks have been repelled. Our losses are high, very high. But still: the enemy is impressed by the strength of our attacks. He will think twice before moving out of his positions.

* * *

Now begins the mental, the intellectual struggle between the two commanders. It concerns the coastal plane to the south of Tel Aviv. At the

HQ near Rehovot gray-blue eyes are studying the maps, calculating and planning. And in a house in Majdal dark brown eyes are looking at the same map – the eyes of the Egyptian division commander

How can one prevent the enemy breaking through to the north, to Tel Aviv, with insufficient forces against his aircraft, tanks, and artillery? One must throw him off balance. How can that be done? By attacking his rear area, his transport and supply routes.

About three kilometers south of Isdud, between Be'er Tuvia and Nitzanim, there is a hill which is labeled with the figure 69 on the map. It is a low, flat hill with three old water towers. It has a controlling view over the road between Isdud, where the Egyptian forces are assembled, and Majdal, where the Egyptian HQ is located.

On 7 June, two days after the fighting around Isdud, a small group of Israeli soldiers climbs this hill in the dead of night and digs in. In the early morning they cut the road. First round to the Israelis.

The Egyptians react to the blow with preparations for a counter blow. Two days later, at dawn, they throw their whole weight against this hill. For the first time, an Israeli position is exposed to a concentrated blow with all modern weapons at the same time: artillery, bombardment from the air, an assault by heavy tanks. The defenders use whatever they have, clawing themselves to the ground with their fingernails. And at this fateful moment the chain breaks at its weakest link: a man in a responsible position makes a mistake. The defense collapses. Hill 69 falls to the enemy. The Egyptians have won the second round

The report hits brigade HQ like a thunderbolt. A moment of naked horror. They were all sure that the hill would hold. All military logic said so. But it has fallen.

They can all feel it: in the first real confrontation between Israeli fighter and Egyptian steel, the steel has overcome the human factor. Maybe the spirit is not superior to the material? Was it a mistake to believe that fighting men can overcome fighting machines?

The commander and his deputy stand in their small office and see themselves confronted with a second fact: at this moment the fate of the young state is being decided. If the Egyptians march on against Be'er Tuvia, they will break through the front. There are no Israeli reserve forces there which could stop them. If the Egyptians reach Be'er Tuvia, then the whole front will collapse. The south will fall and then Tel Aviv.

There are almost no soldiers left in the region of the brigade. Forces of the Arab Legion and local fighters have occupied Gezer in the east. The kibbutzim of Gat and Gal'on are holding on as if by a miracle. There too, there are hardly any soldiers. All the forces are concentrated in the section between Isdud and Hill 69 against the Egyptians. There is no reserve.

Tomorrow the ceasefire is due to come into force. But will the Egyptians respect the ceasefire, if it is clear to them that just one more blow is all that is needed to seal Israel's fate?

* * *

Slowly the awful day drags by. Each second is an eternity. The commander himself has driven to Be'er Tuvia. The third and decisive round has begun.

In Beit Daras, between Be'er Tuvia and Hill 69, are two Israeli companies. One of them went to the hill to provide supporting fire for the company that abandoned the position there. They reach the edge of an apricot orchard about two hundred meters away from the hill.

One PIAT, which is something like a bazooka , three machine guns and eighty Israeli boys are the defenses of the State of Israel at this moment.

The Egyptians occupy the hill. Their spearhead, the tanks, is advancing toward Beit Daras. Suddenly they meet unexpected resistance. Three PIAT rounds hit the tank but don't explode. Machine gun bullets scratch the steel. A moment between life and death. The tanks halt. The Egyptian commander thinks for a moment, then the command arrives by radio: back to Hill 69 to take position there.

The Israeli commander grabs the opportunity and strikes again. A small unit of jeeps together with half-track vehicles from a Palmach battalion attacks the hill, pours heavy fire onto it, and returns.

Again the Egyptian army halts. The aggressiveness of little David has impressed the cautious, heavily armed Goliath. Round three to the Israelis.

The ceasefire comes into effect.

* * *

The ceasefire is no time for relaxation. Both sides prepare for the next confrontation. Both analyze the consequences of past battles, draw their own conclusions, and correct their faults.

The Egyptians strengthen their forces. They give up the idea of break-ing through the front at Isdud, and redeploy their troops further south. That is where they are planning the decisive blow.

The Israeli commander knows that a confrontation is coming that will overshadow all the battles so far. He knows that he will again have no reserves, that again he will only have the same rather ragged infantry battalions, along with a few out-of-date field guns. He will have no tanks, no aircraft.

He draws the conclusions from the "Day of Isdud" and establishes a "Battle HQ" to control all movements, even those of smaller units, during the fighting, and to coordinate all the action all the time. The units train. The positions are reinforced. Everything awaits the first shot.

* * *

At this moment comes a blow from an unexpected direction. Reports come in that the inhabitants of some villages in the south want to leave their houses. They have no illusions. The people in Gan-Yavne, in Be'er Tuvia, and in Negba know how things stand. They know that the tanks won against the fighters on Hill 69. They know that the troops who are supposed to protect their houses are weak. They also know that there are no reserves. The few soldiers in the positions will have to hold out – on their own.

The inhabitants are tired. Since the Egyptian invasion they have been helping to build fortifications – without pause. And they also had their agricultural work to do. Not only did the military not feed them, it even seized some of their stores of food. In Gan-Yavne some of the houses have been hit by Egyptian shells. And now the citizens also know that the enemy they are facing has brought in a gigantic force equipped with the most modern weapons.

The local commanders ask the chief to come and talk with the population, and he comes. He didn't learn the art of war from books. He believes in people. In soldiers and in citizens. He knows that this is pri-marily a collision of different aims, and that in the end the side with the strongest will, the most convincing, is going to win. He believes that no army can win without the support of the population. And he knows that the population must stay in their houses of their own free will and with-out pressure.

The chief wanders around and talks. Tired citizens, worried about their families, about their houses, and their own lives, give him a hearing. He doesn't promise any reinforcements. He doesn't promise them the heavy weapons we don't have. He promises only one thing – that he and his men will stand firm to the last, to the last bullet, to the last breath.

The citizens hear his words. And they see the gray-blue eyes, these steely eyes that are so human. They are not certain that his army will win. But they are certain that his army will fight to the end. And they decide: we will stay, together with the soldiers.

It may be that in this instant the real decision was made. It is possible that Shimon Avidan achieved his greatest victory at this moment. Not in the field, not in battle. But in talks with the citizens of the south, who remain voluntarily in their houses.

* * *

On 8 July, at dawn, thirty hours before the end of the agreed ceasefire, the Egyptians attack Beit Daras. A selected company of Sudanese soldiers assaults the positions. In man-to-man fighting they are driven back. Dozens die or are wounded in this battle. With their last energy the defenders beat off the attack. The enemy withdraws.

The chief and his deputy are in the new battle HQ near Kfar Warburg. And they decide: attack immediately, before the Egyptians are ready for another attack. The brigade is prepared. Everything is planned. All that is needed is the order. And it comes.

In the night of 8 July, brigade units attack Position 113, Hatta, and Karatiyya. And at the same time other units capture the villages of Iraq Suweidan, Beit Affa, and Ibdis in the Negba region, while a Palmach unit attacks the police station of Iraq Suweidan, that terrible fortress that controls the whole of the south.

The attack on the fortress was not successful. In the morning the forces leave the villages of Beit Affa and Iraq Suweidan, which are indefensible as long as the enemy occupies the fortress. But the Ibdis Position near Negba remains in the hands of the brigade.

Now it is the enemy's turn. In great strength he attacks Ibdis and Negba from his base in the fortress. In Ibdis the fighters had no time to organize themselves and dig in properly. The capture of the village was not complete until eleven o'clock, at which time the approaching Egyptian units could already be seen in the distance.

The intention is clear, even without having seen the Egyptian battle plan, which later fell into the hands of the Israelis in Ibdis. The plan is for a pincer movement. If this is successful the whole Israeli front would collapse and the wide plain would be open all the way to Tel Aviv.

The failure of the attack on Beit Daras and the Israeli attack in the region of Negba have messed up this plan. But the Egyptians rely on their large quantities of arms. If the first blow fails, they follow up with a second, a third. And if that, too, is insufficient, then they will attack four, five, or ten times. They have enough reserves.

The fighting around Ibdis and Negba raged for four days and four nights. A battle that cannot be compared with any other in this war. On the second day it reached its hellish high point. To divert the Israeli forces, the Egyptians attack the village of Julis, which controls the western part of the front. With the help of this diversionary tactic, the decisive attack on Ibdis is carried out.

An attack? No. Eight attacks on a single day, one after the other. Artillery, mortars, and aircraft turn the position into hell. And then come the tanks and behind them the infantry assault. They come once, three times, five times, eight times.

Since the morning a continuous stream of wounded flows out of the position. The company commander is among them. To replace him, another company commander is sent over. Between the explosions of the shells and bombs, the radio reports: the squad leaders and the ordinary soldiers wish to report that they are managing. They can be relied on. Toward the evening the company that defended Ibdis during the day is reduced to a few squads. A replacement company is sent. The same fate awaits them. But the soldiers take over the position without grumbling.

* * *

The battle HQ is located a few kilometers behind the front. It is the control center for the whole front. Here decisions that are made in seconds affect the fate of the state. On the radio here the heartbeat of the bleeding front can be heard. And like in a power station, the power is produced here to drive the units.

At ten o'clock in the morning there is a meeting of battalion commanders and their deputies. They are simple young men who bend over the map. One is a farmer, another a philosophy student. But they are in command of men in this hell. They see the personal example of Shimon Avidan and "Me'irke," his deputy. They discuss the plans for the next twenty-four hours and make the necessary decisions.

They return to their units, visit the places where their troops will be in action in the coming hours, issue orders, complete the last preparations. At the same time the brigade staff discuss various topics with the commanders of the service units – the sappers, the medics, the communication services – such as supply routes, the transport of ammunition to the units, and unsatisfied requirements for intelligence.

At five o'clock in the evening the battalion commanders return for a last meeting. They report on the situation. The final arrangements are made. At six o'clock they set off. One last check. The men's tasks are explained to them.

Zero hour. The first shots, assaults, hours between life and death, losses, evacuation of wounded, resupply of ammunition and equipment, fighting. The battle HQ is directly in touch with all this via radio contact with the fighting units. The brigade commander and the chief of operations can hear and feel the pain, the fire, the blood as though they were in the middle of the battle. They get involved in the details of actions and adjust the plan while the fighting rages.

In the early hours of the morning the fate of the night has been decided. Their nerves as ragged as if they had been in the thick of the battle themselves, they both leave the HQ to grab a few hours' sleep.

The battle lasted four days and three nights. Negba and Ibdis held out.

On the fourth day the Egyptians were approaching their limits, and summoned up all their remaining energy for one last major effort. The road to Negba. The fate of the front depends on this village. A section of the road there is dominated by the fortress of Iraq Suweidan. This section goes past a little hill, number 105 on the map. On the fourth day the Egyptians capture this hill. Negba is cut off.

The story of Hill 69 repeats itself – but this time the other way round. The brigade commander realizes that he has no choice. He has to attack. Directly and frontally. No maneuver will be of any use here. He has to attack the enemy exactly at the point where he is expecting it.

What forces does the brigade commander have available for this attack, whose chances are so remote? One company of infantry and two units of fighting jeeps. They receive the order to attack, which ends with three words that have a terrible meaning at the front – "at any price." This "price" is measured in blood and death.

The night of 12 July is dark when the fighters launch their assault on the hill. And then the jeeps appear. Strange apparitions that spit fire, drive over positions, over people. Panic grips the hearts of the Egyptians.

They run for their life, leaving field guns, PIATs, machine guns, and ammunition behind – and the dead.

* * *

The next morning the artillery along the whole front is quiet. Without understanding how it happened, everyone between Gal'on and Julis knows the tables have been turned. Something big has happened. Time for a moment's pause. The units need a rest. There is not a single company that is still fit for battle. The people who are still alive need a break.

But the commander, who is just as tired as all the others, knows that this is not the time to take it easy. Now we have to attack, attack, attack. Give the enemy no rest, no chance to reorganize, to recover from that blow. The commander asks his battalion commanders. And they, ready to drop, answer: Yes!

Again they are bending over maps, marking, drawing, calculating. Fingers follow lines on the map and come to a halt at one point: Beit Affa.

The talks are over. Then the commander mentions a small detail: yesterday, on the third day of the battle for Ibdis, members of the General Staff visited the front: General Yigael Yadin,[2] the Chief of the Operations Department of the General Staff, and Israel Galili,[3] the man whose name had been synonymous with the Haganah, who uttered the sentence that went down in history: "Your ranks are fairly thin. But your spirit fills the gaps."

* * *

13 July, six o'clock in the evening. A company of infantry, which has been in action every night for the last five nights and which yesterday attacked Hill 105, gets ready for the attack on Beit Affa. The soldiers are making the last preparations.

Next to the battle HQ, near the front, two men are standing. One is blond, with a hooked nose and gray-blue eyes, and the other, his deputy, has brown hair, lively eyes, and an athletic build. They know their responsibility – the responsibility for the state on whose behalf they are at this place. For a short moment everything depends on them, on their command. They give the command: attack! And although this one engagement is not particularly important, it is a historic command. For, this night, the initiative on the southern front has come into Israeli hands – to remain there. The danger to the Israeli state from the largest and strongest Arab army has been deflected. Tel Aviv is no longer threatened.

Blood and Muck

We had already experienced two severe crises in the army. The first was during our first few days in the training camp. The second was when we went into battle for the first time. And now, after eleven terrible days of fighting, we headed for Tel Aviv for a short leave – and the third crisis, which was to be the most difficult of all.

In celebration of the unbelievable fact that we were still alive, still breathing, and still able to walk on our own two legs, we went to Tel Aviv. Our heads were still full of our awful experiences in Ibdis and Beit Affa, where the unit had been bloodied and lost half its strength, and the front was desperate for reserves.

When we reached the city, we saw hundreds and thousands of healthy young men, who hadn't the slightest intention of following our example. We saw smartly dressed men sporting officer's insignia, who engaged in "important" tasks in their offices.

We had been practically cut off from headquarters for months. We came home for short leaves, "organized" ourselves an evening in the town, and returned to the front. The slogan went: "the whole people – one army." We were told that the whole nation was fighting, that the shortage of manpower was a general shortage.

And then we discovered that this was a lie. Only part of the nation, only part of the youth went to fight. And behind their backs there arose and thrived the "headquarters." A gigantic structure which had produced its own lifestyle, its own philosophy of life.

We remembered going into action night after night, for lack of reserves. We thought of the fate of our company number one, which twice had to suffer defeat for the same reason.

And in the city we heard from self-appointed aristocrats in fine uniforms that in every army in the world, for every soldier at the front

there are seven or seventeen or twenty-seven people at the rear ... many
of us began to wonder why we had to be the one against the seventeen
on the other side? Why shouldn't one of the seventeen change places
with us?

Some of those among us could not withstand this temptation. They
found themselves a position at the rear, or in the navy or the air force.
They invented a black joke about our brigade: DAWDUFG – "Death
alone will discharge us from Givati."

Most stood firm in this critical situation. They returned to the front.
But a bitterness took root in their hearts that would darken the mood at
the front in the coming days. They hated the rear. They turned their
backs on it.

22 July 1948
Battalion HQ

Front and Rear

They are driving to Tel Aviv. For weeks they have been dreaming
about this break, were longing for it in their positions and during the
battle. Now they are singing.

On the way back from Tel Aviv they are silent. Depressed and
weighed down by their thoughts.

* * *

I want to buy tickets for the movies. The line for soldiers is twice as
long as the civilian one. Soldiers in smartly pressed uniforms. But
something is missing from their faces: that particular expression,
that special something which frontline soldiers immediately recognize in each other.

I see many familiar faces and ask the men what they are doing.
They answer proudly that they are working in an important ministry
or a very important institution. I hear about important duties that
sound impressive and very significant. And they all have one thing in
common – they are far removed from the places where the bullets
whistle and the shells explode.

Can anyone at the rear imagine the feelings of a frontline soldier?

He signed on for military training when the call came. He spent
months in filthy villages and took part in eight, twelve, or maybe fifteen battles. He saw his comrades die and could not imagine that one

could "organize" oneself some fine task. Maybe he could even have got "protection" for himself, if he were an expert or had some particular talent. Instead of all that he just went to the front. And in his naivety he thought that everyone else was doing the same.

When he was on leave at home he first noticed that not everyone had signed up after all. Some were waiting for the right moment, had applied for a temporary exemption. And as the military bureaucracy came into being, they were among the first who jumped in. They had time to go from office to office and make the necessary contacts, to get the right words whispered in the right ear at the right time. And nobody thought about those who were lying under cannon and mortar fire and didn't even have the time to think about the distant rear.

But now that they had the time to catch their breath, to ponder, and to discuss, a bitterness crept into their hearts that would affect their activity at the front. They saw how less talented colleagues quickly climbed the career ladder while they remained in the lowest ranks. They discovered how low their chances of promotion were. This particularly affected those who distinguished themselves in combat, who volunteered for particularly dangerous tasks, and who naturally knew that they were good soldiers. For their career advancement this was of no significance.

* * *

In the early days, when we came home on leave, we would see friends in civilian clothes. At that time they had a strange look, as though they were embarrassed. And without being asked, they rushed to excuse themselves and to explain that they were going to sign up soon.

Now it is different. These friends all wear uniform and are soldiers – better turned out and more "martial" in appearance than the front-line soldiers. A rear aristocracy has formed. And now when you come to the city on leave, you have to explain why you are out there on the front, instead of having organized a good and important job in the city. And you feel what they are silently thinking: "Ah well, a talented lad. But he just can't get himself organized ..."

In his book *All Quiet on the Western Front* Erich Maria Remarque describes how a veteran from the front comes home on leave. He comes across an elegant young major who has never been at the front but attaches great importance to the correct execution of a smart salute. It seems that this relationship between the gray front mice and the staff-room studs is the same in all wars and peoples. But that this has appeared here with all its consequences fills me with gloomy thoughts.

Something new and significant has arisen at the front. But only a part of our young people has experienced this. At the rear quite different things have been "experienced," a different style of life and behavior. Two different worlds, whose inhabitants will soon be incapable of understanding each other.

The front found ways to express its silent protest against these developments. The soldiers from the front emphasized the difference with torn, dirty uniforms, unruly hairstyles, and wild beards. If the government refused to grant them a special front badge, well, they would have to do it themselves. Just as the sock hat was a symbol of the people's army in the early days, the beard became a symbol of the front, which despised the spit and polish of the rear.

An undeclared competition between the lifestyle of the front and that of the rear broke out. Some officers at the front took a liking to the rear style, and felt uncomfortable with the indiscipline of the frontline soldiers. They didn't notice that the "rebels" tended to be exactly those soldiers who distinguished themselves in combat. And thus began the attempt to introduce the so-called discipline of the rear into the fighting units. Its first victim was – the beard.

24 July 1948
Battalion HQ

The story of a beard

Time to write an obituary. An obituary for my beard. Because it is with us no longer.

It was no simple beard. It had a history.

I always wanted to grow a beard. Perhaps it began with that sweet girl's whisper in my ear; a beard would suit me, with my narrow face. From that day on, the thought would not leave me. It gave me no rest.

The first opportunity presented itself during the days of the Nachshon operation. For three weeks we were in Deir Muheisin and in the positions on the road to Jerusalem. My beard grew all by itself. But at that time I didn't dare. I played with the idea, but … whenever I went "home" for a short time to Hulda, I would pick up my razor and the beard was gone.

Days passed. I saw a lot of beards. Goatees which only just covered the chin, beards which formed a narrow frame around the face, and the impressively full beards of the Palmach people from the Negev, the so-called Negev Animals. And also simple beards without any tradition or meaning. A decision was slowly taking shape to grow myself a fine, proper beard at the next opportunity. And the opportunity came.

It was before the first ceasefire. We were positioned outside Beit Daras, a village without compare in the whole of the southern region, as far as fleas go. We had no water, didn't wash, and of course we didn't shave. We were five whole days there before the ceasefire came into force. On the next day, so we were told, we would go on leave to Tel Aviv.

I stood in front of the mirror for a long time, pondering. I felt sorry to lose my beard. On the other hand I didn't want to turn up in Tel Aviv with a half-finished product. I had no choice – and so I shaved.

At some point the first ceasefire came to an end, and the war of eleven days began. All the battles of the past paled into insignificance next to the battles of Negba, Ibdis, Beit Daras, Hill 105, and Beit Affa. Now we were commandos racing here and there in our jeeps. The days flew past, with three or four actions a day. And after each action you look at yourself and ask: what, still alive? Nobody thought of shaving, nobody even thought of washing.

When the next ceasefire began, we awoke as if from a bad dream. And I became aware that my face was adorned with a proper and handsome beard. I contemplated it with pleasure. That girl was right: I needed a beard.

By now we had acquired the name "Samson's Foxes." People admired us, the way we had admired the Palmach people when we were raw recruits. This beard, I told myself, is just right. That's what a commando needs.

My beard came with me the next time I went to Tel Aviv. My parents got a shock. Acquaintances worried that there had been a death in the family.[1] And a dark-haired girl, whose opinion was very important to me, implored me to shave it off. But when I was back in the camp I regretted my rash promise. Am I a woman's slave or a frontline soldier? In brief, I broke my promise and left the beard where it was. It flourished splendidly.

But I had left one thing out of account – the ceasefire. This brought some things that we didn't like at all. Being woken early, morning roll call, a thousand little rituals from earlier times that we had long forgotten during the fighting and that we had hoped we would never have to submit to again.

In short, our commanders had decided that it was time to put an end to our partisan existence and to reintroduce what they, for unknown reasons, called "military order." This order is very popular among the superiors. And if it didn't occasionally happen that an army also has to fight – which disturbs the boring routine seriously – they would have introduced this "order" at the front too.

The first victim of this order was my beard. First to come to me was my immediate superior, then the sarge, followed in the end by an official order from the company commander. No lesser person than the battalion commander made his remarks when he visited our company. They had all decided that my beard symbolized this damned "partisan spirit." So it had to go.

I am a soldier, dear reader. And an order is an order, whatever you think about it. My comrades stood around me. Some felt sorry for me, others radiated schadenfreude. The news spread quickly, and my naked face became a popular theme for gibes and various kinds of joke.

Poor beard. With a heavy heart I write your obituary. You were a good friend to me, a source of comfort and joy on difficult days. And now you have met your fate …

Why are my comrades suddenly looking so sad? Have the Egyptians broken the ceasefire? Has the fighting started again? … Maybe, after all, my beard will get another chance to grow …

This mental crisis strengthened the comradeship and the esprit de corps among those left in the fighting units. They despised the "HQ heroes" more and more. We carried in our hearts the words of the Russian song that Abba Kovner brought us during the eleven days in the trenches:

only at the front can you tell/who is a friend and a brother/only at the front can you see/it does exist – the soldiers' love …

Comradeship is more intense than any other feeling at the front. It is an elementary necessity. Without it we would have had no chance of survival.

My friend Jochanan Silbermann was a private in the company that defended Beit Daras when it was massively attacked. On that day he was sent to Tel Aviv to take part in a military parade. Together with his comrades he was told to leave the parade and return to his battalion. That's how it happened that he suddenly appeared next to me. I was already sitting in the jeep, ready to set off for the forward base. We chatted a bit until the order to set off arrived.

*   *   *

That night marked the start of the big attack on Iraq al-Manshiyya. At last we were fighting to open the road to the Negev. Jochanan's company was at the spearhead of the assault. Our jeeps were deployed to bring in the wounded.

The next morning I learned that Jochanan had fallen.

28 July 1948
Geladiyeh

Portrait of a hero

You ask: who granted us this state, this free life in safety? You ask: who stood firm in the bombarded positions, in the hail of bullets, against tanks, aircraft, and artillery? You ask: who opened the roads to Jerusalem and into the Negev? Who repelled the attacks of the enemy?

It was not the quality of the weapons, nor was it their number or greater professionalism. It was the simple soldiers. I would like to talk about one of these unknown soldiers, my friend Jochanan. Of all the experienced frontline soldiers, Jochanan was one who managed to survive so long just by chance.

With the second ceasefire he thought it was his turn to take a break, to get some leave, to spend a few days with his beloved. But when the reports came in that the Egyptians were blocking the way to the Negev, and the order came to attack, he did not complain and did not hesitate.

The company had many "green" soldiers, raw recruits who were filling the gaps resulting from the recent fighting. A murderous carpet of fire from the fortified positions in Iraq al-Manshiyya covered them, and many of them were terrified. That's when Jochanan stood up, to be an example for them, to overcome their fear. A burst of machine gun fire hit him in the chest, killing him instantly.

He wasn't the garrulous type, unlike those who sit in the cafes of Tel Aviv and boast about their heroic deeds. He often wore a shy smile on his face. The smile of someone who values modesty as a fundamental virtue.

He signed up shortly after me, and I felt sorry for him deep in my heart. "He is too good natured and won't be able to stand up for himself in the army," I thought to myself. "His superiors and his peers will tease him and take advantage of him."

After about a month I happened to meet a common friend in the company, and asked him how Jochanan was doing. "Jochanan?" he asked. "He is a real soldier. A wonderful fellow." In the course of one month he had made his mark. Instead of teasing him and exploiting him, his comrades and superiors envied him his quiet bravery. He didn't like military life. But he was an exemplary soldier.

* * *

Music was what filled his life with meaning. He could forget himself at the piano. And during the long weeks when he and his comrades were besieged in Gat, he could soothe his troubled comrades with his music.

Some weeks before the war started, be began to perform in public. A glowing future was painted for him. Great things were expected of him, as a composer too. But then his long fingers began to play on the trigger of an automatic weapon. It is hard to imagine a stranger character in this destructive task. But still, he proved himself in battle. What is special about such people, that gives them the power to hold their own in battle? What is it that makes them into model soldiers?

It is certainly not ideological commitment. Jochanan didn't understand much about politics. It did not interest him. What motivated him was human decency. He could have "arranged" something in an office of the army culture department. But he signed up as a matter of course. His brother was a member of one of the kibbutzim in the Negev. It was quite clear to him that he, too, had a duty to fulfill.

* * *

If the war had not broken out, one day we would have heard of the composer Jochanan Silbermann, renowned throughout the world. But now he is lying somewhere in the south of the country, his handsome face calmly facing the stars, and his chest riddled with bullets. One of many who don't come back from the field of battle.

That is a very high price that you pay, homeland, for your freedom.

The death of Jochanan moved me to describe a soldier who hates war, who is a pacifist deep in his heart, but still distinguished himself in battle. In the war we learned to behave like cynics and pour scorn on ideals. But that was just pretense. The experience of the war made idealists of the fighters.

29 July 1948
Jaladiyya

Fatima

She sat on the jeep, shook her curly head, and watched us through humorous eyes. They were the eyes of a clown, and the bandages on her legs and neck underlined this impression.

We laughed out loud. Who has ever seen a dog bandaged up like a soldier returning from battle? But then we looked into the eyes of the soldier sitting next to her, and stood with open mouths. Something about those eyes killed our laughter stone dead.

"A strange fellow" I said to Menashke. "Who is that?"

Menashke was the biggest scandalmonger of the brigade. He knew everybody. No one knew exactly what his duties were supposed to be. But when we wanted to know what had happened to someone, where somebody had been wounded, or who was going with who, we knew that all we had to do was ask him. He was a modern information system on two legs.

"What, you don't know Eli?" asked Menashke. "There's a good story for you."

* * *

This Eli was was an unusual character. A giant of two meters or so, with broad shoulders and a prodigious mustache. He looked like one of those who spend their leave in the beach cafes of Tel Aviv, loudly recounting how they killed at least a dozen Arabs and captured an artillery piece. Eli, in fact, was exactly the opposite: taciturn, restrained, solitary.

He was a machine gunner. A real one. Not simply a soldier who can operate an automatic weapon. The weapon lay in his hand like the brush in the hand of a painter. It was said of him that even if he wanted to, he could not miss his target. But Eli did not enjoy his task. His comrades envied him. But when they sat on their beds discussing how to destroy the enemy more quickly, he turned his back or went to take a shower. In brief: a strange fellow ...

* * *

The story of him and Fatima began with the assault on Deir-Mussah. Eli was in the first wave. He ran with the machine gun, stooping, ahead of his squad. Flat on the ground – jump up – flat – jump, until he reached the first houses.

The resistance from the village got weaker and weaker. It looked as though the last few Arab fighters wanted to get out. People's spirits were high, soon they would ... suddenly the chattering of a machine gun opened up from the left. The fire came from a shabby house standing beneath a big leafy tree. Eli turned his gun, fired a short burst and quiet fell on the front at Deir-Mussah. Nobody took much notice. The comrades stormed onward and broke open the houses. Here and there they found souvenirs. Nobody asked about Eli.

Eli went to the isolated house. Something drew him there. He stood there, looking at the young Arab lying face down on the floor. It was a silent dialogue between Eli, the machine gunner, and the man he had just killed.

But suddenly Eli was awoken from his reverie. A little dog jumped from the house and ran to the dead Arab. With howls of desperation she licked his face and prodded his body with her paws. She looked as though she wanted to bring him back to life. Eli stood there for a long time, silent and still. Then he picked up the dog and returned to the company.

* * *

Days passed. The war went on. In place of local fighters the enemy was now the Arab Legion and the Egyptian Army. Eli didn't carry his machine gun on his back any longer, but used the one mounted on the jeep.

"Eli's jeep" it was called, even if Shmuel, the squad leader, was the actual head of the team. In time he became known throughout the brigade. The machine gun just spat out its bullets, whether stationary or on the move, and never missed its target. But the more Eli's renown spread, the worse his mood became.

People wanted to make fun of him for his softness. But nobody dared to say a word. Because in combat he was in a class of his own. So they had to face the facts and accept that he was just different.

But Eli was no longer on his own. He had a little girlfriend. The dog from Deir-Mussah. He never went into battle without her. She slept next to him. And the bond between them seemed to become stronger with every enemy that Eli struck. It would happen that someone surprised him sitting and talking with the dog in a language that no human understood.

* * *

One day Eli's jeep was driving on a patrol through Deir-Mussah. The task was to provoke the enemy into a firefight, to test their strength.

As the jeep approached the village, it was greeted with unexpectedly heavy fire. The first bullet hit a tire. Ephraim, the driver, just managed to bring the vehicle to a halt, and Shmuel gave the order to take cover. Eli grabbed the machine gun, jumped out of the jeep, and fired one salvo after another. Fatima also jumped out of the jeep and then disappeared.

Covered by the automatic fire, Ephraim worked fast. Bullets may have been whizzing past his head, but he knew his job. He replaced the damaged wheel with the reserve.

"Prepare to withdraw!" shouted Shmuel, and then "Into the jeep!" Eli jumped on, then paused. Fatima was not there. For a moment he flattened himself out on the ground, then he jumped up and ran to the house at the edge of the village.

"Are you crazy?" shouted Shmuel. "Come back immediately!"

But Eli didn't hear him. He ran toward the house, without

stooping, as if unaware of the bullets flying around. There he found Fatima, lying on her side, bleeding from a bullet wound.

Shmuel waited for him. What else could he do? You can't just leave a comrade behind, even when he has taken leave of his senses. And so Eli jumped back onto the jeep, with Fatima in his arms and her blood dripping on the machine gun.

* * *

It was Menashke who told me this story. Usually I was rather skeptical about his stories. Experience had taught me to discount 50% of everything he said. But this story was somehow convincing. Hadn't I seen the wounded dog with my own eyes? And the strange eyes of the machine gunner, this giant with a facial expression all his own, sadly resolute? The expression of a lonely person ...

31 July 1948
Jaladiyya

The soldier at home

When a frontline soldier says "I would like to be back home again," it is not clear what he means.

If it is spoken during combat operations, it means his forward base, a trench six feet long and two feet wide, laboriously dug near a tree in the forlorn hope of some shade. If at the forward base, it probably means the base camp with its tents or barracks. And if he is at the base, it means his real home – his parents, his wife, his family. The domestic instinct comes to the surface in the most unlikely places.

Say a unit reaches its forward position, a great wide field with a scattering of trees. The commander distributes the squads: from this tree to that one – squad number one, from here to there – squad number two and so on. The soldier dumps his things on the ground, wanders around a bit, visits his friends, and already he feels like going "home," to that tree which is no different from the other trees.

* * *

In the training camp there was no room for expressions of individuality. On the long rows of beds, things were positioned on the mattresses in the specified arrangement – and that was your home. Every

morning there was an inspection to make sure that the sacred tidi-
ness was observed. Feeling at home was excluded.

* * *

At the forward base before our first battle, sixteen of us were
lying in a tent together with the squad leader and longing to be
back in the training camp. But even this was heaven compared with
our "homes" during the first days of the Nachshon or the Maccabi
operations, those damned little tents which let the rain in and were
suffocating on hot days. How we cursed those little tents!

A lot changed after the Maccabi operation. We were allocated a
permanent base, which we left for battle and returned to afterwards.
We left our private things "at home" and took only the absolute
necessities with us – sometimes less.

We were lucky. We managed to take over living quarters that had
once been intended for officers. We lived six to a room, and immediately set about putting our stamp on the place. We hung the photo of
a pretty dancer from an American magazine on the wall. We stole
two large maps from an Arab village, for the development of our
inspired strategic plans. One night we raided the storeroom and
returned with a large table, two chairs, and two armchairs. A gray
blanket served as our tablecloth. We made vases out of old brandy
bottles, and every morning one of us was selected to wash the floor
and get some flowers.

When we were out in the fields in those days, we used to say:
"We'll soon be home." That was no empty phrase. We knew
that a real home awaited us, in which we could feel like human
beings.

When the commando unit was formed, our unit, which had lived
in this beautiful room, fell apart. Each of us took with him a part of
our common property. And since we had been told that the new
arrangements would not last for long, we didn't make any efforts to
make our new "residence" comfortable.

Then we were reassigned to new barracks. We didn't like that. But
we were experienced front mice, no longer green recruits. So the two
of us – my friend Shalom Cohen and I – laid claim to a small room.
We organized three armchairs and a table, brought two mats from a
captured Arab village, hung three maps on the walls, and built ourselves a little bookshelf for the books we had collected over time. And

now we lay on our beds under mosquito nets and felt like the masters of creation. Our greatest pleasure was provided whenever a "green" comrade accidentally came into our room. Seeing the luxury and the maps, he apologized in embarrassment, and left with the firm impression that he had stumbled on the room of no less than the brigade commander.

One late evening the composer Mordechai Zeira[2] appeared in the "villa" near Jaladiyya. We assembled around a burning candle and listened to the tender notes he conjured out of his harmonica. It was a special atmosphere – the darkness, the tones, the forms of the comrades, the comradeship that surrounded us. In my head, words were coming together as verses. The Foxes' song was taking form.

In the jeep's headlights, which I turned on from time to time, I wrote the words with pencil and paper. When I was ready I gave Zeira the sheet. He was also drawn into the atmosphere, and so the song got a tune – a melody of roaring jeeps, howling foxes, and the nocturnal sounds of the southern landscape.

* * *

Later I wondered whether anyone had ever thought about the feelings of the foxes as the torches were tied to their tails. And what happened to them? There is nothing about that in the Old Testament. But we were given the name "Samson's Foxes" ...

4 August 1948
Battalion headquarters

Convoy into the Negev

"Oh how sick I am of that ..." complained Freddy Regenstreif and put his cards on the ground.

* * *

The company was stationed in a large Arab house on the path to Jaladiyya, near the road to Castina. Freddy had a good reason to curse life. He lost a pile of money at poker. But we were all sick of this kind of life. We longed for action, followed by the two or three days' leave that would follow. Since the start of the ceasefire we hadn't had any leave. And I was weighed down by the sad duty of bringing the news of the death of Jochanan Silbermann to his parents. "If only we had something to do," continued Freddy. But Reuven had already dealt the cards again and Freddy was drawn back into the game.

* * *

I go into what used to be the boiler room in the cellar, which the staff have taken over. Aryeh Spack, the company commander, Chaim Poltorek, the sarge, and a few squad leaders are lying about on the ground and trying to find something interesting in some old newspapers. Miriam Feinstein and Miriam Milstein, the two secretaries, who at least bring a bit of life to the staff, are using the chance of a lift to the camp to take a shower. The rest of us have long passed that threshold, when you no longer even notice your own filth.

I take the newspaper from the hands of a sleeping squad leader. There is no war in it. Two parties are arguing about something that I don't understand. There is some excitement about a football game. At the front – according to the paper – a ceasefire is in force.

The telephone rings. Since I am the nearest, I pick up the receiver, even though the call has nothing to do with me.

"Samson's Foxes."

"Battalion HQ. Is Aryeh there?"

"Yes."

"Then pass him to me"

"Is it important?" I ask. The battalion is often bothering us.

"Any other questions?" in a cutting tone. I pass the receiver to Aryeh.

"Aryeh here," the company commander says in a sleepy voice. Then he is suddenly wide awake. After a minute he puts the receiver down.

"Get Elieser!" he commands. Elieser Lasky has been in command of the jeeps since the assault on Beit Affa. "He is coming with me to battalion HQ ... and the jeeps should be made ready for a night operation."

* * *

"OK, listen ..." Elieser begins. His face was beaming as he returned from battalion HQ. We already knew that something was afoot, and gathered around his jeep.

"Tonight we are making a resupply expedition into the Negev. For the people there it is a matter of life or ..." he paused briefly. He didn't like empty words. "Well, it is really very important. They have run out of food and they are even short of clothing. It will be a convoy of twenty trucks. We are taking a new route and will break through the Egyptian lines between Iraq al-Manshiyya and Qubeiba. The jeeps will be divided into two groups: four at the front of the convoy and three at the rear. We will use two small radio sets for internal communication and two large ones for contact with the base. The convoy will be under the command of someone from Palmach. I will be in charge of the jeeps."

Elieser pauses and smiles. He knows that what is coming is the most important part.

"We hand over the trucks to the Negev Animals[3] at a rendezvous north of Ruchamah.[4] If everything goes smoothly, we will take the same way back. Then we pack our things and leave this shi… place. We return to battalion HQ."

* * *

The jeeps steal out into the night. We sit in silence, thinking about the operation ahead of us. For many months we have been fighting over the Negev, but have never actually been in the Negev itself. This night we will break through the thin Egyptian line separating our southern front from the Negev.

We know from experience that it doesn't take much more than a little courage to drive between two Egyptian positions in the dead of night. But for a long convoy with umpteen trucks it is rather a different matter. Is it possible that the Egyptians would not guard the road that carries all their supplies and which connects their position from Majdal to Beit Jibrin?

A jeep is a special kind of "weapon" which is very vulnerable. Its only defense is speed and agility. But this time we will be attached to the clumsy trucks. Still, our morale is high. Not many know how weak our forces in the Negev are at this moment. We have already transported food to besieged and hungry Jerusalem. And this time too, we will bring our fighting comrades what they need.

If we get involved in a fight tonight and cannot return by the same route, we will have to stay in the Negev for some time.

Jassir and Gat are behind us. Ahijah, the commander of our squad, is at the wheel. I am sitting next to him as the forward machine gunner. In the back sits Moshe Kimpinski, our radio operator. He holds a machine gun with one hand and the radio mouthpiece in the other. On the floor are cartridge cases, ammunition boxes, steel helmets, and maps – in our typical untidy style.

A dark shape signals with a flashlight – a battalion policeman. Strange to see one so near the front. I look at the sky. We are to the south of Zeitah, about a kilometer away from the Egyptian road. Here we should meet up with the trucks. The jeeps drive off the path and line up in the order they will take in the convoy.

Some way away the superiors are sitting, standing, and crouching around a darkened petrol lamp, with the intelligence officer and the scouts. Maps, aerial photos, and notes lie on the ground. They are whispering together.

"… these positions will be captured tonight …"

"…there could be old mines around here …"

"…the scouts noticed some traces around here …"

"…and what if the advance guard runs into enemy fire? …"

"…leave behind any broken down or damaged vehicle …"

Photos are passed around. Some bright dots are the subject of discussion. The scouts, who know the location, explain and discuss among themselves. The commanders of the forward and the rear parties come to a consensus about tactics. It is clear to everyone that this is a journey into the unknown and that chance and luck will be decisive.

The officers have concluded their discussions. A deep silence surrounds us and fatigue dulls the tension. The supply trucks are late. The hell with them. We all want to grab a few precious minutes' sleep. I lie down on the hood and drift away.

When I awake, I hear a faint humming in the distance, which increases in volume. The convoy is here.

We all liven up. Motors are started. Now every minute counts. We are at least two hours behind schedule. Elieser takes four jeeps to the front of the convoy. My jeep and two others form the rearguard. Our drivers are pessimistic. The trucks are old, their drivers are raw recruits, and they don't like the idea of this midnight cruise at all. It looks like trouble. The comrades who are staying behind wave. "Good luck!" We are off.

* * *

Now we are wide awake. We are approaching the Egyptian road. We have taken the covers off the machine guns and the cartridge belts are within easy reach. An occasional colorful Egyptian rocket sails into the air. The red one on the right comes from Iraq al-Manshiyya, the green one on the left from Qubab. If they keep on like this, it will be easy to find our way. Let's hope they continue.

Some figures wave to us from the side of the road. Palmach people who have taken position along the road. The convoy stops. The first problems with the drivers. Two trucks get stuck in a steep wadi. We swear. With every minute the chance reduces that we will be able to return during the night. If we don't make it back today – when will we be able to? And leave is beckoning in the distance ...

Chadad, one of our best drivers, replaces the other driver at the wheel and has a go himself. The truck does not move. Ahijah talks on the radio with the commander of the convoy. We hear him discussing the situation with HQ. We recognize the voice. The brigade commander in person is talking over the radio. We finally realize how important this operation is.

The order is to leave the faulty vehicles and drive on. The convoy slowly gets under way. We are used to driving fast in the jeeps. This crawling behind prehistoric trucks is getting on our nerves. A light colored strip crosses our path. Is that the Egyptian road? Yes! Two Palmach soldiers wave us through. That is the last wave. From now on we are on our own.

* * *

The tension rises. If something is going to happen, then this is the place. This is enemy territory.

But nothing happens. In Iraq al-Manshiyya the Egyptians are still having fun with their colorful rockets. Suddenly, without any warning, there is a massive explosion directly in front of us. The first thought is: a shell. Instinctively I put on my steel helmet, the machine gun is ready. Where is the enemy?

Everything is quiet around us. The convoy has stopped. We are nervous and want to know what is happening. Ahijah leaves the road and drives beside the convoy toward the front. Some of the men have collected around one truck.

"Halt! Don't move!" someone shouts at us. "You are standing in a minefield!" The jeep stands where it is. We don't move. Some sappers who are attached to the convoy clear the ground ahead of us.

Mines then. A strange life. At least four jeeps and ten heavy trucks drove over that point. Why did this particular truck catch it?

"Anyone wounded?"

"Two dead."

The ground has been cleared. I get out and walk to the truck. The two dead will be carried in the ambulance that is placed in the middle of the convoy. One of them had been sitting on the wing to show the driver the way. He was torn to pieces.

"Hey, you there, can you give us a hand?" The commander of the sappers addressed me.

"What then?"

"Have a look at the truck, and see if we can unload anything."

I climb onto the truck, and see boxes of clothes, some food, and four engines. I call some people to unload the engines. The rest is not worth it. Ahijah comes with the Palmach commander. He wants to burn the truck. I am horrified. "Burn it? Do you want to call the Egyptians, so they set an ambush for our return?" He considers. He hadn't thought of that. Since he is a Palmach man, he accepts suggestions even from an ordinary soldier. The truck will not be burned.

At HQ they are getting nervous. The commander orders us to drive on immediately. One after the other the heavy trucks drive around the wreck. We return to our places. We are on our way again.

* * *

We are also getting nervous. Time is passing. The convoy keeps stopping. Then it is our turn. The jeep runs roughly for a moment and then stutters to a halt. I look at Ahijah. It is not schadenfreude, but I know what has happened. He had taken a container from the truck that hit the mine, sniffed it, and emptied it into our petrol tank. Apparently it contained water, even if it still smelt of petrol.

Amid curses and insults fired in both directions, we connect our jeep with a chain to the truck in front of us. Reuven Huber is its driver. He is not a trained driver, and this is his first attempt. Every time he pulls away, his vehicle gives a jerk. What if a battle were to start now?

Hardly has the idea entered my head when the first bullets are flying past our ears. According to the map the little hill on our left is the location of a camp of Bedouins[5] and refugees. From the noises we can tell what is going on ahead. The jeeps race forward with all eight machine guns barking at once. The enemy falls silent. It seems they were just a few gunmen.

That was no real battle, but the trucks now drive faster, without stopping. Judging by the colorful rockets, we are now to the south of Iraq al-Manshiyya. We drive on for another hour. More trucks break down.

From the radio traffic it sounds as though we are near our goal. The Negev brigade suddenly joins the net. HQ asks where we are exactly, and the Palmach forces occupying the positions north of the road want to know if it is OK for them to withdraw.

From the front of the convoy comes a radio message that they have met the Negev people. The convoy halts. We drive forwards. A few half-track vehicles are waiting there. The commanders are deep in discussion. Both their and our soldiers have got out.

"Greetings Animal!"

"Greetings Fox!"

"What's the news from the Land of Israel?" asks a bearded Negev man.

"What are your girls like?" asks a Fox.

Discussions take place but there is no easy conclusion: to return immediately or not? Two of the eight jeeps have to be towed. It is four o'clock in the morning with only ninety minutes till sunrise. The enemy might have found the abandoned trucks or heard from the Bedouins and set a trap for us.

On the other hand: if we don't return straight away, this route will be of no more use to us. We would have to find another, and no one knows how long we would then have to stay in the Negev. We could forget about any leave.

We ask HQ. They leave the decision to Elieser. He is an old Haganah man and asks for our opinions. Two camps develop. I am convinced that we should return immediately. That would be a brave decision. But it is exactly that which gives us a chance. This opinion gains the upper hand. Now every minute counts. We set off.

* * *

This time we enjoy the drive. We are free of the heavy trucks and drive at full speed. Whenever Reuven slows for a moment, our jeep jumps. Our bodies have long been mashed to pulp. We laugh and swear. Suddenly Elieser halts. We have gone the wrong way. Hell. We turn back and find our earlier tire tracks. It is easy to lose your direction in this desert. I look at the time: fifty minutes to sunrise.

"Meirke" Davidsohn, the Operations Chief of the brigade, is still sitting by the radio. Apparently the people at HQ are not sleeping tonight. He urges us on. Later we hear that they all remained in the radio room till the last moment – the company commander, the battalion commander, and all of the officers of the brigade.

We race past the Bedouin camp, without incident. Onward. We make a wide detour around the abandoned truck. We would dearly like to blow it up, but it is too late. It will fall into the hands of the Egyptians. A pity.

Finally we find the road. No ambush here either. Luckily for us the Egyptians are very reluctant to leave their positions during the night. Strange for an army that is not at all bad in other respects. A first silvery line on the horizon. There are the two trucks that broke down first. Blow them up? No. They may be recoverable later. We load what we can into the jeeps, until we have almost no room to move. But here we are safe from surprises. When it gets light we are somewhere near Zeita. We look at each other and can't help laughing. We look as though we have been rolled in flour. Everything is covered in the white dust of the Negev – the jeeps, our weapons, ourselves.

We break into song. The tension is gone. We are filled with an exaggerated cheerfulness, almost hysteria. As we approach Gat we can see the jeep of the company commander coming toward us. We know what he must be feeling – some pride and great joy: we are back without losses.

We stop singing. And the battle cry of the Foxes spreads across the plane. A strange, wild rendering of the foxes' natural cry: "Heiii, Haiii …!"

After we got back I was given twenty-four hours special leave, to notify the parents of Jochanan Silbermann. Not a pleasant duty. It was the first time that I had been in contact with the relatives of one of our fallen. It shook me. And for the first time I thought about what would be the best way to grieve for the dead of this war. How would I want to be mourned if I were to die tomorrow? In tearful hysteria or through an active struggle for definite ideals?

*   *   *

The Foxes' company was not stationed in the most forward positions. It acted in accordance with its special capabilities. We were connected with battalion HQ and sent on daily patrols along the border of our territory. We monitored the wide no-man's-land to the north of Beit Jibrin, as well as being sent on special missions.

These were our happiest three weeks in the army. We enjoyed almost complete freedom, our food supplies were plentiful, and our military duties were light. I lived together with two friends, Shalom Cohen and Israel Lebertov, in a small Arab house. We cleaned it and furnished it and called it "the Castle."

9 August 1948
Jassir

Humor at the front

We are in the mosque at Jaladiyya. Four idle men with a field telephone which connects the front positions. A ceasefire is in force. But by every phone in the region a bored man or woman is sitting. I pick up the receiver.

"Do you really have green eyes?" asks a warm male voice.

"Look into the telephone," the girl answers.

"And what about your hair?"

"Black as the night."

"What's your name, then?"

"My name," she giggles, "is Jocheved."

"Don't believe it," a third voice breaks in, "Judith is her name!"

"Hallo HQ," says another new voice, "I have an urgent report for you."

"Oh please," says the warm male voice, "can't you see that we are busy? The report can wait."

"Stop! Stop!" says Jocheved/Judith. "Give me the report."

The coded message bores me since I understand nothing: "Bravo, Whiskey, Juliet, Sierra, Alpha ..."

Time passes. A jeep arrives to relieve us.

* * *

That was our chance to disappear for a few hours. We raced to Tel Aviv, went for a meal in the town – and returned again.

In Rehovot we picked up a hitcher, a farmer heading for Be'er

Tuvia. As we made room for him he was impressed by our friendliness. In addition it seemed to be an honor for him to travel in a jeep of the Foxes.

There were four of us: Freddy Regenstreif, the driver, Shlomo Apfelbaum, a quiet, blond squad leader, Shalom Cohen, a roundish, self-satisfied fellow with a gigantic mustache, and me. In Gedera we stopped for a quick popsicle. Gedera marked the frontier between the civilized world and the "wild South."

Before we drove on, we got ourselves ready: Freddy pulled an enormous, rather dirty red cloth from under his seat, and wrapped it around his head. Shlomo rolled his sleeves right up to his armpits. Shalom took off his shirt and sat there half naked and we all put on our green driving glasses. The farmer watched us in puzzlement.

Freddy drove off at full speed. Just beyond Gedera there were deep pits in the road – tank traps. Normally you would drive through or around them in first gear. But not Freddy! Without slowing down, the jeep flew to the left, then to the right, and then to the left again. We knew Freddy and the tank traps, and were ready for it. But not our passenger. He nearly made a premature exit. At the last moment I managed to grab his collar and return him to his place.

After a while the fun really started. Freddy roared along. You need some practice to survive in a jeep like this at fifty miles an hour. For example you should not hold on to the machine gun, because it can spin around. Not to the machine gun mount, either, because it doesn't do your fingertips any good. And you should try and stop your head getting too near to the stock. All this theory was learned by our guest in a matter of seconds. Not that he enjoyed the lesson.

At sixty miles an hour we reached a state of ecstasy, which discharged itself in the Foxes' battle cries. Since the farmer was the only one without goggles, his eyes were running. He was hardly aware of his surroundings.

At seventy miles an hour it was Shalom Cohen's turn. That speed always has a strange effect on him. He pulled out his private Luger[6] and began firing into the air. And since we were approaching the front, it was time to try out the machine guns. One salvo after another.

Just then we were approaching the Be'er Tuvia turn-off. "This is where I get out" said our guest. The speedometer was reading over seventy-five miles per hour, but a second later we were at a standstill. We were all ready for it. But our passenger was not. He flew forwards and warmly embraced Freddy. The meeting of their skulls produced an interesting noise.

"Here you are," said Freddy.

"Actually I wanted to get out by that house over there."

"Certainly. Wait a moment," said Freddy politely.

"No! No! I'll get out here!"

"Are you sure?" asked Freddy in a friendly tone.

"Yes. Completely. Thank you very much."

We laughed all the rest of the way.

The humor of the front was a cover for the reality, which was not in the least funny. The Negev was still cut off, and we knew that the fighting could start again at any moment. All our operations had been nothing more than preparations. At night we would set off, four or six of us, to check on the enemy lines. We crept past their positions, looking for their telephone cables, and tapped them if we found one.

* * *

Between these activities we had time to work through our impressions. We sat on the balcony of our "castle" and talked. Never before had we had the time to talk about serious matters: our relations with Army HQ, the point of the war, our plans for the time after ...

11 August 1948
Jassir

After the war ...

"If I am still alive at the end of the war ..." said Yaakov Malishewitz with the faint smile of a daydream spreading across his face. The eternal theme of the frontline soldier, like Erich Maria Remarque's soldiers sitting in their trenches on the Western Front, or the Desert Foxes of the Second World War. Today it is we who are sitting in an Arab house full of fleas, in a miserable, deserted village on the Southern Front.

"If I am still alive ..." with the stress on the "If." Like every frontline soldier, Yaakov is certain, absolutely certain, that nothing is going to happen to him, of all people. But his brain tells him that the fighting will start up again, and that his chances of surviving to the end of the war are fairly slight.

Now we are all dreaming. After the war ... peace ...

"Anyone who has seen war with his own eyes and is not a pacifist is mentally ill" said Shalom. "Or a sadist" added Yaakov.

"First we have to return to civilian life" I say.

Long, deep silence. Everyone is imagining what that is like – to sit in a narrow, dusty office, to work eight hours in a factory, routine, day after day.

"You know what," says Yaakov, "it won't be easy for me, going back to all that."

* * *

We know what he means. We all feel the same. We have got used to a life of tension, life at the front. Our life is based on a few simple and unshakable principles: friendship until death; the mutual respect of soldiers who have been through umpteen battles; the sense of honor of people who don't want to die, but who regularly volunteer for highly dangerous missions. How will we be able to change our lifestyle for one completely different and alien to us?

"I spent two days in Tel Aviv. The life they lead there makes me sick. Schemes, patronage, sloth ... I don't know, I really feel that I won't be able to get used to that kind of life. If I say that I am at the front, they laugh at me and think I'm an idiot. If I went back there tomorrow, they would be making a fool of me at work and everywhere else ..."

"If only the comradeship that grew up here could continue ..." I dream.

"I don't believe it could," said Shalom. "It developed at the front, and after half a year of peaceful life it would be gone."

"I would love to travel the world. To see everything ..."

"You can't just run away from it," I start preaching. "We will have to make sure that the ideals we fought for become reality." But the idea is tempting. To travel, to hang around somewhere with no responsibilities. "I don't have the money for that," says Yaakov. "And I wouldn't take any from my father."

"Who needs money?" asks Shalom. He used to be in the British Navy and has seen a lot of the world. "You work on a ship, arrive in some harbor, Rome for example, and stay there until your money runs out. Then you get work on another ship. You can do that for six months or even a full year."

We dream. We are sitting on the deck of a ship, watching the sun go down, puffing on a pipe, and listening to the waves. No artillery, no tanks, no aircraft. Our lives are not threatened. Everything is OK.

"We could set off with a whole group of friends," adds Shalom. "We don't need anything. If there is no food, we just don't eat. That would be nothing new ..." "But then we would be adventurers," warns Yaakov, "and the way back would be even harder." "To hell with the way back," counters Shalom. "If we don't get what we are entitled to, we'll take it. Take my word for it." "But only if we are agreed on it," says Yaakov. He is watching a fly. Suddenly his hand slams down. The fly is squashed. We are experts at that.

"What are you talking about?" says Shalom. "The war is not over yet." Suddenly we all come to ourselves again. No one believes that the war is over. We are too near the front. In the distance we hear occasional shots.

With the words "if we are still alive after the war ..." Yaakov closes the discussion. We can all feel this "if" hanging over our heads.

It was exactly these "happy" days at Jassir that really brought home to us the awful side of war. Our main task was to prevent Arab civilians from entering the areas we had conquered. Hungry Arabs were crossing daily over the no-man's-land from Beit Jibrin, Agur, and Zakariyya into our areas around Kedima, Tel al-Safi, and Kfar Menachem. We were supposed to stop these movements.

On one of our patrols we stopped off at the Tel al-Safi position. Suddenly we noticed two Arab children running around among the soldiers and serving them. This unusual sight is imprinted in my memory. I wrote a little story about it.

13 August 1948
Jassir

Little prisoners

The resistance was broken. The enemy had evacuated the village. Now only occasional shots were coming from the mountain opposite. Now and then a bullet hummed past at a great height, with the sound of a tired bee. They were just firing at random without taking into account the distance. A counter-attack was no longer to be feared.

The men dispersed around the village and walked through the narrow alleys looking for prisoners, ammunition, and souvenirs. In particular for souvenirs. They were not looking for valuables. An Arab headdress, a dagger, some prayer beads were enough. One day the explosives expert came back with a decorative water pipe – that was something special.

Rafi split off from his group and headed down a dark alley. He wanted to be alone. The reason he gave was to check even the darkest alley, that his comrades were happy to ignore. After all, snipers might be lurking there. But that was just an excuse. What really drove him, as always, was a mixture of curiosity and a sense of adventure.

"At the front you can't afford to be an adventurer," his friends used to preach as he volunteered once again for a special task. "At the front you have to be an ordinary soldier, you understand? You get an order – then you go. No order – then keep your nose out of things that are nothing to do with you." And Joske the clown added dryly, "If I were to be killed on a job like that, it would annoy me till the end of my days."

Rafi cocked his Sten gun. Behind any of these wooden doors there could be an Arab sniper or just a Fellah who didn't want to leave the village of his ancestors. Strange that so very few had chosen this way. That must be an inheritance of slavery. They never were free. For generations they were the victims of foreign rulers.

What the hell, Rafi grumbled. These philosophical thoughts always descended on him when he made his way alone through an Arab village. It was like a curse. You shouldn't think too much about the dark side of war. It just makes your life more difficult. Maybe the others think the same, just don't dare talk about it because they don't want to appear soft?

Behind him a door clattered. A second later he was standing in front of a corpse dressed in black. For one moment he was a wild animal, with a well-oiled instinct for self preservation. In a single movement he had jumped to one side, turned, and shot. And now the corpse was lying there.

His heart had missed a beat, but now resumed. His first reaction was joy. His natural reflexes had worked. You could rely on them – in case of need, they would save him. That is the reward for a man who exposes himself to danger. The feeling that he has escaped from danger. Danger? What danger? He looks at the corpse. An old, emaciated Arab woman. She had probably stayed behind because she didn't have the strength to keep up with the others.

How could he have known that it wasn't an armed man? Self defense, that was all.

* * *

The old woman looked at him through half-closed eyes. Her mouth was askew, as if scornful of his feeble excuses. He wanted to run away. But he could not. Something drew him, forced him to enter that low, disorderly little room. An almost empty room. A broken scythe, a pile of straw in the corner, a torn, filthy mattress, a dirty plate, and a large mirror. The mirror annoyed him. Why was there a mirror in every Arab room? Rafi had no desire to see himself at that moment. The Sten was still loaded. He fired at the mirror and destroyed it.

* * *

On the ground lay a string of red prayer beads. That was one of the reasons he had gone away from the group. He wanted to find some prayer beads for Rinah. With childish pride she had shown him a keffiyeh[7] that Moshe had given her, and had asked him for some prayer beads. And he, the great war hero, did not tell her that Moshe had probably got it from a dead soldier or a fleeing Fellah. He had kept quiet about that and promised her the prayer beads. Now he had them. Probably the old woman's only inheritance. He kicked the prayer beads into the pile of hay.

Outside he heard loud voices. He leapt out and saw one of his comrades struggling with an Arab boy of about twelve years of age, with black hair and dark eyes. Even in this moment of extreme fear his dirty face was beautiful. And the fear in his eyes was contradicted by the pride in his face.

"What are you doing with him?" asked Rafi.

"I'm telling you, he's a spy. Just a dirty Arab spy. Hiding in dark rooms, to disappear in the night and betray our positions to the Egyptians!"

"You can't do anything to him," said Rafi with apparent

calm. "You must have heard what Israel said last time. He would chew the head off anyone who maltreats a prisoner. We will have to hand him in."

Under interrogation the boy said almost nothing. He hadn't left the village, because it was his village. Just that – his. Moshe, who was cross-questioning him in fluent Arabic, looked at him in amazement. He had never heard this simple argument from an Arab prisoner before.

"What shall we do with him?" he asked. That was one of the nice things about him. He discussed things with his subordinates, as though he were still in the Haganah. "I think we should send him to the other refugees. He can't tell the Egyptians anything that they don't already know."

The boy, understanding nothing, looked at the group of wildly bearded soldiers, one after another. "This is my village," he murmured. "Mine! Mine!"

Rafi gazed at him. In his mouth he still had that bitter taste from earlier on. He liked the boy. Perhaps he is an orphan. If he goes to the refugees, he will starve like them. Rafi had an idea.

"Maybe he can stay with us?" he suggested.

His comrades looked at him as if he was mad. "What do you mean – stay with us? What on earth for? So that he can run over to the enemy at any moment and provide them with information?"

Rafi tried to convince the others. "All this talk of spying, that's just rubbish. An idiotic idea. And if he stays here," with the right argument at last, "he could serve us. Bring food. Wash the dishes and simply make our life easier. Why should we send him away? So that he can serve the Egyptians?"

"That is an idea," said Shmulik. And a general discussion broke out. Pro-Hassan (for that was his name) and anti-Hassan parties quickly formed. And it was the wildest who spoke in favor of Hassan. It soon became clear: Hassan would stay.

* * *

The village stood on a hill. One of those special hills that decorate the south of the country, and under which lie the ancient cities of the Israelites and the Philistines. Most of the houses were built into the slope. At the top stood some ruins from earlier times, overlooking a wonderful view across the landscape. Down below, at the foot of the hill, stood a few new houses belonging to the more prosperous farmers.

As usual the command post occupied the beautiful houses near the well. Next to them was the kitchen, the makeshift showers, the mess, and first company's quarters. The two other companies settled in around the top of the hill, and took it in turns to man the observation post.

Hassan's main duty was to bring the meals up the hill from the kitchen. Everyone was pleased with him. Three times a day he would appear at the top, riding a white donkey which carried the containers. Between mealtimes he washed the dishes, cleaned the showers – which he very rarely used himself – polished our shoes, and occupied himself with similar tasks.

Although he was at everybody's service, he displayed a natural pride which amused everyone. He never refused a task. But he did everything proudly, as though he was a host doing his guests a favor to emphasize his hospitality.

In time we all started to spoil him, with the "wild" ones taking the lead.

They bought chocolate for him in the little canteen, and taught him to smoke cigarettes. The "softies" accused the "wild" ones of doing it to soothe their consciences. But in fact he was just as pampered by all of us.

Hassan accepted the chocolate with the gesture of a patronizing lord. He didn't make friends with anyone. Except Rafi. He literally worshiped Rafi. He cleaned his shoes and washed his clothes, without being asked to. The fact that Rafi was just a private soldier had nothing to do with this. Although comrades sometimes laughed about Rafi and his servant, they got used to the fact that Hassan belonged to Rafi, just as Nero, the company's little dog, was attached to Moshe.

* * *

Suddenly this idyll was destroyed. Jeeps appeared and conducted daily patrols, probing and observing the villages in no-man's-land and testing the strength of the enemy. After them appeared the officers from battalion HQ, a sign that usually meant that something was going to happen soon on this part of the front.

Then the details of the planned operation were announced. In two days, two battalions were to attack and capture the area up to the mountain peaks. In the morning came the jeeps, and a general discussion started next to the canteen about the details of the operation.

"The Egyptians are completely in the dark," said Rubke, a jeep driver, who always covered his head with a red cloth. "We were in Agija just now, and the Fellaheen ran away after the first shots. There weren't even any Egyptian sentries. It will be like a hot knife through butter this time." And as if to emphasize his satisfaction, he handed Hassan a big piece of chocolate.

"If you keep messing around in no-man's-land, they are bound to get an idea that something's going on," said Moshe in an unfriendly tone. The self-confidence of the jeep crews annoyed him. "Don't worry," said Rubke, "they think it's just our usual harassment."

* * *

"What is happening? Where's the food?" The typically hoarse voice of Janek, the commander of the second section, rang out over the hilltop. "No need to make a fuss! It's on its way!" said Moshe absent-mindedly and put down the receiver. He was engrossed in the details of the upcoming operation. "Hey, Dudik," he called outside, "tell Hassan to hurry up and take the food up to the top." A few minutes later Dudik poked his head into the tent. "Don't bother me," grumbled Moshe, "can't you see that I'm busy?"

"Hassan is not there," Dudik reported.

"Shall I go and have a look for him?" asked Moshe in a mean and ironic tone. "Have a look in the kitchen or in the mess and find him. They are getting hungry up there."

Dudik didn't move. "I have looked everywhere. Hassan has disappeared. And the Messiah is gone too." "The Messiah" – that was his white donkey.

This time Moshe woke up. "Get Rafi. Quick. And tell Jossi to get a jeep ready."

Rafi was pale. Dudik had already told him. "When did you last see him?" asked Moshe. His voice, usually so sleepy, was suddenly sharp and clear.

"I don't know … three hours ago he was still in the mess … what do you intend to do?"

"What can I do? I will go after him in the jeep."

Rafi hesitated for a moment. "Moshe, take me with you" he said quietly, almost in a whisper.

Moshe looked at him for a long time, his eyes expressing something like pity. "Listen to me," in an unusually gentle tone, "it would be better for you to stay here. You can't make any friends at the front. That only causes problems. Particularly if you are talking about an Arab boy. It was a crazy idea from the start. I should never have allowed it. Now it can cost us lives … if I find him near the front line, I will have to shoot him from a distance." Moshe was known in the battalion as a good shot.

"Still …" Rafi begged.

"Tfaddal.[8] But don't forget: I warned you. You are too sentimental for things like this."

* * *

When they were standing on the second hill, they saw the white donkey and its rider disappear between the houses of the village of Agija – the village that was cleared that morning by the jeeps. Moshe, himself at the wheel, raced across the field at seventy miles an hour. The jeep was bouncing like crazy.

In the main street of the village they suddenly spotted the donkey Messiah on its own. Moshe stopped. Rafi jumped out and disappeared between the houses. Moshe cut the motor and followed him. Rafi stood still and listened. From one of the windows he heard a rustling. He approached on tiptoe, holding the Sten at the ready. He stopped by the narrow window and looked in cautiously.

At first he saw nothing. Then his eyes slowly adapted to the darkness in the room. He could make out Hassan, on his knees before a figure lying in a dark corner.

"Abu Musa," he whispered, but his voice echoed in the little room. "Can you hear me? It is me, Hassan. Hassan Ibn Darwisch …" The figure muttered something. It had probably not heard Hassan at all.

"You must be able to remember me. I am Hassan, you taught me to read and write …" The figure stirred and raised itself into a sitting position. It was a very old Arab with a thin white beard. Old and blind. He smiled, revealing his two remaining teeth. His hands groped in the dark until they found Hassan's head. "Hassan. Hassan Ibn Darwisch. God bless you."

"They have all run away," said Hassan tearfully. "They all fled and the Yahud[9] are laughing about them. Only you remained."

"Inshallah – it is God's will," murmured the old man. Did he understand the boy at all?

"I have brought you something to eat. Good food," said Hassan. "I took it from the Yahud. I'll bring you some more tomorrow. Every day I will bring something." Rafi jumped. Someone was touching him. It was Moshe. He was also listening through the window.

Slowly they walked back to the jeep.

In the vehicle Moshe burst out laughing. "You are sentimental and crazy. You have almost infected me." But his laugh sounded somehow artificial … "Doesn't matter," he said after a while. "Main thing is, he'll come back."

Apart from the military operations and occasional serious discussions, we led our "normal" life in Jassir. We had disputes and friendships, we had a "home" to live in, and there were a few girls there for us to compete over. And above everything hung the great motto, the existential wisdom of a forward base "Eat and drink – you might be dead tomorrow."

Front Ants

The heavy losses of the eleven days between the two ceasefires had depleted the lower command level. Many squad leaders had fallen. Leaders were missing from all the battalions of the brigade. To fill these gaps a special course for squad leaders was organized at brigade level. In its three months' duration it was to cover (nearly) all topics which used to be reserved for officers' courses.

Most of the veterans of the brigade were selected for the course. They met each other again in the tents for the trainees. They were the ones who had survived dozens of engagements and who had also refused all the chances of setting themselves up at the rear. This group consisted of fighters with a clear attitude: they came from the front, and to the front they would return.

5 September 1948
Training course for squad leaders

School for combat leaders

The time for lights out is approaching. The men are lying on their beds, exhausted from the long day's training. Their muscles are aching. They are not used to courses and hard training any more. The two on watch duty take their rifles, swear in the best army tradition, and go out.

"What a dark night," grumbles one of them, "almost like in Isdud."

"What?" comes a voice from a far corner of the big tent. "You were at Isdud? Which unit?"

A discussion quickly starts about that operation. Two others in the tent were also there. Each recounts what they experienced on that night. One who took part in the northern assault compares notes with the one from the west. Together they piece together a more complete picture of the operation.

* * *

That is typical for the conversations in this tent. A chance remark develops into something more serious. Mistakes that have been made become clear, and the analysis covers successes, characters, and commanders. The people here are no simple soldiers. The ones who live here will be commanding units in future battles. This is the school for future leaders of combat units.

* * *

There isn't a battle on the southern front that is not represented here. The ten of us here have been everywhere, have seen everything – as simple infantry soldiers, in the crews of heavy weapons, in armored units, or on the jeeps. All are battle hardened.

A training exercise: you jump up, run a few steps, and throw yourself to the ground. On the right the machine gun unit runs, takes position, and fires at the imaginary enemy. And suddenly reality dissolves and another scene comes to mind: Deir Muheisin, the first days of "Nachshon," the rows of the assault, snipers from the left, automatic fire from the right, you jump forwards …

* * *

Or you sit in the theory tent – with paper and pencil in front of you. An officer with glasses draws the lines of an imaginary landscape on the board: a gentle slope, a steep hill, a valley, a wadi that snakes through the area. And again you are in another world: in the dark of night, returning from an operation behind enemy lines, you notice that you have lost your way. The jeep drives slowly, crosses a wadi, you examine the map in the feeble light of a lamp, you scan the sky for the Pole Star, shrug your shoulders, and drive on. Maybe you'll get through. Maybe not. And when you eventually find your unit, your comrades embrace you like a lost son …

* * *

These men are here out of conviction. They didn't come in search of promotion. They could easily have "arranged" a comfortable life for themselves. They know the responsibility a commander bears in combat. And they still chose this route. But if anyone says he likes war, they would regard him as mad.

They are sitting in the big tent. Tanned, tired faces are turned toward David Shani. He is responsible for the training course, the defender of Ibdis, and gives a talk about "leadership." Everyone knows that they will soon be responsible for the lives of hundreds of young men. They all wonder: are we capable of that? Will we be successful? And if you look at their faces the answer is clear. Yes. They will succeed.

Everyone knew how great was the responsibility that he would have to take after the course finished. We all tried to imagine what an ideal commander would be, how he would behave in this or that situation. At night we lay on our beds and discussed this. And slowly we formed an image of a good commander, liked by his men, a leader and friend for them. But who behaves independently in relation to his own superiors. A commander with all the characteristics which distinguish the brigade as a whole.

A long time ago, after the death of Menachem Brotzki in Iraq Suweidan, I wrote a story about the commander who is loved by his men. Now I reformulated this story in an attempt to present my idea of a good commander.

16 September 1948
Squad leader course

The reprimand

"I don't know how he does it," said Israel in a voice dripping with envy. "When my people have kitchen duty, they get ill. His wash the dishes and sing. I need three squad leaders to haul my men out of bed in the morning. His men jump up happily, as if they had been dreaming of going for the morning run. He is a magician!"

"And I'm telling you," company commander Shmuel joined in, "he is stirring the people up. He is spoiling them. Do you know what he did yesterday? At lunchtime he sat with the ordinary soldiers and left the squad leaders alone at the commanders' table."

Shmuel, the company commander, was getting worked up. He always got excited when he talked about Menashke. And that means that he was always excited when he was in the Officers' Club. Because when he was there, he never talked about anything else.

This Menashke. Devil take him! He had discovered a new idea of leadership and took no notice of theory. His colleagues could not deny that his unit was the best and acted in combat as though they had made a pact with the devil. But after the fighting Menashke allowed his people unbelievable things.

"It can't carry on like that," said Shmuel and raised his voice, so that the battalion commander, who was sitting in a corner, could also hear him. "He is demoralizing our people. You can't spoil soldiers like that. We'll all pay for it in the end ..."

The battalion commander raised his eyebrows, but behaved as though he hadn't heard anything. He didn't like Shmuel, this chubby commander of the HQ company, who never saw combat. He smelled of bureaucracy. And he was always the first to add new stripes to his shoulder straps. But in this case he was right, absolutely right.

There was no doubt about it. Menashke was going too far. Alright, if he didn't want to appear in the Officers' Club and preferred to spend his free time with the ordinary soldiers – that was his business. But what happened last week, that was something else altogether. Menashke set off with his people for a night exercise, even though rest had been ordered for that evening. And the radio officer had reported to him later that the night exercise had finished up in Tel Aviv's Mugrabi Square.[1]

Why didn't I say anything at the time? he asked himself. Ah yes, I remember. The next day the company was in action and Menashke's unit captured Position Number 37. That was very good. Two men fell and Menashke himself received a light head wound. After that it didn't make any sense to reopen the matter.

The murmur of conversation fell silent. Menashke stood in the doorway. He smiled, as though appearing in this place was the most normal thing in the world, walked across to the company commander, and asked him some questions about the planned operation. In his hand he was holding a colorful map.

The first to recover from his paralysis was Shmuel. With a false smile he opened his arms and approached Menashke. "Welcome!" he called. "A hearty welcome, Menashke! So you finally decided to honor us with your presence! Take a seat. Make yourself at home. Would you like a cup of tea, perhaps?" And with exaggerated gestures he summoned the young girl who served the officers.

"No, thanks," Menashke answered briskly. "I just want to clarify a few points. The map seems to be inaccurate here ..." Shmuel didn't give up. "A pity, really a great pity," he said pompously, "we would so dearly like to know why it is that you sit at a table together with the ordinary soldiers. We would really be very interested to hear. Perhaps we can learn something from you ..."

That hit a nerve. Menashke flushed bright red, and the scar on his forehead shone like the rising sun. "Oh, you don't like that? That I sit together with the ordinary soldiers? Ordinary soldiers, eh?" His calm was icy.

"Were you at Ibdis? Oh, excuse me. At that time you had an important position in Tel Aviv. As for me, I happen to have been there. That wasn't at all pleasant, incidentally. It was more like hell. Artillery, mortars, aircraft, tanks. One assault after the other ... On the hill were eighty ordinary soldiers. Just ordinary soldiers. What I mean is, in the morning there were eighty. In the evening there were only twenty. The next morning eighty new ones arrived, and they knew that they would only be twenty by evening.

"And I ask you, why did they come? They could have left. Any one of them could have left. Did they remain because of this bullshit that you call discipline? That evaporates when the first shell lands in your trench?

"So, what kept them in that hell? I will tell you: it was decency. The self-respect of the ordinary soldier. They didn't run away because they wouldn't leave their comrades in a mess, they wouldn't disgrace the honor of their unit. They simply had a bit of conscience. That is all.

"And you are so superior you think you can trample on the self-respect and honor of the ordinary soldier. You want to make a machine out of him, an order-obeying machine. But if there is a new Ibdis tomorrow, nothing will keep the men in that hell. Nothing. Not your bullshit, no standing to attention, no military saluting, and not even the olive leaves[2] on your shoulders."

The club had fallen silent. Menashke walked to the door. Then he looked again at the astonished officers and continued:

"A month ago, in Isdud, I was lying wounded in the field. Five meters from the Egyptian positions. Four ordinary soldiers got me out of there. One of them was himself seriously wounded in the process. God help you if you find yourselves in battle without such ordinary soldiers around you, and only obedient robots."

* * *

The next night the company set out again. The aim was to capture one of the big police stations that the British had left to the Arabs.

Menashke's unit was to lead the assault. His people would crawl to the fence and, while armored vehicles attracted the enemy fire, blow a hole and capture the building.

The men crawled for almost two hours. Any other unit would have long since changed to jumping. But the men were well trained and used to long periods of crawling. They reached the fence without losses.

With their elbows and heels the men scraped at the ground. There was no natural cover. Bullets whistled over them, mortar shells thundered, and machine guns rattled. The soldiers lay motionless on the ground. They wanted to begin the assault and put an end to the intolerable tension. Menashke was lying in the first row, with the runner, the radio operator, and the medic directly behind him. In the hellish noise the radio operator shouted reports to him. The din was too loud for the enemy to hear him.

"Ask if we can begin the attack!" shouted Menashke.

"The order is: withdraw immediately!" called the radio operator after a minute.

Menashke couldn't believe his ears. He crawled back to the radio to make sure that he had heard correctly. Maybe the armored vehicles had been hit so the chief had decided to call off the assault?

Menashke was boiling with anger. To withdraw – now? He considered for a moment. Then he had made his decision and called to the radio operator: "You didn't hear that message. Understood?"

"No," said the operator.

"I am deaf. You are wounded. The radio is not working. OK?"

"No," he answered.

"Go to hell!" shouted Menashke and gave the sappers the sign to blow the fence. The way was free for his people to begin the assault.

* * *

The next morning the unit was relieved in the captured building, and Menashke returned to base with his men. Everyone was excited about the dramatic success. The building was an important strategic position and three attacks had already failed.

"Ah, there you are," said the company commander. "The battalion commander keeps asking for you. You are to report to him immediately." And his expression said: "I'm sorry, my friend. We are in the army. Where would we be if everyone just went his own way?"

As Menashke entered the chief's room, he knew that he had gone too far this time. The long-awaited collision between them was unavoidable. He, the product of the Palmach, and his boss, who tried to emulate the traditions of the British Army.

"Menasheh Jaari" said the chief. In critical moments he always called sinners by their full names. "You have committed a serious misdemeanor. You have contravened a fundamental principle of the army – discipline. You did not execute a clear command ..."

He spoke for almost a quarter of an hour, and each word was like a hammer blow. This is the end of me, thought Menashke. I will be demoted, thrown out of the army, perhaps even sent to prison. This is the end of my military career.

"Menasheh Jaari," the chief wound up his talk, "in accordance with an order from the brigade commander, I hereby reprimand you severely for violation of the rules of discipline of the Israel Defense Forces!" Menashke was as red as a tomato, but in his head a glimmer of hope was flickering.

The chief busied himself with the papers on his desk, as though he had a lot to do. "By the way," he added as an afterthought, "before I forget: this morning I received the confirmation from the brigade commander: you are promoted to company commander."

One day I had organized a "story evening." The comrades took it in turns to recount their memories of earlier battles. The idea was to learn from our experiences. The evening was dedicated to the topic "The good commander."

Passing scenes appeared before us. Commanders whose behavior in combat had made an unforgettable impression. The wounded David Shani, in defense of Ibdis. Aryeh Kotzer, who saved a unit of jeeps in Beit Affa at the cost of his own life. Avraham Pulvermacher, known as Polli, who was mortally wounded in the final assault on Beit Affa, but wouldn't himself to be evacuated before the other wounded had been treated. Yitzhak Pundik, who led a unit's assault from the front, to save his people who were surrounded by Arabs and British.

* * *

One day I discovered a harrowing document in a newspaper: the obituary written by Dr Elieser Rachmilevitch for his son Yaakov, our company medic, who had fallen in Isdud. He wrote:

"Your commanders, my son, did not mourn you. The battalions of the Haganah, in whose ranks you fought for several years, did not honor you. Your comrades too, who you treated in battle and whose lives you perhaps saved, have forgotten you. Your parents learnt the terrible news that you had fallen on 4 July 1948, in a chance encounter with a young woman in the street. "The news is already three weeks old that Yaakov, the medical orderly, fell in the battle for Isdud," she told us ...

Don't be sad, my son. Do not grieve. One day Israel will live in peace. Then a new generation will honor those who gave their lives for freedom. This new generation will appreciate your kind, will recognize you as heroes who saved Israel and brought freedom.

And I, your bereaved father, what can I say to you? No gravestone will commemorate you, because we don't know your resting place. Only your image, my son, I will carry that in my heart till the last of my days.

With love, your father Dr Elieser Rachmilevitch."

* * *

During the fighting we often thought of our parents. If we thought about the possibility of dying in battle, we didn't think about ourselves, but about them. And if one of our comrades fell, our first thoughts were for the father, the mother. But we never dared to visit the parents of our fallen.

I had the feeling that the time had come to explain the attitude of our fighting comrades to the bereaved parents. Not to comfort them. But to free them of the terrible fear that his comrades had forgotten their fallen son.

22 September 1948
Squad leader course

Letter to a bereaved father

I felt shame in the depths of my heart as I read the awful words you used to formulate your obituary for your son, company medical orderly Yaakov Rachmilevitch.

Yaakov, the medic …

I can remember that night. It was very dark. We are marching in a long column and making a detour around the Egyptian tanks. We cross a deep wadi. Visual contact between the vanguard and those following is lost. I run forward to report this. A hand grenade falls from my belt. I bend down to pick it up, and at that moment we come under fire from close by. I lie on the ground. Someone falls on me. I want to push him to one side, but he says quietly: "I have been hit in the back. Bandage me." I know this voice. It is Yaakov, the medic. He is treated quickly. A few minutes later I notice him marching on with the others as if nothing has happened.

Eight hours later the fighting is still intense. We lie in soft sand and wait. Ahead of us two companies have already been committed to the battle. Suddenly we hear our commander: "All medics over here!" One unit has heavy losses, their medic has fallen. All the medics run over. Yaakov too. The unit in question is about a kilometer away from us. The ground between us is flat, with no cover. Yaakov runs crouching over to the company that needs help. After that I didn't see him any more …

* * *

"Your commanders, my son, did not mourn you. The battalions of the Haganah, in whose ranks you fought for several years, did not honor you. Your comrades too … have forgotten you" you, the father, wrote.

I can remember another scene: we have just returned from action. We are lying beneath trees and expecting enemy aircraft. Filthy, hungry, with red eyes, and shaken by the experiences of the last twelve hours, we comrades sit there. The tension has not yet faded. We say what we have seen. We give the names of the dead, the wounded.

Anyone who could hear us would think – as you would too – that we had hearts of stone, that the fate of our comrades left us cold. But that is not true. We are just trying to fool ourselves. Because every name is a heavy blow for us. Each name brings thousands of memories.

We, who have seen our comrades die, we know the same thing can happen to us tomorrow or the day after. We talk in tones of indifference. But no one apart from us knows the truth about these moments. The shock of the first hours that saves us from going mad.

No, bereaved father, we have not forgotten Yaakov! We have forgotten no one who was torn from our ranks. How could we forget? When every hour, every minute, experiences like this mark us for life.

* * *

Another unforgettable scene: the evening when we saw combat for the first time.

The whole battalion is stretched out in a long column heading for the forward base. On our backs we are carrying a heavy burden: our weapons, our equipment, and our personal things. We are almost collapsing under the load, staggering like drunks. Our brains have stopped working. Somewhere in this area is the enemy. Our unit is securing the head of the column. The damp earth sticks to our soles.

Suddenly we come under fire. From so near, that we can see the flames from the muzzles. We fall instinctively to the ground. Our pulses race. It is our baptism of fire.

We stick to the ground, press our faces into the mud, dig ourselves in with our fingernails and the toes of our shoes. Someone near us is groaning and calls in a whisper "Medic!" And one of us gets up from the protective ground, runs stooping to the wounded man, lies next to him, and treats his wounds.

Yaakov, the medic.

Do you think, bereaved father, that scenes like this will be forgotten? Can be forgotten? These are really moments when our personality is shaped and formed on the anvil of life.

* * *

Why, you ask, did we not visit you? Why did we not try to console you? Do you have an idea, can you imagine how we feel in front of the relatives of our fallen comrades? How we stand there and are ashamed to be still alive? We are embarrassed to be spared by the bullet that deprived you of your dearest. A fighting soldier knows this look because it is so understandable, so natural. This expression which says to him "My God. Why did the bullet have to hit my son. And you stand there so healthy and lively, while our son is mouldering in his grave ..."

Yes, father. Even the bravest soldier, who has carried dozens of his comrades on his back away from the firing line, who has charged the enemy, and withstood the attacks of tanks. This soldier is afraid of the family of a fallen man. That is why he does not visit the relatives of his fallen comrades. Even though he knows that his honor makes it his duty.

* * *

"We don't know your resting place ..." With these words you end your obituary.

It is a terrible tragedy for the parents when their fallen son is left in the field because there is no possibility of recovering his body. We know your feelings, father, because they are our own as well. How many of us have been hit while attempting to recover the body of a fallen comrade? How often have the best among us volunteered to look for a comrade who was left just a few meters from the enemy lines?

"Then a new generation will honor those who gave their lives for freedom," you write. No, it won't take future generations to commemorate and honor him. The fallen will first of all be honored by those who have suffered with them, who shared their joy and pain. Those who survive, those who come through this terrible test, they will remember.

The End of the Ceasefire

*O*n the evening of 14 October 1948, a Saturday, we assembled on *the parade ground for our usual celebration of the Sabbath. David Shani stood up and read us in a quivering voice the following battle bulletin.*

> **COMBAT HQ DEATH TO THE INVADERS**
> **BATTLE BULLETIN**
> **15 October 1948**
> **FORWARDS TO THE DAY OF DECISION**
>
> *The ceasefire is dead. The war goes on. The decisive battle has begun. We have had enough of attacks without retaliation! Bombardment and shelling without an answer! Destruction of our farms without a chance of peace! The ceasefire is dead and its body will be buried.*
>
> *The Egyptian Army is facing us and preparing a campaign to destroy our settlements in the south and to capture the Negev. We are the only ones who can hold back the enemy. They will not withdraw until we smash their illusions. We didn't want this war. They chose it! The enemy began it. We will finish it!*
>
> *We had to win – and we have won!*
>
> *We had to defeat the enemy – and we have defeated them!*
>
> *We said at the time: if the war starts again, we will commit ourselves forcefully and with even more energy. And if necessary, we will eradicate the enemy.*
>
> *Brothers, the hour has come! We were called upon to drive the enemy out of our homeland. Day after day they bombarded our*

villages under the guise of the ceasefire, and fired on our positions. Farouk's slaves, do they want war? Then they will get it!
And they will savor every last drop of it. We will commit ourselves with all our strength from today. We shall not rest before
we can deliver to the State of Israel the liberated Negev.

Soldiers! Officers!
All our experience – one fist!
All our strength – one fist!
All our hate – one fist!
All our love – one fist!
And with this fist, and in the certain knowledge that this will
be the last battle –
On to the liberation of the Negev!

The enthusiasm was enormous. It was clear to us: this was the time of
harvest for the seed we had sown in Ibdis, in Negba, and on Hill 105. At
last the initiative was in our hands. We packed our things. We were sure
that the battalion would recall us. How could they fight with the most
experienced men sitting in a training course?

Then came the disappointment. It was decided not to break off the
course. The battalion commanders explained that the need for trained
leaders was greater than that for fighting soldiers.

On 16 October an infantry unit captured Beit Chanun and thus cut
off the Egyptian forces between Isdud and Huleiqat from their HQ in
Gaza. On the next day the brigade fulfilled its historic task and kicked
open the door to the Negev with tremendous force.

Josh's company took Hill 113 and Matti's company captured the
position on the big crossroads in an assault with fixed bayonets. That
was the same company whose darkest hour was the surrender of Hill 69
due to an incompetent commander.

One blow followed another. Units of our battalion captured
Kawkaba; the jeeps, Samson's Foxes, chased the enemy and captured
Beit Tima. The next day two battalions of the brigade captured the positions around the village of Huleiqat. It was man-to-man fighting with
knives, claws, and teeth, a brutal fight, like hardly any other in this war.

* * *

In the course a rebellion broke out. We were involved only in small operations in the eastern part of the front, we harassed the enemy near

Zakariyya, helped our comrades to establish themselves in Qubeiba, and carried out long patrols in the area around Agur and Zakariyya. But our comrades were involved in heavy fighting. David Shani's explanations that the battalion was in great need of trained superiors did not help. A "secret" committee, with representatives from all battalions, had decided to press decisively for our return to our units and to the front.

The first lists of dead and wounded had meanwhile reached us. The losses were heavy. In the battle for Huleiqat our "Bulli," Chaim Bulman, fell together with many of his people. Yaakov Burstein, "Meshi," "Musa" Wassermann, Yaakov Velichkovski, all members of our former company, were wounded. Shlomo Apfelbaum, my jeep commander in the Jassir days, was mortally hit.

When we got this news, we declared unambiguously: with or without permission, we are going to "desert" and return to our units. We packed the essentials in little bags and agreed to leave that night.

At the last moment the brigade gave in. They did refuse to terminate the course and send us back to our old units. But the participants in the course would be sent to the front as a separate fighting company.

* * *

We were to replace the ravaged company that had captured Huleiqat. The whole front was awaiting an Egyptian counter-attack. We knew that a whole Egyptian brigade was trapped between Isdud and Majdal. They would not surrender before making a desperate attempt to break out. We set up the Vickers[1] that the enemy had left behind and waited.

The unburied bodies of dead Egyptians were scattered all over the field around us. It was a sight that would have engendered pacifistic thoughts in the most hard-hearted.

21 October 1948
A trench in Huleiqat

Conversation with the dead

A cloud of smoke rises from the Gaza to Majdal road. The men keep their heads down in their trenches. The shell whistles in and explodes ten meters away. The heads are raised again. No casualties. The trenches, constructed by the Egyptians with great care and expertise, have proven their high quality.

In front of us the great plain of the land of the Philistines. Ahead of us the blue sea. To the right, Majdal, the center of the trapped enemy forces. To the left of us, Nir Am, Gvaram, and Yad Mordechai.[2] Somewhere to the north the police station of Iraq Suweidan winks at us as if the enemy wanted to remind us that the fighting is not yet over.

All around us the debris of the recent battle. Bloody knives, ammunition boxes, discarded water bottles, knapsacks, a small artillery piece disabled by its fleeing crew.

Just two days ago Egyptian soldiers were here. They were the ones who kept the Negev isolated and maintained the connection between their forward units and the rear. All that remains of them is the signs of their flight. A dirt-covered rifle is lying over there. Someone brought it here from a foreign country, kept it clean, and wrote his name on its shoulder sling. Where is this someone now? Was he killed? Or did he run away leaving his rifle behind?

This is the slope where Bulli fell. I remember the song that he taught us in those distant days: "The world is so beautiful and so good ..." I shake off the memory. Over there is the Vickers that mowed him down with his people. The barrel is still pointing at the slope they stormed. The Egyptian was standing here and firing until the last, when they reached him and left him dead beside his weapon.

Behind the positions lies a row of the enemy dead, still unburied. The stink is awful. Still something draws me there. I want to look into their faces.

A broad-shouldered Arab with a pointed beard is lying on his back. The bullets hit him in the stomach and his trousers are stained with blood. His twisted face could almost be laughing. His eyes are wide open – the glassy eyes of a corpse.

For a moment I converse with him, this dead enemy. What brought him here? Military obedience? Idealism? Was he married? Perhaps he had children? The ways of Fate are curious. If our comrade had just held his weapon a few millimeters differently, this man might have now been sitting in a cafe in Majdal writing a letter to his wife, or dreaming about other women. Now he is lying here. His fingers are clutching at the ground, and it is hard to say whether what is lying here is a man or simply something in the form of a man.

Another is lying over there. Black face, mangled with knife cuts. Evidently one of those who did not run away, who made a last stand fighting with teeth and claws. What was it that made him prefer death to life? An order? His sense of honor?

There a young woman is lying. What is she doing here? Was she seeking pleasure, was she accompanying a young officer – and did she die because a bullet fired from a distance cannot distinguish between male and female? She looks lost among all the male corpses.

I turn my back on the dead. Five yards from here life is in full swing. Unshaved young men make jokes, examine captured weapons, investigate the heavy Vickers. This Vickers, which caused many casualties in our own ranks, also saved many lives. When our comrades had just established themselves here and the Egyptian counter-attack began, an Egyptian prisoner showed our people how to use the weapon. And since there was plenty of ammunition, the heavy automatic weapon was immediately turned on its previous owners.

On the ground a booklet in Arabic. I try to decipher the title: Wasarat al-difa al-watani – the Art of War.

At a desk, in a world of words and ideas, perhaps war is an "art." Here it is brutal reality: life against life, fragments of steel that bore into living flesh, the whistle of approaching death, and foxholes for protection or for dying in.

On 22 October another ceasefire was announced. But we remained in our position at Huleiqat. We were sure that the enemy would violate the ceasefire to free his trapped forces.

In a brave and risky operation the enemy succeeded in escaping the siege without a fight. On a dark night their sappers laid wire nets over the soft sand of the beach at Beit Chanun. All their forces and their heavy weapons got out. Only along the road, between the police station of Iraq Suweidan and Iraq al-Manshiyya did a large unit of three thousand men remain behind, and held on without any chance of escape.

The losses of the big operation, which bore the name "the Ten Plagues," were immense and particularly heavy in the ranks of the lower commanders. Brigade HQ gave the order for the course to be continued and speeded up.

* * *

We learn from the newspaper that the General Staff has introduced new regulations for leadership and conduct. We, the veterans of the southern front, rejected these regulations from the depths of our hearts. They would mean the beginning of the end of the peoples' army that saved the state in its most critical days, that routed the enemy, and that fought successfully to open the way to the Negev.

Animated discussions broke out among the participants in the course. Most of us didn't take it seriously. Is there anything more ridiculous than forbidding a soldier to grow a beard? But I knew: it was a considered decision, and the result would be a complete change in the spirit of the army. It would mean the final victory of the rear over the front.

3 November 1948
Squad leader course

The soul of Nachshon

The first drops of rain fall on the tent. Someone wakes me – it is my turn for guard duty. It is cold outside. The wind is howling, and it looks as though the whole camp will soon be blown right over the next hill.

I feel cold. I rummage in my box until I can feel the softness of wool. There is the pullover. I fold it in two, clap the edges together, and pull the result over my head.

Sock hat! Sock hat! … in the darkness I begin to dream. And in this dreamy state a longing makes itself felt, a yearning for bygone days, for the days that were our finest in the army.

I look at my comrade's face and remember another night of guard duty. It was six months ago, in Hulda. He remembers it too. And we begin to remind each other of forgotten details of those days, we laugh, we are happy, our voices rise until someone complains from the neighboring tent: "What the hell! What is going on?"

Nachshon … a meal of dry bread and tinned sardines is consumed by the squad with grumbles and laughs … we march through the mud which sticks to our boots until we are walking as if we had high heels, like a pretty Parisienne … one hundred and fifty rounds and three hand grenades in the pockets of our Australian army jackets, and we look like bosomy girls … the hours of oppressive fear before our first engagement and the outbreak of joy during the assault, as we realize that our baptism of fire is behind us ... the meal of chicken in Deir Muheisin, the first Arab village that the Israeli army captured with the clear intention of conquest ... waiting endlessly in ambush, plagued by the burning sun and deadly boredom ... the drive to Jerusalem in a truck loaded with cheese ... the wonderful reception in Jerusalem, with the whole town standing there to cheer us on ... meeting our comrades of the Palmach at Castel, when all the earlier rivalry between Palmach and HISH was forgotten ... our first leave, when we sang "Believe me, the day will come" until we were hoarse, and the civilians on the road waved to us with love ... firing the salute at the grave of a fallen friend ... the patrol between the positions in the kibbutz, regularly passing the canteen where a pretty girl served cocoa and sandwiches, but refused to tell us her name ...

A whole generation pioneered a new yest for life. A generation that had grown up in the land, and whose nature first became clear when they set out for battle singing and laughing, who fell asleep in the forward bases half an hour before the decisive assault, who cursed lovingly and complained, but accepted the shortcomings of this unorganized army and who lived the special comradeship between soldier and soldier, and between soldier and commander.

* * *

The most striking phenomenon of those days was the relationship between soldiers and their superiors. The commanders did not yet have any stripes or olive leaves on their shoulders. The private was a fighting soldier, and the commander slept in the same tent as him (if there were any tents at all) and told stories about earlier battles. He was nothing more than a comrade with a bit more experience, whose authority came from his personality.

I can remember that day at a forward base, shortly before an operation, when we saw, for the first time, an officer with insignia – and we heard, for the first time, the command: "Officers – take your places." Not only did that seem absurd to us, but also to our commanders who fought side by side with us.

* * *

A further special feature of the Nachshon days was the absence of a military bureaucracy. This resulted in monotonous meals of sardines or bully beef, and the need to lug heavy equipment around on our backs. But in those days there was also another atmosphere in the army.

When we drove into town, we were the only ones in uniform. We walked through the streets with the sock hats on our heads and felt like kings. In street cafes no one asked us whether we had stripes or oak leaves. We would be asked whether we were at the front or not. Being at the front was the decisive thing, not the indications of rank, which didn't exist yet. It would never have occurred to anyone that a nice job in the bureaucracy would be more pleasant than lying in a damp tent at the front.

* * *

The days changed: artillery, aircraft, and tanks appeared. The sock hat disappeared. The steel helmet appeared. Perhaps steel protects our heads better than wool. But steel is cold. One helmet is like the next. They lack the individuality that distinguished thousands of sock hats, which were all different.

Of course it was absolutely necessary to replace the sock hat with the steel helmet. But were there not other ways to keep alive the spirit of the sock hat? The spirit of Nachshon, the spirit of this free army – even in a time when steel helmets were necessary?

The course ended on 6 November.

We were sent to the combat headquarters of our battalion, that was then situated in the ruins of Kawkaba. In the road next to the police station of Iraq Suweidan we met a soldier who was crying bitterly. He told us that barely an hour ago the police station had been taken.

There is no way to describe the feelings that were shared by all the soldiers of the brigade at that moment. Since May the fort had been a symbol of the superiority of the enemy. Wherever you stand in that region, south of Gedera or on the plains of the Negev, this fort is always visible on the horizon. Attack after attack broke on its walls. The best of our brigade died on its barbed wire.

And then something happened which shook us to the core. The population, drunk with victory, forgot the infantry which had made such sacrifices in the battle for this fortress. All credit was given to the tank unit which had taken the fort without losses, after most of the enemy forces had been destroyed by continuous barrages of heavy artillery.

Samson's Foxes came from the infantry. All the members of the company had fought as infantry soldiers in numerous battles. Even if we sat in jeeps, we saw ourselves as part of the infantry. We belonged to an infantry battalion in an infantry brigade. And even if we attracted a lot of attention, we still knew that we did no more and certainly suffered less than the other companies of the brigade. The "front ant," the simple infantry soldier, he was the real hero of this war.

I felt particularly bitter about the "Writers of the Israel Defense Force," who never took part in combat, but who provided the public with detailed reports. They did not see their task as accompanying the units in a night attack or in the assault on a fort, as thousands of reporters had done in the last world war.

A few days after the capture of the fort of Iraq Suweidan I sent the newspaper an article with the title "Honor the ants of the front!" I am sure the whole brigade stood behind its sentiments.

13 November 1948
Battalion HQ

Honor the ants of the front!

I flick through a magazine which has found its way along some tortuous path to our position on the front. So this is the way the front appears to our citizens.

Pretty pictures surround bombastic articles. The photographer and the writer may not themselves have driven to the front, but they still provide the public with the required "delicacies." Tanks, armored vehicles, jeeps, artillery pieces, aircraft, even horses! Also "Desert Animals" and "Samson's Foxes" – only one creature is missing: the front ant or, better, the infantry. The infantry soldier was not romantic enough, neither bombastic nor sufficiently attractive. "Why should I waste my efforts on this dingy creature," the photographer thought, "when there is a fine collection here of everything the public is interested in." And the writer did the same.

* * *

Days passed. The first aircraft crossed the sky. A boy smiled from the armored "Bren carrier." The poor infantry soldier has been forgotten. But even without the attention of photographers and reporters he carries out his task. In the bloody fighting around

Latrun it was he who made possible the opening of the Burma road to Jerusalem. He stormed the enemy at Isdud and stopped his advance. He assaulted Iraq Suweidan two, three, four times. He was not always successful. He often failed. His equipment was pitiful next to the Egyptian. He had – it was said – only two legs and a rifle. Not even a bayonet did he have in those days.

* * *

There, another picture: "The victors over the fortress of Iraq Suweidan." A wall perforated by tank shells, a tank, and a young soldier with goggles.

* * *

"Victor over the fortress of Iraq Suweidan" – doesn't Menachem Brotzki also deserve this title, he who ran at the head of one of the unsuccessful assaults and fell by the fence of the fortress? He was no tank driver, just a simple infantry soldier with healthy legs. If you want to publish photos, why not one of Ephraim Makovsky, who fell in the battle for Negba, trying to rescue a wounded comrade. Or one of Moshe ben-Moshe, a quiet and modest soldier, who met his end in a similar way? After all they are the ones who saved Negba from falling to the enemy, at a time when none of our aircraft could be seen in the sky.

Pilot, tank driver, man in a jeep, and gunner. They gave their all. They made an important contribution to victory. But don't forget – these are all just supporting weapons.

Support for whom? For those who have been forgotten from your beautiful photos. For that king in sackcloth, this thousand-footed giant, who sacrifices blood and sweat, who digs himself into the ground, the one who shoots a rifle, who storms and conquers – the soldiers of the infantry.

Honor the gray ants of the front! The fairytale figures that you are looking for with your cameras are supported by the millions of grains of sand of victory.

On my return to the battalion I received the order to report, together with my friend Shalom Cohen, to company number three and to take over command of a squad of infantry.

The order plunged me into a serious crisis. I knew that the use of the bayonet as an important weapon had reduced the value of the jeeps in relation to the value of the simple infantry soldiers. I knew that it was an important task to communicate the spirit of the brigade to newly arrived volunteers from abroad.

On the other hand I felt as if the door of my house had been slammed in my face. The company "Samson's Foxes" – in all its different forms – had been my home since my first days in the army. I felt close to the comrades there, as one can only feel close to comrades in a company. And now I was expected to join a company where I knew hardly anyone.

But an order is an order. I became squad leader in Company No. 3.

16 November 1948
Battalion HQ

A squad of foreign volunteers

During the course I had imagined my first appearance before the new squad in detail. "Comrades," I would say, "I am not just a trainer. I have been given the responsibility for this squad, to lead it into battle." A deliberate and dramatic pause here, with a clear and resolute expression. "And don't forget: starting today, you belong to a fighting unit with a proud tradition. From now on everything you hear, see, or learn has only one purpose – to prepare you for the moment when you go into battle ..."

And there were other things I would say to them. Sublime words, that would touch their hearts. But like all the other fine speeches that one prepares for the right moment, this one too was never spoken because things did not happen the way I expected ...

I was lying in a position opposite Faluja. Here and there the enemy was firing colorful rockets, and occasionally I would hear the bark of a machine gun. So there must be a freezing machine gunner lying somewhere. I snuggle up in my sleeping bag and hope for a few hours' rest.

Suddenly someone rouses me. "Get up. Order from the company commander. You are to go straight back to the base, to pick up the new recruits."

Wrapped in a blanket I drive along lonely sand roads and arrive at the base after midnight. The new unit has already moved into their barracks. They have just received their mattresses and blankets. I open the door and stand rooted to the spot. It is hellish loud. It seems that everybody is talking at the same time. I can't understand a word. At least five languages are competing with one another. Hebrew is not among them.

I blow my whistle. It is like magic. The sound means authority, and its language is international. It is immediately quiet. I say a few words in Hebrew. They listen to me. But don't seem to understand a word.

"Anyone here understand Hebrew?" I ask. A man with a mustache on his intelligent face springs to attention before me. His Hebrew is terribly limited, but he understands more or less what is required and translates it into French. Another translates it on into Spanish. Another French speaker translates it into Italian. So we have a training method – I say a sentence in Hebrew which is passed on in several languages. This gives me enough time to think about what I am going to say next.

* * *

They came to this country to fight. But they didn't imagine the war like this. They expected some kind of movie war: dramatic confrontations with the enemy, heroic deeds ... compared with that the reality is rather gray. Boring positions, endless sentry duty, digging trenches. Jumping up and staging assaults are just the highlights, little red dots in a sea of gray.

Here's an example of an extremely prosaic and not at all amusing activity: crawling through a field of thistles. Why don't we crawl comfortably through grass? No use explaining that you can't choose the most pleasant field at the front.

Explaining is absolutely pointless. The sense is quickly lost in our cumbersome translation procedures. Everything has to be demonstrated, to be seen. We march back to camp, and I give them a ten-minute break. Those who want to can put on some long trousers. Ten minutes later we march back to the thistle field. Most are wearing long trousers – I have short ones.

"So! Pay attention! On the command "drop!" you fall to the ground. Like this. Watch out for the details. My heels are flat on the ground ..." They watch and understand.

"Now you fall at the same time as me. Drop! Quicker!" This time they fall into the thistles. I have won. A small, important victory.

* * *

I have learned what I have to do to command a squad in an assault. I have also learned how to find my bearings on a cloudy night and how to solve complicated tactical problems.

But they forgot to teach me how to feed forty hungry soldiers without any mess tins. Or how to motivate them for sentry duty or a night exercise when they are shivering with cold because we haven't provided them with any winter clothing.

Still. Somehow the problems are solved. In half legal ways I organize some mess tins. And if there are not enough to go around, we just have to take it in turns to eat. I can hear some whispering in French. Some plot is being hatched. But what? In the end one of them approaches me – as a representative. "Commander" he says, and hands me a mess tin. I pass it on to someone else. He tries to explain to me in French that I should be the first to eat. I refuse. The ones who are standing at the end of the queue and waiting ill-temperedly say nothing.

After we have eaten our job is to load sand onto a truck, to fill the bases of our tents with, and so prepare them for the rainy season. I tell them what we have to do. They grumble. They came here to fight, not to work. How can I explain to them that an infantry soldier is at the same time a fighter, a worker, and a beast of burden?

When we reach the place, they don't want to get out. I shout. A few get out and stand around and wait. I realize that words won't help here. I grab a shovel and set to work, as if I were unaware of them. The men whisper to each other, point their fingers at me, and discuss the matter. One of them picks up a shovel and joins in, then a second, a third, and a fourth follow suit. Another little victory!

* * *

Without intending to, I compare them with the group that was inducted with me a year ago. Melancholy seizes me. How many of the veterans are still with us? Some are fallen, many wounded. A few have found themselves jobs at HQ. There are not many familiar faces from those days still around. And this lot? They have good intentions. Most of them want to fight and to be good soldiers. But they are different from us. They don't have that open laugh, that healthy cheerfulness. They are missing that natural, rebellious pride which needs no discipline.

After just a few days of exercises came the order for us to take over a sec-

tion of the front south of Iraq al-Manshiyya. An Egyptian brigade was surrounded there, and skirmishes were continually flaring up. They would make occasional attempts to break out, and we did our best to prevent this. We also tried to prevent the smuggling in of food during the night. At the same time we admired the Egyptians for the way they held out under these conditions.

I set off with my squad in an anxious state of mind. For the first time I had people under my command at the front. The fact that they were not trained Israelis but foreign volunteers, who didn't know the conditions in our country, weighed on my spirits. I took over a position about a kilometer away from the encircled enemy.

28 November 1948
Position opposite Iraq al-Manshiyya

Rain

In the evening we took over the position. We distribute the men in small bivouac tents, organize sentries, and get the machine guns set up.

The tents are situated on the back slope, the trenches for the look-outs were dug out on the forward slope. Since the men have to be near the positions, to be ready for an enemy attack at any time, they cannot sleep in the tents. They drag the mattresses and the blankets near the positions.

The first evening at the front. "This is all like … like … like a dream," says Jehoshua, a little man from Paris who has picked up a few words of Hebrew. Then he continues in French. I understand only the occasional word: "immigration," "war," "front," "attack."

I lie between the positions. It would set a bad example to sleep in a tent. If words are not persuasive, you have to do it with actions. I find a comfortable place in a connecting trench, lay the mattress there, crawl into the sleeping bag, and spread the blankets on top. It is forbidden to remove your shoes or clothing. So it soon gets really warm.

But still I can't go to sleep. Now and then I get up and go to the positions. The sentries are alert. In the evening I told them about a position where the guards were killed in their sleep. That did the job!

After midnight I find myself awake. No idea what has woken me. I listen. Not a sound. No shots. Then I become aware of it – tap, tap, tap. Raindrops on the tarp.

The sky is heavily overcast. What should I do? I know exactly how I should behave if we are attacked from the left or from the right, if we are bombarded by mortars or artillery. What we are now facing is worse. Our positions are open, without any protection from the rain, and the people have no winter equipment.

The raindrops develop into a shower, the shower into a flood. I know that I have to get up, somehow rally the people to hold the position – but my willpower has left my body. I lie there feeling terribly unhappy. The water slowly seeps through the covers, the sleeping bag, and my clothing. A little stream runs from my neck along my back. Other streams flow down my socks into my shoes. Still I can't get up.

I don't know how long I lay like that. Maybe ten minutes? It seems like an eternity to me. Images appear before my eyes, as if I had a fever. I see myself in a dry bed in Tel Aviv. I listen to the rain tapping on the window, and pull the warm blankets over my head. I can't even get annoyed. The water drowns all feeling.

Then I see myself at my desk. A lamp illuminates the book in front of me. A radio is playing a quiet melody, and the tapping of the rain on the window pane increases the feeling of cosiness ...

This time I swear and get up. My body is shivering with cold and wet. I sink up to my calves in mud, take a few steps, slip, and fall in the muck. Somehow I reach the next position.

The men have pulled the covers over their heads. They also have the unhappy feeling of helplessness. But the guards are at their posts. I compose my face as if I hadn't noticed the rain, put a tarp over the wet machine gun, and say a few words intended to convey firmness and confidence.

On the way to the platoon commander's tent I fall into the mud. Twice. My rubber soles slip at each step. I know he can't help me. But I have the need to lean against someone, to exchange a few consoling curses. I find the chief in a corner of his tent. Here, too, everything is wet. After a while Shalom Cohen, the leader of the second squad, also appears. He is just as muddy and wet as I am.

What can we do? Nothing. We cannot leave our positions. The enemy might attack at any moment, under protection of the rain. And most of the tents, which were put up hastily and without much experience, have collapsed long ago. Our equipment is lying in dirt and in puddles.

The first night at the front. This is certainly not the way they imagined war. The front ants are lying in the mud. They are freezing, wet, and helpless. A surprise attack by the enemy would amount to a blessing. The rain, the mud, the cold – they are much worse. Somehow they will be overcome. But this victory will cause no anthems to be written, no films will be made about that, even if this victory sometimes takes more courage than any battle.

After a few days it became clear that my people were sticking it out despite all their weaknesses. The situation at the front had shown that Shalom Cohen and I were right when we decided to treat the newcomers with the same generosity and friendship that we had experienced in our former units.

Shalom Cohen and I felt very lonely here. Apart from two or three comrades we were the only veterans in the company. Our memories, our jokes, and experiences were alien to the others.

In the evenings we "assembled" in one of the tents with a bottle of stolen cognac or a tin of fruit and exchanged memories. Those were gloomy evenings. One after another we saw the faces of fallen comrades before us. We recalled the wonderful feeling of life in the early days, the wonderful comradeship in the peoples' army. We shed a silent tear.

4 December 1948
Position opposite Iraq al-Manshiyya

The veterans

The company is like a big lake with some rocks protruding. The lake is the new soldiers, the volunteers from abroad. They are good lads, mainly, but they lack individual features. From close up you can see that they each have their own characteristics, but in the distance they are all the same, like a calm, shallow lake. The rocks, on the other hand, are recognizable from far away – they are the veterans, the lads from the Land of Israel, with plenty of experience from more than ten months of war.

It is not easy to say what makes them stand out. But if you meet one you notice immediately: that is one. They are men who reject all order and discipline and who for this very reason are promoted. They have their own humor, they have guts. And that means a taste for adventure. Apart from that they have an enviable tolerance for suffering. But, as I said, you can't talk about them in the plural. Only the singular is applicable.

Take, for example, my friend Shalom Cohen. Shalom comes from a little kibbutz of Hashomer Hatzair.[3] He was born in this land but spent a large part of his youth in Egypt where he enjoyed a British high school education.

He looks as though he has just stepped out of a Western. On his head he wears a strange Australian hat. Around his neck an Arab headscarf, and from his belt hangs a splendid Luger, which swings against his thigh at each step. He has also picked up an impressive map case somewhere. But if you look into it, you'll only find a map of Ramle, although we are on the southern front. He just hasn't found a map of our area yet. Is that showing off?

But that is only one side of him. Beyond that Shalom belongs, like me, to the founding members of Samson's Foxes and has a good fifty or sixty battles under his belt. In none of these was he ever seen to be frightened or even nervous.

* * *

Aryeh Langmann is quite different. He was a member of Aryeh Kotzer's legendary company, was wounded twice, and came with us to the Foxes. He too now belongs to our new company. His body contains some shell splinters.

The squad Aryeh was allocated consists of wild immigrants from Morocco, who have already "worn out" several squad leaders. Nobody really expected him to get his squad under control. He is not capable of shouting, and his orders sound more like modest requests. One day, after he and his squad had taken over a position, they were attacked by the Egyptians who had approached in a wadi to as near as thirty yards. Aryeh advanced – alone – against the attackers, with a hand grenade in each hand. Since then his people have followed him.

* * *

On the same day I brought "Shwok" – that is Zvi Bruk – to the medical station. Nobody knows why he is called "Shwok." He got the name during the Maccabi operation.

Shwok is the only one of the veterans who wears the official army headgear. With that he looks as though he belongs to the Foreign Legion. He has a wild mustache and resembles an old Red Indian.

For a long time he was the company runner. Then he got fed up with this duty and applied for a transfer to the jeeps. In that tragic night in Beit Affa, when we lost Aryeh Kotzer and Moshe Wantzover, he was with us. Now it has got him too – a bullet shot his nose off.

* * *

Those are the rocks in the sea – the veterans, the remnants of that unit formed of the youth at the start of the war, that escorted the convoys to Jerusalem, that carried out the Nachshon and Maccabi operations.

We used to be many. Many individualists, who found themselves together in the units. At that time one person was seen almost as a squad, a squad almost as a company, and a company almost as a whole army. At that time also, as Schiller wrote: "In the field, there a man is still worth something/there the heart still has its weight ..."

Meanwhile the army has changed. Of the many individualists only a few remain. Many have fallen, many wounded, and some others couldn't take it. What remains are the rocks in the sea. Rather sad rocks, and in the storm of battle, in its thunder and lightning, some of them disappear and leave a gap. They are irreplaceable.

One of the few who joined the "Order of the Veterans" was Jack Schack, a Dutchman with a legendary past. He had fled to England, became a medic in a British commando unit, fell into German captivity, escaped, and traveled through half Europe before joining the Yugoslav partisans. Now he is with us. After a few days I wrote his obituary ...

4 December 1948
Position opposite Iraq al-Manshiyya

The medic Jack Schack

We are walking along, following a telephone cable. The night is unusually dark. Rain clouds cover the sky and hide the stars. Occasionally a lone bullet whistles over our heads. The Egyptians are shooting in the direction of our positions without having a real target. But the men, who are new at the front, duck each time. They think that each bullet is aimed directly at them.

During the night we are to move from our positions into "Position Hell," which is particularly near to the trapped Egyptians. Our job will be to help with digging trenches. The old saying "sweat saves blood" is the awful truth here. But the people have no experience. They have also never experienced heavy shelling. A shape looms on the horizon. We have reached the position. Three hundred yards away is the position of the trapped enemy, who are preparing a breakout attempt.

We discuss where the new position should be dug. The last attack by the Egyptians, which came to within thirty yards of our lines, showed that something needed changing. In the meantime we stay in the wadi on the rear slope and wait for orders. The men are tired, they lie down, and fall asleep immediately despite the biting cold. Shalom Cohen and I sit to one side. Someone joins us there.

"Who is that?" I ask. In the darkness the faces are hard to recognize.

"Me. Jack."

"What are you doing here?"

Jack, our company medic, tells us that he has joined us. "I just decided to come along. I'll go back with you tomorrow. I have to be somewhere near HQ to deal with the transport for the wounded."

We have heard a lot about this fellow. A youth from western Europe, whose Hebrew (still) sounds strange. But he already looks like one of the veterans. "A lad with guts!" is what they say about him. During the attack on Huleiqat he ran around under fire and took care of the wounded, which was actually the task of the more junior medics. He received a commendation for this day.

"When did you last clean your Sten?" he asks me.

"About a week ago" I admit to my shame. I tend to neglect my Sten. I only take the weapon with me to avoid having to carry a rifle.

"Only a week ago? I haven't cleaned mine for at least two weeks." And hugging his medic's bag, he adds "This is my weapon." I look at the bag. It is marked and torn in places. "You know what, the first time I was in action I had a nice shiny new bag. And when I treated the first wounded man, I could hardly open it. The man almost bled to death." He hugged his battered bag lovingly. "Since then, my friend, I have learned my lesson. See this tear? I ripped the bag open here so that I can get at the things quickly and without delay." He pulled a rubber pipe, which served as a tourniquet, out through the gap. "But in an emergency I don't need the bag at all. I carry this tourniquet on my body. A movement of my hand, and I am ready to use it. And in my trouser pockets I have a pair of scissors and some bandages. In difficult cases I just leave the bag and the Sten behind me and crawl quickly and unencumbered to the wounded man …"

I really like him at this moment. He is one of us, I think full of pride. One of the veterans who has learned the right thing not from training courses but from combat experience. Each one has his methods, each his own peculiarities. These veterans are individualists. Their experience is beyond price.

We sit there and tell stories. About brave medics and those who did not distinguish themselves with bravery, about cases of wounding that we have seen, about how to treat a comrade in shock and what the "best" method is to die quickly.

At last we are called. We distribute the tasks, urge the men on, support them, swear, join in with the work to set an example, praise, and admonish. We make slow progress. The men are discontented. They have not yet learned to suffer and continue smiling. Toward morning we arrive back. We are all dog tired. No one notices that Jack is not with us. At the last moment he decided to stay at the forward position.

It is only in the afternoon that we remember him. The report comes in over the field telephone that he was running to a lightly wounded man when an Egyptian sniper shot him.

The White Front

*I*n the early afternoon of 8 December I was wounded in the belly and the arm. It happened about three hundred meters from the enemy lines at Iraq al-Manshiyya. I was hit by a salvo from a Browning machine gun. The place I lay could not be reached by anyone without them putting their life in extreme danger. Still I was rescued thanks to the personal bravery of Aryeh Langmann. He was also a squad leader and one of the veterans of the battalion. Three hours after being wounded I was already lying on the operating table in a military hospital.

For half an hour I lay on the ground writhing in pain, without knowing exactly what damage the bullets had done to my insides, but sure that no one could get me out of there. This half hour was the worst experience of my whole life. But when I arrived at the hospital I was quite sure that the danger was over. Only later did I learn that for twelve days the doctors and my family had been extremely concerned about me. During this period my digestive system was out of action and I could neither eat nor drink.

Since I did not lose consciousness for a moment, I made use of the time to think about the war. I was not happy with what I thought.

For three weeks I didn't write a single line. I lay almost motionless in bed and had nothing else to do than to think about life. After this period the pain retreated, my body slowly started working again. And I started writing again.

A salvo

Around midday I received the order to pick four men from my squad, and go with them to relieve the group which had held "Position Hell" since the morning.

This position was situated on a low hill. The trenches were about one hundred meters long and completely in view of the enemy, who was well dug in about three hundred meters away. The position was not continuously manned. But from time to time a small unit would be sent there to observe the enemy.

Luckily we found a free Bren carrier, so we loaded up our weapons and drove out to the hill. I left the men on the rear slope and went up alone. I wanted to check out the trenches and decide where to station the men.

At the top I met my friend Aryeh Langmann, the leader of the squad we had come to replace. We ran from trench to trench, and he explained the layout to me. Here was the command post with the field telephone. It worked. Further. There is the machine gun stand. We run along the pathetic connecting trench. It is just a foot deep. No point crawling. That would take too long. So you have to run and trust to luck.

Rat-tat-tat-tat. I feel something warm on my belly and fall into the connecting trench.

"I have been hit!" I shout.

Aryeh is also lying in the trench. For a moment I think he has also been hit. He crawls to me. He is unhurt.

"Where?" he asks.

I point to my stomach. He undoes my trousers, takes my emergency dressing, and puts it on the wound. I see a big bleeding hole on the right side of my belly. Then I notice that my sleeve is also dripping with warm blood. Aryeh takes off my battle dress and bandages the wound on my arm.

He jumps up and runs to the field telephone. Again the machine gun barks. A bullet goes through his coat, but misses him.

The pain is terrible. I cannot move, but my head is clear. I keep thinking the same thought: how are they going to get me out of here?

My men are far away. Only Aryeh is near me, and one thing is clear, shockingly clear. In this place, in full view of the enemy, it would be deadly for anyone to come anywhere near us. There is no cover at all.

I have no idea how serious the wound is. Am I going to die? It is strange that this thought does not shock me. But the certainty that I cannot be rescued before darkness falls makes me desperate.

I shout. With pain. Somehow that makes me feel better. I have a childish feeling that somehow my cries will affect someone and they will find a way to get me out of here.

"Where is the jeep?" I ask. I believe that the jeep could somehow rescue me.

"Come on," Aryeh consoles me. "I have phoned HQ." He tries to get me on his back and to crawl. The pain is unbearable. He lays me back on the ground.

"Don't stand up!" I tell him. "They will kill you." But Aryeh is one of the old school. He has been wounded twice. A quiet man who has often displayed admirable courage.

He gets up and runs. The machine gun rattles.

I keep on screaming. The time is endless. I am surprised that I have not died yet. But somewhere deep inside me a thought is lurking: I will survive!

Aryeh is back again with my four men who had waited behind in the wadi. They are recruits and have never been so near to the enemy. They look at me. In their faces I can see their concern. I can feel that they like me. They are endangering their lives to get me out of here.

They take me by my arms and legs, and run with me to the rearward slope. The pain is awful. I groan. I don't want them to hear me scream. Somehow we reach the slope. There the Bren carrier is waiting. They put me on it. One of the men gets on and puts my head in his lap. I hold the bandage on my stomach to stop it shifting.

We drive off. The vehicle rolls and shakes crazily. The pain gets worse. I start screaming again.

At the command post some men are waiting. Half conscious I recognize their worried faces, as they transfer me to the jeep of the medical unit. The drive to the collection point is hell. The sand road is full of potholes and boulders, the jeep jumps like mad. I feel as if my body is breaking apart.

"We'll soon be there," says the comrade soothingly, holding my head. But the drive continues. Finally we reach the tent of the collecting point. They carry me in and put me on the operating table. Rafael, the battalion medic, cuts open my clothing, examines the wound, and bandages it neatly.

"That is nothing," he says in a confident tone. "In a month you'll be back with us."

I know him and his habit of saying that to any man who is seriously wounded. I have often brought him wounded comrades! But still his words calm me. I am a child again. I w-a-n-t to believe him, so I believe him.

"Give me some morphine," I beg him.

"That's just what I am doing," he says and injects me with something. The pain doesn't stop. Was that really morphine he gave me?

We start a crazy drive. We use the road the Egyptians constructed. But they didn't finish the job and it is now in a terrible condition. The vehicle jumps around and with each bump the pain gets worse.

"Slower!" I beg the driver. He is a friend. He slows down a bit, but after a few minutes it is the same as it was before. He knows that he is causing me pain. But he also knows that my life depends on how quickly he can get me to the hospital.

That awful journey is never-ending. The medic who is accompanying me tells me several times that we will soon reach the better section of road. I don't believe him any more. The shaking is endless. At last the village of Iraq Suweidan appears. Here the main road begins. The bouncing reduces. The pain too. We are driving along the main road. How many hundred times have I already driven along this road? One after another the familiar villages. The pain too comes and goes. I become apathetic.

There is the crossing. Not far from the hospital. Just a few minutes.

The vehicle stops. Whispering outside. The door opens. Medics in white slide out the stretcher.

In the reception ward they lay me on a bed. Nurses in white come and go. A medic asks me some questions. They remove what remains of my clothing, wash me, and shave the area around the wound.

"You will be operated on soon," says a medic. "You are in luck. Our doc is wonderful. A specialist for stomach wounds. In two weeks you'll be fit again!"

I hardly hear his words. A strange tranquility comes over me, my senses relax. This atmosphere of quiet efficiency, of safety, fills me with trust. A nurse comes with the anesthetic injection. I close my eyes. The last words I hear are "Afterwards you can put him in bed 23."

The battle with the injuries is fought by the wounded man alone. The doctors and nurses do their duty, and sometimes they achieve wonders. But in the end it is the wounded man alone, his willpower – success depends on him. This explains the excitement the patient feels at every sign of life from "outside." Every visit from comrades, from friends and acquaintances. And the visitor often does not realize how grateful the patient is.

1 January 1949
Military Hospital Number 8

Chocolate

From that day on, when an armor-piercing bullet from a heavy automatic weapon confused me with a tank and lost its way in my stomach, the doctors forbade me to eat. As compensation they stuck a needle into my leg and connected this with a container of glucose solution. In this way I had only one meal a day, lasting twenty-four hours.

My friends and relations came to visit me. They stood around me making strenuous efforts to radiate optimism and to hide their discomfort. One day in the first week, a girlfriend visited me. After she had recovered from the initial shock and had got used to my appearance, I explained to her the purpose of the various tubes decorating me. One of them fed me continually without burdening my stomach or intestines. A second one, which made my nose look like an elephant's trunk, continually sucked the juices out of my stomach.

We spoke about this and that, about friends and acquaintances, and I described for her in detail the twelve-course meal that I intended to consume on my recovery. I also described my keen anticipation of the first glass of beer, and the whole time I kept my melancholy eye on the container with my liquid "nourishment" above my head.

Then she pulled a little packet from her pocket – a small box of chocolates. I didn't know what to say – at that moment it was not a very useful present. My young friend turned such a bright red that I was reminded of a ripe tomato (all my fantasies at that time had something to do with food), she stuttered that she had forgotten that I couldn't eat anything, and suggested that I could perhaps share out the chocolates among the nurses. I smiled gratefully to her, accepted the present, and declared firmly "The day is certainly not far away, when I can eat that!"

The visitors left. The pain returned. I held the chocolate in my hand and gazed at it. It was nicely packaged and had something provocative about it. And as I examined the chocolate, a remarkable change came over me …

There are three phases in recovering from a serious wound.

The first phase is complete apathy. Everything apart from pain is unimportant. The doctors and nurses can do what they want with the patient.

When the patient has overcome this phase, the second begins. He starts to develop an interest in his surroundings, but mainly its disadvantages. He doesn't feel well, which has an effect on his attitude.

The third phase is recovery. The attractions of the world re-emerge. The nurses are suddenly pretty and nice. He gets hungry. In short, the spirits of life awake …

That bar of chocolate propelled me from the first into the second phase. Until then I was indifferent to everything. My world had shrunk – to my bed, the doctor who tortured me twice a day, and the nurses who kept watch around my bed twenty-four hours a day. I didn't dare to believe that my body could ever work properly again.

My will awoke while I was looking at the chocolate. "What the hell," I said to myself, "one day I am going to eat it!" I didn't give it to the nurses or to my neighbor who had lost his legs. I put it in my drawer.

This chocolate became a symbol: for health, home, Tel Aviv, the full life that I wanted to rejoin. I would regularly bring it out, look at it, and dream.

Two and a half weeks after I was wounded the doctor decided that it was time for my stomach and intestines to start working again. On the same day the needle was removed from my leg, and I was presented with my first meal in a festive ceremony. Maybe it was only some mush and a soft-boiled egg. But it was godly! Then the big day came unexpectedly and on my tray lay the first slice of bread! And it was no mistake by an over-tired nurse. I was really allowed to eat it. From that point things advanced by leaps and bounds. I could sit, then take a few steps and one day the tray came with a piece of chocolate. A small one perhaps, but real chocolate!

On the next day I got the chocolate out of my drawer. I looked at it for a long time. Each piece was wrapped in colorful paper. I decided to eat one piece. But which? I can't eat any nuts nor any chocolate with cognac. I closed my eyes and took a piece blindly. I unwrapped it. Then came the great moment. I hesitated, and then, as if in a religious ceremony, I raised my hand and placed the piece of chocolate on my tongue ...

In the hospital, the soldier faces his ultimate test. In battle he has something he can rely on: comrades who fight next to him, faith in his leaders ... but who was there to comfort that anonymous Etzel man who suffered terribly with thirst until he was taken to the operating theater and did not come back?

3 January 1949
Military Hospital Number 8

One-legged hero

He was lying in the room next to mine and I never saw him. But I heard his shouting. This woke me up in the middle of the night, about a week after I was wounded. "Yitzhak ... help me! What should I do ... Oh! ... My leg! My leg! ... What can I tell my parents? ... Who is going to look after them? ..." The nurse whispered me the information that he was an explosives specialist who had lost a leg and most of the fingers of one hand.

A day later I was moved into his room. He was depressed and could not be comforted. His hands were bandaged. He did not know that he had also lost his fingers.

Whenever his pain or his desperation became too much for him he began to shout. But he never called to his parents, always to "Yitzhak." That seemed strange to me. I knew from experience that a wounded man, and in particular a severely wounded man, returns to his childhood. He forgets his unit and his comrades and longs for his family. Even I, who had never had particularly strong connections with my family, spent the first few days in the hospital thinking only about home.

Who was this mysterious "Yitzhak"? One day he appeared and was none other than my old explosives trainer Itshe.

This Itshe was a special character. One of the very few old veterans left. A comrade who would stand by you through thick and thin. Yitzhak had an artificial leg. Unless you knew him well you wouldn't know it. He drove a car (like the devil), jumped over fences, and had been decorated more than once for particular daring in the use of explosives. He was the Explosives Officer of the battalion.

"What can I do?" my room-mate cried. "How can I manage with only one leg? How can I support my parents? They have only just arrived in this country. What will they do without my help? What on earth can I do?"

"Stop crying like a baby!" Yitzhak shouted at him with simulated anger. "Look at me! I have only one leg – so what?" I had never heard Itshe mention his missing leg. In his presence the subject was strenuously avoided. "I drive a car, as you know very well. The wound will heal. They will give you an artificial leg and you will be able to do everything!"

The wounded man was not convinced.

"Listen to me!" continued Itshe. "We are in the army. We are all comrades here. We look after each other. We will look after you too. You will see. Tomorrow the whole squad will be here."

And the next day the whole squad really did come. Eight explosives experts with Itshe at the head. They filed in and stood around his bed. Itshe talked. The others keep quiet. Like every healthy soldier who visits a wounded comrade, they felt guilty – as though their own good health required justification.

"Would you like us to inform anyone?" asked Itshe.

"Not my parents! Just let my sister know."

"You can rely on us," said Itshe, and made a note of the address.

But the military machine has its own logic. There are social officers, there are lists of addresses ("to be informed in case of ..."). And so one evening, while I was dozing after a bad attack of pain, a man of about fifty appeared, with a wrinkled face and a leather cap on his head like the ones worn by coachmen in Europe. With him was the mother. Small, fat, and gray haired.

The parents had known nothing. Just now, in the corridor, the nurse had explained the situation to them. They still had not got over the shock.

Their son felt like crying, but could not do so in front of his parents. He didn't want to worry them. The father wanted to cry, but not in front of his son. Only the mother could not control herself. She kept turning her face away, wiping away the tears, and murmuring the eternal question of a soldier's mother: "Oh God, why did it have to be my son?"

"Don't worry about me," he consoled them in Yiddish. "I'll get an artificial leg and become a driver."

"And what about your hands?"

"Oh that's nothing. Just a couple of wounds that had to be bandaged."

"Don't you worry" said the father in a faltering voice. "We will look after you, the same as we did when you were small. We'll manage."

Time did its job. Moshe slowly recovered. The pain faded. He was served a hearty meal three times a day, and the sisters fed him. And I, who had been fed intravenously for three weeks, watched each mouthful as it disappeared. Then he told me his story. Mine clearance. Inaccurate maps. A tank mine with a foot trigger. The explosion ...

After a few days he was transferred from the severe injuries ward to the recovery ward. When I was allowed to get up, I went to see him. His head bandage was gone, and his face was dotted with scars.

"How are things?"

He smiled. He really smiled. "Good. The pain is gone. And the doctors says that my wounds are making good progress."

"And your hands?" I didn't know if they had told him yet. A shadow passed over his face. "You know, they removed nearly all my fingers. But somehow I'll manage."

I looked into his face – the face of a twenty-year-old. Until recently he had had a life full of adventure ahead of him. What kind of a life could he now expect? And a second thought went through my head.

What kind of a life will the country offer him? Will he receive any gratitude for his sacrifice? Is there any suitable way at all to show gratitude for a sacrifice like that?

I thought of the books about World War II. About war invalids. How quickly they had been forgotten! And we? Would we forget too?

... back in the ward. A lively discussion is going on. What about? Who is happier – someone who has lost a leg, both legs, or just an arm? They were arranged in order – an arm was more important than two legs and so on. A horrifying calculation. And that question floated back into my head: will the state remember? Will the hundreds of thousands remember, the public? Will the citizens remember those who are responsible for their security, their freedom?

Five weeks after being wounded I was transferred to a convalescent home. There I ran into many of my old friends from the brigade. We were glad to see each other again. We knew that each of us had been very lucky to have been at the front for a year and have survived. In whatever form.

From the convalescent home I escaped for a few hours into town. The journey was not pleasant. My body was unused to the shaking around. It was painful. Worse still was something that happened. I wrote a short story to draw public attention to it.

20 January 1949
Convalescent home

An ill-mannered young man

He sat in the bus which serves the southern settlements. His mere presence was remarkable. What is a soldier doing in a "civilian" bus? His comrades preferred to hitch a lift. But he sat in the bus, behind the driver, by the aisle. Dark haired with a reddish, wild beard and blue eyes. He was leaning back, his eyes half closed.

* * *

The rest of the world did not seem to interest him. This lack of interest was rather arrogant, irritating. At the station in Gedera, next to the kiosk, the soldier opened his eyes and showed a little interest. For over a year it had become habitual for the soldiers, before setting out on an operation, to stop at this kiosk and drink a juice or eat an ice cream. This was their last contact with the civilized world. Gedera was like a border post. To the north lay the Land of Israel and to the south, beyond the great roadblocks, lay "the Front."

As the soldier, sunk in reminiscences, gazed at the kiosk, an elderly woman got into the bus. She was one of those women whose faces are deeply marked by hard work. She bought her ticket and looked around for a place to sit.

All the seats were taken, which did not trouble her. Her eyes settled on the soldier. He woke briefly from his thoughts, glanced at the old woman, and returned his gaze to the kiosk. The bus drove off. The old woman squeezed in somehow. The soldier returned to his reverie.

In Rehovot a young woman got on. She was pretty or even more than that: and you could see that she knew it. She appeared very self-confident. A quick glance told her that no seats were free. But she also registered something else: that the soldier was the only young person on the bus. He looked at her discreetly through half-closed eyes. The way a man looks at a pretty woman. He naively thought she would not notice. Their eyes met, and she smiled at him. His face stiffened. He closed his eyes, let his head sink onto his chest as if in sleep, but his cheeks reddened.

The woman went further and soon found an elderly gentleman who offered her his place. The bus drove down the hill to the railway and then through the abandoned orange groves of Ness Ziona.

There a middle-aged couple was waiting. A respectable woman and a man with a stomach decorated with a golden watch chain. They were obviously Germans and it was difficult to make a connection between their appearance and the small, poverty-stricken settlement where the only attractive building was a minaret. Maybe they were visiting some new immigrants who had moved into the abandoned Arab village?

The woman got in and stood next to the soldier. He didn't open his eyes. Maybe he had not seen her. She hesitated, and then coughed. He didn't move. She got annoyed and said to her husband in German: "Nothing is more ludicrous than a young man pretending to be asleep!"

Her high-pitched voice resounded through the bus, but still the soldier did not move. Maybe he didn't understand German? "What behavior!" the man declared pompously. "In Europe I have never seen a young man who wouldn't offer his place to a lady."

One of the passengers was pleased at the chance to teach the soldier a lesson, and answered in Yiddish: "It is the army that spoils them. As soon as they put on a uniform they think they are the most important thing in the world."

"Yes," said the lady, "that's the sabras[1] for you. They haven't been brought up properly."

The soldier who was the center of attention seemed unaffected. Was he really asleep? But shortly before Rishon LeZion he suddenly opened his eyes and pressed the button. The soldier slowly got up, holding onto the driver's seat, shuffled to the door, and climbed out cautiously. Outside he stood still for a moment and then went off slowly, his body strangely twisted.

The driver cast a cursory glance after him and drove on.

On 25 January elections took place for the first parliament of the State of Israel, which was built on the blood of the frontline soldiers. The soldiers regarded this election with indifference and scorn. It was the first official demonstration of the chasm that had opened up between the front and the rear.

The election campaigns dealt with unimportant themes. The writers of the election posters competed with each other in total ignorance of the military reality. The worst thing was that none of the parties realized that a group of people had been formed at the front with their own attitude to things, with their own style and their own leadership. The parties carried on with business as usual. And a parliament was elected without a single person who could legitimately speak in the name of the frontline soldiers. None of the new representatives was in a position to formulate the thoughts and feelings of those who had founded the state.

25 January 1949
Convalescent home

Election day

"We have brought you thus far!" screamed the loudspeaker. "We have founded the state!" boomed another. "Your vote for the founder of the state!" said the headline of a newspaper.

In the streets of Tel Aviv is a soldier on crutches. His uniform is too big for him – he has a poor relationship with the quartermaster and also no significant rank. He is watching and listening and doesn't know what to think. For a whole year he knew nothing about parties. He imagined them as something far away behind the lines, arguing about traffic on the roads, and whether people should be allowed to raise pigs.

So which one was right? Which party was it that founded the state? The soldier wrinkled his forehead and thought hard. Thinking in these categories did not come naturally.

There is that photo of Ben-Gurion on 14 May 1948. Where was he on that day? The soldier racked his brains. That must have been ... this filthy village they had captured in the morning. Not many losses. Only three dead. Joske, Yaakov, and Mishka. The soldier smiled at the thought of Mishka. He was a joker. A pity he is dead. For certain he would have cracked a wonderful joke about this election.

The soldier drifts off in thought. That village now belongs to the state of Israel. So Mishka also played his part in the founding of the state of Israel. But Mishka is lying somewhere in the place where they buried him, and red flowers are growing on his grave.

Which party would Mishka have voted for, if he were still alive today? No. It is unimaginable that Mishka would have got enthusiastic about any party. He was interested in quite different things. He would have said, in his typical way: "Soldiers are only interested in two things. The second of these is leave ..." And still he played his part in the founding of the state.

But maybe the state was not founded on that day at all? After all, the armies of the neighboring states only marched in on the next day, and that was when the real war for the state began.

The soldier could remember that evening very clearly. The chief storming into the room and announcing that the enemy had marched all the way to Yavne. "Less than twenty kilometers from Tel Aviv!" They spent the whole night talking about Molotov cocktails: the only anti-tank weapon that they had at the time. Did anyone really believe that these bottles could stop tanks?

In the morning they set off for the defense of Gedera. They dug trenches and waited for the tanks. One company, less than one hundred young men, stood between Tel Aviv and the Egyptians. In the night they attacked the Egyptians, and also in the second and third nights. They beat the Egyptians by Isdud and left behind a few dozen dead.

After all that, the soldier thinks, they must be the founders of the state. The real founders. The politicians didn't help then. A miracle decided the war at that time. This miracle was Mishka and his comrades. Those that fell and those who survived. Those who came from the factories, from the dance halls, and from the schools, who put on badly fitting uniforms and suddenly looked like soldiers.

No. The posters don't talk about this miracle. Nor about Mishka. On the posters everything is quite simple: one party said this, another that, and the political leader something else – that's the way the state of Israel was founded. The miracle of the night at Isdud is not mentioned at all. And neither is Eli mentioned, who was hit in the belly by seven bullets and now writes satirical verses.

The soldier flicks through the list of candidates. He accepted it from the hand of an enthusiastic youth so as not to offend him. No. The miracle by the name of Mishka is not on the list.

The soldier is surprised. Something has really happened during the last year? A new spirit has arisen, a whole generation has had its say. Even if the thunder of artillery made it hard to hear. Can it really be so, that of all the thousands of Mishka's comrades not one is fit to appear on the list of candidates and to be mentioned as a "Founder of the State" on the placards and in the speeches?

The soldier tries to work out which party would get the support of the comrades in his squad. The four who fell, the two who were wounded, or the two who went on the squad leader training course. He doesn't know. It is interesting to note that parties were never mentioned in their discussions. Did they talk about politics at all? Certainly. Quite a lot in fact. Because Itzik, who later became a squad leader, was a passionate debater and could never sit still. But their politics was so different from that of the posters on the wall …

At first they talked about the possibility of fighting to clear the road to Jerusalem. Then they discussed whether the Negev should be liberated immediately, or if they should wait until they had tanks. It was quite a different politics. Perhaps because they knew that they were the ones who would have to pay the price for this politics. And they were prepared to pay the price. They knew the facts, too – the strength of the enemy and their own weakness.

But here it seems to be a different matter. It is no problem talking about conquest if you are editing a newspaper or sitting in the office of a party. It is easy to compose the text of a poster, when those who write it haven't the slightest idea what it is like at the front or how victories are really won.

But those who paid that price or who are going to pay it – their voices are not to be found among this noisy chorus. They don't speak from the tribune, they don't write placards, they don't formulate headlines. They are at the front.

The soldier reflects. Yes, he thinks. We are at the front. And that is far away. Maybe that is the root of the problem? The front is too far away. And the frontline soldiers, on the occasions they come to the city, are submerged in the sea of neatly ironed uniforms that is the military in town. Earlier on, when the front still ran through the Hatikva quarter and Yasur,[2] it was quite a different matter …

Fatigue suddenly overcomes the soldier. I'll head for home, he decides. The clicking of his crutches fills the street with echoes. Pity that Mishka isn't around any more. He would have known how to put it.

Plate 1. Samson's Foxes. Avnery as temporary communication man, fourth from the left, with his friend and later deputy editor Shalom Cohen on the far right. Third from the left is the future General Albert Mandler, killed in the Yom Kippur war

Plate 2. Avnery's camp in Kibbutz Hulda, just before he left for the battle of Latrun, May 1948

Plate 3. Returning from the battle of Latrun. A moment of rest during the tiring retreat on foot. Avnery is first on the right

Plate 4. Avnery's squad during the retreat, exhausted. Everybody wears the famous "sock hats," a symbol of the war. In the background is the Arab village of Hulda

Plate 5. During the second ceasefire, a "Day of the Brigade" is held in Rehovot, and Samson's Foxes are part of the parade

Plate 6. An official army issue photo, showing soldiers of the Givati brigade on parade. The slogan, right, says "For a Year of Victory and Peace." The emblem of the Givati brigade, a sword and cactus branches, is displayed top left

Plate 7. Reclining on the hay in an abandoned Arab village. The photo shows Avnery with his peaked cap, Shalom Cohen with his Australian hat, and Mira, Mira, and Jocheved, the three female members of Avnery's company

Plate 8. The truck with armoured cabin, loaded with cheese, arriving in Jerusalem with the convoy that broke the blockade, April 1948. Avnery is first on the right

Plate 9. In the field. Shalom Cohen interrogates a blindfolded Arab villager

Plate 10. The battle of Latrun, May 1948. Soldiers carry a wounded comrade who has been shot in the chest. The angry soldier on the left, with a Sten gun on his back, tells Avnery: "Stop taking pictures, help us carry the stretcher!"

Plate 11. "Captured" photo of an Arab woman, found by Avnery in an abandoned Arab village

Plate 12. Palestinian Arab leader Haj Amin al-Husseini, Grand Mufti of Jerusalem, with the Jerusalem Dome of the Rock on his breast

Plate 13. "Captured" photo of an Arab family, found by Avnery in an abandoned Arab village

Plate 14. Temporary grave of an unknown soldier near Hill 105, with grave number and Egyptian flag. One foot is just visible

Plate 15. An abandoned well among the trees, all that now remains of the large Arab village of Faluja, near the hill where Avnery was wounded

PART TWO

The Other Side of the Coin

The Long Nights

It is ten o'clock in the evening.

In the big ward next door, where the less serious cases are, the lights are being put out. A female voice says "Good night" and is answered by a choir of the wounded. I have never seen any of those who are lying there, but I know all their voices. It begins with the bass of Shosho who has lost a leg, and ascends to the hoarse whisper of Uzi, the seventeen-year-old, who played with a hand grenade and now has only one eye.

"So, what I was going to tell you," in Shosho's voice, "the nurse was very cautious. She asked the doctor if you can catch syphilis from the toilet seat. The doctor said: of course it is possible. But very uncomfortable."

A thin voice that I didn't recognize laughed wildly and loudly. Someone new it seems. The others can't produce more than a desperate groan. It must be the tenth time they have heard this joke.

"Put on a new record!" demand the sardonic tones of Ulcus. This "Ulcus" is a major who hasn't yet got used to lying among ordinary soldiers, who, what is more, go so far as to make jokes about his not-so-military illness. "Come on," says Shosho soothingly. "So: one day the battalion quartermaster goes into a brothel ..."

"Oh, no, can't you shut up for once?" groans Uzi.

"That's enough – we want to get some sleep," adds the choir.

"Miserable creatures," Shosho rejoins, not giving up so easily. "One could almost imagine that you lot had done something apart from shitting today."

"Quiet please, children!" The nurse's voice.

"Sister, pot!" calls the major.

"Ass!" Shosho gladly takes the opportunity for revenge. "Been busy up to now, have you?"

"He has invented a new procedure that enables you to salute while you are sitting on the pot," Uzi whispered.

"Go to hell," grumbled the major and did his business.

Here and there the squeaking of a bed as one of the wounded men tries to find a more comfortable position for his wounds.

Quiet envelops the ward.

* * *

It is ten o'clock in the evening.

Rachel enters the room where the critical cases are lying. She always leaves this room till last, so that she can devote more time to the two of us, the "critical cases."

Through half-opened eyes I follow her movements over at the other bed. She inserts a thermometer between the teeth of the wounded man to take his temperature, and holds his hand to take his pulse. He just lies flat. His breathing rasps like a door that hasn't been oiled for a long time. It was only half an hour ago that he was brought into this room. For two days he lay in the room opposite. He was shot in the chest.

Rachel lets go of his hand and writes something on the board which hangs from his bed. Her reddish face is remarkably unexpressive. She tries not to show any feelings. It is the expression of someone who knows that the other is lost and thinks, "I'm not going to let that affect me." A trick of repression which never works.

"Drink," croaks the wounded man.

Rachel goes to the head of the bed and lays her little hand on his glowing brow. "In a minute," she says. Liar, I think to myself. Didn't the doctor tell you not to give him a drop to drink?

Now it is my turn. I smile. Rachel smiles back. We two have a secret. Like children in the kindergarten. I cling to the ridiculous belief that only Rachel can help me to go to sleep, that without her I won't be able to sleep a wink. A childish belief. One of those tiresome thoughts that a wounded man hangs onto without having the faintest idea why. Twice in the last week , when other nurses were on night duty, I called for Rachel for so long that she got out of her bed, came to me, and told me off. But still it meant something to her. Most of the wounded men treat the nurses as though they were mechanical parts of the system. And if a troublesome patient treats them as individuals, they feel flattered.

"What's the reading?" I ask.

"Quiet! You know that I can't show you." Every evening Rachel repeats the same words, before showing me the chart. That is part of our ritual. If she just showed me the chart without refusing first, then I would be disappointed. Like a lady-killer whose new lover surrenders to him without resistance.

"Do you want a sleeping pill?" It is a rhetorical question. I swallow the pill automatically, while Rachel moves the cover aside and looks for a place on my left leg where she can give me two injections. The leg is covered with little pinholes, there is hardly any room for more. Since I have been here I have had two injections every three hours, that's eight every twenty-four hours: one of penicillin and one painkiller. Sixteen holes a day.

"Owwwwww!" I groan, even though I hardly feel anything from Rachel's injections.

"Are you afraid of needles?"

"Yes, really," I admit. "Like going to the dentist."

Rachel laughs. She raises my head with one hand, and arranges the pillow with the other. She smooths the cover, strokes my hair, and regards me like an artist whose work is complete.

"Now be a good boy and go to sleep!"

"Certainly," I promise.

She turns off the main light and turns on the small table lamp. The lights are never turned off completely in the rooms of the critical cases. During the night the nurse has to make regular checks on the patient.

"Good night," says Rachel.

"Good night," I answer.

"Drink," mumbles the other, as if in a trance.

* * *

I know I won't go to sleep.

The whole day I have been afraid of this moment. The long night is torture. In the day there is always something happening. You can talk with the doctors or nurses, listen to other voices, read a book, or leaf through a magazine.

In the night the minutes drag endlessly, and the pain feels doubly bad. My right leg, the one with the tube for intravenous feeding, hurts and itches. I can't lie on my stomach or my side, and my back is burning even after Rachel has rubbed it with alcohol.

There are things I don't want to think about. During the day I can avoid them. But at night they catch up with me, grab hold of me, and won't let go. Damned memories. Why is it so hard to forget?

It is the eighth night since I was wounded. The eighth night that I can't sleep. And every night the same memories haunt me. They are clearer and sharper than reality itself. Maybe it is the fever that makes them so colorful that each detail, however small, acquires tremendous significance.

During the day pleasant memories predominate: smiling comrades, a landscape flying past at high speed in a jeep, the battalion mess, nice, funny events. In the night other memories take over. Sometimes I try to imagine that I am asleep and it is all a nightmare. But I know that I am not asleep and that what I can see is not a dream.

I stare at the dim light. My eyes fixate on the little light that shrinks, retreats, approaches, and is once again far away. It is flickering, flickering, flickering ...

* * *

... the light flickers and flickers and flickers.

I am in Camp "Jonah" in Tel Aviv. The wind is howling outside. February wind, announcing the end of the winter. It is pleasantly warm in the tent. Only a slight draft gets through and plays with the petrol lamp that is hanging from the ridge pole.

I am lying on the bed in my dirty clothes, reading (for the thousandth time) *All Quiet on the Western Front* by Erich Maria Remarque. Actually I am not reading. I am scanning the lines and absorbing none of the content. I am overcome by fatigue, and have lost all motivation. This is more than the physical tiredness of a recruit who has worked his whole life with his head and suddenly has to take part in physically demanding exercises. It is more a mental helplessness, the first shock. For three weeks my soul has been suffocating in the grip of military discipline, confronted with the cruel herd mentality. Your own will is suspended. Any idiot who happens to be appointed a squad leader can push you around any way he wants.

The squad leaders ... with relief I remember that our chiefs are not there. They have been unexpectedly called upon as a reserve force, when fighting broke out in the Keren Kayemet[1] House in Beit Dagon.[2]

A gust of wind in the tent and the flame of the petrol lamp flickers wildly. Without looking around I know that Sancho is back.

"What? Twelve o'clock already?" I close the book and yawn. Seems I haven't noticed the passing of time.

"No. It's only eleven," Sancho answers in an odd voice.

The meaning of his words is also strange. His leave didn't end till midnight. Why should a soldier with his wits about him return from leave a whole hour early, with girls and cafes in the world outside and here just boredom? That is a breach of trust! It wasn't easy for me to organize this six-hour break for him. The company commander, who can't stand the officials responsible for culture, knew I was a member of the "intelligentsia" in civil life. So he appointed me as part-time "cultural attaché" for the company. In this capacity I could occasionally sneak comrades out with some implausible pretense. Officially Sancho had gone to town to fetch an accordion for a party. If he arrives back a whole hour early, then something terrible must have happened.

"Stomach ache?" I suggest gingerly.

"Yob tvoyu Mat,"[3] retorts Sancho and lies on his bed fully clothed.

"You lost, you lost" crows Zuzik, who has woken up and is sitting on his bed. Sancho made a bet with him at lunchtime, that he would make it with a girl that evening if only he could get a few hours leave. For the purposes of the bet, Zuzik and Nachshe, the other two who shared the tent, had talked me into arranging a free evening for Sancho. Sancho and I are a strange pair. He calls me "Don Quixote" and says that I am one of those lunatics who meet an early death in a fight or on the gallows. I call him "Sancho Panza" because he is so materialistic. Sancho is blond, short, and thin. He owns a workshop for precision engineering and regularly proclaims that he has no desire to die for the damned homeland just so the shirkers can have a good time. If he was really a coward he could easily have found a way to avoid the fighting. So the name I gave him does not really fit.

"Tell us what happened," demands Zuzik.

"Go and screw yourself." Sancho's answer was unambiguous.

"What is that supposed to mean?" Zuzik is angry, it is clear from his childish, freckled face. "Did we have a bet or not? If you have lost, then you have to admit it."

"He's right," I decide, relying on my authority as informal acting squad leader. "A bet is a bet!" Sancho's behavior has aroused my curiosity. I would really like to know what has shaken up this cool-headed man.

Suddenly Sancho bursts out laughing. I don't like the sound of it. There is something dirty, malevolent in it. "You want to hear the truth? Our Don Quixote wants the truth about pure, true love? OK. Listen and enjoy!"

In the meantime the other members of the squad have come over from their nearby tent. Joker, tall and wearing a nightshirt that covers him down to his ankles, chases me out of my bed and gets in himself. The atmosphere is tense. The fighting, which is going on at this moment in the Keren Kayemet House, seems to be forgotten. As witnesses to the bet we have a right to our share of Sancho's love affairs. If you have no chance to commit your own sins, you can at least enjoy the sins of others.

"OK, listen!" starts Sancho. His voice sounds indifferent, as if he is going to read us one of those reports which we have to learn in the idiotic radio exercises: "To command post two – from command post three – the enemy is attacking from the south – I have three dead and two wounded – send ammunition and a pretty medic."

"After leaving here I went straight to Amos," recounts Sancho. "You know Amos?" I know him. He is one of those who avoid call-up because he is registered at some higher institution of learning, which he sees from the inside twice a year at the most. "I was sure that I would find some girls at his place. Around him there are always a few pretty girls who recognize their national duty to open their legs whenever a poor soldier comes by in search of love. They are not always pretty, but that is not so important."

"Not in the least!" shouts Zuzik. He is seventeen years old, from a respectable household, and his parents have tried too hard to bring him up well. We suspect that he is still a virgin, and feels obliged to take every opportunity to prove how masculine, adult, and experienced he is.

"But," Sancho continues, "that was a mistake. No girls there. So I suggested going to the movie theater. I knew that we would find some there."

"And how!" says Zuzik with enthusiasm. "If you sit next to a girl in the movies and you don't start smooching as soon as the lights go out, she will be insulted." The great know-all.

"We went to the Kessem movie theater. I stand in line for tickets and Amos goes off for cigarettes. Then I notice that some woman is watching me."

"A woman?" asks Zuzik doubtfully.

"She looked about twenty-two or twenty-five. Face slightly too round, but her body was another matter! A body that shouts out that it knows what things are about." Sancho falls silent for a moment, apparently considering this philosophical expression.

"And then? And then?" Zuzik could hardly contain his impatience.

"What can I say? She looks at me. I look at her. Then she comes over and asks if I can get her tickets. 'How many?' I ask. 'One,' she says. 'Sure,' I say. I get the tickets and we go in. Amos on the left, me on the right, with the woman in the middle. She says her name is Schoschanah. I call her Shosch … she smiles. And I tell here that I arrived this morning from the Negev and have to return tomorrow. 'Really?' she asks and puts her hand on my back as if to protect me. I gaze into her eyes which look like a leave pass for a whole week. Then the lights go out."

"What was the film about?" asks Joker naively.

"The film?" Sancho returns the question. "No idea! I lean a bit to the left, and she does not pull back. So I put my hand on her knee and she covers it with her jacket. So my hand wanders across her thigh, I investigate her knickers, and she joins in with enthusiasm. At that moment I was almost ready to give thanks for this damned war."

"And then what?" Zuzik probed. His green eyes are gleaming and he looks rather ridiculous. I turn over a page of my book and act as if I am not listening. But in fact we are all too excited to miss a moment.

"Well, the film comes to an end," Sancho groaned. "We go out and she asks if we feel like coffee at her place. Amos winks at me and says 'For sure!' So she takes us along Ben-Jehuda Street to a neat little flat.

Amos and I sink into the comfortable armchairs and she goes into the kitchen to make coffee. After a while she calls to me to come and help. Amos winks again and whispers to me that I should leave something for him to help with. Then I go into the kitchen and close the door behind me.

What can I say? She has changed into a shiny red housecoat. There is hardly any room in the kitchen and with every movement I touch her. Suddenly I notice that she is wearing a wedding ring. 'Are you married?' I ask. 'Yes,' she answers, 'but that is not important. My husband is not in town. He disappeared quite some time ago. And he is totally inconsiderate.' She smiles from ear to ear and I can see her teeth with her tongue gliding between them. So I say to myself: 'What the hell. What do I care for her bourgeois husband. This idiot is enjoying his life with some woman or other and I am soon going to fall in battle for this donkey.' So I put my arms around her, she presses herself against me, and I kiss her. She has her tongue down my throat, I can hardly breathe. I can feel her tense in my arms, her housecoat opens and reveals her naked body. I forget the world around me. Have you ever done it standing?"

For a moment the only sound in the tent is Zuzik's quiet moaning.

"Then we make the coffee, I carry the tray into the room, and we drink it. I tell Amos that he should help her later to wash the dishes. Then we talk about the adventure that I am supposed to have experienced in the Negev. She says 'My God!' and 'No, really?!' and 'That's incredible!' and then she says that it will all be over soon. When I laugh and ask her how she can be so sure about that, she says that her husband told her. Her husband is certain about that. He is an officer in the HISH by the name of Rashke.

"At first that means nothing to me. Then I remember: Rashke is the company commander who pulled the wounded men out of the burning armored car the day before yesterday, in the Jerusalem valley, and got a bullet in the face. I can feel my stomach turning and want to vomit. I get up and leave the house staggering like a drunk. I can still see her astonished expression and Amos beginning to stroke her ... and now: back to your stinking beds. Let me sleep."

"What's the matter with you?" said Zuzik enviously. "What do you care? And anyway, Rashke had no idea, that you ..."

I turn out the light. It is cold in the tent. I think about Rashke, how he crawls to the armored car under enemy fire. The cries of the wounded. Suddenly his nose explodes , his jaw is smashed, and his face is just a pulp of blood and flesh. And the diesel from the tank flows onto the road and burns ...

The Radio

"Water, water, water!"

My room-mate has recovered consciousness. At first he groaned, now he is howling more than shouting. Like a wounded animal. And between the howls his breathing is labored. It sounds like a blunt, rusty saw.

Rachel comes at a run. She still has the magazine she was reading in her hand. The sweaty face of a soldier is smiling out from the front page. A rifle with mounted bayonet is meant to lend the picture a certain glamor.

"Water … Give me waaaater!" cries the wounded man.

If he keeps on shouting like that he will wake all the other wounded men in the big room. Rachel tries to calm him down, without success.

"Give him something to drink and be done with it," I feel like telling her. "He won't survive the night!" But I keep my mouth shut. I am not quite that crazy.

A sentence comes to me, that I read once, written by some general: "The soldier must die with dignity." It must have seemed pretty simple to the general at his desk. A bullet hits you in the chest, you raise your arms, shout "It is good to die for the fatherland!" – and you sink, as in the movies, gracefully to the ground. But if the bullet hits you in the face and not in the chest, then your dignified death doesn't look quite so fine. In Ibdis there were two in a trench, arm in arm, but without heads. It was not easy to tell if they died with dignity. How can a man die with dignity when his body is racked with pain and he is not allowed anything to drink?

Rachel groans and sits on my bed. Nurses often appear to have no feelings for the suffering around them. That is not so. It is not possible to get used to this misery. Nor to the sight of death in the field. You just get used to controlling your face and suppressing your feelings. The only alternative is to go mad.

"Why is he moaning like an old woman?" I am not angry. I screamed too. But I want the nurse to talk to me. I want her to sit there and help me to fight against the night.

"You should be ashamed of yourself!" she rebukes me. "He is in a very, very bad way."

"What's the matter with him?"

A bullet hit him in the chest. Two holes – in front the entry point, the exit from his back. He was treated like anyone with an injured lung. It was not until this evening, when the records of liquid intake and output were checked, that it was noticed that he was drinking far too much. A clear sign of a stomach wound. He was given another thorough examination. It was found the bullet had indeed entered his chest and exited through his back, but on its way it severely damaged nearly all his internal organs.

Tomorrow morning a desperate attempt will be made to operate on him. Rachel did not say "if he is still alive." But it was clearly written in her face. Tomorrow morning. Still ten hours to go ... an eternity for someone who is fighting for his life.

I am on my own. Rachel has left. The sound of the saw fills the room. It seems to be getting louder all the time. Soon my skull will burst. It will drive me mad if it does not stop. You should be able to close your ears. Doesn't work. Concentrate on other sounds. There are other sounds. There always are. You just have to listen properly.

Where did I hear that before? The start of the first night exercise. Twelve young city boys in a dark field, feeling nervous. Silence all around. Not a sound. We hear nothing. "Listen," says Musa, the squad leader. "Nature is noisy. Thousands of sounds. You just have to listen properly. Can you hear? This whistling, that is the wind in the trees over there. Listen: one, two, three dogs are barking to the north-east. There must be a house there. And now – the distant rattle of a car. You must learn to open your dirty ears to these noises. That can save your life. They will hide the noise of your steps from the enemy, and they will betray the enemy. Pay attention to the cicadas ..."

The cicadas. The cicadas chirp. And they never stop, not for a moment, during all the nights of battle. People died and the cicadas sang. The wounded are left in the field and the cicadas sing them a lullaby, till they fall asleep and die. No. I don't want to think about it. Shut up, damned cicada! There, far away, a radio is playing. Where? Perhaps in the nurses' tents? No. They have no radio. In the mess hall of the neighboring barracks? It is a tango. That should remind me of something nice. But what? I always was a poor dancer. I just lack the talent. So I act as though these things are beneath me. What it is really? A socially acceptable form of petting in public! But secretly I am jealous of the dancers, of course ...

The tango stops. Someone laughs. The radio plays an Arab melody. Immigrants from Morocco must be sitting there. An Arab tune ... Arab, Arab ... what kind of face emerges from the sea of memories? The turncoat from Sudan who came to Negba with the machine gun in his hand? A pleasant face. Under the heavy mortar bombardment he was next to me in the trench. We smoked together. We cursed the Egyptians and talked about home ... No! Not him. It is a different face.

Perhaps the Sudanese major we captured in Beit Daras? He was old. Over fifty. He came all the way from Khartoum to take part in the Holy War. What a strange combination of words: Holy War. A brave man. When we captured him, he was wounded. But he would not let us treat his wounds before a more seriously wounded private from his unit, who lay next to him, had been looked after.

No. It is not the major's face either. A different one. Before that. The first I saw. Latrun? No, before Latrun. Earlier, before Maccabi. Nachshon? Yes. That's it. An Arab face ...

Arab face.

Since the early hours of the morning the company has occupied the position overlooking the road to Latrun, waiting. Everyone knows that there is no point waiting. Someone "up top" had this glorious idea that the Arabs might go for a stroll around here, although any idiot can see the Arabs know that stretches of this road are in our hand. And so the company lies here the whole day, from early morning till sunset, in this ridiculous position, to trick the naive Arabs. But the Arabs are not naive. Only the British occasionally drive around here. The observation posts radio a report of vehicles on the road.

The men get their heads down and load their weapons. After a few tense moments some vehicles appear – but at the last moment the observation post tells us to keep our cover and do nothing. British faces have been recognized in the vehicles.

Each soldier is lying on his own, a few meters apart from the others. Each one has found a rock for cover. There is no shortage of rocks around here, thank God. The sun beats down. Some have taken off their shirts and are baking half naked in the sun. Drinking is, of course, forbidden. Water is valuable. All that remains is dreaming – nebulous, short-lived, meaningless.

Far away, on the horizon, we can see Arabs tending their fields. The look like miniature chess pieces moved by invisible hands. I am lying behind a machine gun and aiming. Of course you are not allowed to shoot. We have to maintain the illusion that no one knows about our ambush. The bullets couldn't reach anyone. The distance is over two kilometers. Or is it less than that? I change the weapon's setting to one and a half kilometers. Even that is much too far to have much effect. Doesn't matter. The safety is on in any case. Now the Arab is directly on the back sight. The front sight is getting nearer. Too high. A bit lower. Just right. Now it would be simple to hit him. One bullet and that's it. An idiotic thought. That's what boredom makes you do – silly things.

I lie on my belly with the sun burning my sweating back. I can't turn over. I have an impressive boil on my backside. Nothing to be embarrassed about.

That is definitely a front wound. That comes from getting sardines to eat three times a day, two weeks long. Three varied meals a day: for breakfast sauerkraut with sardines, for lunch sardines and sauerkraut, and for dinner you get not only sauerkraut but also sardines. We are all suffering from vitamin deficiency. Some of us suffer from heartburn, which makes the nightly guard duty hell. Diarrhea is another front illness. My boil is the pinnacle of the romance of war. If I don't see the medic tomorrow the sore will spread over my whole body.

Behind the next rock Farouk is lying. He was born in Damascus and owes his name to his plump, Arab-looking face. He looks like a pimp, and that was in fact the way he earned his money in Damascus. He prefers not to talk about this phase of his life. To make up for that, he is quite happy to talk in detail about other activities. How during

World War II he conned British officers into buying worthless items at horrendous prices. He tells these stories over and over in an attempt to prove that he is the equal of the "white" comrades of the battalion. I listen with half an ear, I have nothing better to do in any case. Here you can hear the most amazing stories from people you would never meet under normal circumstances. Farouk and I are worlds apart. But here, lying behind these rocks, the differences shrink into meaninglessness.

Hours pass. I remember that I have some photos in my pocket. I get them out and look at them. Photos I took of girls on my last leave. Meaningless acquaintanceships. But here they all look especially pretty and I fall in love with all of them at the same time. Lying on the warm ground I am suddenly overcome by desire.

"Show me!" demands Farouk. He examines the pictures and whistles quietly, purses his lips. "Wow! What a chassis!" – which is supposed to be a compliment.

Slowly the position turns into a photo market. The girls are passed from hand to hand. "Oh, she is good," groans Jamus. "Her?" answers Kebab contemptuously. " I wouldn't touch her with a barge pole." Jamus doesn't give in. "Not with a barge pole. But maybe with something else." But Kebab acts bored. "I wouldn't take her to bed for one hundred pounds."

"Quiet!" shouts the company commander. "Nobody is interested in your sexual exploits!"

War is a sandwich – a thin slice of danger between two thick slices of boredom.

* * *

"Incoming message!"

The radio operator whispered to the commander, who called to the men that the lookouts had seen movement on the road.

At last. Hands load rifles. The men lower their heads behind the cover and point their weapons toward the curve where the enemy must appear. Thirty rifles are ready. Hands are shaking.

On the road a single man appears.

He is walking in the direction of Latrun as though unaware that fighting is going on here. He doesn't see the unit. He has no idea that thirty rifles are aimed at him and that at least three pairs of binoculars are watching him – from various directions.

A single person is walking along the road.

"Two hundred meters – enemy on the road – one bullet – fire!"

All thirty rifles fire as one. The man stands there for a moment. Then he breaks into a run. Hell! All the bullets missed their target. But his fate is sealed. The rifles fire like crazy. Bullet. Bullet. Another bullet. The machine gun coughs. At least one hundred and fifty rounds are fired.

The man is lying on the ground.

* * *

A truck comes to take the wounded man to HQ. He is lying on the road, surrounded by the curious. The wounded man writhes in pain, cries, shouts. His right leg has been hit by several machine gun bullets. The medic tries to stop the bleeding. There is not much chance of saving his leg. It will probably have to be amputated.

"Why is he being treated? He is an Arab after all," shouts a short man. "Wounded is wounded," says the medic censoriously. "All over the world wounded prisoners are treated."

"Don't be childish. Who cares if he dies?"

"Is that also a human being? This stinking Arab?"

The medic takes no notice. He moves quickly and bandages the wound.

"What he needs is a bullet," announces Kebab. And plays with the safety catch of his rifle. Kebab is tall and dark, his voice always hoarse, and his eyes in continual movement. Nobody knows exactly what he was in civilian life.

"Enough," Sancho interjects. "We are not savages."

"What does that mean?" objected the short man. "What did the Arabs do in Yasur? And in the Hayotzek foundry? Are they not slaughterers? They slaughter and we slaughter as well. That is all!"

"Shut your mouth," growled the commander from some distance. "Prisoners are not killed because we need to extract information from them. Is that clear?" And that is now really clear to all.

The medic completes his work. The blood-covered man is loaded into the jeep. The medic sits next to him. Someone else has to help by holding the wounded man.

"You there!" the commander remembers me. "You have this decoration don't you, this boil on your bottom. Get up and have yourself treated." Everyone laughs.

"Tomorrow I'm going to get myself a boil on the balls," muttered Kebab.

* * *

The journey is awful. The vehicle jumps around, the wounded man moans and groans. We want to help him, but what on earth can we do? "Mayia, mayia"[1] the Arab moans. We have no water. We hold him firmly so he is shaken around less. Our hands are covered in his blood.

"I am going to die," he whispers. "You won't die" the medic tries to comfort him with the little Arabic he has picked up. "Wait a moment. The doctor will come soon."

"I am going to die. Going to die!" the wounded man repeats.

Strange thoughts dance through my head. We ought to tell him that everything will be OK. That he will soon be treated, that we will take him to a hospital. But my mouth is sealed. I hold him firmly, feel his writhing body and his pain. A revolting brown liquid flows over my hands. And I always thought that blood was red.

* * *

We carry him into the medical tent. The doctor examines him and puts on a new bandage. The doctor is very unpopular. A short man from Poland who treats every sick or wounded patient as though he was a shirker.

I drop my trousers and show him my bottom. The boil is red and swollen. A little nurse tries to treat it. She is young and embarrassed. After two weeks on the front my body is not particularly clean. I don't care. I look at the wounded Arab. An officer of the intelligence corps comes in. "How does it look?" he asks the doctor, who shrugs his shoulders as though the matter had nothing to do with him.

"Where do you come from?" he asks the wounded man in Arabic. He doesn't answer. Just whimpers to himself like a whipped dog.

"Min wien inta,"[2] shouts the officer.

Now the wounded man answers, falteringly. He is a Fellah from Masmiyya. He has a wife and two small children. He was going to the town of Lod to earn some money. He doesn't know where the Arab fighters are. He doesn't know anything about the war. He is a simple Fellah who wants to feed his wife and two children.

The officer is annoyed.

"How many Iraqi soldiers are in Wadi Sarar?" he asks.

"Bi-hayat Allah, ma b'aref"[3] the Arab yammers.

"Qadesh Iraqi fi Wadi Sarar?"[4] the officer shouts, hitting him on the chest. The wounded man moans and says nothing.

"Don't give him anything to eat or drink," say the officer and prepares to leave.

The doctor shrugs his shoulders. The whole thing is nothing to do with him.

"But … but he is wounded, isn't he?" the squeaky voice of the little nurse suddenly burst out. Her face is red.

As if bitten by a tarantula the officer whips round: "Why are you interfering?" he screams. "In a week we will attack Wadi Sarar. Do you want our people to be killed?"

"No," admits the shocked nurse.

"Then shut your mouth and mind your own business!" says the officer and leaves.

The next morning I feign blood poisoning and am returned to the medical tent. The nurse is not there. A nice, fat medic removes my plaster, spreads some colorful ointment, mumbles something about poor diet and vitamin deficiency, and covers the painful area with a new plaster.

I want to ask about the wounded man. But I dare not introduce the subject. I wait until the medic has completed his work. Then I offer him a cigarette and casually ask about him.

"Oh, that Arab?" asks the medic indifferently, "he's buried."

"What, buried?" I ask.

"Of course," says the medic. "That's what you have to do. Or should we preserve him in alcohol?"

I feel like asking whether he died of his wounds or whether he was finished off. But I don't ask. I am afraid of the answer.

* * *

A person has died.

If he had remained in Masmiyya, he would be still alive. His wife would have a husband, his children a father. I try and imagine his departure. He tells his wife that he is going to Lod to earn some money. The children run after him. A boy and a girl. He sends them back to their mother, half laughing and half strict. "When is Papa coming back?" asks the girl. "In a few days" says the mother. "He will bring money and we will have something to eat ..." He harmed no one. So why did he die?

It is war. That means we have to kill each other. That's the way it is. But this person, this one individual, did he *want* war? That is unimportant. Of those who die in war only very few really wanted it. Those who wanted it are very rarely among the victims.

So why did he have to die? I know, there is a simple answer: he was an enemy.

A strange word. Enemy. It can mean anything. And really it means nothing at all. Think the word "enemy" and your heart fills with hate. You want to kill, to destroy. But when you see the enemy with your own eyes, you see a person – like yourself. If you get to know them, you can't hate them any more. How would it be if all of us – the Arabic speakers and the Hebrew speakers – got to know each other? Could we still hate each other then, kill each other?

Stupid ideas. He is dead and that's all.

Yes. Of course. Finito. But why did this poor man die? Why is his wife a widow and his children orphans? What has our fight to do with him? Is he the *enemy*?

* * *

We are on guard duty tonight, four men at the southern gate. Actually only two of us should be here, the other two should be patrolling the fence. Ramle is not far away. And Sukreir is very near. But we are neglecting our duties. Nothing has happened in this area since Nachshon. Why should today be any different? The Fellaheen are happy if we don't attack them and never stick their noses outside their villages.

We are sitting at the foot of an old British water tower. Sancho has stolen some tins of Australian emergency rations from the mess hall. From pure boredom we are chewing the stone hard sweets and the dry fruit. Joker has brought some cognac which helps us to keep out the cold.

"Total bullshit," remarks Sancho between two gulps. "Here we stand like telephone poles, and the camp is so big that any stinking Arab could climb over the fence at any place."

"Bullshit!" agrees Joker. "I am going to lie down."

"That's just what we'll do," Sancho decides. "One sentry is enough. Every half hour we'll change around. Me first, then Joker. Uzi third and Zuzik fourth."

Joker wakes me after an hour exactly. I sit there, wrapped in a woolen blanket and still freezing. The night is dark. In the distance the lights of the Kibbutz twinkle. The cicadas chirp. I try to eat up the rest of the emergency rations but they have no taste at all. I try to think about something. But my thoughts have no shape.

Strange. Only five months ago I would have enjoyed reading a serious book. Now it is too much for me to concentrate on a cheap novel. We don't even have girls in our heads any more. They appear more often in dirty jokes than as the object of real lust.

What did Freud have to say about that? No idea. If Freud had been a private in the infantry, and had to keep watch for four hours every night, then he would not have had the time or the energy to worry about the psychopathology of everyday (or every night's) life.

The hands of the clock move agonizingly slowly. Ten more minutes, eight more, five, three. I can wake Zuzik now. He needs three minutes to wake up. He is lying rolled up like a hedgehog, and I give him a kick in the bump I assume to be his backside.

"Yob tvoyu Mat. Pigdog" he curses in his sleep.

"Yob tvoyu yourself! Get up. You're on!"

"What time is it?"

"Three minutes before half past."

"Why are you waking me up now, you ass?" He wobbles his head and blinks. I lie down, pull the covers over my head, and fall asleep.

I dream about school. We are in the sixth or seventh class and the teacher is explaining to us something from the Talmud, about a bull or a cow. Nobody is listening, we all find it deadly boring. The red-headed boy sitting next to me has a pistol bullet with him, which we are examining surreptitiously. Disturbances are sweeping the land, our older brothers are auxiliary policemen, and we are getting bored at school. Suddenly I hear my name. "What did Rabbi Gamliel say about that?" asks the teacher. I don't know what he is talking about. The whole class is staring at me and grinning with schadenfreude. The bullet falls to the ground with a clatter. "What was that?" asks the teacher. "A Mauser cartridge caliber 11.56," I stutter. "No: caliber 11.54," shouts the redhead. "Quiet!" roars the teacher. "Shame on you. Go to the director."

Someone nudges me. "Rabbi Gamliel said ... he said ..." but

standing in front of me is Musa, the squad leader. I look for my rifle.
It is not there. The others' rifles are also gone.

"Wake your friends up!" Musa laughs. "Four sleeping men on
watch. Four Arab battalions could have marched in and slaughtered
the lot of us – and all thanks to you pigdogs." I wake up the other
three. We stand in the first light of dawn and shiver.

"Go to the chief and report that you were asleep on watch and that
your rifles were taken away."

The chief is a major, a former officer of the Jewish Brigade.[5] We go
to his barracks and squint through the window. He is lying in bed
with his mouth half open. The colorful sleeves of his pajamas lend
him a totally non-military appearance. When we see him like that, we
get angry. Why can he sleep and we can't? What is better about him?
It is just a matter of chance that he is an officer and we are ordinary
soldiers.

I curse Zuzik for not getting up when I woke him, and he attacks
me for waking him too early and not waiting until he got up. We
argue for a long time, getting louder and louder until the door opens
and the sleepy face of the chief appears. He yells at us, his face red with
anger: "To hell with you stinking farts. You have been disturbing my
sleep for the last hour. What do you think you are doing here?"

Sancho puts on his most subservient expression and explains:
"Musa, the squad leader, sent us here to wake you."

"I haven't the faintest idea who Musa is. To hell with him!" His
voice cracks. "Get away from here, and make sure I don't see your
dirty faces again today." We run away. When we have turned the corner of the barracks we collapse with laughter.

* * *

As a punishment Musa gives us twelve hours' guard duty. Zuzik and
Joker stand at the southern gate, opposite the kibbutz, while Sancho
and I guard the northern gate facing Sukreir. We are bored and chew
a brick of dried fruit that got stuck in my trouser pocket.

Just before midnight two figures approach the gate. We can hardly
believe our eyes. One of them is an old Fellah wearing a keffiyeh and
an Agal,[6] the other is dressed like a townie, probably a Jew. He
explains to us that the old man is the Mukhtar[7] of Sukreir. He has to
talk with the chief. Sancho seizes the opportunity and sets off with
the two. He forgets to come back.

After three hours he turns up again; full after a heavy meal and very pleased with himself. He heard everything that was said. The old man came to offer peace. The village of Sukreir doesn't want war. The villagers are prepared to surrender under the condition that we protect them. In the village there is only one warlike person who supports the Mufti.[8] The Mukhtar suggests setting a trap for him, so that we can take care of him. He has a long list with him covering all the weapons in the village.

Sancho scratches his ear – a sign that he is inclined to philosophize. "Listen, my friend" – full of enthusiasm – "I am wasting my time here. The infantry is OK for Zuzik and that donkey Musa, but not for someone with my intelligence."

"The infantry is the queen of the battlefield," I quote from a book whose title I have forgotten.

"Yes, because she gets fucked by everybody," explains Sancho. "In brief, that's nothing for me. I have discovered my true military calling. Can you guess what that is?"

I have no idea.

"We need a special unit for political work among the Arabs," he explains. "That is the job for me! These Fellaheen have no taste at all for war. We could make peace with them in a moment. We just have to find out who wants peace in each village, give them some money, and wipe out the Effendis[9] who still support the Mufti. In a month our regime will be recognized by all villages."

"And if the Arab states march in with their armies?"

"If the population is on our side there will be no invasion. And if it did come to an invasion, we'll arrange a civil war among the Arabs. We will always be able to find some to fight on our side. They just have to see that we support the Fellaheen and fight against the Effendis. All we need is a little intelligence."

"You should take some leave and explain that to Ben-Gurion," I suggest.

Sancho's enthusiasm wilts. "There's no point. You don't understand anything," he complains. "It would be much better to work with the Arabs rather than attacking them and dying. If you want to die – I don't care. You can all die and set up your own tombstones. But count me out. The infantry is not my thing."

*   *   *

In the evening the whole company – apart from us four criminals – is going to the movies in Rehovot.

But at the last moment it is canceled. The company is planned as a reserve. Rumor has it that another company is to attack Sukreir. Sancho and I stare at each other. Why attack? Haven't they offered peace?

The whole company is in uproar. "To hell with them," shouts Tarzan. "I'm going to beat up these commanders. Why won't they let us go to the movies? How many battalions do we need to take this lousy village?"

"Only a dog remains as a reserve!" Tarzan continues to shout. Suddenly he smiles. "You know what?" he explains. "We'll have a party and finish off the wine that was left over from Pesach."[10]

We storm the stores and purloin about fifty bottles of red wine. We take it to the little room that is set up as our "hall of culture." We have furnished it with things we found in a deserted cafe. There are stools, a radio we got from the battalion, and a carpet that somehow found its way here.

We begin with a few gulps, passing the bottle around. We roar the company song, the radio plays at full volume, a really cosy atmosphere fills the room.

"Call yourselves drinkers?" Tarzan shouts. "For ten piasters I'll finish off a whole bottle in one go."

"So will I, so will I!" squeaks Zuzik.

"I'll give you five, if you manage that." Sancho likes to bargain.

Tarzan pours the wine down his throat, coughs, and empties the bottle. He takes his money. Zuzik manages half a bottle, then slams it on the floor and runs out. Everybody laughs.

We stand up, staggering and supporting ourselves against the walls. Sancho, the only one who is not dead drunk, grabs me by the collar, leads me to the company barracks, and throws me on my bed. I fall asleep immediately, fully clothed. After less than an hour he wakes me up.

"What is going on? Are you crazy, waking me up in the middle of the night?" I feel sick. Something is pressing on my stomach, like on the evening before our first battle.

"Get up." Sancho shakes me. "Can't you remember? We are on sentry duty." I groan. Get up, find my rifle, and stagger along behind him to the warehouse that we are supposed to guard. There I hug a wooden post and spew.

"I think I am dying" is all I can mumble. My stomach is turning over.

"I hope so," Sancho answers mercilessly.

I lie down on a pile of sacks of flour and go straight back to sleep.

* * *

When I wake up the sun is beating down on my face. The warehouse is deserted. Sancho is not there and my mind is clear again.

In front of the headquarters stands a convoy looking like something out of *The Thousand and One Nights*. The company which was in Sukreir during the night has returned in their armored vehicles. They look like figures from a fairy story: turbans and keffiyehs on their heads, sparkling daggers in their belts. And the vehicles are sparkling too: long swords, water pipes, masbahas.[11]

A soldier with a walrus mustache – wearing a yellow keffiyeh and a square agal with silver threads, like those worn by respected sheikhs – fills Sancho in with the details.

"Without these bloody British we would have had no trouble. We had surrounded this shitty village and called through loudhailers for them to bring out their weapons. You should have seen how they ran to give up their weapons. It was a joy to watch. Then we went from house to house to search them. Then we suddenly learned that the damned Brits were approaching with their tanks from the direction of Sarafand. So we beat it quickly."

"To hell with these Brits," cursed someone in the next vehicle. "I had just got my eyes on a nice little one, well rounded with really dark eyes. Just when I was about to grab her we had to disappear."

"Ugh! Do you want to rape Arab women?" The man with the mustache played holier-than-thou.

"So what? War is war. I can't see what's wrong with that!"

"Why not?" a third joined in. "If you can kill, you can also rape."

"That is something different. In war you have to kill. But to rape – that is disgusting."

"Especially with a stinking Arab woman!" sneered the man with the mustache.

"There is no arguing about taste" added another philosophically.

* * *

At lunch in the canteen we hear that three Arabs were taken prisoner and that Jamus, our Egyptian, is guarding them.

"Come on, let's go and see," says Tarzan.

The three Arabs are in one of the empty barracks. They are sitting on the ground and talking quietly. All three are very young, between fifteen and twenty-five years old. Good looking lads, well built. Fear is written on their faces.

Jamus is listening to them but pretending not to understand. He was born in Egypt and looks like an Arab Effendi. Rather fat and sporting a very impressive black mustache. He used to work illegally in Arab countries. That got too boring for him, so he signed up for the army when the war broke out. An outsider would not recognize him as the most interesting person in the company: he studied at a British college in Egypt, and had a higher rank in the British Navy. He is a member of a kibbutz near the border and is an ordinary soldier here.

The Arabs are discussing something inside, and outside Jamus translates their words for us. The three are brothers. They were arrested during the night, because the machine gun could not be found, that was on the Mukhtar's list.

"Why did Jaber run off with the machine gun?" asks the eldest, the one with the curly hair and the gigantic mustache. "We should get him back."

"He must have run away to Ramle."

"The Jews will beat us up first and then kill us."

"No they won't. The Jews know that we are innocent."

"The Jews wouldn't do a thing like that. They will put us on trial and so find out that we are innocent."

"But before that they will beat us up."

Tarzan goes in and offers them cigarettes. "Mayia. Mayia." pleads the youngest.

Tarzan picks up an empty jug and walks past us without looking at us. "I was going to the mess hall in any case, to drink something." He returns with lemonade.

The eldest stands up and wants to go to the toilet. He puts a blindfold on himself. I take him by the arm and guide him to the latrine on the other side of the road. I wait until he has finished. I even give him an old newspaper.

On the way back the Arab forgets to put on his blindfold and it makes no difference to me. Why shouldn't he see the sun once more? Suddenly he begins to shout "Khawaja[12] Cohn, Khawaja Cohn" and points excitedly at a group of civilians on the road.

We call the man named Cohn to us. He talks with the prisoner. Cohn is a farmer from Rehovot, and the Arab once worked in his orange grove. He tells us that he knows the Arab as a friend of the Jews. He can vouch for him.

Tarzan and I run to the company commander and tell him. But he is not interested and sends us to the intelligence specialist.

When we storm into the intelligence office someone is sitting there whom we don't know. Presumably he belongs to one of the non-combatant branches. We quickly tell him the whole story.

When he realizes that we are ordinary soldiers he goes red: "You dare to come crashing in here! Where did you learn to talk to an officer without reporting? Back to the door and stand to attention!"

We feel like giving him a punch on the nose. But we don't want to annoy him. That could harm the prisoner. We go to the door and stand to attention. "We thought it our duty to report this. Otherwise the men could be killed for no reason."

"What has that got to do with you? Are you trying to tell me how to do my job? Get out before I write a complaint!"

We go out and stay by the door. We don't know whether to go back in and give him a thrashing or to let matters rest. I console myself with the fact that he did at least make a note of the farmer's name. Maybe his statement could help after all …

* * *

What happened to the three? I forgot about the matter long ago. Now it suddenly appears very important. Were they set free? Did they return to Sukreir? Then I remember that Sukreir does not exist any more. Before the Egyptians even invaded, the inhabitants were driven out. Two days before I was wounded I was there by chance and saw the new inhabitants of the village. They spoke some strange Slavic language. An abandoned village. One of many.

Another three people. Three drops in this murky sea that is called war …

* * *

What the hell! That's enough of this tune!

I don't want to think about Arabs. Not these Arabs. Is it impossible to think of Arabs without remembering something awful? I want pleasant memories, funny ones. I'll have to search for them. I'm sure they exist. You just have to work at it. Arab voices, laughs ...

Yes! Here ... we are in the village of Manzuva. The sun slowly rises. In the faint morning light the Egyptian positions appear before us, about a kilometer away. We are tired and content. Yesterday evening we did our work well. Six of us crawled to the Egyptian positions until we could feel the barbed wire and hear the coughing of the bored sentry at the machine gun. We crawled among the thorns until we found the telephone cable connecting this position with its neighbor. The specialists joined up the cable with our own one which we had laid from our positions in Manzuva. Nothing happened. We crawled back along the cable, covering it all with sand. Nice work.

Now we are sitting and waiting for the Egyptians to talk on the line. Jamus is holding the receiver in his hand. Out of curiosity I have volunteered to help him. He will translate and I will write it all down.

"Hallo Falluga! Hallo Falluga!" The voice of a young Egyptian. The Palestinians pronounce the name of the place as "Falluja."

"Naam ya sayyedi"[13] answers a rather distinguished voice. Wonderful! Seems to be a staff officer in Majdal.[14] We have really tapped the main link connecting all the Egyptian positions on the front.

"What's the news?" Jamus translates for us.

"Alhamdulillah."[15] A philosophical, rather vague expression.

"Isma ya Suleiman"[16] in a submissive tone. Why is it that, in all the armies of the world, the frontline soldiers lick the asses of the heroes of HQ?

"What's up?" The staff man knows his value.

"Suleiman, you are there at HQ and know everything. When are we going to get leave?"

The magic word "leave." Suleiman's heart melts. He groans. "God knows when. I have no idea."

Jamus and I smile. For a moment they are not our "enemies," people who could kill us tomorrow – or we them. They are comrades in the Internationale of the gray front mice, who have everything in common – suffering, longing, the experiences, the fear.

"When will this war be over?" groans the man in Falluga.

"Shut up!" complains the staff man. "That is in the hands of Allah."

I write zealously. This is important for our intelligence people. Despondency. War weariness. And that is the best brigade in the Egyptian army ... Nonsense! I suddenly say to myself. Those are the very same words that we use. War weariness? Who is not tired of this war? Wouldn't we break into a wild dance of jubilation if someone told us that a peace agreement had been signed?

And anyway – why not? Why are we fighting? Why do they aim their British weapons at us, and we our Czech machine guns at them?

Do we really have any conflict with each other? Isn't what they want the same as what we want – to drive out the British, the Americans, and the French and to develop Egypt, Palestine, Syria, and Iraq?

For a moment I have the crazy idea of taking the receiver from Jamus's hand and talking with them. "Listen to me, Suleiman," I would say, "we are wasting our time here. You won't really be serving your homeland, nor I mine, if we kill each other. Your father is a Muslim and mine a heathen and they hate each other. But you and I, Suleiman, what have we got against each other? Don't we belong to the same patch of earth? We speak (almost) the same language. And if we argue, the Brits, the Yanks, or the Moujiks will come and swallow us up. If we had a little sense, Suleiman, we would organize a Sulha.[17] I would help you to drive the British out of Sudan and you would help me to irrigate my land. Then we could work together to make this sleepy region blossom and live peacefully and amicably ..."

An idiotic idea. You can't speak to the enemy on the telephone, or they will know that we have tapped their line. And anyway: what can we achieve – Suleiman, Jamus, and I, and all the hundreds who are lying around here and trying to kill each other? What is our opinion worth? We are just little pawns on the great chessboard, moved by someone who finds the opinions of Suleiman and me as important as the sex life of the fleas which are biting us here.

"Quick. Write it down!" calls Jamus.

Iraq Suweidan is speaking with Beit Jibrin. They are talking about light tanks and heavy automatic Vickers machine guns. Apparently senior officers. They have more refined voices than the two we just heard. One of our pilots has been shot down near Beit Jibrin. He is about to be taken for interrogation to Iraq Suweidan. Very good! We'll have to inform the brigade staff straight away. Maybe he can be rescued while he is being transferred.

"When was the last time you were in Egypt?" asks Beit Jibrin.

"Oh, Egypt," Iraq Suweidan moans longingly. "Just two weeks ago."

"Really?" Beit Jibrin is full of envy. "What is Groupi like?" When he mentions the well-known cafe in Cairo, his voice is suddenly wide awake.

"Full of life! You can hardly tell that a war is on."

"These shirkers! Damn them!" Beit Jibrin burst out. "Here we are lying in the dirt and they are enjoying a life of paradise. I would send my company there and finish off the lot of them." Cairo or Tel Aviv. Groupi or Pilz. The relation between the front and the rear is identical.

"And how is your wife?"

"My God!" Iraq Suweidan tries to sound shocked. But it doesn't work. With them, too, there are no love secrets between soldiers. "You know what? It was like the days after the wedding. For four whole days I didn't leave the bed …"

"You lucky fellow. And the children …"

"They are both fine. The little one already calls me 'Papa.' He takes after me. A little devil."

"Egypt," Beit Jibrin dreamed, "home, girls, cafes, music. What a dream!"

I have stopped writing. And Jamus is translating the words in a trance. Home, girls, cafes, music. What a dream!

We, however, are in neither Cairo nor Tel Aviv, but in Beit Jibrin and in Manzuva, only a few kilometers apart. And we live in two different worlds, ready, in the name of Arab freedom or Zionist progress, to kill each other, ready to subordinate ourselves to any foreign power, just to prolong this idiotic fratricidal war for years and generations …

* * *

I only experienced it once, such a bridge from front to front, an invisible bridge that lasted for several days.

We were in a position opposite the encircled Falluga. The days dragged past in endless boredom. Never-ending rain turned the earth into deep mud which stuck to your boots, the little tents were soaked day and night and the sentries in the trenches stood up to their knees in water. The only pleasure that Jamus and I had – congratulations, we had just been promoted to squad leader! – was the odd visit to the mess tent where we secretly emptied a tin of pineapple. Or we would spend a quarter of an hour in the company commander's tent and talk with Tucki.[18] Tucki was crazy, like all radio operators. A tall, thin youth with sad, deep-set eyes, he looked like a living corpse. He got his name from his inability to remain still for three minutes.

One morning Jamus and I were on our way to the kitchen to check on the preparations for lunch. Tucki called us to him excitedly. He had picked up the call sign of an Arab station and realized it must come from the surrounded units. They were trying to set up a connection with Gaza or Hebron. Jamus seized the opportunity, and provided us with some interesting minutes in this sea of boredom.

"Hello – Bravo Alpha One – Bravo Alpha One, keif tismaini, keif tismaini?[19] Can you hear me, can you hear me – over."[19] The Egyptian net used British procedures just as we did. The language is the only difference – even the voices of the operators are similar.

Jamus puts on the headphones and holds the microphone firmly. His face betrays the struggle going on inside him. We have clear orders not to use the Egyptian frequencies, to avoid giving them any indication that our intelligence is listening in. But everyone knows that this is a senseless order. Because the Egyptian operators will certainly know, just as our operators know, that the enemy is listening.

The struggle doesn't last long. The curse on his tongue breaks free: "Hello, ya misril. Teezak hamra lesh?[20] You Egyptians! Why is your arse so red? Over"

Silence. Just as Tucki is not allowed to use the Egyptian frequencies, the Egyptian cannot answer the Israeli. But can a soldier restrain himself from answering such a nice insult? Especially when the answer is obvious.

"Because you have licked it too much, you Jew, you dog – Over."

"Uskut, ya ibn kelb!²¹ You dirty son of a bitch! Over." Jamus is warming up. After all, he completed his studies in Egypt with distinction.

The Egyptian feels that such simple insults are beneath him and searches for something special, something that cannot be answered. "When I find out which of your mother's ninety-nine lovers is your father, only then would I answer you, you Akrut,²² you pimp – Over."

If he thought that he would be able to end the discussion with this respectable formulation, then he made a serious mistake. Jamus scratched his head and was soon ready to cap that one.

"For sure your mother sleeps with men on credit, you ass. Over."

This nasty insult annoyed the Egyptian. "Get your sister ready for when we conquer Tel Aviv. Over."

Jamus laughs out loud into the microphone. This boastfulness of the besieged Egyptian is really too cheeky. "The whole Egyptian fleet can't pull your mustache out of my behind, you bastard. Over."

This delicate reference to his desperate situation really stung the Egyptian. "You son of a bitch. Tomorrow we will drown the lot of you in the sea of shit you came from. Over."

The ether crackles. Atmospheric disturbances. This damned rain. Jamus presses the headphones firmly against his ears. "Hello, Egyptian. I can only hear you faintly. Repeat your words, you cesspit. Over."

A moment's silence. The Egyptian is probably realigning his antenna.

"I will be glad to shit into both your ears, you syphilitic Jew. Over." The voice is clearer again.

"What is all this filth in your mouth? Is that all you get to eat over there, eh, Ahmed?"

"My name is Ibrahim, you Jewish son of a bitch. Over."

"Welcome, castrated Ibrahim. Over."

This time the Arab is really upset. "Your father is castrated. I already have three children and two wives in Tanta, curse you. Over."

Jamus considers for a split second. His face is glowing red, and his eyes are sparkling with pleasure. It is a long time since he had such an interesting conversation. "If God wills, you will find three more waiting for you when you get back. Over."

"Don't judge our women by your own, you pimp. Our women are waiting for us with open arms. Over."

"And when do you think you will see these arms again, you madman? You'll still be stuck here in ten years' time. Over."

The Egyptian knows that there is some truth in this. His chances of reaching home soon are slim. There is almost no chance of breaking the siege. And if the war is not over soon, he will either be shot, starved, or will end up as a prisoner of war. He tries to escape through optimism: "I will get out of here. But before you get home your wife will be an old woman. Over."

Everything has its limits. For the sake of entertainment Jamus is quite happy to exchange compliments about parents and siblings. But if his girlfriend is involved, it is a different matter. He has little trust in her faithfulness. And he has no desire to spend five more years on the front. He forgets his Egyptian origins and changes to pure Hebrew. "Yob tvoyu Mat – you dirty Arab!"

"Shut up you Jew, you dog."

* * *

This first radio dialogue was the start of a special relationship between Jamus and Ibrahim. Every morning since then, at around ten o'clock, Jamus and Tucki tune in their radio sets. At ten on the dot they hear loud crackling on the Egyptian frequency, and then Ibrahim's call comes clearly over the ether: "Hello, hello – Bravo Alpha One, hello – Bravo Alpha One, hello – Bravo Alpha One …" Tucki hands the headset over to Jamus and the exchange of juicy curses begins.

This daily entertainment gives Jamus's life new content. He transfers most of his duties as squad leader over to me. I take charge of the distribution of food and the organization of sentry duty. Jamus is busy. He sits in his little tent holding what remains of a pencil, busily scribbling down ancient curses on an old piece of newspaper. He sorts through the memories of his schooldays, or he invents new curses. His highest ambition is to formulate the ultimate, final curse. The one that will shake Ibrahim and shock him so much that he won't be able to find an answer and will have to admit defeat.

But Ibrahim also has talent – and time. Every morning he too has a newly prepared list. Both mothers and fathers to the fifth generation, brothers and sisters, uncles and aunts, religion, nationality, homeland – everything is a target for endless curses and insults, without the duel reaching a decisive point.

And amid all these insults Jamus and Ibrahim are telling each other about their lives. If they ever happened to meet, they would surely recognize each other.

On the fifth day of the dialogue Jamus gets a day's leave. During the morning talk, between cursing and swearing, Jamus informs Ibrahim. He falls silent, lost in thought. The situation is desperate under the siege. Now the last route is blocked, where some supplies could be smuggled on camels in the dead of night. There is now an acute shortage of food, medicine, and ammunition.

"Listen Jamus, you pimp …" Ibrahim pauses. For the first time he expresses a personal request. It is not easy for him. He has a sister in Jaffa. He hasn't heard anything from her since the war started. If Jamus is prepared to look into the matter for him, he will call again in half an hour with the address. Jamus has no time. The jeep to Gedera is just about to leave. Still he waits.

When he returns the next day, his face is grim. I am sitting in the little tent, trying to find a fair way of allocating guard duty, when he comes in.

"Well?" I ask.

"Nothing!" he says.

"You found nothing?"

"Not there!"

"Did you ask at the military governor's office?"

"I went everywhere. There are new immigrants living in the house. The Arabs can remember having seen her in the town after Jaffa was already taken. They think she is dead."

At ten o'clock the three of us are again sitting by the radio. "Hello – Bravo Alpha One, hello – Bravo Alpha One," we hear Ibrahim's voice. Jamus holds the headset firmly. But he does not answer. The call is repeated again and again, until Ibrahim gives up hopelessly.

The next morning he tries again. And again Jamus sits by the radio with his grim expression and says nothing. "Fein inta ya Jamus,"[23] Ibrahim begs. Jamus keeps silent.

"What has it got to do with you?" asks Tucki, who is unnerved by the silence. "Tell him the truth and be done with it."

"Kiss my ass!" Jamus spits back.

On the third day Ibrahim's voice sounds like a distant echo. The batteries of his radio are nearly dead. For a few moments we hear his weakening calls, until they get mixed up with the atmospherics and fade away beneath them. There are no spare batteries.

The invisible bridge between the fronts has collapsed ...

The Irgun Youth

"Nurse! Nurse!"

My call came too late. For a few minutes the wounded man has been directing his empty gaze at the glass on his bedside table. Then he tries to prop himself up on his elbow. He grimaces with pain. Slowly, with great efforts, he raises himself. But before he can reach the glass, he sinks back onto the pillows.

Rachel comes running and turns on the main light. The wounded man's face is red with fever. His mouth is open. He lies there motionless. Only his eyes are alive, as though his whole existence was concentrated there. They fill the room with a silent scream.

"Why – do – you – torture – me?" he mumbles.

Rachel strokes his hair. She talks to him as if he were a small child. "Don't talk nonsense. We don't want to torture you. We want to help you get better." She talks quietly, and I don't know if she is trying to convince him or herself.

"What have I done to you? What have I done?" He tries to shout, but he is already too weak. His words are chopped up by the rasp of his breath – worse than any cry.

"You have to hold out!" says Rachel. "Everything will be fine. Tomorrow the pain will be gone. Now you have to hold out."

The wounded man ignores her. A new thought has come into his head. He doesn't have the strength for two thoughts. "You – hate – me," he coughs out. "You – all – hate – me ..." Rachel is horrified. She stares at him helplessly. "You – are – killing – me – because – I – am – an – Etzel – man ..."

The horrible words hang in the air.

Rachel runs out of the room. Perhaps she is crying. The ceiling light remains on.

We are alone – he, me, and his tortured breathing.

Suddenly he is aware of me. Very slowly he turns his head in my direction. Our eyes meet and his gaze pierces my eyes. A look full of hate – primitive, simple, boundless hate.

A terrible feeling of guilt. Why does he hate me? Maybe he can sense that my chances of surviving are better than his? I feel I should apologize to him, tell him that I might die too, I would tell him anything – just to escape his accusing eye.

Maybe he hates me because I was a soldier in the Haganah, while he was in the Irgun? Should I tell him that I was in the Irgun too, many years ago?

*   *   *

An Irgun man.

August 1938. In one month I will be fifteen years old. For two years the land has been in turmoil. The leadership of the Yishuv is preaching restraint and demanding help from the British. They are hoping for a partition of the land. A radical minority is demanding punitive actions and opposes the partition. I am fourteen years old and identify with this minority.

It is eight in the evening. I am walking along Kalisher Street and approaching the old school at the corner of Hatavor Street. My pulse is racing and my knees are trembling. It is the greatest hour of my life. Behind me are boring school years which have left no impression on me. Then a few months of work, at first in a workshop, then an office. Now a new life stretches before me. A life full of danger and purpose. Like everyone else in my age group I am magically attracted to politics. Without politics, life is empty, devoid of meaning and pointless.

At the entrance of the school a few boys are lounging, and send me scornful glances. Trembling, I walk past them. On watch! In the underground! Romantic books and films go through my head. Danger! That is really living! I am overcome with the will to fight for something, without exactly knowing what.

At the foot of the staircase a boy and a girl are standing. They are older than I am.

"Password!" demands the boy.

"Ye – ho – ash," I stutter. I have repeated this word at least a hundred times since this morning, when a mistrustful boy gave me the paper.

"Upstairs! Second floor, on the right!"

"Wait there until you are called," adds the girl.

I climb the dark staircase. A few boys of my age are sitting on a bench in the corridor, just as nervous as I am, all trying unsuccessfully to appear experienced and knowledgeable. From the end of the corridor, through a closed door, we hear occasional stamping. Like exercises on a parade ground. I am getting more and more excited. I can hardly breathe.

A group of young people goes up the stairs whispering to each other. Scraps of conversation reach my ears:

"... the one with red hair was arrested yesterday ..."

"... he won't talk ..."

"... they will beat him up ..."

"... they should have used their guns ..."

One of them looks across to us and sneers: "It looks as though they are starting a kindergarten here!"

"No need to be so proud of yourself," answers one of the others. "They will soon be better shots than you are!"

Arrest! Shots! Beatings! We will have our tasks. Something that makes life worth living, makes it worth taking risks.

A door opens, and a beam of light illuminates me for a moment. "You there, come in!" Someone grips my arm, guides me into the room, pushes me onto a chair, and disappears.

I can't see anything. A bright light on the table in front of me is shining straight into my eyes. But I can feel that there are people sitting in front of me. Maybe three, maybe four. A deep, unnatural voice announces my name and my address. I nod. I am afraid to speak in case my voice is hoarse. My throat is dry.

"Where do you go to school?" asks the voice.

"I ... I don't go to school. I work for a lawyer." Thank God I can speak. My voice sounds almost normal.

"You are working? Hmmmm ... for how long?" It seems that the Irgun people are not used to young people working.

"More than a year."

There is whispering behind the table. One of the voices is that of a woman. Then the deep voice asks me some questions about my political views. When I decided to join the Irgun. If I know its aims. If I am prepared to put myself in danger.

"Do you hate the Arabs?" The voice sounds bored, it seems to be a routine question.

"No," I say.

I notice immediately that I have made a mistake. Silence falls on the room. I curse myself. Why didn't I just say that I hate the Arabs? They are not going to take me now!

"And the British, do you hate them?"

"No!" I answer automatically. Now everything is lost. I can feel that the people on the other side of the table are looking at me with pity. Like a cripple with an important part of the body missing.

They cross-question me. I try and explain my half-baked thoughts. The British should be expelled. And the Arab Effendis too. Then we could come to an agreement with the ordinary Arabs and found a state together with them. I stutter, stumble over my words, despise myself. After half an hour they let me go. I feel like a wrung-out rag.

The next morning a dark-haired girl appears in my office and gives me a piece of paper. "Next Sunday, at twenty hours zero-zero, you are to appear at the usual location, neatly dressed. Password: Rosh Pina."

* * *

Sabbath eve. Quarter to eight. I am strolling along Allenby Street with Rivka. I am wearing the only good suit that I possess – the result of half a year's saving. And I am wearing a tie for the first time. Rivka is the same age as me, fifteen. She is wearing lipstick for the first time. She is carrying a small parcel under her arm, wrapped in brown paper.

My heart is beating fast. It is my first real operation. I am afraid, but I put on a face like a movie hero to impress Rivka.

We are standing next to Witmann's kiosk. The hands of the big clock on the other side of the street move awfully slowly. A fat man with a red face walks past us and examines me closely. For a moment I think of Wilkins, the famous inspector that everyone is talking about. Thank God he goes away. Youths in blue shirts[1] are pushing and shoving around the ice cream stands. Maybe members of the Haganah?[2]

I try to calm my nerves. We were told that there would be armed adults around, in order – if necessary – to protect us. The awful moment is getting closer. Will I do OK? I have a funny feeling in my belly and my knees are knocking.

"Now," says Rivka. The clock shows eight exactly.

"Tshhhhhhhhhhhhhhhhhhhhhhhhh!" All eyes turn to the sky. From the direction of the beach a red firework rocket climbs into the air. That is the work of Joram, the commander. I take the parcel from Rivka, pull off the wrapping paper, and throw the contents in the air. The leaflets fly apart and float to the ground like snow. People rush to grab them, some trying to catch them in the air. I also bend down and pick one up. We walk on, acting as though we are interested in what we read.

My movements were automatic. At the critical moment I did not feel anything. I am filled with unbelievable pride. I am not a coward. I can act no less than the others.

"Hey, you, come over here!" A policeman appears from Shenkin Street. My heart stops. We will have to try a trick. Maybe he saw me throwing the leaflets in the air.

"What do you want?" I smile bravely and throw a meaningful glance over my shoulder. I am surprised at how firm my voice sounds. I am very frightened. The policeman opens his mouth to say something, but changes his mind. We walk past him into Shenkin Street, toward the meeting place.

The leaflet says that the soldiers of the National Military Organization,[3] as a reprisal for the attacks of the Arabs, have exploded a bomb at an Arab market and killed so and so many Arabs.

I am bursting with pride, feel like a hero, in the best possible mood. I have taken part in a dangerous operation, I say to myself. I am a man. I slip my arm around Rivka's waist.

"Stop it!" she says and turns away from me.

"We are being followed," I lie. Our orders are to act like lovers when in danger.

We are supposed to go to a small park behind the health center, on Mazeh Street. It is dark in the corner. We are the first there. We had the shortest distance to go. I lead Rivka to a hidden bench next to some bushes and push her into the place next to me. She moves away. I pull her back toward me.

"Have you gone mad?" she exclaims, but stays in my arms. There is a rustling in the bushes. The second couple has arrived.

"How was it?" asks Joske.

"Nothing special." I try and appear uninterested, as if unimpressed by such small exercises. "A policeman wanted to stop us, but we tricked him."

"Joram promised that we could work with pistols in six months," Rivka says.

"Hopefully," I reply, trying hard to yawn.

* * *

I am lying on my bed at home, waiting for my parents to go to sleep. They both do hard physical work and go to bed early.

Below us, on the second floor, a gramophone is playing. A boy shouts something and a woman laughs loudly and provocatively. She is my red-haired neighbor. Every evening there is dancing at her place. Spoiled youth, with nothing to do. The red-head is tall and pretty. We pass several times a day on the stairs and she looks at me scornfully. She thinks I must be shy because I have not tried to make her "acquaintance" and go to her parties. If she knew what I get up to in the evenings ... I am often tempted to hint to her about my membership of the underground. If she discovered a pistol in my pocket, wouldn't she have a different opinion of me! But you have to be discreet.

Again this loud laughing.

We members of the Irgun don't need to wonder what we are going to do with our time. We live under permanent tension, from action to action, in constant danger. Irgun is job, entertainment, love – all of those. It fills our days, absorbs all our energy. The goal is defined. We are clear about all problems and their solutions. We have no need to investigate matters deeply.

In the office I occasionally nod off. My boss has already asked me to explain this and threatened to fire me. As if the job is important. I'll find another one. The main thing is keep up the action. Particularly now that the British have published the White Paper[4] and the Irgun has started a major offensive.

* * *

The light goes out in my parents' room. I get up and open my closet. It is divided into sections. The three upper ones are full of books. My clothes and my personal things are in the fourth section.

My eyes glide over the books. I bought them one after the other and have read them all. To save the money for them I did without new clothes or trips to the movies.

The books are ordered according to size and subject. The two top sections include the political books. And politics is revolution: Machiavelli, Marx, Lenin, Gandhi, Stalin, Hitler. The section beneath has books about the history of war and military leadership.

I am sixteen years old. Not all the books could be understood easily. Some of them I read two or three times before I believed I had understood the content. The authors are my teachers.

Poems, music, painting, or other beautiful things are unimportant for me. I was born just when Mussolini was marching on Rome. When I was ten, Hitler came to power. And when I was thirteen the disturbances started here and the war in Abyssinia.

We were not brought up to seek the beautiful or the sublime. Certainly we were taught songs. They were not songs about beauty but national songs. They taught us to sacrifice ourselves for the motherland. The interest of our teachers didn't extend any further than this. "It is good to die for the motherland." That was the essence of our education. That replaced music, painting, aesthetics, and the poetry of world literature.

My parents work from dawn to dusk. They have no time to look after me. And if they had the time – what would that change? None of us is pampered in our parents' lap. The gap between the generations is too wide. As children we already turned away from our parents.

* * *

Between the books there are some packages. They look like books wrapped in paper. There are six of them – pistols! Our group's weapon store!

I open one of the packages. A shining German Luger. It comes apart easily. Lovingly I wipe off the oil, lubricate the parts, and reassemble the weapon. Actually, that is not permitted. The weapons are stored at my place. But only Joram, our group leader, is allowed to use them. There is something attractive about them, hypnotic. Or maybe it is just the knowledge that any one of these weapons can land you in Acre[5] for many years.

I clean all six weapons – one after the other. The Luger, which I particularly like for its handiness and beauty, the German Mauser,

which we all hate for its complicated construction, the nice "P.B.,"
the Colt, which reminds us of forgotten cowboy movies, the out-
dated Russian Nagan, and the Belgian "F.N." that gives you a sense of
security. I study them all during evenings at home. The fact that,
as a result, I am more familiar with their handling than the other
members of the group, is naturally a great source of pride.

After cleaning them I release the safety catch of each weapon,
lower it slowly to the horizontal, take aim, and squeeze the
trigger. Someone is standing in the window opposite. If the gun
had been loaded I would have hit them. A shudder runs down my
spine.

* * *

The next evening I walk along Allenby Street carrying two large
books under my arm, with a third book between them, wrapped in
brown paper. Now and then I stop in front of a shop window and
glance around idly. Every man who is walking behind me looks like a
secret policeman. I bend down and tighten my shoelaces, until he has
gone past.

That is the house. A girl and a boy are standing and talking.
They look like all the other couples hanging around the houses at this
time of the evening, smooching. But a secret button is mounted on
the inside of the fence, on the same level as the boy's hand. Joske, who
is studying in a technical school, mounted it there as an alarm
button.

I climb the stairs to the top. The meeting point is the washroom, in
the feeble light of an oil lamp. A dozen members of the group are
already there. Joram, our commander, a twenty-five-year-old post-
man, explains to us the basics of aiming and firing. With a pencil he
draws a little cross on the door. We support the weapon on the cush-
ions, which serve as sandbags, and aim at the cross. Joram checks our
accuracy.

Our movements are like those of a religious ritual. We close one
eye, hold our breath, and aim. It is not easy to hold the weapon still
on the cushion. The smallest movement throws off the aim. Joram
closes one eye and and checks the position. "Excellent," he says,
"exactly in the center."

My comrades, who don't know how many times I have practiced
this exercise at home, look on enviously. I am very proud. At this

moment I despise from the depths of my heart all those who are not members of the Irgun.

* * *

1940. In the world outside a war is raging and the Irgun has called a ceasefire. We continue our intensive training, undertake strenuous hikes and prepare ourselves. My main task is to infiltrate other youth organizations and to set up underground cells. One after the other I become a sportsman in the "Maccabi," a sailor in "Zebulun," and a youth leader in the "Zionist Youth."

The Irgun does not supply me with much information material. Most of the time I have to rely on my own knowledge. Occasionally I notice discrepancies between the official Irgun positions and those I propagate in its name. But I suppress my doubts.

One day I am marching with the Zionist Youth in a mass demonstration of the youth movements. I have forgotten what it was about. The law of land purchase or an immigrant ship that was prevented from docking. The "Institutions of the Yishuv" have called a strike. We are carrying flags and many boastful placards, with slogans that no one believes in. Next to the Muslim graveyard, by the beach, empty speeches are made by some personalities. They look rather pitiful and none of us pays them any attention. One of them, a short man with a big nose, is almost dancing with enthusiasm. He stirs the air with his arms and his voice cracks. He is promising a war to the last drop of blood.

"Big mouth," sneers Srulik, a Zionist youth who appears in my notebook as a Haganah member. "They are always talking, but they never do anything!" "The Haganah should do something," I remark casually. "Do what, with these old people in control?" he answers hopelessly. I make a note of what he said, to include in my next report.

The hysterical leader suddenly lowers his voice and asks us to fold up the flags and banners. We sing *Ha Tikva*[6] and are asked to disperse gradually.

"What a scandal" complains Srulik.

"Come on! Let's organize something!" I suggest.

"But what could we do?" he asks sceptically. I know that the Haganah has forbidden its members to cause trouble. The Irgun has also forbidden us from taking part in demonstrations.

I hold the flag in my hand. I don't fold it up. With the flag flutter-ing above our heads I march off toward Ben Yahuda Street. Since the street we are walking along is narrow and the only way into town, a large number of youths collect around us. Without planning any-thing, we have suddenly become a demonstration.

One of the leaders of the Zionist Youth pushes his way through to me and demands that I should fold up the flag. I ignore him. The feel-ing that I am leading a demonstration almost drives me out of my mind.

He has no choice but to walk alongside me.

* * *

"Free Im-mig-rat-ion!" I yell. "Free Im-mig-rat-ion!"

"Free Im-mig-rat-ion!" repeats the crowd.

"Set-tle-ment!" "Def-ense!" someone calls.

"Free-dom o-or death!" roars the crowd behind me.

Word quickly spreads through the little town that a demonstra-tion is under way. On both sides of Allenby Street people are watch-ing and trying to work out whether it is a Haganah or an Irgun march. Joske, my comrade from the Irgun group, is standing at the side of the street and looking on disdainfully. Suddenly he recognizes me and waves. I ignore him. He struggles through the crowd to me and shouts in my ear "Are you crazy? The Irgun has forbidden any kind of participation!"

I don't care at all. I am drunk with joy. "Go to hell!" I shout back. He stares at me, appalled. The very idea that one could disobey an order of the Irgun has never occurred to him. He disappears.

The leaders of the Zionist Youth, who are marching behind me and who don't like the look of this "breach of national discipline," are holding council. "What can we do?" I can hear behind me. "He is crazy. He won't put down the flag!"

A group leader tries to persuade me to stop the madness. There is a rumor that British policemen are waiting by the railway tracks ready to shoot if we approach the District Commissioner's office. I would be responsible for any blood shed. I hesitate, then give in. We will finish the demonstration at the main synagogue.

The youth leaders and I climb the steps. Someone gives me a shoulder up onto the railings. Around me the area falls silent. Hundreds of pairs of eyes are staring at me and trying to guess whether I represent the Haganah or the Irgun. I know that I will have to say something. But I have no idea what. It is so quiet I cannot think. Then I remember our demonstration a year ago, on the evening the White Paper appeared, when the District Commissioner's offices were set on fire. At that time someone got us to swear our loyalty to Jerusalem.

A weight is off my shoulders. I shout: "If I forget thee, O Jerusalem, let my right hand wither!" There is silence as the crowd waits for the rest. I am horrified, because I have forgotten the second half. " Let my tongue ..." Srulik whispers. I raise my head. "Let my tongue cleave to my palate, if I do not remember you!" The crowd is satisfied. Some shout "Bravo!" and others "Boo!" We fold up the flags and go home.

* * *

Something is brewing. First there were odd rumors about differences of opinion among the leadership of the Irgun. And one day everyone knows: there is a split.

Names that we had never heard before, or which were always spoken quietly and respectfully, are all of a sudden pronounced loudly and clearly and covered in mud. The younger ones like us stumble around aimlessly as if our world has collapsed. Until today everything was clear and definite: the supermen are in command, wise and totally fearless, who know exactly how we can conquer the land on both sides of the Jordan river in three, or at most six months. All we have to do is to follow their commands. Now these superhumans are accusing each other of all possible crimes – from murder and informing to corruption.

I wake up as if from a long dream. I try not to let it go, even though I know that it will never return. The doubts that kept surfacing over the last two years, and that I suppressed, return with redoubled strength. What does the Irgun really want? Do I know all its aims? Does it even have a clear goal, a thought-out ideal?

Haven't we been building up illusions simply because we needed them, because we wanted something we could subordinate ourselves to, to give us an aim in our lives and a purpose for our actions?

* * *

The whole company, the seventh company, is summoned to a meeting in the evening in the Bilu school. The guards at the gate neglect their duties. About eighty boys and forty girls are sitting in the hall – sections 25, 26, and 27 of the Irgun. When I go in, discussions are raging everywhere.

"That Rasiel of yours is a disgusting fellow!" the little blond-haired boy from the Montefiori School is shouting. "Definitely an agent of the British secret service ..."

"You ass!" snaps Joske. "How dare you talk like that?"

"Didn't he send us out to inform on Jewish communists? Yes or no? Didn't he deliver these Jews into the hands of the British military? Yes or no?"

"What are you getting excited about? These communists are enemies of Zionism and Russian agents. And your Yair[7] too is a foreign agent, not of the Russians this time but of the Nazis, the fascists!"

"What do you know about it, you stupid donkey? The Germans have conquered France. Do you know what that means? The Germans will win the war! And we can make a deal with the Italians. They are not at all anti-Semitic and they support the idea of a Jewish state."

"Aha! Avraham Stern wants to set himself up as a little Mussolini, eh?"

"Idiot! Jabotinsky[8] said that he would make a deal with the Devil himself if that would help us."

"Atten-tion!" Joram calls out. We jump up automatically, line up, stand to attention.

Ehud, the company commander, receives the reports. His handsome face looks confused and sad. The way I imagine a commander after a defeat. He informs us that he has handed over command of the company to someone else, who will be named by the leadership of the new organization – the "National Military Organization in Israel." We are to go to the room next door where we will be addressed by a leading member of the new organization.

We sit there in the darkness on school benches and whisper to one another. Suddenly a voice emerges from the darkness. It is the deepest voice I have ever heard.

"We follow our commanders into battle, as long as they really lead us into battle ..."

The voice makes a speech. The depth of feeling is unbelievable, and I can feel how the speaker slowly gains control of those sitting around me, hypnotically dispelling their doubts. For some reason this annoys me. The voice fills the room and I am sure that it can be heard on the street and in the neighboring houses. A complete disregard for rules of conspiracy which have shaped our lives for the last two years. Occasionally I notice that I am also being swept away. But I pull myself together and resist the hypnotism, analyzing the sentences and differentiating between demagogy and logical argument.

"You are the chosen few, whose blood will build the new state …" For the first time a few clear questions form themselves in my head. State? What kind of a state? What form will it take? How will it be governed? Will it be a repressive regime or one of justice? Does the Irgun really have a clear idea about the future society?

"And if the old Zionists stand in our way, we will sweep them from the stage …"

The Irgun has already acted against the orders of the Old Man. Has he not disregarded its ideas? Isn't he basing himself on those narrow nationalist ideas, combined with a shallow religiosity? Isn't he also hemmed in by the narrow-mindedness of the Jewish ghetto? Has he any new ideas which the masses could follow? How can a struggle for freedom be led without offering the masses new ideas?

"We will break the Arab resistance with an iron fist …"

It may be that we will be able to found a state against the resistance of the Arabs. But then what? How will we be able to exist in a sea of Arabs full of hate? Do we want to fight an endless war? Do we want to be dependent for ever on foreign help? Today from the Italians, tomorrow from the Russians or the Americans, and the day after tomorrow, perhaps, from a new league of nations? Is it not our task to get the masses of the Arab world on our side? Should we not be developing a new idea, a vision that includes the Arabs? A vision that won't lead to the founding of a new chauvinist ghetto state, but one that can breathe new life into the whole region around us?

The deep voice doesn't answer any of these questions. It gets high on its own words – state, liberation, kingdom, Zion, artillery, submarines. I can see in the semi-dark how the eyes of my comrades are shining, how their muscles are tensed.

The speaker can feel in the darkness that he has conquered their hearts. He winds up his speech with a clever trick. "… and any of you who is afraid to accompany us on this road of sacrifice and suffering, let him get up and leave."

No one stands up. Everyone is hypnotized. Even if their heads had been clear they wouldn't have dared to get up. No one wants to appear cowardly.

I can feel my heart pumping. I know that I have to stand up and leave behind me everything that has given my life a purpose for the last two and a half years. Fine years full of danger, romance, and noble friendship in the underground. I am afraid I won't have the strength to stand up in front of my comrades – but some secret power beyond my control makes me stand up. One hundred and twenty pairs of eyes are staring at me in the gloom.

"You are free!" says the deep voice with infinite contempt.

I walk to the door. I don't know how I manage that. My knees are trembling and my legs are weak.

I walk down the stairs, past the guards who are still engaged in a discussion, and find myself on the street.

I am mixed up. Something in me is crying. Something in me is smashed, something beautiful, important, and great – and simple. But still – in another corner of my heart I feel joy. I know that this crisis had to come, and I am happy that it is over and that I have won. The illusions are shattered, the dream is over. We believed in them. We hoped the grown-ups would show us the direction. But they have nothing, nothing at all, which could give our lives a new content.

We must find the truth ourselves. In ourselves. My heart is joyful because the new truth is still fresh and unused. Only we will understand it. It will break out of the walls of the ghetto and spread across the whole region. Morality and peace and partnership – together they will show us the way to a new life.

* * *

Years pass. Terror. Curfew. British military rule. Kidnapping.

We are all "busy." Everyone is doing "something." Some are organized in the Etzel, others in Lehi, as Avraham Stern's organization is now known. Some belong to the Palmach and still others to the HISH. Here and there new groups are forming, seeking a new ideological path.

Almost all of us are prepared to die for something or other. Only a few have something that is worth living for.

1947. The UN resolution. The war.

It looks as if the nightmare of a civil war, which has cast its shadow over the youth for ten years, has disappeared. The Etzel is responsible for the massacre of Deir Yassin.[9] But the Etzel is not much worse than the others. There is an agreement. Its battalions will be incorporated in the newly founded army.

* * *

In the morning we receive orders to leave our barracks for a camp where a battalion of the Etzel is stationed. They have recently been incorporated into the brigade. We don't know what is going on. In the camp a radio car is standing, with two blond men next to it. One is the brigade commander, the other his adjutant. Fantastic rumors fill the air: a lot of Etzel men are deserting, leaving their positions on the front, great gaps are appearing in our lines.

About a kilometer before our forward positions we come across the end of a long marching column. We drive slowly behind them in our new jeeps, which we only got a week ago. Our automatic weapons are loaded and ready in our hands. The column is headed for the road to Tel Aviv. The marchers are unarmed. They are walking in silence. No one says a word. From time to time they cast hateful glances at us.

At the crossroads we stop and take up a position. The column also stops. Its head has run up against another unit of ours.

We stay like that for several hours. They – unarmed, surrounded, full of hate. We – uncertain, not knowing what orders we will get. Fire? And if so – what will each individual do?

In the afternoon we withdraw. It has been agreed with the Etzel that they will return to camp. As prisoners. We breathe a sigh of relief.

* * *

We have had enough of discussions. They last the whole day, because we have nothing else to do. Sometimes we go on patrol around the Etzel camp. And we debate, debate, debate.

Some in the company, the veterans of the HISH from Tel Aviv, hate the Etzel people from the depths of their heart. For years they have fought a running battle with them. They kidnapped and were kidnapped, beat the others up and were beaten up, tortured and were tortured. They envy the Palmach people who were posted to Tel Aviv. Rumor has it that battles are fought out there on the beach, with real weapons.

"I would kill them like dogs," says Kebab. When he was in the Haganah he was involved in the fighting against the rebels. More than once he has boasted about the new techniques of torture that he claims to have invented.

"What? You are prepared to kill Jews?" asks Nachshe, visibly enraged.

"Jews or not Jews, it doesn't matter to me. They keep causing trouble. You have to deal with them once and for all."

Killing – the solution to all problems. If you get used to the idea of killing for the motherland, you lose all sense of limits. You start with killing Arabs – the "enemy," the "savages of the desert," "intruders," "bandits," "subhumans" – and then you can't see why you shouldn't kill Jews who you think are harming the motherland. In the end you are prepared to kill anyone you don't agree with.

And if killing is OK, then of course rape is no problem. Because rape is, of course, not so terrible as murder. And if you start with abusing Arab women in captured villages – and society smiles about it and winks at you – then of course you can steal. And if it is OK to steal from Arabs, why only Arabs?

* * *

The sun is setting. Time for us to patrol the fence around the camp.

Two Etzel people are standing by the fence, obviously new immigrants. "Heil Hitler!" shouts one of them. "Gestapo," shouts the other. Both of them raise their arm in the fascist salute, as if we were SS guards. That reminds me that we recently used to greet the soldiers of the British brigade the same way ourselves.

"To hell with you! Let's beat them up!" Kebab shouts and tries to get out of the jeep. We have a hard job holding him back.

* * *

It is a cold night. We are freezing pitifully in our thin summer shirts. We are not yet used to operations in the jeep. On our route there are still a few cafes from the days of the British. We have heard that one of them is supposed to be a brothel. Kebab is enthusiastic. First he wanted to chase the cursing Etzel people. Now he has forgotten about that. He talks us into stopping and having a look. We get out, but take our automatic weapons with us – just in case.

The room was once a primitive cafe. A few rickety tables still remain, along with some equally dilapidated chairs. A board for darts, a game that the British love, is still hanging on the wall. But the darts themselves are missing. In the corner is an old gramophone. I try to get it going, but it emits only an irritating clicking. The atmosphere is sad enough to make one cry.

* * *

The next morning I am to accompany an Etzel officer in his car to town. He is responsible for organizing rations for his people. When I enter the command center of the battalion I can't believe my eyes. Joske is sitting there. Eight years ago he was in the same group as me in the Etzel.

"What are you doing here?"

"Yob tvoyu Mat, what about you?"

"I never expected to find you in the Haganah."

"And I didn't know that you are still with the Etzel ..."

"Are you going to keep me under control with that?" he asks me bitterly.

"No, of course not." I leave my rifle with one of my comrades.

We go. At the entrance a man stops us and talks quietly with Joske. Then he turns to me: "That is the battalion commander of the Etzel. Can you help him to get out of here?" I try to find an excuse to refuse. The Palmach people at the gate will check our papers. But actually I don't care. Joske drives on. We talk. But I feel bad and have the impression that Joske also finds it unpleasant.

"So you became an officer?" I ask.

"Yes. If you had stayed, you might also be in command of a battalion." He is trying to be funny.

"And someone else would now be guarding us."

Suddenly it bursts out of him. "You have no idea what was happening here yesterday. The night before last, Palmach people stormed our barracks. We didn't know what they wanted. They just started shooting in all directions. Some of us tried to break through the barbed wire in a car. They shot two of our men. A girl gave the command ..."

"Etzel also had girls who gave orders to kill British men, didn't they?"

"What has that got to do with it?" he answers in amazement. "They were British. But she got the men to shoot at Jews." I have no answer to that and keep quiet.

"And in addition, they stole cars, a motorcycle, watches, and even fountain pens," he continued. "They are worse than the British."

"It seems to me," I think out loud, "that the British were not so terrible at all. We treat the Arabs less sensitively than the British treated us."

"That may be," he says doubtfully. "I have never thought about that."

I know that our people stole some items from the Etzel battalion. One of them took a motorbike. Jamus and I also got our hands on a nice armchair for our room. We didn't think twice about it, after spending months stealing the property of the Arabs.

"What do you think of this whole business?" ventures Joske.

"Shall I tell you the truth? Your Begin[10] doesn't appeal to me at all. I don't like people who keep talking about war and conquest, and then, when the war comes, they leave the dirty work to others."

"And what about your Ben-Gurion?"

"Quite honestly, I can do without the two of them. They should fight it out between themselves."

* * *

When we get back I notice that one of our people is missing.

"Where is Nachshe?"

Tarzan stares at me. "You didn't hear what happened?"

"No. I was in Tel Aviv. What was it?"

Tarzan looks at the blue sky, as though there was something interesting to see there.

"It was in the evening paper. His brother was killed in Kfar Vitkin."[11]

"What, was he in the Etzel?"

"Yes. He joined them more by chance than calculation, when the war began."

I turn around and sit down in the jeep. I feel like crying.

The Village and the Cows

My stomach ache is getting worse. I feel sick. But I have nothing in my stomach to vomit.

Eight days ago I stopped eating and drinking, and the accumulating stomach juices make me feel sick. During the day a narrow tube is put in to pump out the fluid. In the evening the doctors remove the tube. My stomach is supposed to get used to working normally. But it doesn't seem to want to.

I try to put up with it. I don't want to cause trouble. And the tube also scares me. But the main thing I am afraid of, is that the man in the next bed will start shouting again if the nurse comes into the room.

"N-u-r-s-e!"

I can't stand it any longer. My stomach is turning. Like being drunk or seasick. If only I could puke!

Rachel comes into the room. Her eyes are red with fatigue. She glances at the other wounded man. He looks at us blankly. Is he sleeping? Or is his mind in a world we don't know?

"Do me a favor," I ask of her. "I feel terrible. I need the tube."

"Don't talk nonsense," she laughs at me. "It is just that you can't sleep, and you are annoyed that the doctor is sleeping peacefully."

"Be a good girl," I say and smile through the pain. "When I get out of here I'll give you a really nice kiss."

"Promise?"

"I promise!" She laughs and goes to fetch the doctor. I like her because she makes fun of me, as if I was healthy and just pretending to be a patient.

Doctor Karni comes running. He is wearing striped pajamas under his blue coat. In his hand he holds the tube and a bowl. Rachel is carrying a glass of water.

"You want the tube?"

"Yes."

"In my whole medical career you are the first patient who has asked me to introduce a tube through his nose," he says with a smile. His mockery doesn't change my opinion. Better to have a moment of fear than many hours of pain. "Normally we have to hold the patients down and force them to take the tube," Rachel remarks.

Doctor Karni is short and seems nervous. He is the only doctor whose words I believe. He tells the patients and their relatives the truth. As my sister informed me, he told my parents that my life is in danger until my intestines start working again. I hate doctors who always tell their patients that they are getting better, and who leave them in permanent uncertainty.

He feeds the tube into my nose. That is the moment I am afraid of. I feel as though I am choking. I roll from side to side, open my mouth, and make noises like a man dangling from the gallows.

"Drink!" orders Rachel and hands me the glass.

I swallow some water and can feel how the cold tube slides into my stomach. I feel better already.

Doctor Karni connects the tube to an apparatus consisting of several containers. It is a complicated pump that empties my stomach automatically. One part produces the necessary reduced pressure and the other sucks the juices out of my stomach. I can see the greenish liquid coming up and mixing with the clear water.

"That better?" asks the doctor.

"Yes. Thanks."

The doctor and the nurses don't get many thanks. They have to cause pain and the patients resent this. Even if they know that it is for their own good. "Now you look like an elephant," says Rachel. "A really sweet trunk."

"Just a moment, doctor," I say as he is preparing to leave. "When do you think I will be able to eat again?"

"That depends." I can see that he is thinking. "You have been making good progress so far. Really good progress. If there are no … er …

complications, we will be able to give you light food in, shall we say, a week or two."

"And in three months you'll get a roast chicken," Rachel adds.

"And a cold beer," I dream.

"And potato salad with mayonnaise."

"Stop tickling his appetite." Doctor Karni smiles and turns off the ceiling light.

I stare at the lamp and dream about the first meal I will order as soon as I am back in Tel Aviv. First course: chicken soup with noodles. No, first, potato salad with chopped liver. Then the soup. A main course of roast chicken. A whole one. Well browned on all sides. Like that chicken ...

* * *

That chicken ...

It is roasting over a Primus stove. Four more butchered chickens are lying on the floor. Sancho, bloody and plastered with feathers, is in charge of the roasting.

It is a day to celebrate. First, because we have captured this village – without a fight. Twenty rifle bullets and two grenades did the job. After the terrible massacre in Latrun we needed an easy victory to improve our morale. Only twelve hours ago, when we climbed into the damned armored vehicles – those "mobile coffins" – we were expecting hard fighting with heavy losses. The intelligence reports suggested stiff resistance. These intelligence people. Because of them four companies had to be assembled for the "big operation."

And we have another reason to celebrate. It is the first day of the State of Israel. Yesterday evening we heard the news as we sat on the lawns in Hulda – young men, whose whole purpose in life for the last few months had been the fight for the state. Perhaps they understood that the declaration would change nothing in the real situation. The state was really founded on the day we marched off to the first battle. The battles between the politicians, who, if rumor was to be believed, were fighting right up to the day before about whether the declaration of the state was right or not, have become meaningless. After all it is not political declarations that will decide the future, but the facts. And these facts were established by us, the soldiers.

"There is a rumor that the Egyptians have invaded tonight," reports Zuzik as he comes back from a "reconnaissance patrol."

"Then there will be a real war," Nachshe explains. "But we'll get that over with in no time."

"Do you think so?" asks Sancho doubtfully. "Don't get too optimistic. It will be like in Latrun. Only far worse. Artillery, aircraft, and all that."

"What do you know about it?" Zuzik tries to look important. "We have everything that we need. American aircraft, British artillery, Russian katyushas, even parachutists. I have an uncle who is a high-up in the Haganah. He told me that the only reason we haven't used these things yet is not to warn the Arabs. But now – you'll see!"

"Rubbish!" Sancho makes an obscene sign with his hand. "Those are fairy tales. The leadership has prepared nothing at all. They didn't even believe that there was going to be a war. They thought that everything would be presented to them on a silver platter."

"And so we heroes will have to save the motherland," Zuzik bitches, his tone completely altered.

"Do we have a choice? When the old people make a mess of things, the young become heroes and march off to death." Sancho has been playing the philosopher ever since he butchered the chickens.

"Do you think the war will last for long?" Zuzik gazes thoughtfully at Sancho, as though he were the supreme commander. The latter turns over the chicken and scratches his left ear. His expression becomes even more serious.

"Who knows? Perhaps we won't be able to conquer Cairo and Baghdad, and I hope that they will also be unable to take Tel Aviv. Then the war will last a long time, until … until peace comes."

We all laugh. But I know what he means. Neither we nor the Arabs will be able to win a victory that destroys the other side. So this war will continue, with interruptions, until we die. Or until the Russians or the Americans take over the whole region.

"You are talking nonsense," Sancho declares. He is disappointed because we haven't been taking him seriously. "Come and eat and shut up!" We sit in a circle in the filthy room and devour the chickens.

"You know what?" I think out loud. "We eat the chickens. Then the Arabs will kill us and bury us. Our corpses will fertilize the corn fields. The corn will then be eaten by chickens, and a new battalion will come and eat the chickens."

"Oh, please!" exclaims Sancho, sinking his teeth into a meaty chicken leg. "Tell us something funny."

"One of us will have to eat up and take Joker's place," Sancho reminds us. After all we are on duty. Our building is the last one in the village and overlooks the road to Ramle. Outside we have built a rather feeble road block. One man is on guard.

"I quite forgot to tell you," pipes up Zuzik. "You wouldn't guess what is going on in the village. We are the only ones on duty. All the other companies are ransacking the houses. Scheike's company found a doctor's house. I'm telling you – a dream. They confiscated two pianos, beautiful oil paintings, armchairs, fountain pens, everything. This is a really rich village!"

"Damn the Chinaman!" Kebab bursts out. The Chinaman is our company commander, who has an oriental face. "He is always taking on the most ridiculous tasks. We are always the ones on duty while the others are enjoying themselves."

* * *

After the meal it is my turn to wander through the village. I get on the bicycle that we found this morning. A lot of bicycles have been found. Because this is not really a village at all, but rather a little suburb, whose inhabitants worked in Ramle and Lod.[1]

The whole area is crawling with our soldiers. Some are relaxing in armchairs, sporting an incredible variety of head coverings, daggers, and swords. Other comrades are proudly showing off their watches and fountain pens.

In front of the doctor's house, Yashke's company is sitting and keeping an eye on their treasures. The men are discussing the price of the looted piano. They have had to accept surrendering one of them for the battalion's culture room. They intend to sell the other.

Fat Shmuel calls to me. The last time I saw him was in Latrun, when he was trying to rescue a wounded man. He was carrying him on his back. When he heard a shell approaching, he threw him on the ground and himself next to him. After the explosion he got up. The wounded man was gone. All that was left were some strange stains on the ground.

Now Shmuel is beaming. "Have you heard the latest?" he calls out as I approach him. "Our little Benjamin found a hole in a wall somewhere in a house, with a rusty iron box in it. He worked on it for two hours, before he could get it open. And you know what was in it?"

"I don't know."

"A pile of mil² coins," Shmuel laughed. "Together with about five grush. It must have been a little boy's savings."

Everybody laughs.

On the way back to our position I discover a house situated slightly out of the way, whose doors have not been broken open. I lean my bicycle against a tree and run over there. The wooden front door is strong and well secured. I hit it with the stock of my rifle, without effect. Is there another door? I walk around the house. Yes there is, but it is also locked.

I am now convinced that this house contains valuables. Why else would the owner have secured it so carefully when our shots were already whistling through the village? I must get in. But how? There is a window. But there are boards nailed over it. Back to the door. I shoot into the lock. But that too does not help.

In desperation I walk once more around the house. There, at last – a little window, a bit high perhaps, but protected only by one thin board. A few blows with the stock and the window is open. I pull myself up, lose my hold, and scrape my knee. On the second attempt I manage to get in.

A poorly furnished room. A bed, a big closet with a mirror, a stool. The closet is open. There are clothes and papers lying on its floor, as if the Arab had hurriedly searched for something before escaping.

I look in the drawers and the closet. Nothing special. A set of masbaha prayer beads, a dagger, an agal. I am looking for a keffiyeh but can't find one. What a cheek of these Arabs, to leave an agal in the house without a keffiyeh. In my annoyance I smash the mirror.

Among the papers there is an ID card from the time of the British mandate. Aha. Interesting to know whose property I am plundering.

Name: Attalla Abdallah Abu Salem

Pleased to meet you!

Place of residence: Chudad

Nice village. Have to admit it. The nicest Arab village that I have seen since the war started.

Occupation: worker.

Hmm. What did you do? Judging by your room, you were making good money. Maybe you worked on the railway in Lod and rode your bike to work each day. The girl went with you to the road and waved you off with her little hand. In the evening you probably brought her sweets back from Lod. Those bright, tasteless sweets that she liked so much.

Race: Arab.

Rubbish. There is no Arab race. Just as there is no Jewish race. You are a Levantine mixture. A remote ancestor of yours was probably a Canaanite peasant. His daughters were carried off by the Jewish invaders and their great-grandsons served King David and Solomon. Later the Greek soldiers came and the Romans. And they too have left their traces in your veins. And when Khalid won the battle of Yarmouk,[3] the Arabs came, gave your ancestors their religion and their language, and married their daughters. Since then you are an Arab. And if you are an Arab, we must pursue you. And if necessary, kill you. You and your wife and your children. Understand? That is a law of nature. Were your ancestors and mine brothers and sisters? Did they come from the same Israelite family? Or maybe my fore-bears weren't Israelites at all. Perhaps they came from Tyre[4] or Carthage and adopted the Jewish religion only after the Roman conquest. But all that is not important at the moment. The main thing is that you are an Arab and I am an Israeli, and that we have to kill each other as soon as possible. That is the simple logic and all the rest is nonsense.

Height: 5 feet 9 inches. Eye color: dark brown. Hair color: dark brown. Build: normal. Scars or marks: scars on both temples.

Here. Another photo of you. With a mustache. One could say that you are a good-looking fellow. Tall, masculine, broad shoulders. Judging by your scars, you don't go out of your way to avoid a decent fight. Your wife must have liked the look of you, when you bought her from her father.

Don't look at me like that, Attalla. It is not my fault. I didn't want this war. Really I did not. Of course not. I know that stealing is wrong. It says so in the Bible. And in the Qur'an I am sure.

Before each battle we dream about the spoils. Maybe the girls too, that we will find. That is a kind of primitive instinct within us. In quiet times it is hidden and doesn't dare show itself. But in times of war or revolution, then it breaks out and takes us over. Just like our ancestors five thousand years ago.

History is packed with examples. All great commanders knew its use to motivate their armies. "Soldiers!" Napoleon told his hungry troops, "beyond these mountains are rich lands. Food, drink, clothing, it will all belong to you when you arrive in the place I am taking you to."

Enough of that. I have nothing at all against you. Really I don't. I wouldn't have minded if you had remained here and we lived next door to each other. It would be fine with me if my son one day married your daughter. No, that wouldn't work. Because your daughter would be much older than my son. He is not even born yet. But anyway: I wish you every success and that your daughter does not starve.

There is the bicycle. It is pleasant to ride around on two wheels. Damn the infantry. Long live wheels. Wheels, wheels, wheels ...

* * *

Wheels. Jeeps. Four jeeps during the first ceasefire. Patrol in Wadi Nisnas. A somewhat delicate task. The area we are driving around in is no-man's-land. If we see UN observers we will have to disappear. The politicians are responsible for political complications. Why shouldn't they too do something for the motherland? They will be able to think of an excuse. Their job is easier than ours. And less dangerous.

We are supposed to attack the three villages on the hills opposite. At maximum range. Our aim is double: to discover their positions and test their strength. And to make clear to the simple peasants the advantages of going elsewhere before the fighting starts up again. Almost a humanitarian task. Because if they stay, we will have to kill them as soon as we take their villages. And that will be pleasant neither for them nor for their daughters. In their favor must be said that they quickly understand our unsubtle suggestion. Not many of them insist on staying after we have sprayed them with bullets.

The road is dusty. Nowhere else in the country is there such fine white dust as in this area. After five minutes' drive you look as though you have been dipped in flour. The dust gets in your eyes, which then start streaming until you can't see anything any more. What the hell! How can you drive in an open jeep without goggles?

There is no chance of getting hold of any goggles. The whole jeep company is actually unauthorized. It does not appear on the staff plan. It was simply one of the brigade commander's brilliant ideas. But HQ did not approve it. And if HQ does not approve something, then you don't get any jeeps, machine guns, or protective goggles. The brigade commander "impounded" the jeeps from battalions under his command. Most of them are old. We expect them to stop working about fifty yards before the enemy lines. That is going to be entertaining.

The machine guns too come from various battalions. That means each infantry battalion is now four machine guns short. The weapon carriers must be glad to be rid of that extra weight. But the poor soldiers will have to attack with correspondingly reduced covering fire. If some of them fall who would not otherwise have done so, their gravestones can carry the inscription: "The soldiers who were sacrificed for the holy organization chart."

The main thing is: we have no goggles. There aren't any in the battalion. So we can't confiscate any. If we get our hands on one of the staff officers responsible, then we'll tie him up and drag him along behind the jeep, so that the dust gives him a good understanding of the significance of the holy organization chart.

There is the first village. A few bullets do the job. Just a few rifles return fire. Not even worth investigating. On to the next village. Three bursts. They don't even respond. Cowards. The third village. Fire! Cease fire! Yawn. A boring little drive.

On the way back the first jeep suddenly races off and the crew begin firing. With our streaming eyes we can hardly see anything. There – some figures running in the direction of the third village. Give me the weapon! One salvo! Another salvo! Quick, let's get there too!

The first jeep has caught a shepherd boy. One bullet has hit his backside. He is still young. Perhaps nine or ten years old. He is shaking with fear, but keeps silent. We are a little ashamed. The medic attends to the wound. Jamus tries to calm the child and we send him on his way. He walks a few steps and looks around nervously, as if he is afraid that we will shoot him in the back. When he sees that we are not going to do anything to him, he runs away quickly.

"God knows how he can run like that with a bullet in his ass," says the medic.

"What do you mean? He was only lightly wounded, wasn't he?" asks Jamus.

"Well," the medic explains, "the bullet is deep. If he is not operated on and the wound gets infected, he will get blood poisoning and die."

"And who is going to operate on him in this shitty village?" asks Jamus.

The medic shrugs his shoulders.

We drive on. Suddenly the first jeep stops. We stop too.

"What is going on?" asks Nachshe. "Have you found another child to shoot in the bottom?"

"Idiot!" Kebab shouts excitedly. "Our goggles are walking over there."

"Where?" I ask and look around. But I can't see anything without goggles.

"There, you fool!" Kebab points at a herd of about twenty cows grazing at the side of the road. Probably the ones looked after by the little boy. I understand. Of course. There are our goggles!

"You know what a cow like that is worth?" asks Kebab enthusiastically. "I'll tell you: a fortune. You just have to sell them to the right dealer. That will be enough for the goggles and some other things besides."

"And where can we get a truck?" asks Nachshe with a worried expression.

"If we report this to the battalion, they will take all the cows for the kitchen" Tarzan predicts.

"You know what?" Sancho has found the solution. "We tell them that we have found five cows. The others we get rid of straight away. We give the battalion five." Agreed. We have no alternative.

"Hello – Tango – Golf – Alpha – Five[5] ..." The battalion is sending a vehicle.

In the meantime we have to keep the cows together. How to convince cows? Quite simple. After all, we have seen lots of cowboy movies! The return of Tom Mix and Buck Jones. The jeeps are our horses. We do live in modern times after all. We surround the herd, chase the cows which try to get away, and drive them all together.

The truck arrives. Now the real work starts. The driver takes command. He claims that he has often transported cows in civilian life. Jamus too, who comes from a kibbutz, plays the expert and makes knowing suggestions.

We pick out one particularly fat cow, which seems to be the leader of the herd. Four men hold it still and then try and push. The cow is not convinced. We rain blows on it, but it does not move. Zuzik tries to pull it by the horns. Like in a bullfight, it almost catches him on its horns.

"You donkeys! This is how you do it," says Nehemia didactically. He takes the cow's tail and twists it. That seems to cause pain and it starts walking slowly. Hurray! The first cow is caught.

The second cow is much more obstinate. Zuzik, keen to show he has been paying attention, grabs the tail and twists it. But at that moment the cow exercises a particular natural function. Zuzik yelps and runs off. We all laugh.

I get the third animal by the tail, but forget to twist it. The cow races off, I hold tight and am dragged twenty yards along the ground until I hit a boulder and let go. Tarzan chases the cow in the jeep, but can't get it to come back. A military defeat. The cow is lost. The work is hard and makes us sweat. When we have the three cows in the truck, they rebel and jump back out. The work starts again from the beginning. It takes a long time to fill the truck.

"Watch out. Here comes an Arab!" Sancho shouts.

On the nearby hill a single Arab appears. He raises both hands above his head. In one hand he is holding a white cloth.

"Fire a round over his head!" someone orders.

We fire one round. The man lowers his head, but keeps coming toward us. A second bullet is not enough to get him to stop. He calls out in Arabic, waves his arms around, seems to be very excited. One of us approaches him. Jamus interprets.

Words pour out of the Arab. His face is stubborn and deeply embittered. He looks quite impoverished. "He says he is a Fellah from the village," Jamus translates. "The herd belongs to him. It is all he has."

"Who's supposed to be interested in that?" asks Kebab.

"He says that if we take his herd away from him, he will be destitute. He has a wife and four children."

"They always have four children," Kebab grumbles. "What does he want from us? Did we father his children?"

"Tell him that the Israeli Army is confiscating his herd and that he should disappear before he gets a bullet in the head." The Arab screams, begs, cries. I only understand some isolated words, "Fellah," "poor," "children."

"He says he won't leave without the herd," Jamus explains.

"Tell him that if he doesn't get out of here quickly, he'll never see his children again," says Kebab.

"He says he would rather die than watch his children starve to death." What can one do with such a stubborn donkey? It is clear to all of us that we have no other course of action but to bump him off. But no one wants to do it. Even the wildest among us are not enthusiastic.

A military vehicle is approaching, manned by several Palmach people. We call to them and they stop.

"What's this stinking Arab doing with you?" They belong to a unit stationed in the area. We tell them the story. "You know what?" they suggest after brief consideration. "Hand him over to us. We'll know what to do with him." We are glad to be rid of him. They get him on their vehicle and drive to the next village.

"At last that's over! Come on, let's get back to work," Nachshe drives us on.

We don't have much time. The sun is already low. We choose the best cows and load them up. We have no patience left. The incident with the Arab played on our nerves. Brutally we beat the cows. In the end eight cows are on the truck. Enough. We will have to do without the rest.

"What about the battalion kitchen?" asks Tarzan.

"They can go to hell," Sancho suggests. "We'll give them two cows and that's it. If we sell six on the black market in Tel Aviv, that'll cover our goggles."

We are tired and thirsty, but in a good mood. Instead of heading back to base, we drive into the next village and drink a cool beer in the soldiers' club. We send Sancho and Nehemia into town with the cows: Nehemia as the expert on cows and Sancho as the expert for black marketeering.

"After the war we can set up a cowboy farm," Zuzik suggests.

Kebab bursts out laughing. "An hour ago a cow was shitting all over him, and now he feels like Buck Jones!"

"That's OK," Joker conciliates. "We all start off in the shit."

"Main thing is, we got our goggles," Jamus ends the discussion.

The First Ceasefire

I am thirsty. I am thirsty.

Actually, it is not really thirst. The liquid which flows down the pipe into the vein in my leg contains everything that my body needs. I just want to drink a few gulps, even if the pipe that goes through my nose would pump everything straight out again.

"Don't be silly," my head tells my body. "It is just your imagination. What's the point of drinking water that's going to be pumped straight out again?"

"Imagination or not," my body answers. "Who are you to judge that? Haven't I already done plenty of things that were totally pointless? Were cigarettes necessary? Or wine? Haven't I gone to sleep often enough on watch, although I was not really tired at all? I feel the need to drink, and I want to indulge it."

"Don't be such a weakling. You know that you are not allowed to drink."

"Why not? With that pipe in my stomach I can drink as much as I like. The pump will just empty it all out again straight away."

"You are not allowed to drink. Because the one over there will see it and start shouting again."

"He's asleep."

"That's what you think. If you move a little bit, he'll open his eyes immediately."

"I have to drink something. Otherwise I'll go mad."

"You have no consideration for others. That is all. If he sees you drinking, that will make him more thirsty. That is maltreatment. Torture. You can't have anything to drink!"

"I don't care about him. He can go to hell. I have my own problems!"

"You should be ashamed of yourself. Talking about a dying man like that!"

I attempt to restrain myself. But that makes me even more thirsty. I must drink. I just must.

"You can talk. It is easier to have a noble conscience than a human body."

I arrange a compromise with myself. I will move my hand very slowly in the direction of the glass. Like in the night exercise, when you have to crawl toward someone in order to stick a knife between his neck and his shoulder. If he wakes up, I will stop moving as if I were frozen.

I listen. His breathing is still grating like a broken saw. Is he really asleep? I move my hand very slowly in the direction of the glass. Thirty centimeters to go. Then twenty. Just about there ...

Suddenly he moves his lips, his eyes are open. He doesn't say a word. Only his lips are moving. Like a fish on the fishmonger's slab. He has seen my hand. He is awake.

Too late. There is no going back. I grab the glass and bring it to my mouth. I spill some on my shirt. Who cares?

I throw it back in great big gulps and replace the glass. Bubbles rise in the container hanging above my head. Ah, what a pleasure to feel the cold water in my stomach, even if it only lasts a moment.

He is staring at me. His lips are still moving. They look blue to me. But perhaps it is just the dim lighting.

Oh God! He might at least say something. He can shout until the walls shake. But he should stop these awful movements and stop looking at me!

What can I do? I can't stand this accusing look. Does he want to punish me? Or is he trying to drive me mad? Is it my fault? I didn't send you off to war. Can you hear me? I didn't tell anybody to torture you like this in your last hours. As far as I am concerned you can drink a whole bucket of water and then die happy.

Light footsteps. Rachel comes into the room with two syringes in her hand.

* * *

This is how, at the end of days, the Messiah will look: with Rachel's face, pretty and pinkish, he will wear a white coat with old, washed-out blood and pus stains, he will have a faint odor of chloroform and disinfectant, and in his hand will be two syringes.

"Already one o'clock in the morning?" I ask.

"Yes," she answers. The injections are my clock. Earlier clocks had one hand and the sun revolved around it. My modern clock has two new hands. One is filled with penicillin, the other with painkiller. Every three hours they each jump ahead, one after the other.

"Slept well?" she asks, as she inserts the first needle.

"Didn't sleep a wink."

"You can't fool me. You slept the whole time. I saw it myself."

"Honestly, I did not. I was thinking."

"What about?"

"All sorts of things."

"Then stop thinking," she says as she gives me the second injection. I hardly feel it.

"Stay here," I beg her.

"I am here the whole time. You must sleep. If only you want to, you can sleep. Just stop thinking. Count sheep."

Sheep ... herd ... robbery ... "I don't want to think about sheep."

"Then count something else. Or count nothing at all. Think of sleep. Think that you are sleeping. That is auto-suggestion. Use your imagination. Concentrate. Think that you are sleeping, that your mother is standing by your bed, you are a little boy, and sleep ..."

I want to think about sleeping. I am sleeping, I am sleeping, I am sleeping ...

* * *

I am sleeping in an orange grove next to the deserted village that serves as our forward base. Everyone is sleeping and snoring. Everyone – the whole company. Those in the company who are still alive and well after these eleven days. The famous company, the men in the jeeps, the heroes.

But they don't look like heroes. This is not the way the rear sees them. The figures sleeping here are pitiful. Sleeping and snoring, turning from one side to the other, talking in their sleep. Their clothes are filthy and foul. Their skin is pale, their faces look tense with their bones showing and their cheeks sunken.

I am sleeping in a trench. I look like all the rest – pale, with an unkempt beard, sunken eyes, and stinking. The trench is not mine. I have never yet dug a decent one. I hate this work. Besides, I am immune. The bombs won't hit me. All the others will be hit. Not me. I cannot die, I can't be wounded, never mind losing a limb. It simply cannot happen that a piece of rough metal, a bit of scrap without any value, could put a sudden end to this complicated organism with its senses, feelings, thoughts, and all its secrets. That simply cannot happen! Of course I know that everyone else thinks the same. All those who have already left us, without legs, without arms, some of them without a head. And still – I am quite certain ...

Why did I get into this trench? I don't know. The fabled sixth sense. The sense that only those with experience have. That's why they keep getting sent out. Again and again and again and again, until the last of them is finished. Who else should be sent out? This logic applies in all the armies of the world: once in combat, always in combat.

Whose trench is this? No idea. Probably one of our comrades who returned later than we did. He saw me asleep and was too tired to chase me out. He didn't have a sixth sense. He did not feel that they had to come this night, to come and bomb us ....

This night ...

What a night! Yet again we attacked that damned Beit Jamal. For the second time, the third time? I can't remember. There was a battle. Battle? More like a slaughter. Healthy boys set off, mostly green recruits. They didn't know about the bright moon, didn't know that the Egyptians were expecting them exactly where they appeared. And not many came back. Some remained there. But most were brought back. Brought back on my jeep. Bleeding flesh, with smashed faces, broken bones, without fingers, without ears. One load after the other. Each time six or eight groaning bodies, crying, screaming – as well as the silent ...

The bunker in the kibbutz, the "collection point," stuffy, with the wounded almost lying on top of one another. They waited, patiently or in shock, till the medic reached them and at least gave them an injection to reduce the pain. The wounded didn't know how lucky they were. If they had had to rely on being carried by their comrades, most of them wouldn't have reached here alive ...

I am sleeping in the trench. Around us are the jeeps, under the trees, more or less hidden.

Sleep is our greatest pleasure. Our only pleasure. We sleep lying down, standing, even walking. Our world is a fog, hazy and unreal. Two or three times a day this fog suddenly lifts and we turn into wild animals. We wound and are wounded, kill and are killed, hunt and are hunted. As long as the action lasts, we are awake. But not normally awake. This kind strains our nerves and sharpens our senses. And as soon as the action is over our consciousness snaps like a spring that has been overstressed for too long. We are already asleep on the way back. Collapsed over the steering wheel or over the machine gun. We sleep and drive, sleep and walk, sleep and lie.

For eleven days we have been living like this.

Eleven days? Is it only twelve days ago that these hunted creatures were sitting in the battalion mess hall, sleek and content after a month's ceasefire? Was it really me twelve days ago, sitting in a cafe in Rehovot[1] eating strawberries and cream with Jamus, commenting on the charms of passing girls? No. It must be twelve years ago. Or perhaps twelve lifetimes.

I sleep. This is not the sweet sleep of forgetfulness. I am awake as I sleep, more awake than I was before I shut my eyes. My dream shows a real world. A hill, a road. Where is this hill? I don't know. I am lying on the ground and a black Sudanese is crawling toward me. I can see his face, want to run away. But I cannot. Am I dead? Paralyzed? The Sudanese crawls slowly, in accordance with all the rules of a field exercise. He is smiling. No, that is no smile. A bullet has ripped his face open from ear to ear. And the hole looks like a laughing mouth. I know this Sudanese. For five days he was lying by the road to the kibbutz. Bloated and stinking. One of the men who defended Hill 125. Now he has come to take his revenge. Someone has told him that I killed him. I know that I can save myself if I can only prove that it wasn't me. But how?

Maybe it really was me. Did I kill him?

Maybe he was it – that dark something that moved five meters in front of me, and into which I emptied a whole salvo of machine gun fire? That was exactly the moment when our jeeps drove over their trenches into the middle of their position.

In a moment he will be upon me. He has a knife in his hand. A knife I recognize. It is my knife. The one I found in Chudad. He holds the knife against my neck and tries to cut into it. The blade is blunt. He starts sawing at my neck as though it were a block of wood. Back and forth. Back and forth. It sounds awful. It whistles and rattles and bangs ...

The world around me explodes.

I open my eyes and at the same moment jump out of the trench. All around me thick, white smoke and the sweetish smell of powder. I run into the orchard without looking around, half blind, unconsciously. I bump into trees and twigs. I run, hear a loud whistle, and throw myself on the ground, press myself against the earth until it fills my ears, nose, and eyes.

The next bomb explodes, sending earth flying and making the air tremble, hiding the trees in thick smoke.

"Medic! Medic!"

Someone is screaming. And another. Two wounded. One is Nehemia the driver. Who is the other? Someone is running. Someone curses.

The roaring in the air is getting louder. An aircraft in a dive. A moment of quiet, as though the world was holding its breath. Then the automatic weapons open up. The bullets whistle, thrash, scream, rustle in the leaves. And the second aircraft is diving toward us. The air trembles. And the earth breathes, groans, embraces me in terror, draws me to itself ...

The aircraft are gone. I run back to the collection point. Comrades stand up. One after the other. Pale and green. They were all asleep until the first bomb woke them up. Nehemia was woken by a piece of shrapnel in his belly. Eli too didn't wake up until his face was smashed. His blue eyes peer at us out of his destroyed face as if he still can't believe that he has been wounded. Two others have also been hit. Drivers who only joined us yesterday to replace our losses. We don't even know their names.

Instinctively I gather my things together. We have to get out of here. To the other side of the village, before the aircraft come back. My bag is lying open and overturned under a tree. The contents are spread over the ground – a clean towel, that I have never used since we left the camp, a completely unnecessary bag with washing things, a dirty paperback book, the stub of a pencil. I have long since lost my mess tin. The whole company eats from three or four metal plates

which are passed around. My steel helmet, rifle, and emergency
bandages are in the jeep. I am ready to move.

"I can't take any more," Zuzik mutters. "I can't take any more. I
just can't take any more!"

We have had all we can take.

* * *

Up to now it was just the odd one of us who had really had enough.

It is a unique sight. You can tell in advance when someone has had
enough. He moves differently from usual. He flinches if he hears a
distant explosion, looks around like a hunted animal. You can
almost count the days. Another two days, another day. And then,
when the time is ripe, the crisis. Some openly admit it. They are the
most pitiful. They beg to be posted away from the front, for some
duty at battalion or even army HQ.

"I was quite OK up to now," they tell everyone in a whining voice.
"I was there in all the battles. Always did my duty. Really. Now I can't
go on. You understand? I can't go on. If I have to go out once more, I
will die. I know that I will die." And you look at him sympathetically,
the way you look at a dog that has been hit by a car.

Sometimes it is all quite true. They were in every battle up to this
day. Some of them are real veterans. And now they are simply
finished.

But most of those who have had enough don't dare to admit it.
They find excuses, sad and transparent excuses. One has toothache.
Another remembers that he is an only child. A third has a stiff leg. Of
course nobody believes them. And they know that no one believes
them. And we are mad at them because every one who leaves us
increases our own chances of being killed.

"You can work it out mathematically," Jamus discovered one day.
"If the squad consists of twelve men, and each day one is hit, then
within twelve days you are either going to be wounded or killed. If the
squad consists of nine men who are hit with the same regularity, then
within nine days you'll either be killed or wounded."

It is quite simple. Everyone who leaves us increases the danger for
the others. Because the same number of deployments is distributed
over a smaller number of people. A company has to fulfill the duties
of a company. It doesn't matter how many people are left in it. And if
most of the company have been hit and there are just a few squads

left, the company still has to act like a company. In attack or in defense.

Even Jamus understands that the men who have had enough have to be sent home. Their presence is even more dangerous than their absence. A coward will not rescue you if you are lying wounded in the field. And a scared driver will land the jeep in a ditch as soon as the first shell whistles over his head.

I have only once seen someone who really was totally shattered. That was Jeshajahu. A nice fellow, a recent immigrant. It happened under artillery fire. A shell landed in the trench where he was lying. But because the trench had a bend in it, he was not hit by the shrapnel. When I saw him his face was greenish gray, he could neither hear nor speak, and his body was trembling. For hours.

Most of us believe that we can't really be hit, even if we spend sixteen hours of each day talking about death. Without believing this we would not go into battle. We are only rarely overcome by fear – like before our first battle. Unless something unusual happens. Like that night when we accidentally found ourselves in the middle of the Egyptian positions, near Beit Jamal. Or when an aircraft is diving steeply toward us. Fear is a terrible feeling. It turns your stomach and makes your body shiver. You are ready to leave a comrade to his fate, just to save your own skin. Fear makes you stupid, paralyzes your willpower just at the moment when you need it most, because only reacting quickly can save your life.

* * *

I can now feel that we have all had enough. Actually we are not even a unit any more. We are just a shrunken group. In the eleven days our number has been halved. Some have fallen, others have been wounded, and still others have just had enough and disappeared.

We are lying beneath the trees with nothing particular to do. It is hot and clammy. The trees don't have many leaves. They don't give much shade. I take off my shirt. It is dirty and sweaty. I have worn it now for twelve successive days.

"Hey – you fart, put your shirt back on immediately," yells Mussa, the squad leader, who is lying under the next tree.

"What's the problem?" I demand to know.

"Do you want to kill us all?"

My vest used to be white. Even if you need a lot of imagination to see that color now. But from the air it might still be visible, and if the aircraft spot us … the thought doesn't affect me. The shirt disgusts me. The heat is worse than death.

"Don't argue with this shit. It's not worth it." Jamus, who is lying next to me, hardly moves his mouth when he talks. His half-closed eyes are gazing skywards, his wild beard makes him ugly, and his mustache, formerly the pride of the company, looks like a filthy weed. I don't have the strength to argue, and cover myself with the damp shirt like a sheet.

No one sleeps. We just lie there motionless. Passive on the hard ground. We haven't even pushed aside the sharp stones which are boring into our backs. Now and then one of us raises his head, listens for a while, and lowers his head again. That is an automatic movement. He thought he heard an aircraft in the distance. There is something in the air. No one talks about it. But everyone is thinking about it. A dull thought that barely manages to reach the margins of consciousness.

Ceasefire!

This evening at seven a ceasefire could begin. We spell that word mentally. It has such a meaning that we don't dare to think it directly.

Ceasefire is safety. Ceasefire is life. Ceasefires are healthy limbs. Ceasefire is the chance to remain human, even if only for a few days. Ceasefire is paradise. You can't even think that or you will go mad. Otherwise we will lose our senses. We would shout and howl, roll around on the ground and stand on our heads – and cry.

We all secretly believe that there will be a ceasefire. We want to believe it! A childish, naive belief: strong, at least if we hide it from each other (and from ourselves). Because if we talk about it, it will take its revenge on us and the ceasefire will disappear.

We don't believe in spirits. We just know for sure that they exist. We are surrounded by spirits of various kinds, some protecting us and some persecuting us. There are good spirits which shield us from bullets. They are to be found in headdresses, in particular hats, sometimes also in shell fragments and old cartridge cases. And there are evil spirits which write names on bullets.

"Every bullet has its address," Dudu, the scout, told us before our first battle. "When it leaves the factory its target is already fixed.

That's why there is no point being afraid. You can run or you can crawl on the ground, but your bullet will find you. They never miss their target."

I have seen them, the little devils in the ordnance factory. No idea where the factory is located. In England or Germany, or even in Czechoslovakia. But I have watched the workers in their monotonous tasks. They don't worry about who the bullet is meant for. Whether for Greeks, Chinese, or Israelis. It doesn't mean a thing to them. They are thinking of their girls in the night, of their pay, of the presents that they will buy their children. And the little devils are swarming everywhere with printed labels in their hands. These carry names: "Jehuda Carmi, Tel Aviv," in red ink. So this one will get the bullet in the head or belly and die. "Moshe Dror, Kfar Saba," in green ink. He will get the bullet in the thigh and only lose a leg. Perhaps Moshe is enjoying himself at this moment with a girl on the beach at Tel Aviv, jumping around and spraying her with water. He doesn't know that his name is on the bullet and that the next time the girl sees him, he will be on crutches. And she will look away, as though she doesn't know him.

Dudu, the scout, knew it all. He knew the work of the little devils in detail. But one thing he did not know: that while he was telling us this, an ammunition case was sitting in Ramallah containing a bullet with his name on it – "David Zioni, Rehovot, twenty-eight years old, left eye." One should avoid annoying the little devils. Especially on a day when a ceasefire could start.

Actually it doesn't matter to us. One thing clear: whether the ceasefire comes into effect or not, we can't go on. If there had been no mention of a ceasefire, then maybe we could have held out for another four or five days. Four or five whole days, in action twelve or fifteen times. But since there has been talk of a ceasefire, we have secretly started to hope that we will survive the week. We can't go back into that hell. The disappointment would tear us apart.

* * *

In La Valletta the little whore
she was just 15, and she cried so
when she slept with a sailor ...

* * *

Jamus and I are talking. We stick to unimportant subjects, distant things that belong to another world.

Jamus describes his service on a British warship. At night the ship sails under a starry sky, while one sailor keeps watch on the bridge, peers into the moonlit sky, and dreams of sad evenings in foreign lands. A group of sailors sit in a bar in Alexandria, cigarette ends lie in a puddle of beer on the table, and a one-eyed boy fills the glasses. Sad Scottish songs fill the air. A little whore timidly offers her thin body to drunken soldiers on the streets of La Valletta. Her cold lips lustlessly kiss their puffy faces ... in the far distance I feel sympathy for her, with her small round breasts and her skinny body.

I am amazed to notice that I have to answer a call of nature. Strange that my body is still functioning normally. "Come and take a shit!" I say to Jamus. He gets up, independent of his own will, like one hypnotized. We are herd animals who instinctively follow each other. If one of us eats, the rest get hungry. If one goes to sleep, the rest feel tired. I cut a path through the cacti with my knife. We walk a little distance, drop our trousers, and crouch.

Earlier, when we were recruits, we found this embarrassing. In Camp "Jonah" the toilets were open and arranged like a carousel. We sat next to each other and could see each other. In the first days we found it revolting. We went to the toilet when our comrades were on an exercise, or we looked for a more distant latrine. We were also shy of washing ourselves in the big common shower room. We stood in the corner and watched enviously as those with experience got undressed and jumped into the shower in full view of all.

"Virgins!" they shouted at us and sprayed us with the cold water. "There's nothing to worry about. We won't eat you!" And we shamefully got undressed, slowly, in the hope that they would be finished and gone before we were completely naked.

Now we would take a shower in front of the whole battalion and we don't mind taking a shit in a long line. It is even pleasant to talk while you are doing it. It encourages a philosophical state of mind.

We crouch for a long time between the cacti. The bad food, the irregular mealtimes, and the huge quantities of watermelon that we have been consuming have done nothing for our digestion. We all suffer from diarrhea. Suddenly Jamus laughs out loud.

"D-d-d-do you r-r-r-r-emember the first c-c-c-company in Y-Y-Y-Y-Yavne?" he stutters between two peals of laughter.

"Ha-ha-ha. What a t-t-t-terrible operation," I laugh back.

Our first company had a loyal secretary who used to accompany the men to the base camp before each action. This time she gave the men, just before they went into action, a whole bucket of hot milk. It took two or three hours, till the time they were approaching the target, before they discovered that the milk was spoiled. All the time during the operation, and on the way back, the men had continuous diarrhea. And we heard that even in the middle of the assault they had to squat periodically.

We laugh hysterically. A fit like that can last half an hour. When did that happen? Ten days ago?

"Do you remember the people you buried in the middle of the kibbutz?"

The laughter, which had just died down, starts again with added vigor. We were lying in a trench during the main assault. Suddenly a wild figure runs up to us and shouts: "Where is Jamus, that damned swine?"

"What do you want?" I ask, and raise my head while Jamus is trying to hide behind me.

"This asshole buried some bodies and left their legs sticking out!" We lay in the trench and laughed. We laughed and laughed until our eyes were running with tears. People crawled out of nearby positions to see what was going on. In the end even the wild kibbutznik was laughing too. We rolled on the ground with mirth, held onto each other, and wiped the tears from our eyes, while around us the barracks were collapsing and blocks of concrete were falling from the water tower.

"That was g-g-good, eh?" Jamus supports himself with his hands, to avoid falling into his own heap.

Over our laughter we suddenly hear a familiar noise. Three Spitfires are approaching. Our first instinct is to run and hide under the bushes. But you can't run with your trousers down. There is also no point. The movement would betray us. We stay where we are.

"Ridiculous to die in this pose."

"You think it makes a difference?"

"It is better to get shrapnel in your belly after you have taken a shit. Then your intestines are empty," Jamus adds.

That is an old piece of lore. When we were green recruits we used to take notice of such things. Before the first battle – just in case – I emptied my bowels. Since then we have become fatalists. You can die with an empty bowel and stay alive with a full one. In general it is better to fill yourself up before each action. You never know when you will next have the chance …

The aircraft fail to discover our new location. They circle a few times over the village, fire a few salvos into the orchard where we were before, and disappear.

"Perhaps they have to use up their munitions before the ceasefire starts?" I suggest.

"There is no ceasefire!" Jamus asserts.

"Why not?"

"There will always be politicians who like war. Particularly among us!" Jamus explains – hoping, of course, that I will contradict him.

But I just get angry. I imagine a disgusting politician sitting in his office in Tel Aviv with a cup of coffee and a buttered roll in front of him. I can see him in front of me. He has a fat face, an ironed shirt, and a gold tooth in his upper jaw. He speaks like a eunuch in a high voice, drinks a noisy mouthful, and explains to his colleagues: "We must fight. The hope of generations depends on our youth which is giving its blood to realize the Zionist dream. With courageous hearts we shall take the path of suffering and honor …" He sits there and we crouch here. He has hemorrhoids and status.

"If only I could get my hands on one of these politicians," I dream.

"What would you do with them?"

"I would … I would …" I search for an image to satisfy my sadistic fantasies.

"I know," says Jamus, "I've thought about this for a long time. Imagine that we put all these war-loving functionaries in a small room. Then we take a hand grenade, remove the charge, and put the detonator back in. Then we drop this hand grenade through a little window into the room. The people see the safety lever come off and then they all die from a heart attack like real heroes."

"But what if they don't even know how a hand grenade works?"

Jamus stops laughing, with his mouth still open. Suddenly he looks very sad.

* * *

We have finished, but don't feel like getting up. This crouching position is comfortable and somehow fits our mood.

"Give me some paper!"

I generously tear off half of a sheet of old newspaper, which I have been keeping in my pocket for this purpose, and hand it to Jamus. We concentrate on reading the headlines.

"Miserable creatures!" Jamus curses. "Listen to what a military expert writes: even if the UN imposes a ceasefire on the two sides for several years, there is no doubt they will both stock up on weapons in preparation for a second round. That will then be decisive ..." Jamus tears up the paper and carefully wipes his bottom. "The war is not yet over, and they are already considering how to kill off the survivors."

"Come on, let's go for a little walk," I suggest.

We don't feel like going back to our comrades who are lying under the trees. We want to be alone and walk through the fields. The ground is covered in rotting watermelons, the other field is a dried-up vegetable plot. There are weeds everywhere. In a few weeks these too will be dried out.

Rotten fruit, deserted houses. The work of generations destroyed. How many hours' hard work does each plant need? I don't like agricultural work. Earlier on, when I was just ten, I worked for half a year in Nahalal.[2] Since then I don't find this work romantic any more. And I can't tell plants apart.

"I don't know," Jamus thinks aloud, "dead plants and fruit are much more sad than a corpse. When you see this here you can't believe in God any more."

"Did you ever believe in God?" I ask with interest.

"I am not talking about some kind of dear father in heaven, who gives his children sweets or a smack like in the Bible. I mean some kind of morality ..."

"Not lighting a light on the Sabbath? Or not eating pork?"

"Don't be childish! What the Jews call a religion is rubbish. A collection of assorted superstitions and rituals. I mean a real religion that tells you what you should do and what you should not."

"Kebab was brought up religious," I remind him. "And Zuzik too, I think."

"What has that got to do with it?"

"Can't you see what that means? If a man like Kebab can kill every Fellah on the road and at the same time be religious, then screw religion!"

"All that shows is that our religion is corrupt. But that also shows that we need a new religion! One that forbids us from killing Fellaheen and prisoners and camels ..." He suddenly begins to laugh. "Oh really, I didn't know that I was religious. We are all going mad here!"

"I read somewhere that a man becomes religious when he feels that he is going to die," I console him.

* * *

We walk back to the collecting point. Maybe there will be new messages on the radio. Our comrades are still lying on the ground. No one wants to listen to the news. We are afraid of what we might hear.

I discreetly look at the time. Still two hours to go. Jamus gets out some biscuits which we chew slowly just for something to do. The minutes creep by. Our comrades also glance secretively at their watches. To cover that up, they stretch or scratch their arms. And smile stupidly when they notice that they have been observed.

From Manzuva, which our comrades captured yesterday, we hear shots. Suddenly our watches are in front of us. As if by command. We cannot lie to ourselves any longer. Our eyes follow the hands. We are no longer thinking of anything else. Ceasefire or no ceasefire. Ceasefire. Ceasefire or no ceasefire ...

Six thirty, six forty-five, forty-six, forty-seven. Still thirty, twenty, ten seconds – six forty-eight ...

At Manzuva heavy firing has broken out. Mortars and artillery – it sounds as though all the weapons of the front have been collected there. Our hopes rise. That could be a good sign. Five minutes before the first ceasefire the Egyptians began a tremendous barrage. An Arab "fantasia." Maybe they just want to show us that they haven't agreed to a ceasefire out of weakness. But this time they are not shooting in the air. The shells are falling within our lines. In Manzuva and in the neighboring kibbutz. And the damned aircraft have returned and are searching. We lie on the ground like the dead.

Oh God, to die now! Oh God …

The aircraft depart. Six fifty-five, -six, -seven, -eight. Two more minutes. One more. The shelling continues.

Seven.

S-e-v-e-n. It is seven o'clock!

The shelling continues.

Maybe our watches are not accurate?

A few minutes of tense waiting. There is heavy fighting in Manzuva. We can clearly hear the machine guns.

The beautiful dream of the ceasefire is extinguished. Only now do we realize how deeply we had believed in it. No one speaks. The whole company is squatting on the ground, motionless. A feeling of profound desperation.

Every one of us is trying to come to terms with the situation, to be able to endure the next few days. You have to be tough. I c-a-n'-t … you – have – to – be – tough. Just a few days. In a few days everything will be over in any case.

"In a week we'll all be finished," I mumble.

"Maybe we'll just be wounded?" Jamus has discovered a ray of hope.

Being wounded – that is the great hope. It means hospital, a white bed … you get away from the front honorably and don't have to be ashamed in front of your comrades.

"With a bit of luck it might be only a leg wound," Jamus thinks aloud. "Below the knee. You lie in hospital for half a year. Most of them recover fully."

Our ideals have changed. Only half a year ago we prayed: let me never become a cripple! Better to die than to lose an arm or a leg. Today we are all prepared to lose arms, legs, eyes – as long as we stay alive.

"But maybe the Egyptians don't know what you want and will shoot you in the belly or the balls?"

I try in my heart to curse the Egyptians. But in my imagination an Egyptian company appears – poor, reduced, and their remaining sol-diers are lying on the ground just like us here. They curse the war with the same words. For them it is even more difficult. Because they lack the feeling that they went to war to defend themselves. Without this feeling we would all have deserted long since.

Suddenly we hear a sharp, hoarse shout. Sancho is standing next to the jeeps with the radio, waving the headset, and shouting. At first it looks as though he is having an epileptic fit. But some comrades gather round him and then they all shout at the same time. They get up one after another – Tarzan, Nachshe, Joker, Kebab, Zuzik. On their faces is written doubt. Then they all grin like little children.

HQ has announced: the ceasefire is in force.

There really is a ceasefire!

Jamus and I stay on the ground. I can feel a massive emptiness. Although we have been given the gift of life, we don't know what to do with it. During the eleven terrible days we lived in total uncertainty. We didn't even think of the next day. The next week seemed to lie in the remote future that you dream about without really believing in it.

Something strange has happened. Something is missing. We don't know what it is. We listen. We narrow our eyes and try to grasp what is happening.

The artillery at Manzuva is silent.

For a brief moment all we can hear is Sancho's cries. Tarzan puts his big hand over his mouth and the shouting stops. The whole area is completely still.

* * *

From the other side of the village, where the battalion staff are stationed, the chief comes over. He is beaming. He has been wounded twice and wants to get married soon.

He has a last task for us. Around Manzuva some fallen Egyptians are lying. He wants us to search them and collect any papers they may have on them. That is a popular job with plenty of volunteers. My jeep goes along too.

Manzuva looks like an Arab souk in a Hollywood film. Yashke's company, which captured the town, is in the process of being relieved. They are assembling in the central square, surrounded by massive piles of booty. A colorful collection. The men are lying on fibrous mats between stools, petrol stoves, chickens, water pipes, swords. Dozens of sheep and goats are running around and making a hellish din.

I look for fat Shmuel. He is sleeping next to his machine gun while goats walk around him and even lick his neck. I give him a kick in the ass.

"How are you?" he asks, smiles, and closes his eyes again.

"Hey man! Are you sleeping? Don't you know that there is a ceasefire?" I shout into his ear.

"Mmmmhhh."

"Ceasefire! Do you hear? Ceasefire!" I yell, shaking him.

"Yes," he says, and goes back to sleep. If he had been sentenced to death and received news of his pardon two hours before his execution, he wouldn't react any differently. A real soldier.

"Leave him alone," says a passing squad leader. "The whole night they were assaulting the village, until they had it under control. And then they spent the whole day fighting off counter-attacks."

We walk through the fields, hither and thither, lose our way, and almost reach the little airfield which is still in Egyptian hands. We don't find any bodies.

"Sons of bitches!" curses Kebab. "These dirty Egyptians have taken their dead with them."

"And I would so much have liked to relieve an officer of his pistol," Zuzik complains.

On the way back we see a suspicious white dot. A Fellah. Before he can get up, Zuzik has jumped on him, punched him in the face, removed his wallet from his pocket, and ripped the keffiyeh from his head.

The peasant is shaking with fear and flooding us with words. His nose is bleeding. Zuzik has let go of him to examine his loot.

"He says," Jamus translates, "that he is a Fellah from Manzuva. Yesterday he ran away and today he came back to get some things from the house."

"An Egyptian spy," says Kebab. "We should finish him off."

"We'll hand him to intelligence. They will deal with it," the company commander decides.

In Manzuva we hand over the man. Our orders are to stay as a reserve over night. We sleep in a big haystack, next to the jeeps. The last thing I remember is the fleas in the hay, and that they bite.

* * *

The next day we all sit in the company's culture room in the camp. We didn't arrive back until eight in the evening, threw our dirty clothes in the corner, and ran naked to the showers. Then we put on clean clothes. Now we are sitting, packed closely together, in the room which is much too small. The chief wants to talk to us.

"What can he want to tell us at such a late hour, it is already after ten?" Zuzik wonders.

"For sure the important news that we start two weeks' leave tomorrow," Nachshe fantasizes.

"Or maybe three weeks? There is a ceasefire after all. We are owed it!"

"There is a rumor that we all get two weeks' leave and then a week in a rest home."

"I don't want any rest home. Let me stay at home. That is restful enough," Tarzan says.

"Don't expect too much," Sancho warns. "A week is the most you'll get. You'll also be complimented on what good soldiers you are and how you have upheld the battalion's honor."

In this moment being praised is also important to us. We are like little children waiting for Papa to come and tell us how good we are. Our faces, too, look like children's faces: smooth cheeks, red from scrubbing, wet, combed hair. I am the only one who hasn't shaved off his beard.

The room is filled with a good atmosphere. Half the company has been destroyed in the eleven days. But we are alive and unharmed! We like each other despite everything.

Tarzan for example. It is quite impossible to discuss anything with him. But after the battle around Position 125 he went on foot to the Egyptian lines to look for wounded. Nachshe is a complete egoist who only thinks of himself. But on the way to Beit Jamal he got out of the jeep in the middle of a storm of bullets to pick up Nuni's body. There is no doubt that Kebab murders because he enjoys killing. But he has remained with us the whole time although everybody knows that he suffers fearful panic before every action. And even Zuzik, our unholy virgin, is loved by all. He simply belongs with us.

"But really," Tarzan whispers, almost to himself. "I wouldn't have believed that I would still be alive."

"You are too heavy for us to carry to the cemetery," says Sancho. But Tarzan has put into words what we are all thinking. None of us has dared to hope that he would still be alive.

The commander comes in, sits down at the table opposite and looks at us sternly.

"Here come the compliments," Sancho whispers.

"You were good soldiers," the chief begins. "You carried out your tasks well. But a good soldier is not just a good fighter. A soldier must also behave well. And you were really terrible. You were wild and undisciplined! You played poker and so violated an explicit order." His gaze rests on Tarzan, our chief poker player.

"All that will have to change. From now on! Tomorrow you will be woken for the morning run at 5:45. At eight is morning roll call. I want the rifles to be shining, the shoes polished, the clothes clean, and the faces shaved." He fixes me with a stare. "Beards are forbidden!"

We look at each other. We don't look like children any more. The faces are tense and red with anger. Our thoughts can be heard like the distant murmuring of the sea.

"From tomorrow onward, military discipline will apply. You will train! Exercise, with and without weapons! Combat skills! We will put an end to this wildness. When you speak to a superior, stand at attention! I don't want to experience any more discussions with squad leaders! Is that clear to everybody?"

"What about leave?" asks Sancho. His voice is calm. But I know that he is as tense as a spring, ready for conflict. He remains seated. An explosion is not far away. The chief has also noticed it. He doesn't react to the style of the question.

"No leave! A ceasefire is not peace, and we will remain prepared for every eventuality. The companies will take twenty-four hours' leave in turns. Our company is the last."

"Why don't they bring a brigade from Tel Aviv to guard the stinking positions during the ceasefire?" Tarzan bursts out.

"If HQ asks for your opinion, you can put forward your suggestions," remarks the chief mockingly. "That is all! You are off duty until five forty-five!"

"Atten-shun!" the sarge roars. The chief leaves.

Pandemonium breaks out. Everyone talks at the same time. After a while our voices assert themselves, the voices of the "veterans."

"Who does he think he is? Our father?" exclaims Kebab.

"I'm not going to ask him whether I can play poker or not!"

"Yob tvoyu Mat. Damn anybody who goes exercising!"

"I'm not getting up before seven. He can go for a run himself!"

"They might as well put us all in prison and be done with it."

"I'm not going to stay one day longer in this shitty battalion. In battle it is like a slaughterhouse, and during a ceasefire they want to treat us like raw recruits!"

Someone pushes a sheet of paper and a pen in front of my face. "Write!" I yawn. This is the fifth or sixth revolt that I have taken part in. I know the text by heart. "Since I joined the jeep company in the certain knowledge that this is a commando unit with special privileges and rights … I request hereby my transfer to the commando unit of another brigade."

Everyone has to write his letter himself, so they can't accuse us of taking part in an organized mutiny. The intelligent ones among us are quickly finished. But some of us have difficulties with reading and writing. Every word has to be dictated to them separately. Just before midnight the package is ready. We put it on the chief's desk in the dark staff room.

In bed we talk some more. "What will be the result?" Jamus asks.

"The same as usual. Tomorrow the chief will call us together and threaten us with half a year in prison. Then he will tell us that we are the best company in the brigade and we shouldn't be stupid. And then he will add that had already planned to give us three days' leave the day after tomorrow."

It is not easy to command a combat battalion. He can't put us in prison, because we are the only veterans left in the battalion. And the brigade can't get along without our jeep company. He can't transfer us, and we don't even want to be transferred. Sancho is right. In the end a compromise will be found. We will behave ourselves and instead of exercises we will drive nice patrols. The whole thing will last two days. But I can't wait two days. I need to get to Tel Aviv. Tomorrow.

"Jamus, you asleep?"

"No. What is it?"

"You coming with me to Tel Aviv tomorrow?"

"Yours eternally. When?"

"We clear off through the hole in the fence in the afternoon, enjoy an evening in Tel Aviv, and come back tomorrow morning through the fence again. No one will notice."

"Tayeb."[3] He yawns. "Let me sleep."

Going home, going home, going home.

The motor roars. On both sides of the road trees are flying toward us and then disappearing behind us.

"What the hell! Drive faster!" These civilian drivers don't know what a decent speed is.

Ness Ziona, Rishon LeZion.[4] I am driving home – therefore I exist.

Three curious words: I exist! I exist! I exist! But why? Why me in particular? Why me and not, for example, Nino? If that Sudanese had aimed his gun a fraction to the right, the situation would be reversed. I would be rotting in the ground and Nino would be driving home. Strange.

In any case I am alive. That's a fact. My body is uninjured. To think that only two days ago I was envious of Nehemia, when a piece of shrapnel ripped up his guts and sent him to the hospital for months!

I must do something. But what? Drink? No. Drinking is a kind of suicide, the senses are damped down. And I don't want to damp down my senses. Quite the opposite. I want them to be at their sharpest today. Girls? That is it! I will find a woman. This very evening. Make love with her until two in the morning. Then four hours' sleep and back to camp before anyone notices my absence.

A woman. Strange. I don't feel any sexual desire. I want to have her to prove to myself that I am alive, that my body works, full of movement and sensation. I want to celebrate this wonderful idea, incomprehensible, strange, surprising: life!

"And you really were not at the front?" asks my mother.

"I really wasn't," I swear. "I was lucky. We were kept in reserve all the time, to protect HQ ..."

My mother would love to kiss me. But she knows that I hate kissing in the family. In our family, feelings are not often displayed. She satisfies herself with my answer and wants to get me something special for dinner.

My father is leafing through a newspaper. I know that he doesn't believe me and that he wants to ask me about the fighting. But he doesn't dare ask, to avoid exposing the fact that I am at the front. I look at him as if he were a stranger. Recently he has aged and his hair has turned white. He works too hard. He worries too much about what goes on around him. Particularly since my brother Avner fell as a British commando.

A strange fellow, my father. For forty-five years he lived in a world of offices and paper. The son of a teacher, he labored for years to build up his own little bank. All of a sudden he decided to emigrate to this place. He claims that he felt the approaching catastrophe in his bones. But I have the suspicion that he had a secret lust for adventure in his veins and found no fulfillment in the bourgeois life he was leading at the time. The money that he brought with him was gone within a few months, because he trusted people too much. Since then he – and my mother too – has had to engage in hard physical work and earns just enough to support us. But still I believe that he is happier today than when he was sitting in an office and shuffling files.

I am a bit envious. He belongs to a generation that got a real education. That humanistic eduction on the basis of classical culture, that somehow produced better people than we are. They have something, my father and the people of his generation, that is missing in us. Perhaps because they had time. Time to form and to develop themselves at an age when we were already soldiers. Or perhaps because our environment is devoid of culture and we go to schools where not even an attempt is made to educate us.

Since I joined the underground about ten years ago, I have been living an independent life and don't talk much at home. I hold it against him that he had to break off my schooling at the age of thirteen. But really I like my parents. And I am ashamed of them, just the same as my comrades.

"Was it really awful where you were?" my father asks. His voice is low and he is not looking at me. He was a soldier in the First World War and has no illusions about the romance of war. I feel that he knows everything and have no desire to lie to him.

"Yes," I say.

He turns a page.

"But now there is a ceasefire," I continue.

"Yes. Thank God!" He says it as if he is trying to convince himself. Deep inside he knows that we will break this ceasefire in order to open the way to the Negev. Then my father goes out and my older sister comes in. She has two daughters and is the most practical woman I have ever met.

"Listen," she comes straight to the point. "You have to stop! In the last week father has almost gone mad. He can hardly work for worry. And if something happens to you, he will kill himself. It is enough that one in the family has fallen. You can't expect more!"

"And what do you want?" I ask.

"You know exactly what I want. You could easily have yourself discharged or at least get a job at HQ. I met a friend of yours a few days ago. He suggested finding a job for you in the office."

I square my shoulders. "That won't work." I can't leave my comrades and take a job in the office. I wouldn't dare to show my face. Now and then I have played with the idea of changing my unit. I could become a war reporter with other commando units. But that's impossible!

My sister is angry. "Idiot! You don't actually like war, do you?"

"No," I admit.

"Or are you trying to do Ben-Gurion a favor?"

"Certainly not!" I can't explain to her that one should hate war and still stay in a combat unit, because one doesn't want to let one's comrades down.

"Why are you at the front at all?" she wants to know. "The son of the neighbor opposite was called up just two weeks ago, and landed straight in an office. Now he has even been made an officer already, because he has a rich father. And you, with all your combat experience, you are still a private."

"Maybe because of that," is my tired answer.

"What are you expecting? That you will get a particularly big gravestone if you fall? No one will thank you! They will all say that you were stupid. And father will get a nice letter, like the one he has already!"

My sister starts to get carried away. "Even if you come out of it alive. Where has it got you? All the important posts will already have been filled by the slackers. They will look down on you and order you around. After the world war the shirkers became famous and the frontline soldiers were all social cases. You think it will be any different here? Two years after the war no one will be interested in whether you fought in Ibdis or were sitting in the Romano House."

I know that she is right. Maybe all of us at the front really are stupid, while the clever ones are constructing the state the way they want it. That's what the stupid ones always do: they form a living ladder which others use to climb to fame. Then monuments will be made to the clever ones and the stupid will be forgotten.

* * *

I pretend to need some rest, send them all out of the room, and lock myself in.

My room is chaotic. The desk is covered in all sorts of things I brought back in previous "leaves" – small items of booty, orders of the day, pages of my diary, letters from friends, and photos that I lifted from Arab houses. That is one of my quirks. I collect pictures of Fellaheen, especially those of women and children. I want to remind myself later who our "enemies" were.

The books are dusty. I look at them without warmth. During the war I have learned more than from all these books. The books about the "art of warfare" annoy me the most. Scribblers who have never experienced what war is really like. Otherwise they couldn't have written such clever books. The political books I also find unattractive. Still I miss the calm of days gone past. How nice it was to read a good book in the light of the table lamp. The radio would play classical music, and I would feel that I understood the world.

I start clearing up. Wipe away the dust, sweep the floor, until the room starts to look pleasant again. I get everything ready for the night. Systematically, like before a particularly dangerous operation. The wineglasses are ready, the cigarettes in the right place. I get some cake from my mother. Then I take a shower. The cold water refreshes me. At the front we say that a cold shower is as good as four hours' sleep.

Then I just have to laugh out loud. It amuses me to be getting everything ready to sleep with a girl without knowing who she is.

* * *

It is eight o'clock and everything is ready. All I have to do now is find a girl.

First I went to Shifra. I like her and enjoy her company. She has a boyfriend who is serving in another brigade and never gets in my way because he is never in town when I am on leave.

I lie on the sofa in her room telling stories from the front, and watch her comb her hair in the big mirror. I creep up on her behind her and put my arms around her. She struggles in my arms, half seriously and half joking.

"You wild man!" she laughs.

Suddenly I feel ashamed of myself. I realize that I couldn't do it with her, and want to leave.

"What? You are going already?" she asks with a disappointed look. Obviously she wanted to spend the evening with me.

"I have to get back this evening," I lie.

"Why do they never give you a reasonable amount of leave?"

"Aren't there enough young men around here?" I ask, laughing.

"There really aren't very many," she admits. "There are some here who work in the offices. But it is no fun with them."

"May a hero from the front kiss you?" I ask.

"No."

"What a pity," I say. "Shalom."

Back on the street I think hard. I could go and see Shifra's girlfriend. But she lives at the other end of town. If I have to take her home afterwards, I won't get any sleep at all tonight.

"Hello, how are you doing?" a seductive voice asks me.

"Wow, hello!" I reply with enthusiasm. It is Yucki. I don't know her real name. She was only in the battalion for a few days, and we all called her that. She'll be OK. I am pleased not to have to walk far. "You must have been sent from heaven," I declare as convincingly as possible.

"You liar!" she replies, smiling.

"No, really. Only this evening I was thinking about you."

"Tell the truth!"

"I am telling the truth. Come on, let's go."

She hesitates. "I already have a date with a handsome man."

"Who is that?"

"An officer from Jaffa."

"That is all?" I ask. "Forget about it." I put my arm around her waist.

"So where shall we go?"

"Anywhere" I reply with an innocent expression. "How about the movies?"

As we are walking along she asks about the battalion. We talk about my photos, and I remind her of the ones I took of her at the radio set. She wants to see the pictures. So I suggest stopping off at my place on the way to the movie theater. Everything is going according to plan. I don't want to waste valuable hours in a dark movie theater.

In my room I get out a pile of photos for her. While she is looking through them I pour two glasses of arak.[5]

"No thanks."

"Are you a soldier or a doll?"

She drinks a glassful. Mozart is playing on the radio. I sit cross-legged in front of her and begin working on the bottle.

Among the photos are some I took of the massacre at Latrun. One of them was taken about a hundred meters from the Arab attackers, after most of our unit had already fled and only very few remained. On the photo are four completely exhausted men. They are carrying a wounded man on a stretcher. The picture was taken with a camera that didn't cost more than three lira. But the image is very sharp – the face of the wounded man, the blood dripping from his chest, and the worn-out faces of his rescuers.

"What a fantastic picture," says Yucki.

I can remember the wounded man and hate her at that moment. To get my revenge I show her some special horror photos – the Egyptian buried by Position 125, with his leg still sticking out of the ground, the Sudanese who was covered in petrol and burned because we were too lazy to dig him a grave, the picture of the three-year-old boy whose father had been shot. She quickly loses all interest in the photos.

"Come on, that's enough of these awful pictures." She sits next to me on the sofa. "This evening there is no war, OK?"

I kiss her. Silly girl. Does she think we can shut the war away in a drawer and open the peace drawer? Her blouse slips out of her skirt. I stroke her back and cover her body with kisses. Why not really? Why can't the war be shut in a drawer?

"If you help me, I will forget the war." I hold her close to me.

"That is not very nice," she moans. I almost laugh out loud. That's not very nice! And sending us to die or to kill others, is that nice? A poor Fellah who is hit in the head by a bullet is also sure to find that not very nice.

I stroke her thighs. In the dim light they are rounded and rosy.

"At least you might turn out the light." I don't want to switch it off. I like the play of muscles on a moving body. That is so different from the bodies I have seen recently by the side of the road or in the field. Why think about the dead? The dead don't have bodies, just stinking corpses. Here is a living body, a beautiful body. I press my face into it.

"You are crude!" Yucki yelps.

"Yes," I reply.

Her eyes are closed, her breathing heavy. But I am not excited in the least. It is as if I was not here at all. I am floating somewhere, smiling at us. I am sleeping with her as though fulfilling a duty, or to store memories that I can recover later when I am back at the front.

* * *

She is lying next to me, smiling very gently. She strokes my hair as though I had done her a favor. I feel sick. How can I get up without upsetting her? She is relaxed and tired. And the dead at the roadside drift back into my mind.

"Come on, let's go to the cafe," I suggest and get up.

"Why?" she asks, showing no desire to get up.

"I arranged to meet some people from the company," I lie.

She groans, gets up, and puts her clothes on. I drink a few more glasses of arak to wash the stale taste out of my mouth.

Despite the blackout the streets are full of life. The cafes are full to overflowing. People are streaming out of the movie theaters. On the other side of the street someone is trying to kiss a young woman who is laughing loudly.

"How much life there is here today!" The air is filled with jubilation and I am cheerful.

"What do you mean – today? It is always like this in the evening."

I get angry. Every evening? The day before yesterday? The day before that? We knew that this Tel Aviv existed somewhere, a paradise of celebration and pleasure. But we were not aware that lively people were enjoying themselves, young and healthy, while we were racing in our jeeps into the enemy fire. Shit!

In Kassit,[6] a large group of soldiers in smart uniforms. They are the ones that we call the "Romano House Foxes." A few young writers and other members of the intelligentsia are among them. A distant acquaintance calls me to the table. Probably to annoy the others. He is tipsy. "This is a real soldier!" he introduces me. I join them.

Those present send me a few unfriendly glances and don't interrupt their conversation. They are talking about the presentation of wartime experiences, about the need to keep some distance from the actual events, about current, epic, and romantic literature. I feel sorry for them. How naive they are. To spend the whole war sitting in a cafe or an office and to believe they could express the experience of war, without ever having dared to get a real taste of it. How can a writer find the way to the hearts of his generation if he is not prepared to accompany them?

Someone mentions a newspaper's suggestion of giving a special medal to the soldiers on the front. At this table the idea arouses only protest.

"We will never allow such discrimination among us!" protests a high voice from a fat face.

"Down with discrimination!" shouts my drunken acquaintance, who plays an important role in some cultural institution or other. "Let's all go to the front!"

The fat face turns on him angrily: "Our duties are too important for us to be wandering around at the front with a rifle. Anyway! Who does go to the front? Only neurotics trying to escape from their own complexes. We are to blame. We have glorified them in literature. And now the general public finds them romantic."

"That's right," I say. "If you hadn't made propaganda for the soldiers at the front, then nobody would know that they exist at all. It is a pity that the frontline soldiers don't appreciate your efforts."

"They are being stirred up!" In his excitement his voice rises even higher. "In the end any rogue who happened to be at the front will think that he deserves privileges. We will have to deal with the inciters. Then everything will fall into place."

"You should let them finish off the fighting before you stick them in prison!"

"We have to deal with the inciters!" he stubbornly repeats.

"OK. But don't forget to put up a notice at the front: fighting is postponed until further notice."

My drunken companion whispers to me the ranks and duties of those present at the table. Judging by the ranks of the officers, it would not be difficult to reorganize those assembled into the staff of a combat battalion.

One of the officers at the other end of the table elaborates on the strategic visions he is drawing on the tablecloth. "First we advance to the Jordan. Jenin and Nablus,[7] we can take without difficulty ..."

"And what losses will that mean in your opinion?" I ask calmly.

"That doesn't matter," he declares with a lofty motion of the hand. "In this historic moment one cannot talk about losses. Our youth is ready for any sacrifice." He looks about twenty-four and I imagine how old he would look during an infantry assault.

"The southern front is not active enough ..." continues the amateur strategist. I would dearly like to simplify matters and beat him up. But if the Military Police catch me, they will find out that I am in town without a pass.

"Come on, I'll take you home," I suggest to Yucki.

"But I would like to stay here," she tries to persuade me. The glorious company of the upper ranks, the famous names have impressed her. She would like to use the opportunity to get to know the famous people a bit closer.

"I can take you home in my car later," proposes the conqueror of the Jordan, pointing at a military vehicle by the side of the road.

"Wonderful," I reply gladly.

"You don't mind?" Yucki asks politely.

"Not at all, not at all," I assure her. Thank God. I can go straight home and get some sleep. I still have five hours.

"So," the strategist elaborates, "after we have taken Jenin and Nablus, we will continue with a pincer movement ..."

Dream of Generations

This smell!

It enters through your nose and fills your whole body – a revolting sweet mixture of chloroform and disinfectant.

If only I could escape it for half an hour and breathe some fresh air.

A hospital is a realm of odors. The red-haired boy who lies in the big room claims he can tell the time of day with his nose. He is seventeen years old. He joined the Palmach in search of adventure. He is said to have been a good-looking youth. Born in one of the agricultural settlements in the Emek.[1] He himself claims to have been the best rider in the area. That was, of course, before "it" happened to him. After the capture of Majdal he found some German hand grenades. He wanted to find out how to take them apart. A grenade exploded in his hand, tearing off most of his fingers and destroying both his eyes. In a few weeks he will be eighteen and admits that he has never slept with a woman.

He is an expert on smells. In the morning, after the floors have been mopped, disinfectant dominates everything else. In the early afternoon this disgusting smell of chloroform and carbolic acid reasserts itself. The stink of excrement, which occasionally wafts through the wards, is less sickening than the chloroform. Those are the chief odors. Blood and pus also have their own smells, as do the secretions of healing wounds.

War is not for people with a sensitive nose. That may be one of the reasons why most people don't understand war. They see the pictures in the movie theater. But movies convey no smells. Nor do books transmit any idea of the emanations of war. A way needs to be discovered of filling the nose with them.

When the girls in town read that we haven't washed for two weeks, they find it romantic. If they could smell us, they would run away in disgust.

"And he smelleth the battle afar off …" it says in the Book of Job.[2] Perhaps Job was once a soldier. Only someone with experience of the front could write such a pacifistic book. How else could he know that war stinks? The others see flashy uniforms in victory parades. That's the way it has always been. The world hasn't changed much since the days of Job.

"And he smelleth the battle afar off …"

* * *

The smell of powder, the king of the war smells, is a sweet perfume.

It is sometimes so prevalent that it covers whole areas: like at Ibdis and Negba. It is a loyal perfume that stays with you everywhere you are on the front. When this perfume reaches your nose, even if only on the shooting range, your nerves tense up and your stomach starts to contract.

When was the first time I met it? Perhaps it was when we fired thousands of rounds at the poor village of Dir Sumin, the first village we took by assault and whose inhabitants we expelled? No. I had smelt it already, two days before that action, on the shooting range, when we felt a rifle in our hands for the first time.

That was really a milestone in our lives. Our own rifle – the ultimate symbol for the reality of the "dream of generations." New rifles, well oiled, some of them still bearing the German swastika. The Czech factory had produced them for the Nazi army. It must have been a tremendous blow for the factory owner when Hitler killed himself before the rifles had been delivered and paid for.

Where did we hold our shooting practice? Up on the hill. The ground was covered in rifles, automatic weapons, and hand grenades. For the first time we really felt like soldiers. Squad after squad we were lined up to try out the new weapons, to feel them kick against our shoulders.

Israel, the company commander, who we met for the first time this morning, walked around showing us how to hold a rifle, how to aim. A good-looking young man he was, this Israel. A real soldier as if he had just jumped out of a recruiting poster. We, the green recruits, were very envious.

Eight hours later he was dead. Our first casualty. To "toughen" us and familiarize us with the difficulties of life at the front, we had to march from kibbutz to kibbutz on foot. The whole battalion marched in an enormously long row through the dark night. In the dark the first company lost contact with the rest. The men took up a circular defensive position on the ground. And when we suddenly appeared in silhouette ten yards in front of them, they panicked and opened fire. Israel was the first to be hit.

*　*　*

Everything in war has its own perfume. Even love. I can remember the first time I kissed Yucki. It was in Beit Sarah. One of the abandoned villages, which distinguished itself with its particularly aggressive fleas. We poured buckets of liquid DDT over ourselves. That didn't bother the fleas at all. Scientists assert that living creatures can adapt to anything in time. These fleas led a wonderful life and thrived in a sea of DDT.

Yucki spent a few days in this damned village with us. Like us she also stank grossly of DDT. The stink was enough kill a steer. Only the fleas didn't mind it. They promenaded all over us while we were running through the village, looking for souvenirs for Yucki. I kissed her in one of the houses, on a pile of hay. The DDT smell combined advantageously with the other domestic smells, the charcoal, the goat droppings. It was a symphony of stink, a symphony of military love. For a few moments we even forgot the fleas.

Strange how all the smells of war are sweetish. Sweetly disgusting. The smell of rotting flesh. Apparently you can get used to it. We never succeeded.

In Iraq-Sharkiah we were stationed for two weeks in a wadi that stank appallingly. The stink came from a small mound in the middle of the wadi. We never found out what it was. A dead donkey, a camel, or maybe even a human. That is also typical for war: you smell death. But you generally don't know who died there, who killed them, or why. Most deaths in war have no reason. You don't even ask yourself what you are killing for. That is a question for your superiors.

"And from afar he smells war ..."? Not always from afar. Sometimes the smell is very close, envelops you, suffocates you, digs its claws into your lungs. Like on that awful day, the day of death.

*　*　*

"Fi! Fi!" Kebab roars and shakes with laughter. "Hat Massari! Fi! Fi!"[3]

"Shut up! That's enough!" Nachshe shouts. "Shut your mouth!"

"Fi! Fi!" Kebab roars once more. "Hat Masari! Fi! Fi!"

"Are you starting again?" Nachshe asks in annoyance.

This morning we attacked Daba. It was almost like in the movies. Some officers and their guests, together with the officer responsible for culture, climbed onto the water tower of the nearby kibbutz to observe the spectacle. We drove toward the village in a broad row of jeeps, with about ten meters between us. While we were driving we fired thousands of rounds. It is difficult to aim an automatic weapon while you are moving. Particularly if you are sitting behind, with the gun barrel continually swinging between the driver's right ear and the left ear of the man next to him. While we were driving, the weapon slipped out of Nachshe's hand and a bullet flew between the legs of Tarzan who was sitting in front of him.

The village was empty. The Fellaheen had run away when they saw us coming. In front of some of the houses the petroleum stoves were still burning. We had interrupted them in the preparation of their lunch.

Rather bored we drove through the narrow alleys which were hardly wide enough for a jeep. We were dreaming of lunch in Rehovot and the shower in the camp. After little operations like this one we tended to "disappear" for a few hours before we returned to base.

Suddenly we saw someone. We were astonished to see a living creature here. It was an old woman. At least eighty years old. Wrapped in rags she sat in front of her house. When they run away the Fellaheen often leave the old and the blind behind.

We in the first jeep stopped immediately. Looked at each other.

"Not worth it," Sancho answered the unspoken question. We drove on.

At the next crossroads we noticed that the second jeep, with Nachshe, Tarzan, and Jamus, was no longer following us. With difficulty we turned and drove back. The second jeep was standing by the old woman's house. Nachshe stood in front of her waving his pistol.

"Hat Masari! Hat Masari! Fi! Fi!" he shouted. Like all of us, he believed that every Arab must have a treasure buried somewhere.

"Ma feesh, ya khawaja!"[4] moaned the old woman in a whiny voice.

"Fi! Fi!" Nachshe shouted angrily and fired four bullets into the old woman. The shots threw her body upwards, as if she was jumping, then she fell dead into the same position we had first seen her in – leaning against the door frame.

Now Nachshe felt ashamed and didn't want to be reminded of what he had done. It's always like that with him. He can't simply kill for pleasure and then feel like a hero the way Kebab can. Whenever he has killed a Fellah or a prisoner, he tries to forget about it and gets annoyed if you remind him.

Kebab won't leave him alone. Nachshe is a member of the "intelligentsia" and has a big office. Kebab finds this murder reassuring. Because if a person like Nachshe is allowed to kill Fellaheen, then he himself, who is just an unskilled worker, can also be counted as a respectable person.

Actually you can't hold it against Nachshe. It is not his fault. Homicidal urges come on him like an illness. He can't do anything about it. Besides that he is a nice fellow. He would never abandon a wounded comrade in the field. At Position 125, did he not get out of his jeep at the worst moment and right between the Egyptian positions, in order to recover Nino's body? I am not so sure about Kebab. I wouldn't be very keen to find myself on patrol behind enemy lines with him.

"What's the matter?" Kebab asks. "Are you ashamed that you finished off this stinking Arab woman?"

"That's enough! Don't you spend your whole day dreaming of Arab women?" Tarzan says in support of Nachshe.

"What has it got to do with you?" Kebab turns on him. "You are not brave enough to finish off just one Arab!" The truth, of course, is that Tarzan cannot kill an Arab, except in battle. Despite his enormous physical power he has a gentle soul, which he finds very embarrassing.

"Do you still remember," Kebab recalls in a dreamy voice, "when we captured Abu-Shubak? No, you weren't there. That was when I was still in the first company. We were supposed to finish off all the men over fifteen. The stupid Arabs didn't even run away. They didn't know us yet. I went into a house and brought out a man around fifty. But a girl of fifteen or so hung onto him and screamed that I shouldn't do anything to him, he was her father."

"So what did you do?" Zuzik can hardly wait to know.

"I passed the father to a comrade and went back into the house with the girl. At first she resisted and bit me in the hand. But when I pointed my gun at her she calmed down. She was horribly dirty, but had a body like a young woman. Pity I had to shoot her."

"What? You killed her?" Zuzik sounded disappointed. As if he had hoped to find the girl somewhere.

"Disgusting!" remarked Tarzan. "Or is that supposed to be a heroic deed?"

"Did I have any choice?" Kebab defended himself. "You don't know our company commander at the time, Addi. That donkey. Actually a nice fellow, but about things like that – just crazy. Before every operation he used to swear that he would shoot any of us who so much as touched a woman. Our orders were to kill only the men. If the girl had run to him – he would have had me up in front of a military court."

"I wouldn't have done that," Tarzan explained. "To fuck a girl and then shoot her? That is too much!"

"Don't pretend to be so saintly!" Kebab said angrily. "I know very well that, before every attack, all of you are dreaming of catching an Arab girl."

"Now we no longer have the chance," said Zuzik sadly. "They all run away before we come. And if one does remain, then it is an old one, like the one in Daba."

"How her body jumped, when Nachshe pumped her full of lead," Kebab mused. "With this weapon you can finish off three donkeys with one bullet."

Nachshe gazed lovingly at his Luger. "At first they wanted to give me a Mauser. But when I saw this Para, I wanted that or the whole business would have come to nothing."

"Idiot!" said Jamus. "A Mauser is much better. I wouldn't swap my Mauser for three of those."

Jamus envied Nachshe. Jamus was, after all, the first in the company to have a pistol. He is the one who started this fashion. One day he came back from leave, with this gigantic Mauser hanging from his belt and almost pulling his trousers down. He claimed that the kibbutz had made him a gift of the weapon. But we are convinced that he stole it. The Mauser was the talk of the company until Nachshe turned up with the Luger. Everyone agrees that the Luger looks much better.

That was the start of the pistol competition. For a member of the company to walk around without a pistol was soon seen as almost dishonorable. The battalion commander had no pistol. Nor had his deputy. But most of our company got themselves a pistol in time. One of the first was Tarzan's rusty weapon, rumored to have been first used by Methuselah. And the last was Nehemia the driver's gleaming Webley, which Sancho inherited from him when he was wounded. It doesn't matter how good the weapon is or where it comes from. As long as the bullets come out of the right end and it makes a hell of a noise, the honor of the bearer is assured.

There are also some unfortunates who have to make do as pistol-less proletarians. Some of these have resigned themselves to their fate and behave as though the whole thing has nothing to do with them. But in the case of Zuzik the matter assumed tragic proportions. He dreamed of his own handgun twenty-four hours a day. Whenever he saw an abandoned house that hadn't yet been ransacked, or a body whose pockets hadn't yet been emptied, the spark of hope would ignite in his breast. But it seems the Arabs had decided to annoy Zuzik. They literally swallowed their weapons before they died. Even when they had to abandon their houses in a hurry, they took the little toys with them. It was only a week ago that Zuzik finally got his pistol. Kebab says he bought it. For twenty lira that he got from his father.

Now Zuzik gets the little pistol out of his trouser pocket. "Only fools lug cannons around with them," he bravely claims, without being able to hide his jealousy. "I prefer a small, handy weapon." He has a little PB, caliber 7.65 millimeter. An old model that was already in use in the First World War.

"Sour grapes," says Nachshe scornfully.

Zuzik is deeply offended. "It does the job. With it I can bump off whoever I want."

"With that?" Kebab laughs loudly. "With that thing you couldn't knock out a fly's tooth." Kebab has a special laugh. His whole face puckers up and all you can see is the small, green eyes.

"I'll show you!" Zuzik is boiling with anger. "The first Arab we meet, I'll lay him out with it."

"I'll pay you five grush for every Arab you bump off with that toy."

"I'll pay ten!" Kebab raises the prize. Everybody laughs. Zuzik seems rather ridiculous. If the war had not broken out, he would probably be studying the history of the Lithuanian Jews in the nineteenth century. Somehow the pistol didn't suit him. It didn't look natural on him, unlike Jamus or Tarzan. Zuzik was the only one who didn't laugh. His expression was cold.

"Don't get excited," Nachshe consoled him. "Come on, let's get something to drink!"

"Cognac is the thing to drink in this brothel!"

"They must have some cognac here."

The waiter is sitting at the counter sorting through bills.

"Hey, you there!" Nachshe calls to him.

"What would you like?" The waiter graces our table with his presence.

"Bring us a glass of cognac!" Nachshe demands.

"We have no cognac. Orders from HQ forbid alcohol in the camp. The beer we procure privately."

"Don't lecture me. Here's a lira!" Nachshe waves a note.

"Good. I'll see what I can do." The waiter goes off and returns with the bottle.

"What a deal!" Sancho expostulated "One lira for a bottle of cognac!"

"What's the use of money? Tomorrow you'll be dead anyway."

"Eat and drink, for tomorrow we shall die," Zuzik declaimed.

"I don't know," said Sancho pensively. "Maybe we will just lose a leg. Then we will need money."

"The motherland will look after you!"

"Don't make me laugh! The motherland will give you a medal and a kick in the butt!"

"May you all soon be stinking corpses," Kebab wished us. "Who'll give me a lira if I empty the bottle in one go?"

"That is daylight robbery! Twenty grush is enough." Sancho is a thrifty fellow. He never misses a chance to haggle.

"Go to hell! Only a dog would drink a whole bottle for less than half a lira."

"Then don't drink it." Sancho withdraws. Then he has an idea. "If everyone pays a shilling,[5] that will make half a lira altogether."

"Okay," Kebab agrees.

We watch him, the way you watch a racehorse. Kebab has already drunk two bottles of beer on an empty stomach. And the little snack we had in Rehovot, on the way back from Daba, was not generous. The civilians are short of food. Half a bottle must be enough to get him blind drunk. We can expect an entertaining spectacle.

The liquid disappears down his throat. At first in large, quick gulps. Then gradually more slowly. The gulps get smaller and slower. He is surrounded by absolute silence. Even the air force people at the next table are staring silently at the bottle. Even after the first third Kebab threatens to give up. It doesn't look as though he will manage even half the bottle.

With "Are you a soldier or a girl guide?" Nachshe tries to motivate him.

"Go on! Go on!" Zuzik shouts, like a spectator at some sport.

He concentrates, takes a few big gulps, reaches the half-way point, reaches two-thirds, and gives up.

"Th-th-that isn-n-n-n't Co-co-cognac," he stutters, "th-th-that is f-f-f-fly's p-p-piss."

We drink the rest. The bottle goes from mouth to mouth and the liquid warms our hearts. Four gulps are enough for Zuzik – the effect is the same as if he had drunk ten glasses.

"I will get you!" he threatens. "I'll finish off the lot of you with my pistol."

"Why don't you challenge Kebab to a duel," Nachshe suggests.

Kebab is in just the right mood. He picks up his weapon and inserts a round.

"Grab him! He is drunk!" Zuzik cries in horror. We laugh and get up. It is time to drive back.

* * *

That night Kebab keeps us all awake. First he was throwing up till ten. I have never seen anyone puke so much. We put him in one of the trenches and thought he would sleep twenty-four hours. But that was too optimistic. Since midnight he has been holding a monologue, like someone with a fever. But he is not talking – he is singing his text. Always with the same, monotonous melody. Like someone praying in the synagogue. Or like an Arabic Qur'an recital on the radio. Two or three verses of singsong. A long pause. Then another two or three verses.

"I used to be a he-ro," Kebab sang–recited–complained. "Now I'm just a cow-ward!"

Long pause. We are enjoying it, like at the movies. Only Zuzik is sleeping.

We always knew that Kebab was a coward deep down. Most people who boast about their misdeeds are cowards, just trying to cover up their anxiety. There are also wild people who are brave, like Nachshe. But they are not boastful.

"My cousin is a h-e-e-e-ro!" Kebab declares. "He killed three British with the Le-hi." We are gradually losing interest. Tomorrow we have a longer patrol. We want to sleep.

"My Miri-am sleeps with my cou-sin!" Kebab is getting louder. Soon he will be sobbing. "She sleeeeeeps with him in the Haaaadaaaaasah Park." The hell with it. Shut up! Nobody is interested in his dismal love life.

"Oh Miriam, o myyyyyy Miiiiiiriaaaaaam, why have you deserted me? I am a coward and my cousin is a pi-ig!"

"That's enough! Shut your mouth!" Nachshe shouts.

"Let's put him far away in the orange orchard," Sancho suggests.

"We can't just leave him there on his own."

"Then put Zuzik next to him."

Zuzik is awake, and agrees. After that much alcohol he could sleep next to a firing howitzer.

"I want to Miriiiiaaaammm," sings Kebab as we carry him to the orchard. "Why do you sleep with my couuuuuuuuusin?"

* * *

They let us sleep until twelve. We have a hearty lunch and set off on patrol. Kebab comes too. He is fully recovered and has no memory of the night before. When we remind him, he laughs like someone who knows that we are just fooling.

We set off with three jeeps. Before we leave someone reads from a typewritten sheet. We are installing the heavy machine guns on the vehicles and listen with half an ear. It is not something we need to be told anyway. "The Arabs who have crossed the border should be prevented from returning to collect the harvest ... kill all people and animals ... burn the barns ..."

The landscape is fantastic. The sun is shining but doesn't worry us. Most of us are walking around shirtless. We are wearing short trousers in violation of our orders. But no orders can compare with our motto: "Fight and die – in comfort!" On patrols like this one our chances of dying are slim, unless in a traffic accident. The Fellaheen, who occasionally sneak back to harvest some grain for their starving families, are no fighters. They mainly arrive overnight and leave at dawn. We are hardly likely to come across them at this time of day.

At the kibbutz gate an old man gets up, and claims to be a scout.

We drive through the village of Daba. The old woman who Nachshe shot yesterday is still sitting in front of her house, leaning against the door post. She has already begun to stink. The sweetish odor fills the narrow alley sickeningly. Without this stink you wouldn't know that she is dead.

At the end of the village there are some big barns. Wonderful – there we have something to set on fire. If you don't have a fit of philosophizing, then it is really fun. You need some experience, which only comes with repeated practice. You have to start it burning on the side away from the wind. But even then it is by no means certain that the whole thing will burn down. And if only part of it has burned, then you just have to try again another time.

After quarter of an hour all twelve barns are burning. A nice, almost aesthetic sight. At such moments you can understand the Emperor Nero watching Rome burn. In their enthusiasm Jamus and our kibbutz guest also set fire to some nearby mud huts.

Onward. We have to cover the range of hills in the direction of the village of Romajel. As we are crossing the third hill we see a donkey in front of us. A donkey never goes for a walk on its own. There must be people in the area. Boby, the young company commander, urges us on. But Zuzik has already drawn his pistol and jumped out of the jeep. We look on with interest. Can you really shoot a donkey with such a small P.B.?

"It won't die," Kebab prophesies.

"We'll see," says Sancho uncertainly.

Zuzik cautiously approaches the donkey. At one meter's range he shoots it between the eyes. The animal raises its head and gazes at

Zuzik with what looks almost like pity. We laugh. Zuzik is angry and fires a second, third, fourth, fifth bullet into the donkey's head. The donkey does not react.

"Get away from there!" Kebab shouts, raising his rifle. The others are also gripped with blood lust. Two automatic weapons and five rifles fill the animal with lead. For a moment the donkey stands there. Then, without any further reaction, it collapses.

* * *

The smugglers are presumably well beyond the second hill. We drive after them.

Behind the hill a camel is standing.

"Wait! Let me!" Nachshe calls and aims his rifle. He claims to be a marksman. The second bullet hits the camel in the neck. A long stream of blood spurts like a fountain. The blood streams and streams. The camel gazes at us with very sad eyes. Then its front legs slowly fold, followed by the back legs. It all happens very slowly, like a slow dance.

There is nothing sadder in the world than a dying animal. It looks at you, as if it wanted to understand what you have done. But it can't understand. Do we understand ourselves?

* * *

We search the wheat field. We know that the Arabs must be hiding somewhere round here. If they have any chance at all, then only by keeping quiet and staying still. There! Something white is moving. We rush over. Two Arabs!

"Get up, you dogs!" Kebab screams. He searches their pockets. One of them is carrying a beautiful dagger. Kebab pockets it. Another souvenir. They are both between fifty and sixty. They are standing, but their knees are trembling. Sweat is running down their faces. They try to smile, but only achieve a grimace.

Idiot! Why did they wear white keffiyehs which make them so conspicuous?

Jamus asks them the routine questions. They come from Daba and ran away to Beit Jibrin. They have nothing to eat. They have wives and children. They came back to harvest some grain.

While they are stumbling over their explanation, Kebab is loading his rifle. Now they have completely lost their wits. They are babbling incoherently. Their eyes are staring with fear.

"Dakhilkum! Ma bidnash namut! Ma bidnash namut!"[6] They don't want to die. At the same time they know with terrible certainty that they are going to die. They keep talking in the desperate hope that nothing will happen to them as long as they are talking.

Kebab raises his rifle. One of the men sinks to his knees, grasps his hand.

"Ya khawaja!"[7] he shrieks. In my life I have never heard such begging and moaning.

"Hey! Look out!" Zuzik shouts.

Some way away, at the other end of the field, an Arab gets up and runs away. My jeep races after him.

Idiot! If he had lain quietly among the wheat we would never have noticed him. Before we catch up with him, from behind us come the sounds of two shots.

* * *

The Arab knows that he has no chance. He stops running and waits until we arrive. He is very calm. Speaks quietly. His name is Ahmed. He lives in Daba and knows the people from the neighboring kibbutz well.

"That's true!" the kibbutz member who is accompanying us confirms. "I know him. He was always OK. He even wanted to sell us some land." Boby, the company commander, hesitates. "Maybe we should take him prisoner?" he asks uncertainly. But Kebab has caught up with us. There is no holding him.

"Don't be childish!" he laughs. That is a deadly argument. Boby is nineteen. Six or seven years younger than most of us. He is very sensitive on this point. Actually he is a good boy, who doesn't like such things. But he is afraid of appearing soft before us, childish, unmanly. And the command …

The Arab smiles. It is that terrible, tortured smile of someone who knows that his fate is being decided at this moment, and who hopes that a calm expression might influence his judges. But the smile only annoys Kebab. "What are you smiling at?" he shouts at him. "Inta bitmut,"[8] with shining eyes like a bird of prey.

"Inshallah," says the Arab. Kebab loads his rifle. I want to turn away, but cannot. I feel sick.

My God! Why will I never be able to get used to this sight?

Tarzan is also pale. The kibbutz member opens his mouth, as if about to say something. But he says nothing. He knows, as I do, that nothing can help here.

Zuzik grabs Kebab's arm. "Let me!" he shouts. "I want to try out my pistol!" His childish schoolboy face has reddened, his pistol is trembling in his hand.

"Go to hell!" says Kebab, giving him a shove.

"You have already killed two," Zuzik insists. He demands his rights. Kebab curses, but lowers his rifle. He seems to be convinced that it is fair to allow Zuzik his share. Zuzik raises his little weapon. The Arab looks at him.

"Turn around!" Zuzik shrieks. His voice is thin and hysterical. He is not brave enough to shoot when his victim is looking at him. The Arab doesn't move. His face is composed in infinite calm. As if he has made his peace with God. Does he despise us? He doesn't even close his eyes.

Zuzik shoots twice. The Arab falls on his back. He groans gently, his body still moving.

"Damned idiot!" says Kebab and gives Zuzik such a push that he almost lands on the dying man. Kebab raises his rifle, places the muzzle against the Arab's head, and shoots. The skull bursts open and something whitish comes out onto the ground. The wounded man stops moving.

Kebab ejects the spent cartridge case and laughs wildly. His expression is that of someone who has successfully performed his duty.

"You see?" he says mockingly to Zuzik. "Your pistol is useless. A rifle is best."

Capturing the Village – on Film

I look at the time. It is ten minutes to four. At four Rachel will give me two injections. Another ten minutes. Six hundred seconds, six hundred rasping breaths from the man in the next bed.

Will this night never end?

Six minutes … In six minutes a battle can be decided. Dozens of people can die and hundreds be wounded. The jeep assault on Position 125. This engagement, decisive for the whole front, lasted less than six minutes. In these six minutes Nino's parents lost their purpose in life, and Pinchas was crippled forever. In these six minutes the lives of countless families were thrown off course. You could write a book about it – about the lives of these families. You would have to tell their life stories twice: the first time, how life would have been if these six minutes had not happened, and then, what actually happened. The young woman in Damietta[1] will not marry the fallen captain, Pinchas will never again be Israeli champion in long-distance running, and no one will ever sing the songs that Nino would have composed had he not fallen. And with the passage of time his fiancée will forget that she almost married a composer.

In every report of a battle the losses are listed: weapons, ammunition, dead, wounded. But who records the real losses? The music that is not composed, the books that are not written, the achievements that are never made, and the discoveries that remain undiscovered – and all because someone, before they could achieve something, was hit by a bullet worth a few pence?

We talk about geniuses like Beethoven, Shakespeare, or Pasteur. How many Beethovens are lying in the graves of Verdun? Are the bones of a Curie mouldering on the slopes of Monte Cassino? Did a new Einstein get caught in the barbed wire of Iraq al-Manshiyya or Beit Affa?

The parents of the man in the next bed are probably sleeping soundly, unaware that their son is grappling with death. Nobody has told them. Otherwise they would have been here the day after he was wounded, stared at him, and sobbed in the corridor outside. Parents cry when their son is on his deathbed. But then it is usually too late. His fate was already decided when he was still healthy and cheerful.

Maybe there is a sealed envelope at my neighbor's unit, with his handwriting on it: "Please forward in the case of my death." Some leave such letters before they go into action. Most of us do not. What's the use? Letters like that are ridiculous and melodramatic. It is embarrassing. What on earth can you write? "Dear parents, if you receive this letter, I am no longer living …" Idiotic. What can you tell your parents? "I apologize for all the worries that I have caused you …" or "… I hope that we will meet again in a better world …" Nobody believes that there is such a "better world." You could finish like a Zionistic obituary with "the construction of the motherland will be a consolation to you."

But we were too superstitious. We simply knew that writing such a letter opens the door to the devil, and you will die in the next battle. We have seen it happen.

Dany died six hours after he handed in his farewell letter. Is that pure imagination? You sit there and write this letter as if you are already dead. When you think that way, you won't have the energy you need to survive in battle. You become timid. And the timid are the first to die, it is well known.

Many say that a soldier can "feel" the approach of death. Dany also felt it and made a great fuss about taking part in this operation. Of course that is nonsense. It may well happen that a soldier has a bad feeling before an operation, without being timid. But the reason is lack of sleep or poor nutrition. One night I, too, felt that I was going to die. Because I hadn't slept for thirty-six hours. But it so happened that we lost our way that night and didn't run into any Egyptian units. On the other hand I had no such "feelings" on the day I was wounded. I set off on that patrol like someone who is going to the toilet or to a roll call – an unpleasant but in no way unusual duty.

Damned patrol. Why haven't we been provided with any automatic weapon support? Why on earth have we been sent into this area in broad daylight? … No! Don't think about it! Otherwise the wound will start hurting again.

Where is Rachel? Four o'clock has already struck. Please, Rachel, come quickly …

* * *

There she is, fresh, smiling. Devil knows how she manages it, always smiling like that. Habit? No. You never get used to things like this. It is professional armor. "I wear a white coat. I am a nurse. I must stay calm!"

"How did you sleep?" smiles Rachel.

"I didn't sleep at all!"

"You are a naughty-naughty-naughty boy," she tells me off.

"Yes, ma."

"As a punishment, Mama will now give you two injections."

"There is no room left on my legs."

"Mama will find a place."

In earlier days men fell in love with women who could cook and knit socks. Then it was respectable virgins who could play the piano and converse in French. What has made me fall in love with Rachel is her skill at giving injections.

"And now my baby will be really, really gooooood and sleep."

"If I do, will you stop giving me injections?"

"No! The injections will be your reward."

"But I can't go to sleep. Really I can't."

"Then I'll sing you a lullaby, OK?"

"Right."

"What would the little one like to hear?"

"Something nice that has nothing to do with the war."

"Good. I'll sing the song about the green eyes."

"Oh no! Not that one!"

"What's the problem?"

"Doesn't matter. Give me a kiss instead."

"What do you want with a kiss from an old woman?"

"Give me a kiss!"

Very carefully she bends the tube that goes into my nose to one side, and her little mouth touches my lips.

"You are a sweet doll!"

"That's no way to talk to a nurse!"

"Just you wait. When I get out of here, I'll give you a proper kiss!"

"Really?"

"Yes! At least a quarter of an hour. Five seconds for every injection you have given me."

"You should be ashamed of yourself!"

"Do you prefer giving injections to an innocent?"

"My poor little one. Go to sleep now."

"I can't."

"Only two hours to go."

"Only!"

"That is not very nice. I did give you a kiss. Now you should go to sleep."

"OK."

Her light footsteps disappear. Someone is snoring in the big room. This song ... what was it she wanted to sing? Green eyes ... Not that song! ...

* * *

Your eyes are flowing with green light
Like sparkling emeralds set to admire.[2]

* * *

I soap my body methodically, like an experienced soldier. Each body part is washed and rinsed in turn. I know the army showers. At the critical moment the water can stop. Nachshe was once standing in the shower covered in soap, when the water stopped flowing. We had to collect all the water bottles in the whole camp. And the pearls which rolled out of Nachshe's mouth could have formed the basis for a dictionary of curses at the linguistic academy.

"Hallo boy!"

Joker comes in. He undresses, stretches, and tests the water temperature with a careful finger.

* * *

I thirst for a minute's rest
you drive so far, so far ...

* * *

"What is that?," asks Joker enthusiastically. "A concert for us two?"

"That is for rude boys who want to share Bambi's shower," I explain.

"That is historical materialism," Joker laughs.

"How do you work that out?"

"You wouldn't understand. The external social conditions determine the development of art."

Joker is usually embarrassed to show off his higher education. He disguises himself with experiences from the time when he was an unskilled worker in Tel Aviv. Just occasionally, in very personal talks between the two of us, does the university shine out through his words.

"Rubbish," I say, and try to involve him in a discussion, "the most important is the individual." Joker soaps himself carefully. He uses the same method as I do.

"A horse is worth more than ten people!" Joker quotes.

"What's that rubbish you're talking!" Bambi protests from behind the partition.

"That is quite simple," Joker explains. "Every nine months you can produce a human being. But you just try to bring a horse into this world."

With "you're a dirty pig!" Bambi terminates the scientific debate.

* * *

Your eyes are flowing with green light.

* * *

L-u-n-c-h-t-i-m-e!

When this magic word sounds, a mass of humanity streams out of the tents. An enormous and very loud line forms by the mess tent. The man on duty, one of the "pupils" who graces this honorable position for twenty-four hours at a time, tries in vain to demonstrate his leadership qualities by imposing some kind of order on the chattering, swearing, laughing line.

Jamus and I are the last to come out of our tent. We stroll slowly toward the kitchen, without bringing any cutlery.

"Disgusting, how people push into the line!" Jamus remarks as loud as he can.

"Herd mentality," I explain scornfully.

The ones at the end of the queue cast angry glances in our direction, which we ignore. We walk round the kitchen tent and enter the holy of holies, take cutlery which is reserved for officers, and pass through the second entrance into the serving room where those at the front of the line are collecting their food.

"Aha! The nobility has appeared!" shouts someone from the end of the line. Jamus glances coolly at him, but doesn't deign to answer.

"Would you mind leaving this place and joining the end of the line?" asks the one on duty.

"Shhh! That's not the way to talk to future brigade commanders," fat Joshua lectures him. "Would your honors perhaps have the grace to join the simple folk in practicing standing in line?"

This ceremony is repeated three times a day. Everyone knows that we will not stand in line, and everyone has long since got used to it. If we did suddenly join the line, they would feel betrayed. As if they had to watch one of the instructional movies about house-to-house fighting without it being followed by the usual cartoon.

Actually we have nothing against standing in line. But we feel that we would somehow be betraying our jeep company which we are, officially as it were, representing. Noblesse oblige! None of us in the company stands in line. The one with the sharpest elbows gets served first. Only occasionally, when one of the officers pushes in front of the ordinary soldiers, will we remind him of the holiness of the line.

We get a reasonable helping of meat, noodles, soup, and desert on our plates. Jamus wrinkles his nose. "This shit again?" he complains, and puts another big lump of meat on his plate.

"What are you complaining about?" asks the cook angrily from the doorway to the kitchen.

"I know you lot," Jamus replies, "you eat the good meat yourselves and give us the leftovers."

"How dare you ..." roars the cook angrily. He wears a kepi on his head, which trembles when he gets excited.

"He is quite right!" bellow supporting voices from the line.

Since we were left hungry on Yom Kippur,[3] the cooks have not been very popular. The soldiers don't like them, apart from the cook of their own forward base. The orthodox cooks, who refuse to prepare food on the Sabbath, are doubly disliked.

"All that you are capable of is mixing soda into the mush," Jamus asserts. "If you come and visit me at my kibbutz, then I will show you how cooking should be done!"

"What do you mean – soda?" asks the cook in an innocent tone.

"You think we don't know that you sprinkle soda over our food?" asks Jamus. There is a rumor that soda or bromide is mixed with the food in the training camps, to damp down the sex drive of the "pupils." There was no evidence for this. But experience has taught us to believe rumors. Most rumors that spread through the army turn out to be true, though nobody knows where and how they arise.

"Of course you do that!" shouts Mundek. "Since I've been on this shit course I haven't had a single hard-on."

"I don't suppose you ever have had a hard-on," sneers the cook.

"Then why did I on Yom Kippur?"

"On Yom Kippur that was the finger of God."

"Your God seems to have plenty of fingers!" Mundek's remark is greeted with a roar of laughter. Everyone is happy to get revenge on the cook.

"Do you want me to prove that there is soda in the tea?" Jamus ventures. "Listen: the day before yesterday we were trying out the Vickers in the field. Then we noticed that it was leaking. The cooling water for the hot barrel had leaked away. Since we still had the tea from breakfast in our water bottles, we poured it in. And you know what happened?"

"What?"

"The barrel bent till it was pointing at the ground!"

The cook blinks, trying to understand the joke. He has no sense of humor. Then he twigs.

"Your brains are like blocked cesspits!" he exclaims. "Get out of here and give the others a chance!"

In the tent there is only one theme of conversation: the attack that began four days ago along the whole length of the front. Those of us who are taking part in the squad leader training course are seen as valuable human material. So we are not allowed to take part in any fighting before the end of the course.

"Only a dog would stay here and train, while fighting is going on over there!" Mundek shouts. He is one of the most popular people on the course since the last lecture on ballistics when he was snoring loudly.

"If they don't let us out of here soon, there will be no one left who can show it to the Egyptians!"

"Who needs this shitty course? Things were much better as ordinary soldiers."

"First we had to do the dirty work, and now some newly arrived immigrants can play the victor at our expense."

I glance over my shoulder. Our superiors are sitting at their table, chewing silently, and trying to look as though they can't hear anything. They too would prefer to rejoin their previous units. But discipline is discipline.

"So, shall we bug off tonight?" Jamus whispers.

"OK, OK! If you really want to die, we can get out." Since yesterday Jamus has been busy trying to organize a mass breakout.

"So, listen" he whispers. "We don't take anything with us. Just the rifles, ammunition, washing things, and steel helmets. We can leave our clothes here."

"How do we find the battalion? Do you even know exactly where the front runs?"

"Doesn't matter. We'll get there. On the main road we just get onto one of the passing supply trucks."

Joker devours his food in record time and lights a cigarette. He rubs his long nose. This shows that he is in a philosophical mood.

"Why have you all suddenly become such heroes?"

"Don't talk nonsense," says Jamus irritably. "It is just more pleasant to race through the countryside in a jeep than to crawl around in the thorns."

"And that's all?" asks Joker disbelievingly.

"Another thing: how can we look them in the face, Tarzan and Nachshe and all the others, if we hang around here while they could be killed at any moment?"

"What honorable sentiments," Joker mocks. "I think you just like war!"

"Idiot!" spits out Jamus in real anger. "I hate war as much as you do. But if I belong to a unit, I can't just lie in a comfortable bed while the others have to get out."

I know what he means. Once, when the company was in camp, I

sneaked out for a night in Tel Aviv. When I got back the next day, I learned that our unit had been sent out at short notice, and that the Chinaman, our commander at the time, had got a bullet in the head. None of my comrades said anything to me. But the way they all looked at me, I was really not far from shooting myself.

"You are deluding yourself," Joker continued to philosophize. "You know as well as I do, that that is not the real reason. In any case not the only one. The truth is, that we can't get by without it. When we scent danger, we start panting like a dog after a bitch on heat. Half a day at the front, and we are cursing war and praying for a ceasefire. But while we are here, we long to be back at the front."

"Perhaps," Jamus admits quietly.

"It is like a mental illness. It had already started at school," Joker continues.

"But you weren't at school here at all," I interject.

"That doesn't mean anything, does it? I went to school in Romania, Jamus in Egypt, and you here in Palestine. But we were brought up the same way. Every shitty people has its legends of heroes, generals, and marshals, and its history of wars and victories. The kids are taught that war is something beautiful and romantic. And the best thing of all is: to die for the motherland. Every shit who has killed a hundred soldiers gets a memorial and a page in the history books."

"Maybe you should change the world?" suggests Jamus.

"The world can go to hell. If I have children, I will never send them to school. In five years' time they will be being told that this war was a great thing and all of them will be praying to take part in such a war."

"You won't have any kids at all," Jamus consoles him. "Because you will go for a stroll along Allenby Street on the day after the war, when a brick falls on your head and smashes your skull."

"And I will shit on your grave …" Joker begins.

But silence falls over the tent. Even Shabtai's chewing stops.

The course commander comes in. He has just come back from brigade HQ.

"Listen, men!" he calls, smiling contentedly. "Last night the brigade forced the route into the Negev! The Egyptians are surrounded at Majdal."

"And here we are playing around ..." Mundek murmured loud enough.

"Shut up!" the commander barks. "Orders from the brigade. In two hours we head for Barchaba. I want all weapons to be clean. We will take supplies and equipment for an operation of two weeks. The rest of your things and the mattresses will be stored in the culture room. Departure at four o'clock in the afternoon. On the dot!"

> Your eyes are flowing with green light
> Like sparkling emeralds set to admire.
> I thirst for a minute's rest
> you drive so far, so far ...

* * *

Bambi and I go on a tour of the positions. We got our lunch early. The cooks are getting ready for a big operation. Some film people, war correspondents, a few culture people, and still other curious creatures have come to the village. Its capture is to be re-enacted for them. Three houses are set on fire for effect. And all members of support services for the course – cooks, drivers, mess attendants – have been equipped with guns and grenades. They are expected to capture the village most spectacularly for the movie.

"What fun!" crows Bambi, watching the spectacle from a distance. One of the cooks is wearing a turban and playing an Egyptian prisoner. A cameraman explains to the cooks exactly how they should capture the village. All the weapons fire at once – rifles, machine guns, pistols.

"If they had an artillery piece, they would be firing that too," said Bambi critically. "And then they distribute that across the world to show how our heroes take over the whole land in no time at all. And to think of the slackers in Tel Aviv applauding. Sickening!"

We climb a hill. In front of us is a wide field. The cinema behind us is forgotten. Scattered about the field in front of us are something like eighty Egyptian corpses.

"What a stink!" says Bambi.

We go closer. The day before yesterday, this was the scene of one of the most horrifying battles of the war. A battle with daggers, knives, and fingernails. Four times the hill changed hands. The next morning our dozens of dead were buried first. The Egyptians were just shifted over here, to stop them fouling the air around our positions. Some unit will have to be brought over here to bury them. We are certainly not going to do it.

Why do we go and look at the dead? We could have walked around the field. Our stomachs feel weak, but we have to have a look. We are like little monkeys, hypnotized by a snake. They know that the snake will eat them, but the monkeys still cannot resist. The dead are lying in various poses. One is covering his face, as if to avoid seeing the dagger thrust into him. Another is rolled up like a hedgehog.

These corpses will not be shown in the movie theater. What you see on the screen are living people who don't move. The dead look different from the living. The dead don't look like people at all. Something is missing. Religion knows it as the "soul." "They returned their souls to the Lord …" This sentence suddenly occurs to me. If that is so, then the Lord surely has strange methods of recovering what he himself has created.

"What is that?" cries Bambi in horror.

Something is moving among the dead. For a second the dark shadow of an old fairy tale brushes over me. But it isn't a ghost. Joker gets up off the ground. His face is red and it is easy to see his discomfort. In his hand he is holding a knife.

"Are you crazy?" Bambi's face shows clearly that she thinks he has gone mad. "What are you doing here with the dead?"

"I … I … I …" he stutters.

Now I can see. He had begun to operate on the fat Egyptian.

"Let's get away from here. I can explain." Joker walks off fast. We go a few hundred yards. We feel bad. We like Joker and can't understand what has got into him. He would be the last of us to torture someone, still less kill them in cold blood.

"So," he stutters his explanation, "I don't know whether I ever told you. In Romania I began to study medicine …. that … that was a long time ago. Before the Germans came. I wanted to be a doctor. My family was well off. You understand … then the Nazis came and I escaped … I was with the partisans … then with the Red Army … later with the Jewish Brigade, which smuggled me to Palestine … of course I didn't have the money to continue studying … and also I couldn't speak Hebrew. That is why I am an unskilled worker. Carry things in a factory … But sometimes … I dream about studying again … and now, when I saw the bodies lying here … I just wanted to see if I could remember the anatomy I learned…"

He gets a dirty handkerchief from his pocket and wipes his sweaty face. Something shiny falls on the ground. Gold teeth. Joker's face again goes red. "I saw this on the dead man … and he doesn't need it any more …"

"Good," said Bambi dryly. "What are you getting excited about? Over there is a dead woman."

"She was with the Egyptians," Joker says. "No one knows what she did there … I don't think that she was raped." The woman is lying on her back. Someone has shot her in the chest. She has black eyes and is surrounded by flies.

* * *

The village is the scene of hectic activity. An hour ago the order came from the brigade to move the positions one and a half kilometers to the west, on the next chain of hills. For this purpose I have been relieved of my duties as runner and I am back with my unit. Everyone is packing.

The men are angry. Of all the orders there are, the one to relocate the positions is the most unpopular. It all seems pointless. You dig trenches, move a few hundred meters, and dig new trenches. Whoever plans this at HQ simply moves a finger from one point on the map to another. For the men it means work day and night: dragging equipment, digging trenches, moving and relaying wire.

We look like loaded mules. On my back I am carrying a rucksack with enough equipment for a "two week deployment" and a rifle. In my belt are a hundred rounds of ammunition, three hand grenades, and a folding spade. My head is squeezed into my steel helmet and in each hand I am carrying a box with PIAT armor-piercing rounds. Others are carrying boxes of ammunition, Molotov cocktails, machine guns, mortars, and spare parts.

After the first fifty meters we are exhausted and staggering like drunks. The ranks break up and the superiors rush here and there trying to restore some order to the unit and shake the men out of their lethargy.

"You are supposed to be squad leaders? I wouldn't even take you on as privates …"

"You there! Don't stagger around like a pregnant hen!"

Despite the cold of the night we are dripping with sweat. Our desire to drop our burdens is growing. You need a strong will to resist the temptation.

"Heroes! You wanted to go to the front ..." Joker grumbles.

"If only we were back in our jeeps. There we would really be kings," Jamus answered.

The march over that short distance takes hours. We reach "our" position around midnight. As soon as we hear that this is our place, we drop everything and fall to the ground ourselves.

"Don't just lie around like whores after work!" the company commander shouts. "Listen: by dawn we have to be prepared for an Egyptian attack. Three hundred and sixty degree defense. I will show you the individual positions in a moment. I want the trenches to be exemplary. Show that you have learned something here. One trench for every two men. Connecting trenches in between. Special trenches for the machine guns. Tomorrow we will lay barbed wire around the whole position. So! Get up! For God's sake ..."

"He knows what he can do," Mundek grumbles. But we all get up and start working. The trench for two is an invention of the devil. If you just have to dig a trench for yourself, you can do it as well or as badly as you like. But when two are digging a trench together, each one keeps an eye on the other, to make sure they are not taking advantage.

Your eyes are flowing with green light ...

I hum idly, lying on my back, with my head resting on a block of wood. My gaze sweeps over the Egyptian-occupied area. Jamus and I have volunteered to spend the whole day in the lookout post. This is situated in a little vineyard, a few meters away from the barbed wire. The quiet is absolute.

For a couple of hours I read an English book of short stories. The stories captured all my attention. Now and then I would glance around the area. But there is nothing to see – only the next village, whose inhabitants fled when we took Barchaba.

Jamus is also reading an English book. Most of us read English books. The few of us who only know Hebrew read trashy novels in translation. Since I joined up I haven't seen anyone reading a work of modern Israeli literature. Somehow there is nothing there to interest young people. If the writers lived with us in the fighting units, then they would notice how empty and overdone their works are.

"Come for a shit!" says Jamus.

"I don't feel like it," I reply. The loneliness is wonderful. In the army you are never alone. Eating, sleeping, showering, loving – everything is done in company. To be alone – two men in a vineyard, warming the half-naked body in the sun, and not lifting a finger – that is heaven. The greatest pleasure in our lives.

"Very strange," Jamus thinks aloud.

"What's that?"

"Two weeks ago we kicked up a hell of a fuss, just to come here …"

Two weeks ago? Since then we have done just about nothing – keeping watch, guard duty, digging trenches. And still we are sick of it all. The front, the whole war. Nor do we feel like going back to the course. Continuing with drill, becoming a squad leader. What for? Life has only one real purpose – lying in the sun, relaxing. The world is a pile of shit. No, the world is OK. It is people who are the shit. They should all be wiped out and a new start made. Beginning with the monkeys …

"Look what is going on over there," Jamus remarks without great interest.

On the Egyptian-controlled road, about two kilometers in front of us, a long column of vehicles is moving southwards.

"They must be heading for Gaza," says Jamus.

"How can they be? I thought they were surrounded."

"They must have found some way. Maybe across the beach?"

I languidly raise the telescope. No doubt about it. They are leaving. That is heavy equipment – artillery, large caliber mortars.

"We'll have to inform HQ …"

"What for?"

"Maybe we can block their retreat."

"It doesn't matter to me if they withdraw. Isn't that the best solution to the whole business? And anyway, HQ can surely see them too?"

Actually he is right. That is the best solution. What's the point in fighting? In killing? If they decide to withdraw – they have our silent blessing. It is all so pointless. The front, the war, all of it. What is the point of fighting? Why work, when today's results will be destroyed tomorrow? The whole world is a heap of shit.

* * *

Your eyes are flowing with green light
Like sparkling emeralds set to admire.

Sancho's Last Words

He groans. His head is hanging to one side, as if he lacks the energy to hold it straight. His face is darker than it was in the evening – reddish-blue, like a drowned man.

A poem is buzzing around my head. Fluttering souls … what poem was that? Where did I hear that song?

> In dem der Tod ist
> Flatternd in seinen Fängen.

* * *

Words. Did the poet hear the fluttering of a soul in the claws of the Angel of Death? In his whole life, did he ever hear this terrible rattle? This awful groaning? Why are poets and writers allowed to write about things that they don't know? Why are they allowed to celebrate war and death, the last terrible suffering of a poor, helpless creature?

Sellers of fake medicines and shopkeepers who use false weights are punished. Why is there no punishment for those who poison our souls with false words?

The room is filled with rasping breathing. For a moment it gets louder, like an airplane in a dive, and the next moment it stops entirely. In my shock I want to call the nurse, when the rusty, scratching sound returns, ends in a long sigh, and starts again.

He breathes in salvos. An idiotic thought that goes through my head. The breathing of a dying man.

I can't think any more. I have to listen to this noise, that sounds like the chirping of a cicada. Does a cicada have a soul? Poor, fluttering soul, that has had enough of life, but still doesn't want to leave it.

Chchchrrrh. Chchchrrrh. Chchchrrrh.

That is the sound of the Angel of Death. He arrives in a destroyed jeep, rattling and squeaking. The panels of the jeep are made of paper – pages of newspaper, song sheets, homework.

Quiet. The rattling has stopped. Has he arrived? No. Not yet. There it is again, this rattling. It becomes more distant and then closer, distant, and then close. Light tapping on the window. Does Death tap on windows? No. Nonsense. Crazy fantasies. It is rain. First the drops tap lightly on the window, then they tap harder and harder. In the end it is really raining. Tap-tap-tap-tap.

A welcome to you, Rain. You drown out the groaning, cover it up with your own sound. Blessed, calming rain. Sounds like machine guns in the remote distance, too far for the bullets to reach me …

* * *

The first raindrops, gentle, caressing …

We are standing in Mugrabi Square. A big, open truck is waiting to take us back to camp. People are assembling in three rows under the big clock, whose hands indicate the approach of midnight. Jamus is standing in front of them. He shouts in French, acting big in the Israeli way, and the people are shivering with cold in their thin shirts. It is hard to tell if anyone is missing. Civilians walk past, wrapped in thick coats, and throw us fleeting glances.

"Attention!" Jamus shouts. He is the only one of us three squad leaders who can speak French. That is why he has taken on the duty of sergeant. He in turn is standing in for the company commander, who is in hospital after his face was ripped up by a hand grenade.

We spent the evening in Tel Aviv. An unofficial absence. Since we know that our company is headed for the front, we decided to allow our Moroccans a little pleasure in life before their baptism of fire.

They don't have much to enjoy, these Moroccans. The Yishuv brought them here to help in the war. They are sent to the front without adequate training, without suitable winter clothing, and the doors of society remain closed to them. Moroccan – a word of disapproval! The French language alone is enough to spoil the chances of a young man with a girl in Tel Aviv.

Actually I didn't do much this evening. I had no desire for a woman and didn't want to get separated from Jamus. We sat in a miserable, small cafe and drank one beer after the other. A strange melancholy has overcome us, without our knowing where it came from. Perhaps from our lonely way of life, where we are responsible for new immigrants who can't speak our language?

"Très bien! On the lorries!" Jamus shouts.

The people climb over one another, pushing and swearing. They are all trying to get to the good place behind the driver's cab where they imagine there may be a little protection from rain and wind.

There is only room for two next to the driver. Normally we remain with our people. That strengthens the esprit de corps and trust. But now that has lost its meaning. All our noble principles are washed out by the rain and the depressing atmosphere. What the hell! We also got wet when we were recruits. They can suffer a bit.

Janek, the third squad leader, volunteers to stay in the open. We feel sorry for Janek. He is supposed to lead a squad of Turks who understand no Polish, while he doesn't understand a word of Turkish.

Jamus and I push our way into the driver's cab. Nehemia starts the motor. Since he was released from hospital, he has been with a transport unit. He is a little ashamed not to have returned to a fighting unit. As if we would hold it against him! Only very few of the seriously wounded return to a fighting unit. It is human nature to be anxious after being wounded. Fear is a loss of faith in your own invulnerability. You can be a hero so long as you are sure that the bullets are not meant for you. Getting wounded destroys this illusion. Everyone who rejoins a fighting unit after being seriously wounded deserves a medal.

"Wait!" Jamus shouts.

"What's up?"

"I saw something ... there." Jamus has sharp eyes. A girl is standing at a corner and casting furtive, hopeful glances in our direction.

Jamus gets out and approaches her. She is pretty, blond, and well-rounded. Jamus is proud of his discovery. "Would you like to join us?" he asks in the tender voice that he reserves for such occasions.

"No ... I mean ... perhaps ... I am going to Sarafand." The hope in her voice is unmistakable.

"Excellent!" Jamus declares. "We can take you as far as Rishon. There you are sure to be able to hitch another ride." He twirls his gigantic mustache and acts big, as though he is at least the company commander.

"Hey, you there, boy!" he says to me over his shoulder. "Climb up with the others behind!" Actually I should obey his "order." We have a long-standing agreement to help each other impress girls. But up behind it is cold and wet, and I feel that the girl belongs to both of us equally.

"Hhhmmmmmmm …" Jamus reflects. He knows how to extract himself elegantly from the business. "I don't want to be like that and play the gentleman at your expense. You can stay," he says to me, and "Please take your place" to the girl. "I will stand on the running board."

"Are you sure you don't mind?" asks the girl shyly and sits next to me. She has no choice. At this time of the day she won't find another lift.

"Quite the opposite!" Jamus assures her. "It is a pleasure for me. And I can also keep an eye on my people."

We drive off. The roads are deserted. At the Abu-Kabir crossroads, on the way out of Tel Aviv, it starts to pour down. The girl feels uncomfortable. Jamus's gentlemanly behavior has visibly impressed her. These days girls traveling on their own don't always run into young men who behave so chivalrously toward them.

"You know what?" she suggests, "why don't you come back in? There must be room for the three of us."

"If it doesn't make you too uncomfortable," says Jamus generously, but gets in. We twist and turn like sardines in a tin. And then we are all sitting comfortably: Jamus and I on the seat and the girl on us – the left side on one of Jamus's legs, the right on mine. Behind her back Jamus winks at me. The dog has a good grasp of psychology.

The girl is embarrassed and tries to find something to talk about which will distract us from our intimate contact. She shifts around in search of a more comfortable sitting position. We don't feel in the least distracted.

"Are you the commander here?" she asks Jamus.

Jamus makes a dismissive gesture. "I am only in command of the company," he admits.

"Really?" The girl gazes at him in admiration. "But why aren't you wearing any marks of rank?"

"Oh, you mean these shoulder straps?" Jamus sticks his hand in his pocket and pulls out the marks of rank of a captain. "I always take them off when I am in Tel Aviv. I don't like wearing them in public."

"How is that?" Such modesty is beyond her comprehension.

James smiles condescendingly. "This is how it is. I prefer people to see me as a human being, not as a particular rank. After all, every shirker in Tel Aviv is wearing something similar. As a fighting officer I don't want to be compared with them." The girl's admiration becomes boundless.

"Doesn't it have a bad influence on your people, when you don't show your rank?"

"The opposite," Jamus assures her. "A good commander doesn't lead his people with his marks of rank, but with the force of his personality. And besides, the men like democratic superiors. And when they see us walking around Tel Aviv in the uniform of ordinary soldiers, they respect us all the more."

"But at camp you wear your marks of rank?"

"Unfortunately we have to," Jamus groans. He winks at me "Maybe we should put the things back on."

"And what are you?" The girl turns to me.

"Who? Him?" Jamus interrupts, before I can present the facts. "He is a military writer."

"Really?" the girl gasps. And I too have risen steeply in her esteem. I feel like telling her that I haven't been awarded this bombastic title by the army. That I am really just the miserable leader of an even more miserable squad in a combat company. But should I really spoil Jamus's wonderful game? So I pull "my" shoulder straps out of my pocket, those of a senior lieutenant, and fix them in their "right" place.

The truth is that we keep these things with us for the sake of survival. We know that both sides tend to kill the lower ranks among the prisoners. Not officers. That has nothing to do with generosity or respect, but simply with military logic. The intelligence corps demands that captured officers should be brought to them – for the extraction of information.

Our calculation, after long consideration and discussion: when it looks as though we are going to be captured, we hope we can put on the marks of rank quickly enough to save our lives. Later on, if we have to explain this to our own side, we will have to think of something.

After we had begun to carry the things around with us, we realized that they could be useful in much less dangerous situations. Dressed as an officer, it is much easier to stop a vehicle. Every asshole who roars past ordinary soldiers regards it as an honor to stop for a captain or senior lieutenant and to be allowed to give them a lift.

But once, we made the mistake of stopping the brigade commander's car. We recognized his face too late. He must have been puzzled to see two officers suddenly turning round and disappearing down the next side road at a sprint.

"Do you happen to have a cigarette?" the girl asks.

The cigarettes are in my pocket. But I can't reach them with the young girl sitting on my leg.

"Can you move a bit to the right" I ask her, and she lands on Jamus's lap. I get the cigarettes out of my pocket and hand out three. "And now," I turn to Jamus, "can you please give us a light." He swallows a curse, pushes the girl onto my lap, and searches his pockets.

We arrive at the crossing of Beit Dagon. Nehemia, who must have been jealous of our company, has been driving like the devil himself.

"Maybe you could take me to Sarafand?" asks the girl. Jamus looks at me. We would certainly like to spend another quarter of an hour in this position. But the men are standing in the open truck, shivering in their wet clothes.

"Unfortunately we won't be able to," Jamus regrets. "We are due on an important patrol. But we can take you as far as Rishon."

"No, thanks!" say the girl angrily. She is clearly used to soldiers fulfilling her wishes. It could also be that she thinks she has a right to it, after she sat on our laps. Jamus, the gentleman, helps her out.

We drive on.

Half-way to Rishon the motor starts coughing and the truck stops. Nehemia curses, gets out, opens the hood, checks some things, and shakes his head. The truck has broken down. That's what happens with military vehicles. The drivers don't care about them and just push them until they break.

The Moroccans are sitting up there like frozen herrings. Janek claims to know something about trucks and starts working on the engine. It is bitterly cold. The men have no winter clothing. Many of the few pieces of equipment that are sent to us get lost on the way. First the workers in the storerooms help themselves, then the higher ranks, then the "veterans," until there is not much left for new immigrants. Jamus and I had already given the people in the back our coats when we set off. We are freezing and our teeth are chattering.

"Give it a try," Janek says. Nehemia turns the key and suddenly everything is brightly illuminated. Janek is simply a column of fire. His gasoline-soaked clothes are burning. Helpless excitement. The Moroccans jump out. I look for a blanket and find none. Janek alone retains his composure. He rolls in the sand and extinguishes the flames.

He needs to be taken to the hospital straight away. His face and hands are black, his clothes torn and burned. Maybe we can take him to the police station at Beit Dagon for first aid? But how can we get him there without a vehicle?

"I will walk," Janek stutters. I go with him. We both walk. Maybe the cold wind will temper his pain a bit. I count the paces out loud to take his mind off it. Janek grits his teeth, and walks in silence.

Half-way there the truck catches up with us. They managed to start the engine. Jamus helps Janek in and they drive off toward Jaffa. I walk back to the men. They are standing by the road like sheep without a shepherd. One of them is lying on the ground. When the shout of "fire" went up, he jumped out like a swimmer, head first. He is probably suffering from concussion.

It has started raining again. All we can do is wait for our truck. In the meantime we might all catch pneumonia. A truck is approaching. I stand in the road and wave. I almost get run over and it races past as if the driver couldn't see me.

Minutes pass. Some of the men are already coughing. Some are whispering in French. I can just make out that they are talking about the good old days in Morocco, before they had the crazy idea of volunteering for the Israeli army. A wet road in the early hours of the morning is not the best place for Zionist education.

Ten minutes. Twenty minutes. In the distance headlights appear. I stand in the middle of the road and wave my arms like a windmill. A respectable private car, which could take the wounded man. The driver goes around me, with two wheels off the road and races past without reducing his speed. It seems he has experience with such maneuvers.

"Damned bastard, dirty son of a bitch!" I swear. "Eight months ago you didn't dare use this road. You bumped along the "secure road" and were happy to see a sock hat. Now you feel like a hero, you ass! Now you don't care that half a company is standing around here. Main thing is, that they are soon back in their stinking position to defend you. If only the Arabs had cut off your ears and stuffed them into your filthy mouth ..."

The rain increases. The driver becomes for me a symbol of the hated "HQ." Those who are lying in their warm beds and who despise us: who destroyed the spirit of our unit and forced the hated military discipline on us, who grew fat on the blood of our comrades even before it was cold. They should be taught a lesson, these ungrateful ...

I draw my pistol. The men fall silent. In the sudden quiet my clicking off of the safety catch sounds like a metallic blow.

I am a soldier. And I know that it is my duty to shoot at those who abandon a wounded comrade. In the squad leader course I was taught to shoot a subordinate if he refuses to advance or if he deserts before the enemy. I knew that such a situation could arise and that then I would have to use a weapon, perhaps even have to become a murderer, to uphold the rules on which our lives depend. That is an unpleasant duty. But this time I feel the blood lust rising in me. It takes control of me. I know that I will use the weapon if I need to.

In the distance another pair of lights is approaching. I notice that people around me are holding their breath. A truck comes toward us. The driver can see me, but does not reduce his speed. I blow my whistle. The headlights illuminate my pistol hand. The driver brakes hard.

"You will take a wounded man to the hospital in Bilu!"

"But that is not my direction. I am driving to Gedera."

I point the pistol at his chest.

"OK, OK," he stutters. "Put him on."

"Climb in!" I order the men. They climb onto the load area.

"I am not taking any passengers. Just the wounded man," the driver objects.

"Oh really?" I ask with a smile. My blood lust has dissipated. I only feel contempt for him. He takes on twenty men and drives off.

There are still twenty-five of us. If we stand around here five minutes more, we'll all be ill. I am totally exhausted. But I know that if half of us get ill, then I can only occupy the position with the other half. That means double watch duty and doubled risk.

"Walk!" I shout.

No one moves. "You! You! And you!" I push them forwards. One of them lies on the ground. "Get up!" I shout at him and fire a bullet into the ground. He gets up. We walk. Our frozen limbs gradually warm up.

"Sing!" I command.

I begin with an indecent French song they taught me. I don't have a good ear. Even on normal days I am no gifted singer. Now my voice sounds like the howling of a jackal with a sore throat. Unimportant! First one, then a second, then a third join in.

* * *

With my blonde
I sleep well, I sleep well ...

* * *

We laugh and walk. Our clothes are soaked through and the road is slippery, but slowly our mood improves.

A vehicle comes up behind us. I wave my pistol around and shoot in the air – as an introduction to the negotiations. But it is no longer fun.

"Are you crazy?" It is Jamus's voice, who has returned from the hospital with our truck.

The men climb on. I sit down next to the driver.

* * *

Rain, rain, rain.

The military bus is overloaded. Early in the morning, before dawn, we will take over the position. For the first time our Moroccans will be at the front. For the first time I will be in command during an operation. We were able to give them a few hours' instruction with the rifle, and one with the machine gun. But not a single hour of field or night exercises. According to instructions we first have to drill them on the parade ground. Apparently that is more important for the army leadership.

This rain. It will turn the positions into hell. The weapons will be smeared with mud, and we will have heavy lumps stuck to the soles of our boots. Fighting in rain is an invention of the devil.

Jamus is standing by the door directing the singing. He has a good voice and likes to hear it. The men are singing. What are they thinking at this moment? Do they think the front will be romantic? In twelve hours they will know that the front is a trench with mud up to your knees. An image appears in my head: a company of recruits is marching toward the assault on Beit Jamal. They are singing cheerfully. About a hundred young men. Ten or twenty of them came back under their own steam. Others came back in my jeep, bloody and groaning. Still others did not come back at all.

In the headlights a stretch of barbed wire and a British steel helmet with holes in it. Where are we? Of course. Position 125. This is where we raced that night in our jeeps, before we drove over the Egyptian trenches. At the side of the road was a body. And we didn't know whether it was an Egyptian or one of ours.

"Attention!" Jamus shouts. "Pay attention. This is where the big night attack started, that …"

We are not only squad leaders, but also political commissars and history teachers. We have to form the men into one body. That is an important task. In our job description it is not mentioned.

Who was the soldier who lay at the side of the road? He was wearing a British steel helmet, like those worn by the Egyptians. But in the battle for Position 125 our soldiers also wore such helmets.

It is dark. Fine drops of rain, singing, the familiar warmth of a group of young men. Words appear in my mind and form themselves into verses. One of my youthful sins. Without having any talent for poetry. I started getting involved with military and political themes too early. Poetry and politics don't go together. Still I can't stop myself.

> He lay at the road side
> As I drove past in my jeep to the battle
> He lay alone, motionless, quiet,
> His eyes closed in death.

* * *

The truck roars. The men are singing. I can see the soldier lying on his back, next to his helmet.

* * *

Was he for me or against me
I will never know
They resemble each other so closely in death
And the color of their blood is the same.

* * *

When was that? Almost five months have passed since then. The family has long since been informed. Some official in some office has picked up the letter, on which was written, "Please inform in case of …"

* * *

But I know – he also had a mother
And a father is waiting for him far away
Somewhere they are sitting and thinking of
The son who does not return.

* * *

Strange. His head lay on his arm as though he was sleeping. A little boy lost, sleeping by the side of the road.

* * *

You, mother – your son is tired and is resting
asleep among the flowers in the field
I greeted your son there
For he was a human being.

* * *

Human – strange word. In our generation there are no humans. There are only Germans, British, Russians, Arabs, or Israelis. They have a right to exist only in the framework of their nation. In their cradles babies already learn to stand to attention. You are an Israeli – stand to attention! You should sing children's songs and read children's books which the nation has composed for you – stand at ease! You can also play – war games of course! Then when you are at school you will learn how, since the creation of the Earth, your people has killed others and been killed by others. The rest is unimportant – line up in three rows! Pay attention to the way the adults of your people move. You will think the same way, talk the same way, move the same way – dress right! The motherland is in danger – eyes front! The terrorists want to destroy us – forward march! If you are lucky, it will last eighty years …[1]

The Moroccans are singing. Let them sing. Tomorrow morning, when I command them to dig trenches, they will be crying. Their French songs are beautiful, even if I can't understand much. They are cheerful songs. We don't have songs like that. Our songs are sad. Even our marching songs. Maybe that is the way it has to be. We can be funny and crack jokes. Even when we are suffering deeply and dog tired. But being happy is far from us. We are a generation without joie de vivre. We don't know how to enjoy life. Our pleasures are pitiful: movies, dancing, and sexual lust. That is all. We didn't have the time to develop fully as human beings. We were too busy: playing with guns, pamphlets, illegal newspapers – those were our pleasures.

* * *

Girls, yes, yes, yes,
Girls, no, no, no,
Girls – on both knees …

* * *

The Moroccans are cheerful. We don't have songs like that. Even our national anthem is a dirge.

My hand touches something warm. Who is that? Oh yes, little Shulah. I stroke her absent-mindedly. She presses against me. Up till then it had never occurred to me that Shulah is a woman. She is small, dark skinned, and quiet. Nobody pays attention to her. She works somewhere in the battalion. In the stores, in the kitchen, in the radio room? I don't know.

* * *

Let us drink – yes, yes, yes
Let us drink – no, no, no,
Let us empty the glasses …

* * *

It is dark all around and the rain is drumming on the roof. Outside it is cold, inside nice and warm. The bodies of fifty men, who tomorrow will be killed or wounded.

My hand slides under Shulah's pullover and glides over her body. She has a sweet little body. And we had no idea. Her hand is resting on my back.

The bus drives into the camp. The lights come on. I withdraw my hand and she turns away. In the light she is embarrassed.

The men climb noisily out of the bus.

"There is work to be done," says Jamus. "At three o'clock it starts. We must supervise the packing of the equipment."

"I'll be right back," I reply without enthusiasm. Jamus looks at me, raises his eyebrows, reconsiders.

"Ehhhh – it doesn't matter," he decides. "There is no hurry. I will manage somehow." Since Janek got ill, we two have been responsible for fifty men who speak five languages.

I take Shulah in the direction of company HQ. It is still drizzling. I hold my thick jacket over our heads. It is a good jacket. I picked it up in Barchaba, from the field with the many dead. It used to belong to a fat sergeant. He was killed with a dagger. His jacket was undamaged because he left it in the bunker. Now it is protecting us above, and below I put my arm around little Shulah.

Shulah slows her paces. Everything is quiet in the staff tents. Here and there a quiet snoring. The only light is in the radio shed where a female voice is murmuring meaningless words. "Hallo – Boas – Gimel – Moshe – Gimel – five – reporting reception – Boas – Gimel – Over."

We walk around the lighted area and lose our directions among the tents. The camp is still new. The girls' tents are better than the boys'. The floor is tiled and there are low stone walls.

"This is where I live," she says.

"Yes."

"Shalom!"

"I'll come with you!"

"No!" She is shocked and holds me tight.

I pick her up in my arms, lower my head, and go in. It takes a moment to get used to the darkness. There are five beds in the tent. Female soldiers are asleep in four of them. I place Shulah on the fifth bed, lie down next to her, and spread the covers over us. The bed springs squeak.

Shulah is nervous. She makes no sound. She is afraid that her neighbors will wake up. I press my mouth on hers. Slowly she opens her teeth and my tongue searches for hers. Our tongues embrace and start talking to each other.

"Leave me alone," says her tongue. "If we get caught, you'll go to prison."

"Silly little thing," my tongue answers. "In the arrest cells it is warm and dry. In the trenches, cold and wet. The guards will bring me beer from the mess. You will come and see me and another squad leader will take my place at the front."

"There will be a scandal," says her tongue.

"Little woman," my tongue answers, "in Iraq-Elmadi there are no scandals. There is only death and shattered limbs …"

"You must not die!" her arms cry and wrap around me.

"We will all die," my hand answers. "All of us. And because we don't want to die, we will hide in the waterlogged trenches, we will crawl through the mud and be worse off than any animal in the field."

"Forget about all that …" her body begs.

"I want to forget about it," my hand answers. "Outside cold and death are waiting and you are so sweet and tender …" The second bed squeaks. A sleepy girl's voice asks: "Are you there, Shulah?" Shulah stiffens with fear next to me.

"Yes," she murmurs.

"Was it nice?"

"Lovely."

The bed squeaks again and soon we can hear deep, quiet breathing.

I kiss Shulah until we are both suffocating, I squeeze her body until her bones crack, and for a moment we forget the world outside, this awful, ugly world, and a beautiful, foaming life force takes hold of us, and explodes, showering us in loving warmth.

Then a deep sadness overcomes us. We lie motionless next to each other, her cheek against mine, her breath caressing my neck. I would so much like to remain like this till the end of the world, till the end of horror. But I know that I will get up in one hour, that I will lead twenty-three innocent young men to the slaughter and that none of us will return without wounds of body or soul.

* * *

Tiny raindrops, gentle, thin …

Jamus and I have decided that one squad leader is sufficient and so we take it in turns to disappear occasionally. Once a week he goes to the eye doctor in Rehovot, and once a week I visit the dentist in Tel Aviv. My teeth are actually quite OK. But I have a slip of paper from the doctor, with some Latin on it. I can use it any time for a short leave – whenever I decide to use it. The sarge understands no Latin.

I glance into my tent, stuff the dirty washing into my bag, together with the paperbacks I have read already, and just need to get the medic to sign my slip before heading off for Tel Aviv. Our tent is an oasis in this desert of a camp. Jamus and I have assembled all our booty from the last year here – the deep armchair that we "borrowed" from the Irgun after Altalena Day,[2] the hubble-bubble I got in Chudad, two chairs from the cafe which charged an extortionate price for two bowls of ice cream, a folding chair from the staff of an Egyptian battalion, and a chest of drawers we found in an abandoned British barracks. We can live quite well with these.

On the way to the medical center I find the eyes of Fini staring at me. Fini belongs to the battalion staff. A boy with a tragic expression and rounded shoulders, whose duties nobody is very clear about.

"Good that you are here," he says to me and slaps me on the shoulder. "I have a little job for you."

"I am sorry," I say quickly. "I have no time!" Fini has no rank. I don't have to take orders from him.

"Don't run away, my friend. First you should hear what it is about. It is a humanitarian matter."

"A humanitarian matter?"

"I need some volunteers for a memorial meeting."

"What sort of a memorial meeting?" I hate memorial meetings! Throughout the whole war I have tried to get out of going to one. "Who for?"

"We are making a pilgrimage to Sancho's grave. In half an hour his parents will arrive."

"Don't talk nonsense. Sancho was not buried at all. He was left in the field."

"My dear friend, you are mistaken!" His voice becomes very gentle. "Sancho was buried in accordance with religion and law!" He names a location in the area.

"Do you take me for an idiot? Sancho was my best friend. I can remember clearly that he was one of the twelve wounded who were left in Beit Jalal!"

Fini loses his patience. "Take a hammer and knock this into your skull: Sancho was buried! We prepared a nice grave for him. We even put an inscription on it."

"That is deception!"

He shrugs his shoulders. "If you like. If you are volunteering to tell them that Sancho was left on the battlefield … you'll get your chance. His parents are coming in half an hour." I shut up. It had never occurred to me that Sancho had parents.

"Listen carefully, my friend." Fini lectures me. "For you and me, it may be enough to know that Sancho is dead. Of course the Egyptians buried him somewhere. But that is not enough for the parents. Parents need a grave."

"Then take them to some pile of dirt and let them cry there."

"I am a psychologist," Fini explains. "The most important thing is belief. The parents will be consoled by the belief that their son is buried there. It will help them to get over the trauma, until they get used to the idea of losing their son."

"Take someone else for this theater."

"Be a nice boy," he said, slapping me on the shoulder. "One friend should help the other. I promise you: if, by God's grace, you are among the next to die, I will make your parents a nice grave with an inscription."

"Thanks a lot."

We drive off. A fresh grave has been built on the little hill. An inscribed panel stands among flowers. None of the comrades knew Sancho's real name. After I had baptized him with this name, on the first day in recruitment camp, it was the only name he had in the whole battalion.

A grave. Strange how our relationship to graves has changed since the first battles. The first to fall were buried with full military honors. The company commander gave a speech and we fired a three-shot salute. In the following months we risked our lives to recover the bodies of fallen comrades. But with the passing of time we began to think that that was stupid. You are not helping a dead man by laying him down next to another. We lost any connection with the graves of the fallen. You collect them and you bury them. We tried to keep away from such places.

* * *

Sancho's parents are simple people. Long years of hard work are written on their faces. Their eyes are red. The mother gives the occasional loud sob. Then the father claps her lovingly on the back and she falls silent. Sancho was an only child.

A strange character, Sancho. He hated the war from the first day. He laughed at the bit of idealism that we all retained within us. Every day he would prove to us again that we were sacrificing ourselves for a band of shirkers. He had no illusions. And he did his best to destroy our illusions.

"Then why are you still here?" we often asked him. "Me?" he brushed his thin hair back from his forehead in astonishment. "I'm not staying here. They just won't let me go. As soon as people are needed for a desertion course, I'm gone."

The first course was for radio operators. "That is one month's life insurance!" said Sancho and volunteered. After one month he came back. And since then he had been going into combat with a thirty-five-pound box on his back.

As radio operator he took part in the bayonet assault in Barchaba. He was one of the very few who returned unscathed. On the next day he told us that he wasn't going to go on.

"What do you mean?" we asked him.

"Trust Sancho," was all he would say.

The next morning he went to see the battalion doctor, a particularly hated character. There would often be people who wanted to shoot him. The story was told of a soldier who went to see him after an Egyptian shell had ripped his head off. "I'm not going to be taken in by shirkers," said the doctor. "I have seen the likes of you. Take an aspirin and get lost before I tell your superior officer to clap you in gaol!"

Sancho went to the doctor and complained of attacks of depression. The doctor gave him aspirin and two days' rest. Sancho threw the aspirin in the latrine and read Henry Miller's *Tropic of Capricorn*.

On the third day he went back to the doctor in the best of moods, invited him to a rumba, and danced with him through the medical rooms. With difficulty the doctor managed to free himself and give Sancho a tranquilizing injection.

The doctor's life was turned into hell. Every morning Sancho would appear with a new idea. Sometimes he heard a shell approaching and hid under the table. On another day he chased the doctor around the whole camp to demonstrate a bayonet attack.

We, the friends of Sancho, enjoyed the duel. We placed bets on who would go mad first – Sancho or the doctor. They were both obstinate and didn't give up easily. In the end the doctor was convinced that Sancho had really lost his reason. He arranged his transfer to a mental hospital.

In the evening Sancho joined in the big attack on Iraq al-Madi. No one knows to this day what made him do it. He did a favor for another radio operator, who had arranged something in Tel Aviv. It is possible that he wanted to take his leave of the front.

Most of the attackers were killed or wounded. The few who remained unhurt could not carry back all the wounded. When they saw that it was starting to get light, they placed twelve of the seriously wounded between cactus stems, only a few paces from the Egyptian lines, until they could be recovered the next night. When they went back there, the wounded were gone. Sancho was among the twelve who were lost …

* * *

An officer makes a speech. The usual one. "He died for the motherland …. Generations will remember him …" Suddenly Sancho is standing next to me. He is leaning against a tree, runs his fingers through his fine blond hair, and winks at me.

"Zionism!" he whispers to me. "Boring. What are you doing here?"

"Sancho," I whisper back. "This is a memorial ceremony for you."

"Memorial ceremony?" He is surprised. "I hate memorial ceremonies. What sort of nonsense is he talking?" The speech continues. I can predict every single sentence in detail. "By your grave we swear to you … we will continue on your path …"

"Idiot!" says Sancho. "What's this rubbish? Are we all supposed to be buried? If we all die there won't be anyone to stand there and salute."

"A loyal sacrifice," the speaker continues. "He sacrificed himself, just as we are all ready to sacrifice ourselves for the motherland …"

Sancho laughs out loud. "Motherland? What sort of motherland? I have no motherland. Only the living have a motherland. Not the dead. If I was still alive, I could do something. Work, to expand my workshop. But what can I do now? Just fertilize the earth."

"He was one of the first to sign up …"

"Did I have any choice?" said Sancho unhappily. "Everyone told me it was the right thing to do. First my parents, then my teachers, then the youth leaders: we live to serve the motherland. I never learned anything else." He scratches his ear as he always did when he was going to say something philosophical. "You know what? You have to die before you know how you should live. You need some distance."

"Our victorious army will never forget …" the speaker is getting carried away.

"Don't try and fool yourselves!" Sancho objected. "You are not victorious, you are defeated. OK, you have held off the Egyptians. But what have you achieved? The state you dreamed of in the trenches is dead, even before it was born. Instead of it a state has been founded, in which the bureaucrats live it up at your expense and deserters give you a kick in the ass. Everything will be the same as before. Only that you have your own flag and coat of arms and you can prepare for the next war yourselves."

"We will honor him by carrying out his will," the speaker continues. "At any time and in any circumstances, until the end of our days, we will be ready to follow the call of the motherland and to march against the enemy …"

"What did I tell you?" Sancho laughs. "You are beyond help. You are already thinking of the next war and a hero's death."

"What do you want then?" I ask him quietly. "Should we not go? Should we wait until the Arabs come and slaughter us all?"

"Idiot!" Sancho swears at me. "You never were very bright! Not until the motherland calls you. Do something now, so the motherland doesn't need to call you! You see that hill over there?" He points at a distant hill. I remember. That's where Barchaba is. "Over there a few Egyptian dead are lying. I go over there sometimes. They are a bit stupid. But you can get on with them. Now they are dead. And I am dead too. We have nothing more to do with the whole business. But you – do something! So that you don't have to die. Come to some settlement with them. Think about ways to avoid a war! Stop playing at heroes! I know you lot – you are all idiots!"

The officer has finished his speech. He wipes the sweat from his forehead. The mother is sobbing loudly. It sounds like a river that was dammed and is now breaking through.

"Quiet, mother!" says the old man, stroking her gently. "Fate has to be accepted."

He covers her face as though her weakness embarrasses him. But then he starts crying as well. "He was so young ..." he murmurs, "what have we got left to live for?"

Sancho looks at them with sympathy.

"Who are they?" he asks.

"You should be ashamed of yourself!" I answer. "They are your parents."

"Really? They look like good people. What are they doing here?"

"They came for your memorial ceremony ..."

"Memorial ceremony? What for? What can they do for me?" He scratches his ear again. "You know what? I have a great idea. I will give them a memorial speech!"

"Don't be crazy. No one can give a memorial speech for himself."

"You'll see." With one jump he leaps onto the pile of earth and speaks to his parents.

"I am dead. You hear me? I am dead. Dead. D-e-a-d! I don't need your memorial ceremonies! I am not accusing you of anything. But you could do something for other sons, for other parents. Take to the streets and shout! You hear me? Shout! That you took care of me for twenty-four years for nothing. That I died before I could do anything in life! Shout at other parents, that they should not allow their children to be sent to war. They should forbid it!"

"And you there," said he, turning to us, "you herd of donkeys, stop spreading the fairy story that war is a wonderful adventure. Go and shout out the truth! That you hate war, that it makes you sick! You have younger brothers. Tell them the truth! So that they don't lust after a new war, where they will die. If you have any life in you, don't just stand around like castrated good-for-nothings. Make sure that your state is a decent state, where you can live like people and not like the dead on holiday, just waiting for their marching orders to heaven. That depends on you – you hear? – on you alone!"

* * *

Someone kicks me in the ass. "What are you doing standing here dreaming? The ceremony is long over," say Fini.

We walk to the car. Fini's face is desperately sad. "I hate memorial ceremonies," he says. "But what can you do? The parents need that."

He stands still as though tired of walking, and looks at the empty grave. With an infinitely troubled, helpless voice he adds: "What can you do? If the war lasts any longer, all our parents are going to need that."

The Soldier

The first rays of light through the window, pale and cold.
   The sun is rising.
   A new day.
   The sixteenth of December, nineteen-hundred-and-forty-eight.
   The rain has stopped.
   The room is strangely still. Unnaturally still.
   Something is missing. Something has gone.
   What can it be?
   The rasping has stopped.
   The wounded man opposite me lies still, his head to one side.
   His breathing has stopped.
   A person is gone.

Endnotes

Preface

1. Zionism – term commonly used in Israel for empty political outpourings.

Introduction

1. Irgun – short for Irgun Zvai Le'umi (the National Military Organization), known in Hebrew by its acronym Etzel, was an underground militant Zionist group opposing British rule
2. Lehi – Hebrew acronym for *Lohamei Herut Israel*, "Fighters for the Freedom of Israel," a radical split-off from the Irgun, also known as the Stern Gang after its leader Avraham Stern.

Part One: In the Fields of the Philistines

Before the Battle

1. Jamal Husseini – Chairman of the Arab Higher Committee, the central political organ of the Arab community of Palestine. After the flight of his uncle Grand Mufti Mohammad Amin al-Husseini, in 1937, he became the political leader of the Arabs in Palestine.
2. Nahariya – small town north of Haifa.
3. The *Exodus* – a ship that carried Jewish emigrants (largely Holocaust survivor refugees without immigration permits) from France to Palestine, then controlled by the British, in 1947. The refugees were refused permission to land by the British authorities, and forced to return to France, to international public outrage.

4. Haganah – (Hebrew) "Defense." Paramilitary organization of the Zionist movement.

5 Haj Amin al-Husseini – the son of the Mufti of Jerusalem and a member of one of the wealthiest, most powerful Arab families in Palestine. Appointed Mufti of Jerusalem by the British in 1921, he became one of the most prominent Arab leaders in the Middle East, President of the Arab Higher Committee, before being forced into exile in 1937 following the Arab Revolt. He continued to promote Arab nationalism from exile, and played a part in the Arab invasion during the 1948 war.

6. Balfour Declaration – official letter of the British Foreign Office, declaring itself to "view with favour the establishment in Palestine of a national home for the Jewish people."

7. Transjordan – the area of the British Mandate east of the Jordan River, now the Kingdom of Jordan.

8. Yishuv – (Hebrew) – "population" or "settlement" – the Jewish population in Palestine before the founding of the State of Israel.

9. Arab Legion – the army of Transjordan, commanded by British officers.

10. Palmach – Hebrew abbreviation for "shock troops." The commando unit of the Haganah.

11. HISH – Hebrew abbreviation for "field troops." The first regular combat troops of the Haganah.

12. Yekkes – German Jewish immigrants.

13. Bamaavak – (Hebrew) – "in the struggle."

Baptism of Fire

1. Eretz Israel – (Hebrew) the Land of Israel. Appelation for Palestine by the Zionist movement before the founding of the state. The country was officially called Palestine in English, Falastin in Arabic, and in Hebrew – Palestine (EI). The abbreviation EI stood for Eretz Israel and was used on stamps and currency.

2. Ramat Aharon – agricultural settlement to the North of Rehovot.

3. Chaim Laskov – later Chief of General Staff of the Israeli army.

4. Shimon Avidan – his underground name "Givati" was later used to name a brigade.

5. Hulda – a kibbutz in the south, near an Arab village of the same name.

6. Wadi – (Arabic) – a river bed that is often dry. Also used in Hebrew.
7. "Ta'al lahon!" – (Arabic) – "come here!"
8. Ramle – Arab town on the road between Tel Aviv and Jerusalem.
9. Latrun – originally "La Touronne." Christian monastery from the time of the Crusades, on the road to Jerusalem. Nearby was a British police fort and a prison camp, originally for Italian POWs.
10. Sten – short for Sten gun. A simple and easily operated submachine gun of British manufacture.
11. Finjan – (Arabic) – can for making coffee on an open fire.
12. Mukhtar – (Arabic) – village headman.
13. Nebi Musa – The Tomb of the Prophet Moses. According to Jewish, Christian, and Islamic tradition, it is said to be located on Mount Nebo, a high ridge in the Judean desert giving a panoramic view from Jericho to Jerusalem.
14. Bab al-Wad – (Arabic) – "The Gate to the Wadi," where the road to Jerusalem enters a narrow gorge and begins the climb away from the plain.
15. Cameri Theater – A travelling group from Cameri Theater, founded in 1944 in Tel Aviv, and now the biggest of Israel's public theaters.
16. Tnuva – trade union-owned collective in dairy production.
17. Bully beef – a dry and almost tasteless sort of corned beef.
18. During the time of the British Mandate, the jail at Latrun was frequently used to hold underground fighters.
19. Shaar Hagai – (Hebrew) – "The Gate to the Wadi" (Arabic: Bab al-Wad).
20. Castel – ruined Crusader castle on a hill near Jerusalem, the scene of fierce fighting for control of the road.
21. Deir Yassin – Arab village which was the scene of a reprisal action by the Irgun on 9 April 1948, in which dozens of men, women, and children were killed. The news of the massacre spread panic among the Arab population, and many of them fled the country.
22. Fawzi al-Qawuqji – Syrian officer who organized his own private army and later came to notice as the leader of a Palestinian group.
23. Burma Road – road through rough mountain country, used by the British to transport war material from Burma to China.
24. Moshe Shertok – the first Israeli Foreign Minister (later changed his name to Sharet).
25. Kol Israel – (Hebrew) – "Voice of Israel," Israeli state radio.
26. Shaj – Hebrew abbreviation for "intelligence service."
27. Primus – kerosene stove, common in the East in this period.

Man against Steel

1. Iraq Suweidan – one of the most important fortifications of the Egyptians on the front. A British-built fort-like police station.
2. Avor: Hebrew equivalent of "Roger" in radio communications procedure.
3. PIAT – Projector, Infantry, Anti Tank. Early anti-tank weapon, a bit like a primitive bazooka
4. "La ilaha illa Allah wa Muhammad rasul Allah" – (Arabic) – "There is no god but God and Muhammad is the messenger of God," the Muslim creed.
5. Defense army – the official name for the Israeli armed forces is "Israel Defense Forces."
6. "Sallim nafsak!" – (Arabic) – "surrender!"
7. Calabush – (Hebrew slang from Arabic) – arrest cell or jail.
8. Nitzanim – Kibbutz South of Tel Aviv. The history of the fighting around this kibbutz and the fact of its surrender still plays an important role in the political-historical discourse in Israel to this day.
9. Czera Czertenko – birth name of Tzvi Tzur, who was later to become the Israeli Defense Force's Chief of the General Staff, and then the Chief of the Mossad, the Israeli external intelligence service.

Eleven Days of Decision

1. Swing boy – 'Swing' was the counter-culture of the '30s and '40s that centered around swing music.
2. Fellah – (Arabic) – peasant or farmer (Fellaheen in the plural).
3. Albert Mandler – a later general of the Israeli army, who fell in the Yom Kippur War of 1973.
4. Ekron – small village south of Tel Aviv.
5. Camp Sarafand – one of the largest military camps in the center of the country, built by the British after the First World War.
6. Farouk – the King of Egypt from 1936 to 1952.
7. Ramat Gan – small town north of Tel Aviv.
8. Gadna – Hebrew abbreviation for "youth battalions," paramilitary training organization.
9. Spitfire – British single-engined fighter aircraft.
10. Samson's Foxes – see Old Testament, Judges 15:4.5 "And Samson went and caught three hundred foxes, and took firebrands, and turned tail to tail, and put a firebrand in the midst between two tails. And when he had set the brands on fire, he let [them] go into the standing corn of the Philistines, and burnt up both the shocks, and also the standing corn, with the vineyards [and] olives."

Samson's Foxes

1. Bren carrier – small British tracked military vehicle often carrying a Bren light machine gun.
2. Yigael Yadin – head of operations in Haganah General Staff (effectively Chief of the General Staff since Yaakov Dori was seriously ill) and later a world-famous archeologist.
3. Israel Galili – Chief of Staff of the Haganah 1946–1948, later held ministerial positions in several governments.

Blood and Muck

1. Mourning – religious Jewish men do not shave for a month after a family death.
2. Mordechai Zeira – a popular composer at the time of folk and soldiers' songs.
3. Negev Animals – nickname for the motorized company of the Palmach brigade in the Negev.
4. Ruchamah – north Negev kibbutz.
5. Bedouins – nomadic people, nominally Arabs but seldom involved in political life.
6. Luger – high quality German semi-automatic pistol.
7. Keffiyeh – (Arabic) – traditional Arab headdress, consisting of a square of cloth held in place by a rope circlet
8. "Tfaddal" – "Please" or (as here) "OK," or "alright then."
9. "Yahud" – (Arabic) – "Jews."

Front Ants

1. Mugrabi Square – the central square of Tel Aviv at the time.
2. Olive leaves – worn by officers of the Israeli army on the shoulders as a sign of rank.

The End of the Ceasefire

1. Vickers – reliable, water-cooled medium machine gun.
2. Nir Am, Gvaram, Yad Mordechai – three kibbutzim in the northwest Negev.
3. Hashomer Hatzair – (Hebrew) – "The Young Guard" – socialist-Zionist youth movement, involved in the founding of kibbutzim.

The White Front

1. Sabra – (Hebrew) – the fruit of the opuntia cactus (prickly pear). Also familiar term for native-born Israeli Jews (thorny on the outside, sweet on the inside).
2. Hatikva quarter and Yasur – suburban areas of Tel Aviv.

Part Two: The Other Side of the Coin

The Long Nights

1. Keren Kayemet LeIsrael – the Jewish National Fund.
2. Beit Dagon – crossroads south of Tel Aviv, where the main roads to Jerusalem and the south divide.
3. "Yob tvoyu Mat" – a Russian expletive roughly translated as "Fuck off" (lit. "fuck your mother").

The Radio

1. Mayia – (Arabic) – water.
2. "Min wein inta?" – (Arabic) – "Where are you from?"
3. "Bi-hayat Allah, ma b'aref!" – (Arabic) – "In God's name, I don't know!"
4. "Qadesh Iraqi fi Wadi Sarar?" – (Arabic) – "How many Iraqis are in Wadi Sarar?"
5. Jewish Brigade – special unit of the British Army, recruited from Jewish inhabitants of Palestine, deployed on various fronts in the Second World War.
6. Agal – (Arabic) – the rope circlet holding the keffiyeh or traditional Arab headdress in place.
7. Mukhtar – (Arabic) – village headman.
8. Mufti – (Arabic) – scholar versed in Islamic law. Here it refers to the Grand Mufti of Jerusalem, a prominent leader of the Palestinian uprising.
9. Effendi – (from the Turkish) – "lord" or "master," used here for landowners.
10. Pesach – the Jewish Passover, when wine is drunk as part of the religious ceremony.
11. Masbaha – (Arabic) – string of prayer beads.
12. "Khawaja" – (Arabic) – "Sir."

13. "Naam ya sayyedi" – (Arabic) – "Yes sir."
14. Majdal – small Arab town in the south.
15. "Alhamdulillah" – (Arabic) – literally, "Praise be to God."
16. "Isma ya Suleiman!" – (Arabic) – "Listen, Suleiman!"
17. Sulha – (Arabic) – traditional meal of reconciliation after a row.
18. Tucki – (Hebrew) – parrot.
19. "Keif tismaini?" – (Arabic) – "Can you hear me?"
20. "Ya misril! Teezak hamra lesh?" – (Arabic) – "You Egyptians! Why is your arse so red?"
21. "Uskut, ya ibn kelb!" – (Arabic) – "Shut up, you son of a bitch!"
22. Akrut – (Arabic) – pimp.
23. "Fein inta ya Jamus" – (Arabic) – "Where are you, Jamus?"

The Irgun Youth

1. Blue shirts – uniform of the socialist youth movements.
2. Haganah – main prestate Jewish paramilitary organization, became the core of the armed forces.
3. National Military Organization – the Irgun.
4. White Paper – 1939 British policy paper favoring a Jewish–Arab Palestine with proportional representation, and restricting Jewish immigration and land purchases.
5. Acre (Akka) – one of the oldest towns in Palestine. The medieval citadel was used as a prison by the British for many years.
6. Ha Tikva – (Hebrew) – "The Hope": a song that was already sung as an anthem during the time of the Mandate, and later became the Israeli national anthem.
7. Yair – underground name of Avraham Stern, the founder of the Irgun split-off known as Lehi.
8. Ze'ev (Vladimir) Jabotinsky – leader of Revisionist Zionism, co-founder of the Irgun.
9. Deir Yassin – Arab village west of Jerusalem that was captured on 9 April 1948, with over a hundred massacred.
10. Menahem Begin – leader of the Etzel. Later long-term opposition leader in the Israeli parliament, and then Prime Minister.
11. Kfar Vitkin – Jewish village north of Tel Aviv

The Village and the Cows

1. Lod (Lydda) – a small Arab town with an important railway junction on the way to Jerusalem.

2. Mil, grush – currency denominations in Palestine and later in Israel. One pound or lira was worth one hundred piasters (grush) or 1000 mil.
3. Battle of Yarmouk – decisive battle in the struggle for Palestine between the Muslim and the Byzantine armies on 20 August 636. The Yarmouk is a tributary of the Jordan River.
4. Tyre – historic city in today's Lebanon
5. Tango–Golf–Alpha–Five – encoded message.

The First Ceasefire

1. Rehovot – small town about 20 km south of Tel Aviv.
2. Nahalal – famous agricultural collective in the north of Israel.
3. Tayeb – (Arabic) – "good."
4. Ness Ziona, Rishon LeZion (or Rishon). Small towns on the road south from Tel Aviv.
5. Arak – aniseed flavored alcoholic spirit.
6. Kassit – for decades the most well-known artists' cafe in Tel Aviv.
7. Jenin and Nablus – two larger Arab towns, in today's West Bank.

Dream of Generations

1. The Emek – (Hebrew) "the valley." The plain in the north of Israel between the Mediterranean and the Sea of Galilee.
2. Book of Job 39:25.
3. Arabic – "Hand over the money."
4. "Ma feesh, ya khawaja" – (Arabic) – "I have nothing, sir."
5. Shilling – coin worth five grush.
6. "Dakhilkum! Ma bidnash namut! Ma bidnash namut!" – (Arabic) – "Please, we're begging you! We don't want to die! We don't want to die!"
7. "Ya khawaja!" – A respectful form of address for Europeans and other foreigners.
8. "Inta bitmut!" – (Arabic) – "You are going to die!"

Capturing the Village – on Film

1. Damietta – small town in Egypt.
2. From a song by Yaffa Yarkoni. Yarkoni served in the Givati Brigade in the War of 1948, was a member of the army choral troupe, and was later dubbed the "War Singer"; she went on to become one of Israel's most respected singers.

3. Yom Kippur – the *Day of Atonement*, the most solemn of the Jewish holidays

Sancho's Last Words

1. Judges 3:30 – "and the land had rest fourscore years."
2. Altalena – a ship transporting weapons for the Irgun, which arrived off the coast after the founding of the state. The refusal of the Irgun to hand over all the weapons to the state triggered a gunbattle with about twenty deaths. This operation is seen as a milestone in the relations between the underground movements and the state.

Chronology of events

1894	Dreyfus trial in Paris with clear anti-Semitic tendencies. Theodor Herzl, a Jewish journalist from Vienna, is present at the trial and reports on it as a correspondent of the newspaper *Neue Freie Presse*
1896	Theodor Herzl publishes his book *Der Judenstaat* ("The Jewish State"), presenting his vision of a Jewish state in Palestine as the solution to the "Jewish problem." At the time of writing he does not know about the existing pre-Zionist movement in Eastern Europe, which has arisen as a reaction to the increase in pogroms. Only after publication and the founding of the Zionist Organization as well as his untiring diplomatic efforts does the Zionist idea of an independent Jewish state receive international recognition. Jewish Colonization Association (JCA) begins operations in Palestine
1897	26–29 August: First World Zionist Congress with 208 delegates from sixteen countries held in Basel. Session adopts the "Basel Program" which demands "for the Jewish people a publicly recognized, legally secure homeland in Palestine." Theodor Herzl elected first president of the World Zionist Organization
1901	Jewish National Fund (JNF) established to acquire land for the Jews in Palestine.
1902	Hertzl's novel *Altneuland* (literally "Old-New Land") sketches out a socio-political structure for an independent Jewish state in Palestine

1917	2 November: British government publishes "Balfour Declaration" which states: "His Majesty's Government view with favour the establishment in Palestine of a national home for the Jewish people, and will use their best endeavours to facilitate the achievement of this object, it being clearly understood that nothing shall be done which may prejudice the civil and religious rights of existing non-Jewish communities in Palestine, or the rights and political status enjoyed by Jews in any other country"
	December: British General Sir Edmund Henry Hynman Allenby captures Jerusalem and establishes martial law. First World War results in collapse of Ottoman Empire
1923	*10 September: Helmut Ostermann, who later changes his name to Josef Ostermann, then to Uri Avnery, born in Beckum, Westfalen*
	29 September: League of Nations Mandate for British rule in Palestine officially comes into force
1933	*Helmut Ostermann (Uri Avnery) changes his name to Josef Ostermann and attends catholic Auguste Viktoria Gymnasium in Hanover as the only Jewish pupil. One of his fellow pupils is Rudolf Augstein (who later founded Der Spiegel)*
	November: Ostermann family emigrates from Hanover to Palestine
1936–1939	The Arab Revolt
1937	*Josef Ostermann (Uri Avnery) leaves school to work and contribute to the support of his impoverished family*
1938	*Josef Ostermann joins underground organization the Irgun – the "National Military Organization"*
1941	*Josef Ostermann changes his name to Uri Avnery. After the Stern Gang splits from the Irgun, Uri Avnery also leaves the organization but does not join the Stern Gang, which calls itself "Lehi" (acronym of "Lohamei Herut Israel" – "Fighters for the Freedom of Israel")*
1947	19 November: UN Partition Resolution is passed, dividing Palestine into a Jewish and an Arab state,

with the Greater Jerusalem Area coming under international control

1948   *Uri Avnery volunteers for the HISH: the troops of the Haganah*

9 April: Massacre of Deir Yassin by units of the Irgun

14 May: End of British Mandate over Palestine. Founding of the State of Israel

11 June: UN imposes a one-month ceasefire. Lasts until 9 July

30 June: Israeli Army officially founded, under the (still valid) name "Israel Defense Forces"

8 December: Uri Avnery severely wounded on the Israeli–Egyptian front

1949   Ceasefire negotiations take place in spring on the Greek island of Rhodes under UN auspices

15 June: Publication of In the Fields of the Philistines *in Israel – quickly becomes a bestseller; reprinted twelve times in quick succession*

1950   *April: Uri Avnery takes over the weekly magazine "Haolam Hazeh," becoming publisher and editor-in-chief*

May: Publication of Uri Avnery's second book The Other Side of the Coin. *Second printing in June 1954*

1953   *12 December: Uri Avnery made an honorary citizen of the village of Abu-Ghosh near Jerusalem in recognition of his part in preventing the expulsion of the Palestinian inhabitants of the village*

1956   29 November: Suez Campaign. In co-ordination with Britain and France, Israeli Army captures most of Sinai Peninsula and Gaza Strip, to pressurize Egypt to reverse nationalization of Suez Canal. Israeli Army withdraws in January 1957 under US pressure

"Semitic Action" founded by Uri Avnery and a number of intellectuals. Its program "The Hebrew manifesto" supports the founding of a Palestinian state next to Israel and proposes a Great Semitic Union of all the states of the Middle East

1959   Secret foundation of "Palestinian Liberation Committee," soon renamed "Fatah" (meaning "conquest," a reverse acronym of "Harakat Al-Tahrir Al-Watani Al-Filastini" – "the Movement for the National Liberation of Palestine") by Yasser Arafat and others

1964   Palestinian Liberation Organization (PLO) founded with aim of destroying Israel

1965   Left-wing political party "Ha-olam Hazeh – Koah Hadash" founded
Uri Avnery elected to Israeli Parliament (the Knesset) to represent the recently founded party. Remains in parliament for two legislative periods until 1973

1967   June: Six Day War. Israeli Army conquers Sinai Peninsula, Gaza Strip, Jordanian-controlled areas West of Jordan River (West Bank), and Golan Heights, after Egyptian government forces expel UN observers from Israeli-Egyptian border and block Israeli shipping through Red Sea
22 November: UN Security Resolution 242 calls for Israeli withdrawal and peace settlement

1973   6 October: Start of "Yom Kippur War" (October War). Egyptian President Anwar al-Sadat launches surprise attack on Israeli Army along Suez Canal on Jewish Day of Atonement, and Syria attacks Golan Heights. Israeli Army initially under threat but finally gains upper hand. Though a military defeat for Sadat, the war is a political success, paving the way for the first negotiations with Israel

1974   *First secret contacts between Uri Avnery and official representatives of the PLO in London*

1975   Israeli Council for Israeli-Palestinian Peace founded

1977   19 November: Surprise visit to Israel by Egyptian President Anwar al-Sadat, opens new stage in relations between Israel and its neighbor. Sadat receives Nobel Peace Prize in 1978 together with Israeli Prime Minister Menachem Begin

1979   26 March: Egypt and Israel sign a peace treaty

Uri Avnery re-elected to parliament. Cedes seat to an Arab colleague two years later, in accordance with a rotation agreement

1981   6 October: Egyptian President Anwar al-Sadat assassinated by members of extremist group Islamic Jihad during military parade

1982   6 June: Israel invades Lebanon to fight PLO following bombing campaign

3 July: Uri Avnery becomes first Israeli ever to meet Yasser Arafat, during Israeli Army's siege of Beirut

1987   9 December: First *Intifada* ("shaking off") begins, following clashes between Israeli soldiers and Palestinian civilians in Gaza Strip. Ensuing conflict quickly spreads to West Bank. Violence diminishes in 1991 and ends temporarily with signing of Oslo Accords in September 1993 and setting up of Palestinian Authority (PA)

1988   Foundation of Hamas ("Islamic Resistance Movement") by the Gaza wing of the Muslim Brotherhood

1990   *20 June: Last edition of "Haolam Hazeh" published under the direction of Uri Avnery*

1993   *Rachel and Uri Avnery and others set up independent peace organization "Gush Shalom" ('Peace Bloc')*

10 September: PLO and State of Israel officially recognize each other

13 September: Declaration of Principles on Interim Self-Government Arrangements (Oslo Accords) signed by representatives of Israeli government and Palestinians after long process of secret negotiation. Administrative powers transferred to elected PA during Israeli withdrawals from Palestinian areas

1994   4 May: Gaza-Jericho agreement (Cairo Agreement)

Nobel Peace Prize jointly awarded to Yitzhak Rabin, Shimon Peres, and Yasser Arafat in recognition of Oslo Accords

1995   4 November: Israeli Prime Minister Yitzhak Rabin assassinated by right-wing extremist in Tel Aviv

1996	*Uri Avnery awarded honorary citizenship of Kafr Qassem on 40th anniversary of Suez Crisis, in recognition of his part in exposing the massacre that took place there on the eve of the fighting*
2000	29 September: Ariel Sharon, chairman of Likud Party and leader of the opposition in Israeli parliament, visits Temple Mount in Jerusalem. Second *Intifada* begins after violent Palestinian reaction that escalates and spreads across Israeli and PA territory. Large numbers of civilians killed on both sides with violence continuing into present day
2001	6 February: Likud leader Ariel Sharon becomes Prime Minister of Israel replacing Ehud Barak
2002	29 March–10 May: "Operation Homat Magen" ('Defensive Shield'). Israeli Army tries to demolish infrastructure of Palestinian resistance. Yasser Arafat under virtual house arrest in his headquarters (the Muqataa) in Ramallah, until flown to Paris in November 2004 for medical treatment
2003	July: Work on controversial "Security Wall" begins, deviating from 1949 Armistice ("Green") Line between Israel and West Bank, and including on the "Israeli" side areas of West Bank territory
2004	Construction of wall declared "contrary to international law" by International Court of Justice *10 September: Uri Avnery receives 80th birthday video message from Palestinian President Yasser Arafat, addressing him as "my friend Uri"* 11 November: Death of President of Palestine and Chairman of PLO, Yasser Arafat, in a Paris hospital, after a mysterious illness. Funeral in Ramallah on 12 November attended by small number of Israelis, including delegation from Gush Shalom led by Uri Avnery
2005	9 January: New Palestinian President Mahmoud Abbas elected with 62.3% of the vote, without Hamas participation, declares readiness for peace talks with Israel
2006	4 January: Israeli Prime Minister Sharon incapacitated by massive stroke; Deputy Ehud Olmert

appointed Acting Prime Minister, assumes post of Prime Minister 13 April

25 January: Elections held in Palestine Authority Legislative, won by Hamas' Change and Reform Party

21 February: Palestinian President Abbas invites Hamas' Ismail Haniyeh to form a government. Hamas-led Cabinet sworn in on 29 March

7 April: United States and European Union cut off all direct aid to Hamas-led government

25 June: Israeli soldier Gilad Shalit captured by Palestinians in Gaza; Israel begins an offensive on Gaza Strip

12 July: Israel-Lebanon War begins

11 September: President Abbas and Prime Minister Haniyeh agree to form a national unity government but, less than two weeks later, violence erupts between Fatah and Hamas in Gaza Strip that continues into 2007

2007   8 February: President Abbas and Prime Minister Haniyeh sign the Mecca agreement, forming a unity government between Hamas and Fatah, brokered by Saudi Arabia. Israel rejects agreement, America expresses some reservations, and EU welcomes it. Clashes between supporters of the two parties continue in Gaza Strip

19 February: A Trilateral Israeli-Palestinian-American summit is held with US Secretary of State Condoleeza Rice, PM Ehud Olmert, and President Abbas, but with no result

31 May: British university professors announce boycott of Israeli universities to demonstrate solidarity with Palestinian people

14 June: After renewed clashes between Fatah and Hamas, Hamas takes control of Gaza Strip. Israel closes all crossings into the area. President Abbas asks Salam Fayad to form emergency government to replace unity government

27 November: US President George W. Bush hosts

Annapolis Conference, aimed at restarting the peace process. Israeli and Palestinian officials joined by members of the Quartet (US, UN, EU, and Russia), the Group of Eight nations, and representatives of more than a dozen Arab countries. Conference marks first time a two-state solution is articulated as the mutually agreed-upon outline for addressing Israeli-Palestinian conflict. Joint Understanding between Israeli and Palestinian leaders to participate in ongoing negotiations with goal of signing peace agreement by end of 2008 is endorsed

2008   14 May: Sixtieth anniversary of the founding of the State of Israel, and the 1948 war

Index: Part One
In the Fields of the Philistines

Index: Part Two
The Other Side of the Coin

About the Author

U ri Avnery, Israeli journalist, writer, politician, and peace activist, was born Helmut Ostermann in Beckum, Germany, in 1923, emigrating with his parents to Palestine on Hitler's rise to power in 1933. At the age of fourteen he joined the Irgun, an underground military organization opposing British rule, and served for three years, leaving in protest against its anti-Arab ideology. In 1946 Avnery founded the Eretz Yisrael Hatz'ira ("Young Palestine") movement, and edited its publication, which promoted a radical view of the Hebrew community in Palestine as a natural ally of the Arab nationalist movements in the region.

At the outbreak of war in 1948, Avnery joined the Israeli army, later volunteering for the legendary commando unit, "Samson's Foxes," before being severely wounded in the closing days of the war.

From 1950 to 1990 Avnery was the owner and editor of the hugely popular progressive weekly newspaper, *Haolam Hazeh* (*This World*), which campaigned for the separation of state and religion; equality for the Arab minority, and social justice. From the early 1950s, it has resolutely advocated the creation of a Palestinian state alongside Israel, and support for the Arab struggles for independence. Its editorial offices and printing facilities were bombed several times, wounding some employees, and in 1972 both its offices and invaluable archives were completely destroyed by arson. Avnery himself was ambushed and both his hands broken in 1953, and two decades later he was seriously wounded in an assassination attempt.

In 1965 he established a new political party named after his newspaper, serving as a member of the Knesset for ten years, and in

1982 he became the first Israeli to meet with Yasser Arafat. One of the most outspoken radical leaders of Israel's peace movement, he went on to found Gush Shalom, the "Peace Bloc," in 1992, which advocates the creation of a Palestinian state in the Occupied Territories and campaigns to improve the day-to-day lives of Palestinians, while promoting reconciliation between the two sides. He and his wife Rachel continue to be active in Gush Shalom, and together they received the alternative Nobel Peace Prize in 2001. They live in Tel Aviv.

Uri Avnery, 2008

The Secret War With Iran
The 30-Year Covert Struggle for Control of a 'Rogue' State
Ronen Bergman

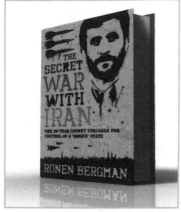

9781851686223 - HB - £16.99

Intelligence expert and Israeli investigative journalist Dr Ronen Bergman draws on a decade of research to deliver a hard-hitting account of a vast conflict being fought under the public's radar.

Unprecedented access to classified documents, interviews with intelligence agents and revelations from political hit men provide an astonishing insight into the stealth tactics deployed by Mossad, the CIA and MI6 in their bid to undermine and control the perceived threat from Iran. Bergman also details the extreme measures taken by Iran as it attempts to outmanoeuvre its enemies in a potentially devastating web of international espionage.

The Secret War With Iran redefines the boundaries of the crisis in the Middle East and its implications worldwide and provides an unflinching examination of the horrors that face us all as diplomacy threatens to collapse into a nuclear standoff.

Following a PhD from Cambridge University, Ronen Bergman teaches investigative jounalism at Tel Aviv University, and is currently the senior security and intelligence correspondent for Israel's largest daily newspaper, *Yedioth Ahronoth*.

"Thoroughly researched and persuasively argued, Bergman's brief against Iran adds a powerful voice to a contentious debate." - *Publishers Weekly*

Browse all our titles at www.oneworld-publications.com

The Diary of Mary Berg
Growing up in the Warsaw Ghetto
Edited by Susan Pentlin

Mary Berg was just fifteen when she was imprisoned in the Warsaw Ghetto. She survived four years of Nazi terror. This is her story.

This is a work remarkable for its detail, authenticity, and poignancy. Not only a factual report on the life and death of a people, this diary is among the most important documents of the Second World War.

"Direct, sharp-eyed and full of compelling detail, this is both a major resource for historians and a richly compelling human document" *Times Literary Supplement*

9781851684724 - HB - £14.99

Sophie Scholl and the White Rose
Annette Dumbach & Jud Newborn

This is the stirring story of five young German students at the University of Munich who started an underground resistance movement, and tried to spark an uprising to overthrow Hitler.

"The animated narrative reads like a suspense novel." *New York Times*

'This book, chapter by chapter, builds into an incontestable argument for the power and possibilities of action over passive acceptance and apathy.' *Jewish Chronicle*

9781851685363 - PB - £7.99

Browse these and other titles at www.oneworld-publications.com